Anonymous

Longworth's American Almanac

New-York Register and City Directory

Anonymous

Longworth's American Almanac
New-York Register and City Directory

ISBN/EAN: 9783337341060

Printed in Europe, USA, Canada, Australia, Japan

Cover: Foto ©Suzi / pixelio.de

More available books at **www.hansebooks.com**

LONGWORTH's

AMERICAN ALMANACK,

NEW-YORK REGISTER.

AND

CITY DIRECTORY,

FOR THE

Twenty-third Year of American Independence.

CONTAINING

MOST THINGS USEFUL IN A WORK OF THE KIND.

Price 5s. stitched—half-bound 6s.

NEW-YORK:

Printed for the Publisher, by T. & J. Swords, No. 99 Pearl-street.

—1798.—

Tammany Society, or Columbian Order.

This national society was instituted in 1789, and is founded on the true and genuine principles of republicanism. It holds out as its objects, the smile of charity, the chain of friendship, and the flame of liberty, and in general, whatever may tend to perpetuate the love of freedom or the political advantages of this country.

Officers for the present year.

Jacob De la Montagnie, Grand Sachem.—Richard Davis, Father of the Council.—William Whitehead, Treasurer.—Daniel Dodge, Secretary.—James Warner, Sagamore.—Joseph Dunkley, Wiskinkie.

Council of Sachems.

Wm. Mooney, Thomas Greenleaf, John Waldron, John P. Pearss, John Mersereau, Richard Davis, Thomas Timpson, Stanton Latham, John Coffin, John Utt, Benjamin Romayne, James D. Bisset, and John Striker.

George J. Warner, Scribe of the Council.

George Clinton, jun. orator for the 4th of July.

ADDITIONAL NAMES.

Abeel, John, butcher, Hester street.
Cannon, Arnout, deputy-sheriff, 343 Broadway.
Dangel, Bent, teacher, removed to 55 Pine-street.
Jackson, John, counting-house, Jackson's-wharf.
Ledet, Isaiah L. merchant, 66 William-street.
Le Roux, Charles, 177 Broadway.
Merrick, Richard, removed to 148 Division-street.
Miller, Andrew, merchant, 89 Maiden-lane.

SICK NURSES.

Letitia Trimper, 52 E. George-street.
Sarah Taylor, Beaver-lane.
Elizabeth Reed, 15 Chesnut-street.
Sarah Buckmaster, 51 Roosevelt
Mary Kelly, 28 Cedar
Widow Schenck, 74 Liberty
A. Day, 7 Chapel
Mary Hutchings, 47 Gold
Widow Snyder, Cross
Margaret Leming, 47 Gold
Hannah Lyon, 17 Division
Widow Lippencot, 69 John
Mary M'Culium, 68 Ann—Mrs. White, 3 Dutch-st.

ASTRONOMICAL CALCULATIONS

FOR THE

TWENTY-THIRD YEAR

OF

AMERICAN INDEPENDENCE,

COMMENCING

THE FOURTH OF JULY, *A.D.* 1798:

Being second after LEAP-YEAR, until the first of January

CONTAINING

The Rising, Setting, Places, and Eclipses of the Sun and Moon; the Rising, Setting, and Southing of the most conspicuous PLANETS and fixed STARS; the Equation of Time; and Time of High Water at New-York, &c.

ALSO,

The Increase, Decrease, and Length of Days; *With the Festivals, &c.*

Calculated for the Latitude and Meridian of
NEW-YORK.

By ABRAHAM SHOEMAKER.

From the Press of T. & J. SWORDS.

Notes to the Reader.

I. THE calculations of this Almanack are made to solar or apparent time; to which, for the mean or clock time, apply the equation given in the fifth column, adding when the Sun is slow, and subtracting when fast.

II. The time of high water, at New-York, is so computed as to serve for either morning or afternoon, sufficiently near for common use; the morning flood being about twelve minutes earlier than the time in the tide-column, and that of the afternoon as much later.

III. The rising, setting, or southing of a star, may be carried several days backward by adding, or forward by subtracting, four minutes per day: for instance, on the 8th of January Sirius is south at 15 minutes past 11; adding 12 minutes for three days sooner, we have 11h. 27m. for the southing on the 5th, and deducting 8 minutes for two later, leaves 11h. 7m. for that of the 10th of the same month, &c.

IV. As the day ends at midnight, the rising, setting and southing of the Moon, when after that time, is found against the succeeding day: so, on the night of (or following) the 14th of January, the Moon sets at 1h. 17m. after midnight, viz. in the morning of the 15th; not 0h. 18m. the time opposite the 14th. which is that of its setting the preceding morning.

Common Notes, &c. for the 23d Year of American Independence.

1799			1799		
Dominical Letter,	G		Dominical Letter,	F	
Golden Number,	13		Golden Number,	14	
Epact, (correct)	13		Epact, (correct)	24	
Solar Cycle,	15		Solar Cycle,	16	
Roman Indiction,	1		Roman Indiction,	2	

Advent,	December 2	Ascension Day,	May 2
Ash Wednesday,	Feb. 6	Whitsunday,	May 12
Easter,	Mar. 24	Trinity,	May 19

Signs and Characters explained.

☽ Moon, ☉ Sun, ♄ Saturn, ♃ Jupiter, ♂ Mars, ♀ Venus, ☿ Mercury, ♅ Georgian Planet, discovered by Herschel.

Signs of the Zodiac.

♈ Aries, ♉ Taurus, ♊ Gemini, ♋ Cancer, ♌ Leo, ♍ Virgo, ♎ Libra, ♏ Scorpio, ♐ Sagittary, ♑ Capricorn, ♒ Aquarius, ♓ Pisces. ☌ Conjunction, ☍ Opposition, □ Quartile.

JULY, 1798—23d Year American Independence.

Laſt Quarter the 6th, at 33 minutes after 1 morning.
New Moon the 13th, at 55 minutes after 10 morning.
Firſt Quarter the 20th, at 51 minutes after 1 morning.
Full Moon the 27th, at 38 minutes after 1 afternoon.

M D	W D	Miſcellaneous Particulars.	Sun riſes and ſets.		☉ ſlow.		☽'s place		☽ riſes.		H[igh] Wa[ter] N.Yo[rk]	
					M.	S.	S.	D.	H.	M.		
4	4	INDEPENDENCE.	4	34	8	3	59	♓ 26	11	24	0	52
5	5	[☽ in apogee.	4	35	8	4	9	♈ 8	11	46	1	32
6	6	Lyra ſouth 11 25	4	35	8	4	19	20	morn.		2	12
7	7	☌ ☉ ♄	4	36	8	4	29	♉ 2	0	8	2	52
8	G	♃ riſes 0 59	4	36	8	4	38	14	0	33	3	32
9	2		4	37	8	4	47	27	1	3	4	22
10	3	Arcturus ſets 2 4	4	37	8	4	56	♊ 10	1	38	5	12
11	4		4	38	8	5	4	23	2	20	6	12
12	5	Spica ♍ ſets 11 11	4	38	8	5	11	♋ 7	3	12	7	2
13	6	♂ ſouth 3 30	4	39	8	5	18	22	ſets.		8	2
14	7	Days decreaſe 16m.	4	40	8	5	25	♌ 6	8	39	9	12
15	G	Swithin. ☽ in perigee.	4	40	8	5	31	21	9	19	10	12
16	2		4	41	8	5	36	♍ 6	9	54	11	0
17	3	Days 14 36	4	42	8	5	41	20	10	24	11	42
18	4		4	42	8	5	46	♎ 5	10	51	0	22
19	5	Bull's eye riſes 1 31	4	43	8	5	50	19	11	17	1	12
20	6	Margaret. ☌ ☉ ☿ ſup.	4	44	8	5	54	♏ 3	11	47	2	2
21	7		4	45	8	5	57	17	morn.		2	52
22	G	Magdalen. ☉ enters ♌	4	46	8	5	59	♐ 3	0	17	3	42
23	2		4	46	8	6	1	13	0	57	4	32
24	3		4	47	8	6	3	26	1	35	5	22
25	4	St. James.	4	48	8	6	4	♑ 9	2	20	6	20
26	5	♃ riſes 11 52	4	49	8	6	4	22	3	15	7	12
27	6		4	50	8	6	3	♒ 4	riſes.		8	2
28	7		4	51	8	6	2	16	8	8	8	52
29	G	Arcturus ſets 0 48	4	52	8	6	1	29	8	30	9	42
30	2	Dog days begin.	4	53	8	5	59	♓ 10	9	0	10	22
31	3	♂ ſtationary. ☽ in ap	4	54	8	5	56	22	9	25	11	22

B

AUGUST, 1798—23d Year American Independ.

Last Quarter the 4th, at 19 minutes after 5 afternoon.
New Moon the 11th, at 31 minutes after 6 afternoon.
First Quarter the 18th, at 9 minutes after 9 morning.
Full Moon the 26th, at 31 minutes after 4 morning.

M D	W D	Miscellaneous Particulars.	Sun rises and sets. M. S.	☉ slow. S. D.	☽'s place H. M.	☽ rises. H. M.	High Water N.Yo.
1	4	Lamma's day.	4 55 8	5 53	♈ 4	9 47	11 51
2	5	Bull's Eye rises 0 37.	4 56 8	5 48	16	10 9	0 19
3	6		4 57 8	5 44	28	10 34	0 47
4	7	7*s rise 11 6	4 58 8	5 39	♉ 10	11 1	1 30
5	G		4 59 8	5 33	22	11 32	2 15
6	2	Transfiguration.	5 0 7	5 26	♊ 5	morn.	3 3
7	3		5 1 7	5 19	18	0 9	3 55
8	4	♂ south 3 57	5 2 7	5 11	♋ 1	0 56	4 53
9	5	Days 13 52	5 4 7	5 3	15	1 53	5 54
10	6	St. Lawrence.	5 5 7	4 54	30	3 0	6 56
11	7		5 6 7	4 45	♌ 15	sets.	7 58
12	G	♃ rises 10 54	5 7 7	4 35	30	7 51	8 56
13	2	☽ in perigee.	5 8 7	4 24	♍ 15	8 24	9 52
14	3	Spica ♍ sets 9 ♎	5 9 7	4 13	30	8 53	10 44
15	4		5 10 7	4 1	♎ 15	9 21	11 35
16	5	Sirius rises 3 51	5 12 7	3 49	29	9 49	0 12
17	6	□ ☉ ♃	5 13 7	3 37	♏ 13	10 19	0 50
18	7	7*s rise 10 10	5 14 7	3 23	27	10 54	1 40
19	G		5 15 7	3 10	♐ 10	11 34	2 33
20	2	♂ south 3 35	5 16 7	2 56	23	morn.	3 26
21	3		5 18 7	2 42	♑ 6	0 21	4 20
22	4	☉ enters ♍	5 19 7	2 27	19	1 14	5 15
23	5		5 20 7	2 11	♒ 1	2 11	6 7
24	6	St. Bartholomew.	5 21 7	1 56	13	3 13	6 58
25	7		5 23 7	1 39	25	4 16	7 46
26	G	♄ rises 7 54	5 24 7	1 22	♓ 7	rises.	8 34
27	2	☽ in apogee.	5 25 7	1 6	19	7 35	9 15
28	3	St. Augustine.	5 27 7	0 49	♈ 1	7 57	9 54
29	4	John Baptist beheaded.	5 28 7	0 31	13	8 19	10 35
30	5		5 29 7	0 13	25	8 41	11 15
31	6	☽'s eclipse.	5 30 7	fast	♉ 6	9 6	11 4

SEPTEMBER, 1798—23d Year American Inde[pendence]

Last Quarter the 3d, at 28 minutes after 7 morning.
New Moon the 10th, at 6 minutes after 2 morning.
First Quarter the 16th, at 50 minutes after 7 afternoon.
Full Moon the 24th, at 7 minutes after 9 afternoon.

M D	W D	Miscellaneous Particulars.	Sun rises and sets.	☉ fast. M. S.	☽'s place S. D.	☽ rises. H. M.	High[tide] N.Y.
1	7		5 32	7 0	24 ♉ 19	9 35	0 1
2	G	♃ south 4 51	5 33	7 0	42 Ⅱ 1	10 10	1 2
3	2	7*s rise 9 14	5 34	7 1	2	13 10 52	1 5
4	3		5 36	7 1	21	26 11 43	2 46
5	4		5 37	7 1	41 ♋ 10	morn.	3 4
6	5	Dog days end.	5 38	7 2	1	24 0 4	4 4
7	6		5 40	7 2	21 ♌ 8	1 5	5 4
8	7	Nativity of V. Mary.	5 41	7 2	41	21 3 1	6 5
9	G		5 42	7 3	2 ♍ 8	4 30	7 4
10	2	☌ ☉ ♅ ☽ in perigee.	5 44	7 3	23	23 sets.	8 5
11	3		5 45	7 3	44 ♎ 9	7 26	9 5
12	4	Bull's Eye rises 10 1	5 46	7 4	5	24 7 55	10 2
13	5	♃ rises 9 3	5 48	7 4	26 ♏ 8	8 26	11 1
14	6	☿ stationary.	5 49	7 4	47	23 9 0	11 5
15	7	♃ stationary.	5 50	7 5	8 ♐ 7	9 38	0 5
16	G	Arcturus sets 9 43	5 52	7 5	30	20 10 24	1 2
17	2	Lambert.	5 53	7 5	50 ♑ 3	11 15	2 2
18	3		5 54	7 6	11	15 morn.	3 1
19	4	♂ south 11 10	5 56	7 6	32	28 0 13	4 1
20	5	♄ south 3 47	5 57	7 6	53 ♒ 10	1 15	5
21	6	St. Matthew.	5 58	7 7	15	22 2 17	5 5
22	7	☉ enters ♎	6 0	6 7	34 ♓ 4	3 18	6
23	G		6 1	6 7	54	16 4 20	7 2
24	2	☽ in apogee.	6 2	6 8	15	28 rises.	8
25	3		5 4	6 8	35 ♈ 10	6 3	9
26	4	Cyprian.	5 5	6 8	55	22 6 5	9 5
27	5	☿ ☿ inferior.	5 7	6 9	15 ♉ 3	7 10	10
28	6	Sirius 1 14	5 8	6 9	35	16 7 40	10 5
29	7	St. Michael.	6 9	6 9	5	28 8 11	11
30	G	St. Jerome. ♂ station.	6 10	6 10	15 Ⅱ 10	8 56	0

OCTOBER, 1798—23d Year American Indep.

Last Quarter the 2d, at 34 minutes after 7 afternoon.
New Moon the 9th, at 40 minutes after 10 morning.
First Quarter the 16th, at 20 minutes after 10 morning.
Full Moon the 24th, at 37 minutes after 2 afternoon.

D D	W D	Miscellaneous Particulars.	Sun rises and sets.	☉ fast. M. S.	☽'s place S. D.	☽ rises. H. M.	High Water N. Yo.
1	2	♃ south 3 6	6 12	10 32	♊ 23	9 44	0 48
2	3		6 13	10 51	♋ 6	10 40	1 44
3	4	Sirius rises 0 58	6 15	11 9	19	11 45	2 42
4	5		6 16	11 27	♌ 3	morn.	3 41
5	6		6 17	11 45	17	0 55	4 38
6	7	☿ stationary.	6 19	12 2	♍ 1	2 11	5 35
7	G		6 20	12 19	16	3 28	6 30
8	2	☽ in perigee.	6 21	12 36	♎ 2	4 46	7 23
9	3	Denys.	6 23	12 51	17	sets.	8 16
10	4	7*'s south 2 33	6 24	13 7	♏ 2	6 31	9 10
11	5		6 25	13 22	17	7 2	10 3
12	6	☿'s elongation.	6 27	13 37	♐ 1	7 39	10 58
13	7	Days decrease 3 52	6 28	13 51	15	8 23	11 11
14	G	♃ south 2 15	6 29	14 2	29	9 14	0 2
15	2		6 31	14 17	♑ 12	10 11	1 1
16	3	Arcturus sets 7 54	6 32	14 29	24	11 12	2 3
17	4		6 33	14 41	♒ 7	morn.	3 5
18	5	St. Luke. □ ☉ ♄	6 35	14 52	19	0 16	4 1
19	6		6 36	15 3	♓ 1	1 19	4 44
20	7	Sirius rises 11 51	6 37	15 12	13	2 20	5 27
21	G	☽ in apogee.	6 39	15 21	26	3 20	6 9
22	2	☉ enters ♏	6 40	15 30	♈ 9	4 20	6 46
23	3		6 41	15 38	19	5 18	7 29
24	4		6 43	15 45	♉ 2	rises.	8 5
25	5		6 44	15 51	♊ 12	5 55	8 5
26	6	♃ south 1 24	6 45	15 56	25	6 21	9 5
27	7		6 46	16 1	♊ 7	7 2	10 2
28	G	Simon and Jude.	6 48	16 5	20	7 45	11 10
29	2		6 49	16 9	♋ 3	8 37	11 11
30	3	Arcturus sets 7 1	6 50	16 11	16	9 38	0 2
31	4		6 51	16 13	29	10 40	1 1

NOVEMBER, 1798—23d Year American Indep.

Last Quarter the 1st, at 35 minutes after 5 morning.
New Moon the 7th, at 55 minutes after 8 afternoon.
First Quarter the 15th, at 25 minutes after 4 morning.
Full Moon the 23d, at 48 minutes after 7 morning.
Last Quarter the 30th, at 58 minutes after 1 afternoon.

M D	W D	Miscellaneous Particulars.	Sun rises and sets.	☉ fast. M. S.	☽'s place ♌ D.	☽ rises. H. M.	High Water N.Yo.
1	5	All Saints.	6 52	6 16 14	♌ 13	11 57	2 35
2	6	♃ south 0 54	6 54	6 16 15	27	morn.	3 30
3	7	Sirius rises 11 1	6 55	6 16 14	♍ 11	1 10	4 22
4	G		6 56	6 16 13	26	2 23	5 12
5	2	Days 10 6	6 57	6 16 11	♎ 10	3 41	6 5
6	3	☽ in perigee.	6 58	6 16 8	25	4 56	6 56
7	4	♄ stationary.	7 0	5 16 4	♏ 10	sets.	7 45
8	5		7 1	5 15 59	25	5 33	8 45
9	6	7*s south 0 42	7 2	5 15 54	♐ 9	6 14	9 45
10	7		7 3	5 15 48	23	7 2	10 3
11	G	Martin.	7 4	5 15 41	♑ 7	7 57	11 3
12	2	Bull's Eye south 1 14	7 5	5 15 32	20	8 58	0 1
13	3	8 ☉ ♃	7 6	5 15 23	♒ 2	10 2	0 57
14	4	☌ ☉ ☿ superior.	7 7	5 15 14	15	11 6	1 52
15	5		7 8	5 15 3	27	morn.	2 35
16	6	Sirius south 3 9	7 9	5 14 52	♓ 9	0 9	3 25
17	7	☽ in apogee.	7 10	5 14 39	21	1 10	4 7
18	G		7 11	5 14 26	♈ 3	2 9	4 7
19	2		7 12	5 14 12	15	3 8	5 5
20	3	♄ south 4 8	7 13	5 13 57	27	4 5	6 5
21	4	☉ enters ♐	7 14	5 13 41	♉ 9	5 8	6 45
22	5		7 15	5 13 25	21	6 10	7 30
23	6	Clement. ☽ eclipsed.	7 16	5 13 7	♊ 4	rises.	8 7
24	7		7 17	5 12 49	16	5 30	9 7
25	G	♃ south 11 2	7 18	5 12 31	29	6 27	9 7
26	2		7 19	5 12 11	♋ 12	7 32	10 7
27	3		7 19	5 11 51	25	8 37	11 7
28	4	Sirius south 2 19	7 20	5 11 30	♌ 10	9 43	0 7
29	5		7 21	5 11 8	22	10 50	1 7
30	6	St. Andrew.	7 21	5 10 46	♍ 7	morn	2 7

DECEMBER, 1798—23d Year American Indep.

New Moon the 7th, at 7 minutes after 9 morning.
First Quarter the 15th, at 10 minutes after 1 morning.
Full Moon the 22d, at 21 minutes after 11 afternoon.
Last Quarter the 29th, at 41 minutes after 9 afternoon.

M.D	W.D	Miscellaneous Particulars.	Sun rises and sets.	⊙ fast. M.S.	☽'s place S.D.	☽ rises. H.M	High Water N.Yo
1	7	♃ south 10 34	7 22	5 10 23	♍ 21	0 6	3 3
2	G	Advent.	7 22	5 10 0	♎ 6	1 18	3 52
3	2		7 23	5 9 36	20	2 30	4 40
4	3	Sirius rises 8 48	7 24	5 9 11	♏ 4	3 42	5 29
5	4	Arcturus rises 2 4	7 24	5 8 46	19	4 57	6 21
6	5	Nicholas.	7 25	5 8 20	♐ 3	6 12	7 16
7	6		7 25	5 7 54	17	sets.	8 14
8	7	Concept. of V. Mary	7 26	5 7 28	♑ 1	5 33	9 13
9	G	2d in Advent.	7 26	5 7 1	14	6 32	10 10
10	2	♄'s south 10 23	7 26	5 6 33	28	7 35	11 4
11	3		7 27	5 6 5	♒ 10	8 37	11 42
12	4	♃ south 9 41	7 27	5 5 37	23	9 45	0 20
13	5	□ ⊙ ♅	7 27	5 5 8	♓ 5	10 48	1 7
14	6	Arcturus south 1 26	7 28	5 4 39	17	11 47	1 51
15	7		7 28	5 4 10	29	morn.	2 32
16	G	Days 9 4	7 28	5 3 41	♈ 11	0 46	3 11
17	2		7 28	5 3 11	23	1 44	3 50
18	3	Sirius rises 7 46	7 28	5 2 41	♉ 5	2 43	4 30
19	4		7 28	5 2 11	17	3 45	5 12
20	5		7 28	5 1 41	29	4 47	5 57
21	6	St. Thomas. ⊙ ent. ♑	7 28	5 1 11	♊ 12	5 52	6 45
22	7		7 28	5 0 41	25	rises.	7 38
23	G		7 28	5 0 11	♋ 8	5 5	8 31
24	2		7 28	5 0. 20	22	6 9	9 32
25	3	Christmas.	7 28	5 0 5	♌ 6	7 16	10 26
26	4	St. Stephen. ♄'s clo	7 28	5 1 20	20	8 31	11 20
27	5	St. John. ♅ station	7 28	5 1 49	♍ 4	9 44	0 8
28	6	Innocents.	7 28	5 2 18	18	10 55	0 47
29	7		7 27	5 2 48	♎ 3	morn.	1 30
30	G	☿ ⊙ ☿ superior.	7 27	5 3 17	17	0 6	2 21
31	2		7 27	5 3 46	♏ 1	1 20	3 5

JANUARY, 1799—23d Year American Indep.

New Moon the 5th, at 17 minutes after 11 afternoon.
First Quarter the 13th, at 1 minute after 11 afternoon.
Full Moon the 21st, at 44 minutes after 12 afternoon.
Last Quarter the 28th, at 53 minutes after 5 morning.

M D	W D	Miscellaneous Particulars.	Sun rises and sets.	☉ slow. M. S	☽'s place S. D	☽ rises. H. M	High Water N. Yo
1	3	Circumcision.	7 26 5	4 14	♏ 15	2 30	4 2
2	4		7 26 5	4 42	29	3 43	4 54
3	5	♄ south 0 46	7 25 5	5 10	♐ 12	4 56	5 49
4	6		7 25 5	5 37	26	6 5	6 45
5	7	Days increase 6 m.	7 25 5	6 3	♑ 9	sets.	7 42
6	F	Epiphany.	7 24 5	6 30	23	5 4	8 35
7	2		7 23 5	6 56	♒ 6	6 11	9 32
8	3	Sirius south 11 15	7 23 5	7 21	18	7 10	10 21
9	4		7 22 5	7 46	♓ 1	8 20	11 7
10	5	♃ stationary.	7 22 5	8 10	13	9 21	11 45
11	6	☌ ☉ ☿ inferior.	7 21 5	8 33	25	10 22	0 3
12	7	☽ in apogee. ☍ ☉ ♄	7 20 5	8 56	♈ 7	11 19	0 54
13	F		7 19 5	9 19	19	morn.	1 35
14	2	♃ south 7 10	7 19 5	9 41	♉ 1	0 18	2 12
15	3		7 18 5	10 2	13	1 17	2 53
16	4	♃ sets 2 0	7 17 5	10 22	25	2 19	3 35
17	5		7 16 5	10 42	♊ 7	3 23	4 23
18	6	♄ south 11 32	7 16 5	11 1	20	4 27	5 5
19	7	☉ enters ♒	7 15 5	11 20	♋ 3	5 29	6 7
20	F	Septuagesima.	7 14 5	11 37	17	6 28	7 5
21	2	Arcturus rises 10 35	7 13 5	11 54	♌ 1	rises	8
22	3	Vincent. ☿ station.	7 12 5	12 10	15	6 3	9
23	4		7 11 5	12 25	30	7 10	10
24	5	☽ in perigee.	7 10 5	12 40	♍ 14	8 35	10 52
25	6	Conversion of St. Paul	7 9 5	12 53	29	9 40	11 45
26	7	Bull's Eye south 7 47	7 8 5	13 6	♎ 13	10 50	0 2
27	F	Sexagesima.	7 7 5	13 18	28	morn.	1 7
28	2		7 6 5	13 29	♏ 12	0 12	1 55
29	3		7 5 5	13 40	26	1 23	2 45
30	4	Spica ♍ rises 10 59	7 4 5	13 49	♐ 9	2 37	3 35
31	5		7 2 5	13 57	23	3 4	

FEBRUARY, 1799—23d Year American Indep.

New Moon the 4th, at 17 minutes after 3 afternoon.
First Quarter the 12th, at 47 minutes after 7 afternoon.
Full Moon the 20th, at 6 minutes after 12 morning.
Last Quarter the 26th, at 25 minutes after 3 afternoon.

M D	W D	Miscellaneous Particulars.	Sun rises and sets.	☉ place. M. S.	☽'s place. S. D.	☽ rises. H. M.	High Water N.Y.
1	6		7 1	5 14	5 ♑ 0	4 50	5 20
2	7	Purificat. of V. Mary.	7 0	5 14	12 19	5 45	6 22
3	F	Quinquagesima.	6 59	6 14	18 ♒ 2	6 31	7 16
4	2	☿'s elongation.	6 58	6 14	23 14	sets.	8 7
5	3		6 57	6 14	26 27	6 0	8 54
6	4	Ash-Wednesday.	6 56	6 14	32 ♓ 9	7 3	9 38
7	5	♄ south 10 2	6 54	6 14	34 21	8 4	10 20
8	6		6 53	6 14	36 ♈ 3	9 4	11 0
9	7	☽ in apogee.	6 52	6 14	35 15	10 2	11 39
10	F	1st in Lent.	6 51	6 14	38 27	11 1	0 13
11	2		6 49	6 14	38 ♉ 9	morn.	8 43
12	3	7 *s set 1 24	6 48	6 14	37 21	0 2	1 23
13	4		6 47	6 14	35 ♊ 3	1 3	2 0
14	5	Valentine.	6 46	6 14	33 15	2 6	2 57
15	6	♄ sets 4 58	6 44	6 14	30 28	3 9	3 49
16	7		6 43	6 14	26 ♋ 11	4 9	4 45
17	F	2d in Lent.	6 42	6 14	21 25	5 3	5 43
18	2	☉ enters ♓	6 40	6 14	16 ♌ 9	5 52	6 43
19	3		6 39	6 14	10 24	6 32	7 42
20	4	Sirius south 8 19	6 38	6 14	3 ♍ 8	rises.	8 39
21	5	☽ in perigee.	6 37	6 13	56 24	7 27	9 33
22	6		6 35	6 13	48 ♎ 9	8 42	10 25
23	7	7 *s set 0 39	6 34	6 13	40 23	9 59	11 10
24	F	St. Matthias.	6 33	6 13	31 ♏ 8	11 15	11 56
25	2	♄ south 8 48	6 31	6 13	21 22	morn.	0 37
26	3		6 30	6 13	10 ♐ 6	0 0	1 30
27	4	Days increase 1 58	6 29	6 12	59 20	1 40	2 23
28	5		6 27	6 12	45 ♑ 3	2 46	3 23

The 22d of this month is observed as the Birth-day of GEORGE WASHINGTON, the Farmer of Mount Vernon.

MARCH, 1799---23d Year American Independ.

New Moon the 6th, at 37 minutes after 8 morning.
First Quarter the 14th, at 25 minutes after 1 afternoon.
Full Moon the 21st, at 56 minutes after 9 morning.
Last Quarter the 28th, at 37 minutes after 2 morning.

M W D D	Miscellaneous Particulars.	Sun rises and sets.	☉ slow. M. S.	☽'s place S. D.	☽ rises. H. M.	High Water. N. Y.
1	David	6 26	6 12 36	♑ 10	3 45	— —
2		6 25	6 12 23	21	4 33	5 14
3 F	Mid-Lent.	6 23	6 12 10	♒ 11	5 13	6 6
4 2	7*s set 0 6	6 22	6 11 56	23	5 44	6 53
5 3	Days 11 20	6 20	6 11 42	♓ 6	6 12	7 33
6 4		6 19	6 11 28	18	sets.	8 20
7 5	Sirius sets 0 27	6 18	6 11 13	30	6 58	9 1
8 6		6 16	6 10 58	♈ 12	7 58	9 43
9 7	☽ in apogee.	6 15	6 10 43	23	8 56	10 26
10 F	4th in Lent.	6 14	6 10 26	♉ 5	9 57	11 2
11 2	Bull's Eye sets 11 56	6 12	6 10 10	17	10 57	11 45
12 3	Gregory M.	6 11	6 9 54	29	11 59	0 25
13 4		6 9	6 9 37	♊ 11	morn.	0 58
14 5	♄ sets 3 14	6 8	6 9 20	23	1 2	1 45
15 6		6 7	6 9 3	♋ 6	2 2	2 5
16 7	Sirius sets 11 51	6 5	6 8 45	19	2 58	3 5
17 F	Palm-Sunday.	6 4	6 8 28	♌ 3	3 47	4 5
18 2		6 3	6 8 10	17	4 31	5 5
19 3	♃ sets 10 34	6 1	6 7 52	♍ 2	5 8	6 2
20 4	☽ enters ♈	6 0	6 7 34	16	5 40	6 22
21 5	Benedict. ♄ station.	5 58	7 7 16	♎ 2	rises.	8 1
22 6	☽ in perigee.	5 57	7 6 57	17	7 42	9 0
23 7	Lyra rises 9 24	5 56	7 6 39	♏ 2	9 0	10 2
24 F	Easter.	5 54	7 6 20	17	10 16	10 0
25 2	Annunc. of V. Mary.	5 53	7 6 2	♐ 1	11 3	11 3
26 3		5 52	7 5 43	16	morn.	
27 4	♄ sets 2 25	5 50	7 5 25	29	0 40	1 2
28 5		5 49	7 5 6	♑ 13	1 41	1 5
29 6		5 48	7 4 47	25	2 40	2 5
30 7	Arcturus south 1 33	5 46	7 4 29	♒ 8	3 30	4 5
31 F	Low Sunday.	5 45	7 4 10	20		

APRIL, 1798—22d Year American Independence

New Moon the 5th, at 24 minutes after 2 morning.
First Quarter the 13th, at 50 minutes after 2 morning.
Full Moon the 19th, at 43 minutes after 6 afternoon.
Last Quarter the 26th, at 33 minutes after 3 afternoon.

M D	W D	Miscellaneous Particulars.	Sun rises and sets.	☉ slow. M. S	☽'s place S. D.	☽ rises H. M.	High Water N. Yo.
1	2	♊ south 10 38	5 44 7	3 52	♓ 3	4 25	5 45
2	3	♄ sets 2 5	5 42 7	3 33	15	4 49	6 27
3	4		5 41 7	3 15	27	5 11	7 8
4	5	Ambrose.	5 39 7	2 57	♈ 8	5 31	7 48
5	6	☽ in apogee.	5 38 7	2 39	20	sets.	8 28
6	7		5 37 7	2 22	♉ 2	7 57	9 8
7	F	♃ sets 10 44	5 36 7	2 4	14	8 58	9 51
8	2		5 34 7	1 47	26	10 0	10 36
9	3	☐ ☉ ♄	5 33 7	1 30	♊ 8	11 2	11 24
10	4	7 *'s set 9 47	5 32 7	1 13	20	morn.	0 2
11	5		5 30 7	0 57	♋ 2	0 3	0 45
12	6	♊ south 9 57	5 29 7	0 41	15	0 59	1 34
13	7		5 28 7	0 25	26	1 49	2 29
14			5 26 7	0 10	♌ 12	2 35	3 27
15	2	Arcturus south 0 34	5 25 7	alt 5	26	3 12	4 21
16	3	☿'s elongation.	5 24 7	0 20	♍ 10	3 45	5 15
17	4		5 22 7	0 34	25	4 15	6 8
18	5	7 *'s set 9 18	5 21 7	0 48	♎ 10	4 43	7 0
19	6	☉ enters ♉ ☽ in per.	5 20 7	1 1	25	rises.	7 53
20	7		5 19 7	1 14	♏ 10	7 59	8 46
21	F	Spica ♍ south 11 16	5 17 7	1 27	25	9 18	9 43
22	2		5 16 7	1 39	♐ 10	10 37	10 1
23	3	St. George.	5 15 7	1 51	24	11 43	11 4
24	4		5 14 7	2 2	♑ 8	morn.	0 20
25	5	St. Mark.	5 13 7	2 13	22	0 42	1 11
26	6	♀ stationary.	5 11 7	2 24	♒ 5	1 25	2 15
27	7		5 10 7	2 34	17	2 5	3 9
28	F	Rogation.	5 9 7	2 43	30	2 35	3 45
29	2		5 8 7	2 53	♓ 12	3 1	4 35
30	3	7 *'s set 8 32	5 7 7	3 0	24	3 24	5 15

MAY, 1799—23d Year American Independence.

New Moon the 4th, at 17 minutes after 7 afternoon.
First Quarter the 12th, at 12 minutes after 12 afternoon.
Full Moon the 19th, at 54 minutes after 2 morning.
Last Quarter the 26th, at 8 minutes after 6 morning.

M D	W D	Miscellaneous Particulars.	Sun rises and sets.	☉ fast. M. S.	☽'s place S. D.	☽ rises. H. M.	High Water N. Yo.
1	4	Philip and James.	5 57	3 8	♈ 5	3 43	5 54
2	5	Ascension Day.	5 4 7	3 15	17	4 4	6 33
3	6	☽ in apogee.	5 3 7	3 22	29	4 25	7 13
4	7	Spica ♍ south 10 27	5 2 7	3 28	♉ 11	sets.	7 55
5	F		5 1 7	3 34	23	7 58	8 30
6	2		5 0 7	3 39	♊ 5	9 1	9 26
7	3	Transit of ☿ over ☉'s	4 59 8	3 44	17	10 2	10 17
8	4	[disk.	4 58 8	3 48	29	11 0	11 10
9	5	♄ sets 11 49	4 57 8	3 51	♋ 12	11 52	11 50
10	6		4 56 8	3 54	25	morn.	0 29
11	7	Arcturus south 10 48	4 54 8	3 56	♌ 8	0 38	1 24
12	F	Whitsunday.	4 53 8	3 58	21	1 17	2 19
13	2		4 52 8	3 59	♍ 5	1 50	3 11
14	3	♂ sets 10 31	4 52 8	3 59	19	2 19	4 2
15	4		4 51 8	3 59	♎ 4	2 46	4 52
16	5	Days 14 20	4 50 8	3 58	19	3 12	5 42
17	6	☽ in perigee.	4 49 8	3 56	♏ 3	3 34	6 32
18	7		4 48 8	3 54	18	4 9	7 27
19	F	Trinity.	4 47 8	3 52	♐ 3	rises.	8 24
20	2	☿ stationary. ☉ ent. ♊	4 46 8	3 49	18	9 24	9 24
21	3		4 45 8	3 45	♑ 2	10 29	10 25
22	4	Lyra south 2 35	4 44 8	3 41	16	11 21	11 20
23	5		4 44 8	3 37	30	morn.	0 13
24	6		4 43 8	3 32	♒ 13	0 4	0 54
25	7	♄ sets 10 53	4 42 8	3 26	26	0 37	1 40
26	F	after Trinity.	4 41 8	3 20	♓ 9	1 5	2 25
27	2	[♄ stationary	4 41 8	3 13	23	1 25	3 5
28	3		4 40 8	3 6	♈ 7	1 49	3 57
29	4	Arcturus south 9 40	4 39 8	2 59	14	2 9	4 37
30	5	☽ in apogee.	4 39 8	2 51	28	2 29	5 30
31	6	☽ ♊	4 38 8	2 8	♉ 8	2 51	6 24

JUNE, 1799—23d Year American Independence.

New Moon the 3d, at 8 minutes after 10 morning.
First Quarter the 10th, at 31 minutes after 6 afternoon.
Full Moon the 17th, at 8 minutes after 11 morning.
Last Quarter the 24th, at 17 minutes after 10 afternoon.

M D	W D	Miscellaneous Particulars.	Sun rises and sets.	☉ fast. M. S.	☽'s place. S. D.	☽ rises. H. M.	Hig. Water N. Yo
1	7		4 37 8	2 34	♌ 20	3 15	6 3
2	F	2d after Trinity.	4 37 8	2 25	♊ 2	3 45	7 2
3	2	☿'s elongation.	4 36 8	2 16	14	sets.	8 1
4	3		4 36 8	2 6	26	8 53	9
5	4	Arcturus south 9 11	4 35 8	1 56	♋ 9	9 47	9 5
6	5		4 35 8	1 45	22	10 33	10 5
7	6		4 34 8	1 34	♌ 5	11 16	11 3
8	7	Spica ♍ sets 1 36	4 34 8	1 23	18	11 50	0
9	F	3d after Trinity.	4 34 8	1 12	♍ 2	morn.	1
10	2	[□ ☉ ☽	4 33 8	1 0	16	0 20	1 5
11	3	St. Barnabas.	4 33 8	0 48	30	0 47	2 4
12	4		4 33 8	0 36	♎ 14	1 12	3 3
13	5		4 32 8	0 23	28	1 37	4 2
14	6	☽ in perigee.	4 32 8	0 11	♏ 13	2 5	5 1
15	7		4 32 8	low 2	27	2 37	6 6
16	F	4th after Trinity.	4 32 8	0 15	♐ 12	3 14	7
17	2	Lyra south 0 49	4 32 8	0 28	26	rises.	8
18	3		4 32 8	0 41	♑ 11	9 5	9
19	4		4 32 8	0 54	24	9 53	10
20	5	Spica ♍ sets 0 46	4 32 8	1 7	♒ 8	10 30	11 2
21	6	☉ enters ♋	4 32 8	1 20	21	11 1	12 4
22	7		4 32 8	1 33	♓ 4	11 25	0 1
23	F	5th after Trinity.	4 32 8	1 46	16	11 47	1
24	2	St. John Baptist.	4 32 8	1 59	28	morn.	1 4
25	3		4 32 8	2 11	♈ 10	0 7	2 2
26	4	☽ in apogee.	4 32 8	2 24	22	0 28	3
27	5		4 32 8	2 36	♉ 4	0 49	5 4
28	6		4 32 8	2 48	16	1 13	4 4
29	7	St. Peter.	4 33 8	3 0	28	1 40	5 10
30	F	6th after Trinity.	4 33 8	3 12	♊ 10	2 11	5 5

JULY, 1799—23d Year American Independence

M|W D|D	Miscellaneous Particulars.	Sun ri- ses and sets.	☉ sow. M. S.	☽'s place S. D.	☽ rises. H. M.	High Water N. Yo.
1|2		4 33 8	3 24	♊ 23	2 52	6 50
2|3	Visitation V. Mary.	4 33 8	3 35	♋ 5	sets	7 45
3|4		4 34 8	3 46	18	8 23	8 41

Eclipses for the 23d Year of American Independence.

FIRST, an eclipse of the Sun, on the 7th of November, 1798, at 55 minutes after 8 in the evening, to us invisible.

Second, of the Moon, on the 23d of November, in the morning, partly visible:

Beginning at . 6 12
Moon sets 6¼ digits eclipsed at 7 14
Duration of visibility, 1 2

Third, of the Sun, on the 4th of May, 1799, at 17 minutes 7 P. M. invisible. This eclipse will be central and annular on the meridian at 13 minutes after 7, in lat. 8° N. and long. 98¼ W. from New-York.

FRENCH CALENDER.

SINCE the establishment of the French Republic, an alteration has been made in their Calender. The National Convention has entirely laid aside the former denominations, and adopted the following—

December 21st. begins the first month of the French year, Nivose, or the snowy month.

January 20th. begins the second month, Pluviose, or the rainy month.
February 19th. begins the third month, Ventose, or the blustering month.
March 21st. begins the fourth month, Germinal, or the budding month.
April 20th. begins the fifth month, Floreal, or the flowering month.
May 20th. begins the sixth month, Prairial, or the meadow month.
June 19th. begins the seventh month, Messidor, or the harvest month.
July 19th. begins the eight month, Thermidor, or the sultry month.
August 18th. begins the ninth month, Fructidor, or the month of fruits.
September 22d. begins the tenth month, Vendemiaire, or the vintage month.
October 22d. begins the eleventh month, Brumaire, or the foggy month.
November 21st. begins the twelfth month, Frimaire, or the frosty month.

N. B. Observe, that no one of the months in the French Calender consists of more than thirty days.—The five superfluous days are termed Sans Culottes, or days appropriated to the Sans Culottes festivals, and reckoned between the 16th and 22d of September, and are intercalated between the two months Fructidor and Vendemiaire.

(16)

Table of High Water at the following Places.

Names of Places.	H. M.	Names of Places.	H. M.
ALBANY,	a. 7 10	Nantucket Shoals,	f. 0 50
Amboy,	f. 0 15	Newbury-Port,	a. 3 25
Annapolis, Maryland,	f. 1 20	New-Haven,	a. 2 30
Annapolis, N. Scotia,	a. 3 40	New-Providence,	f. 0 45
Boston,	a. 2 55	Newtown Landing,	a. 1 40
Bridgetown, E. Jersey,	f. 0 15	Penobscot,	a. 3 40
Burlington,	a. 1 0	Philadelphia,	f. 6 15
Cape Ann,	a. 3 25	Piscataway,	a. 3 20
Cape Fear,	f. 0 30	Plymouth,	a. 2 15
Cape Hatteras,	a. 2 40	Polepel's Island,	a. 3 40
Cape Henry,	a. 2 40	Port-Roseway,	f. 0 10
Casco Bay,	a. 2 55	Port-Royal, S. Carol.	a. 0 10
Charleston Lighthouse,	f. 1 20	Portsmouth,	a. 3 25
Cape May,	f. 0 10	Providence,	f. 0 15
Cape Canso,	a. 0 10	Perryburgh, S. Carol.	f. 1 20
Fairfield,	a. 2 40	Quebec,	a. 3 40
Georgetown Bar,	f. 1 40	Reedy-Island,	a. 2 55
Guildford,	a. 2 10	Rhode-Island,	f. 0 15
Hackensack,	a. 3 40	Salem,	a. 3 25
Halifax,	a. 3 40	Sandy-Hook,	f. 0 15
Hartford,	a. 3 0	Savannah,	f. 0 30
Hell-Gate,	a. 1 10	Saybrook,	a. 2 55
Huntington,	a. 2 40	Sunbury, Georgia,	a. 1 10
Ipswich,	a. 3 25	Tybee Bar,	a. 0 55
James town,	a. 1 30	White-Stone,	a. 3 25
Kingston, Esopus,	a. 6 40	Williamsburg, Virgin.	a. 2 55
Main Ocean,	f. 0 15	Wilmington, Delaw.	a. 4 0

N. B. *The eighth column of the Calendar pages, containing the time of high water at New-York, exhibits also the time of high water at Elizabeth Town-Point, New-London, Topsail, Cape Hatteras, Ockracok Bay, Cockspur in Georgia, and Brunswick in North-Carolina; and, by adding thereto and subtracting therefrom the annexed quantities of time, we have the time of high water at the places above enumerated.* A *shews the quantity of time to be added*—f *subtracted.*

NEW-YORK REGISTER.

For the Year 1798.

STAMP DUTIES.

Treasury Department, March 30th, 1798.

PUBLIC notice is hereby given, that by an act of Congress, passed on the 19th day of March, 1798, the following alterations and amendments have been made to the act passed on the 6th day of July, 1797, entitled, "An act laying duties on stamped vellum, parchment, and paper."

I. The stamp duties on debentures or certificates for the drawback of customs or duties on imports, are repealed.

II. A discount, at the rate of seven and one half per centum, will be allowed by the supervisors or inspectors respectively, to any persons other than officers of the revenue, who may purchase at one time, or procure to be stamped, any quantities of vellum, parchment, or paper, upon which the duties shall amount to ten dollars or upwards.

III. Stamped paper will be provided and sold at the rates prescribed by law, without any additional charge or expence, on account of the price of paper; but for stamped parchment or vellum, an additional price will be demanded at the rate of fifty cents for each skin of parchment, or two hundred cents for each skin of vellum of medium size, which may be furnished at the expence of the United States, and proportionally for any lesser quantity.

Given under my hand, at Philadelphia, the day and year above mentioned.
OLIVER WOLCOTT,
Secretary of the Treasury.

Treasury Department, March 1, 1798.
PUBLIC NOTICE IS HEREBY GIVEN,

In pursuance of the Act of Congress passed on the sixth day of July, one thousand seven hundred and ninety-seven, entitled "An Act for laying duties on stamped Vellum, Parchment, and Paper," and the act passed on the fifteenth day of December, one thousand seven hundred and ninety-seven, entitled, "An Act to postpone, for a limited time, the commencement of the duties imposed by the act entitled, An Act laying Duties on stamped Vellum, Parchment, and Paper," that from and after the first day of July ensuing, the several stamp duties hereafter enumerated, will be levied and collected throughout the United States.

1. For every skin or piece of vellum or parchment, or sheet or piece of paper, upon which shall be written or printed, any or either of the instruments or writings following—to wit:

Any certificate of naturalization, 5 dollars.

Any licence to practice, or certificate of the admission, enrollment, or registry of any counsellor, solicitor, attorney, advocate or proctor, in any court of the United States, 10 dollars.

Provided, that a certificate in any one of the courts of the United States for one of the said offices, shall so far as relates to the payment of the duty aforesaid, be a sufficient admission in all the courts of the United States, for each and every of the said offices.

Any grant or letters patent, under the seal or authority of the United States, (except for lands granted for military services) 4 dollars.

Any exemplification, or certified copy of any such grant or letters patents, (except for lands granted for military services) 2 dolrs.

Any charter-party, bottomry, or respondentia bond, 1 dollar.

Any receipt or other discharge for or on account of any legacy left by any will or other testamentary instrument, or for any share or part of a personal estate divided by force of any statute of distributions, other than to the wife, children, or grand-children of the person deceased, the amount whereof shall be above the value of fifty dollars, and shall not exceed the value of one hundred dollars, 25 cents.

When the amount thereof shall exceed the value of one hundred dollars and shall not exceed five hundred dollars, 50 cents.

And for every further sum of five hundred dollars, the additional sum of 1 dollar.

Any policy of insurance, or instrument in nature thereof, on any ship, vessel or goods insured from one district to another in the United States, 25 cents.

From the United States to any foreign port or place, when the sum for which insurance is made shall not exceed five hundred dollars, 25 cents.

When the sum insured shall exceed five hundred dollars, 1 dol.

Any exemplification, of what nature soever, that shall pass the seal of any court, other than such as it may be the duty of the clerk of such court to furnish for the use of the United States, or some particular state, 50 cents.

Any bond, bill single or penal, foreign or inland bill of exchange, promissory note, or other note, other than any recognizance, bail bond, or other obligation or contract, made to or with the United States, or any state, or for their use respectively:

If above twenty dollars, and not exceeding one hundred dollars, 10 cents.

If above one hundred dollars, and not exceeding five hundred dollars, 25 cents.

If above five hundred dollars, and not exceeding one thousand dollars, 50 cents.

And if above one thousand dollars, 75 cents.

Provided, that if any bonds or notes shall be payable at or within sixty days, such bonds or notes shall be subject to only two-fifth parts of the duty aforesaid, viz.

If above twenty dollars, and not exceeding one hundred dollars, 4 cents.

If above one hundred dollars, and not exceeding five hundred dollars, 10 cents.

If above five hundred dollars, and not exceeding one thousand dollars, 20 cents.

If above one thousand dollars, 30 cents.

Any notes issued by the banks now established, or that may hereafter be established, within the United States, other than the notes of such of the said banks as shall agree to an annual composition of one per cent. on the annual dividends made by such banks to their stockholders respectively, according to the following scale:

On all notes not exceeding fifty dollars, for each dollar, 6 mills.

On all notes above fifty dollars, and not exceeding one hundred dollars, 50 cents.

On all notes above one hundred dollars, and not exceeding five hundred dollars, 1 dollar.

On all notes above five hundred dollars, 2 dollars.

Any protest, or other notarial act, 25 cents.

Any letter for attorney, except for an invalid pension, or to obtain or sell warrants for land granted by the United States as bounty for military services performed in the late war, 25 cents.

Any certificate or debenture for drawback of customs or duties, for less than five hundred dollars, 1 dollar.

For five hundred dollars, and not exceeding two thousand dollars, 2 dollars.

For more than two thousand dollars, 3 dollars.

Any note or bill of lading for goods or merchandize to be exported:

If from one district to another district of the United States, not being in the same state, 10 cents.

If from the United States to any foreign port or place, 25 cents.

Any inventory or catalogue of any furniture, goods, or effects, made in any case required by law, (except in cases of goods and chattles distrained for rent or taxes, and goods taken in virtue of any legal process by any officer) 50 cents.

Any certificate of a share in any insurance company, or a share in the bank of the United States, or of any state or other banks:

If above twenty dollars, and not exceeding one hundred dollars, 10 cents.

If above one hundred dollars, 25 cents.

If under twenty dollars, at the rate of 10 cents per 100 dollars.

II. The duties aforesaid will be collected and received by the supervisors, inspectors, and other officers of inspection, in the several districts, surveys, and divisions of the United States, and by such other persons as shall, from time to time, be specially appointed and employed by the legislatures of the states, for that purpose.

III. The supervisors of the several districts will, prior to the first day of July ensuing, and as soon as may be practicable, mark or stamp, without fee or reward, any quantities or parcels of vellum, parchment, or paper, with any of the rates of duties before enumerated, on payment of the said duties: or stamped vellum, parchment and paper, may, at the option of the citizens of the United States, be obtained at the rates prescribed by law, by application to any supervisor, inspector, officer of inspection, or other person appointed for the distribution of stamps, by the supervisors of districts.

Given under my hand, at Philadelphia, the day and year above mentioned. OLIVER WOLCOTT,
Secretary of the Treasury.

DUTIES

Payable on Goods, Wares, &c. imported into the United States of America, from the first day of April, 1797.

[The inward column exhibits the rates payable on articles imported in ships or vessels of the United States, and the outward column the rates payable in foreign ships or vessels, including the additional duties to which the respective articles are liable.]

ARMS, fire and side, not otherwise enumerated,	free.	free.
Apparatus, philosophical, especially imported for any seminary of learning,	free.	free.
Ale, beer and porter, in casks,	8 cents per gal.	8¾
———————————— in bottles,	10 ditto.	11 and two cents per doz.
Anniseed,	15 p. ct. ad val.	16½
Articles of all kinds of the growth, produce or manufacture of the United States, spirits excepted,	free.	free.
Anchors,	10	11
Boots,	75 cents pr. pair	82½
Books, blank,	10 p. ct. ad val.	11
Buttons of every kind,	15	16½
Buckles, shoe and knee,	15	16½
Bullion,	free.	free.
Brushes,	10	11
Bricks and tiles,	10	16½
Cannon of brass,	free.	free.

Carriages of all kinds,	20	22
Cards, playing,	25 cents p. pack,	27½
—— wool and cotton,	50 cents p. doz.	55
Cabinet wares,	15 p. ct. ad val.	16½
Carpets and carpeting,	15	16½
Candles of tallow,	2 cents per lb.	2⅕
—— of wax or spermaceti,	6	6⅗
Capers,	15 p. ct. ad val.	16½
Canes, walking-sticks and whips,	10	11
Cambricks,	10	11
Cheese,	7 cents per lb.	7⁷⁄₁₀
China ware,	15 p. ct. ad val.	16½
Cinnamon, cloves, currants, and comfits,	15	16½
Cocoa,	4 cents per lb.	4⅖
Chocolate,	3	3³⁄₁₀
Cables and tarred cordage,	180 cts. p. cwt.	198
Coal,	5 cents p. bus.	5½
Copper manufactures,	15 p. ct. ad val.	16½
—— in plates, pigs and bars,	free.	free.
Coffee,	5 cents per lb.	5½
Cotton,	3.	3³⁄₁₀
Clocks and watches, or parts of either,	15 p. ct. ad val.	16½
Clothing ready made,	10	11
Clothes, books, household furniture, and the tools or implements of the trade or profession of persons who come to reside in the United States,	free.	free.
Dolls, dressed and undressed,	15	16½
Drugs, medicinal, except those commonly used for dying,	15	16½
—— and woods for dying,	free.	free.
Fans,	15	16½
Feathers and other ornaments for women's head-dresses,	15	16½
Fringes commonly used by upholsterers, coach makers, and saddlers,	15	16½
Floor-cloths and mats,	15	16½
Fruits of all kinds,	15	16½

Furs of every kind, undreſſed,	free	free.
Glaſs, black quart bottles,	10	11
——window glaſs,	15	16½
——all other glaſs, and manufactures thereof,	20	22
Glaubers Salts,	200 cts. p. cwt. and ¾ p. ct. ad val.	220
Gauzes,	10 p. ct. ad val.	11
Ginger,	15	16½
Gloves of leather,	15	16½
All other gloves and mittens,	15	16½
Gold, ſilver, and plated ware,	15	16½
Gold and ſilver lace,	15	16½
Glue,	15	16½
Hats, caps, and bonnets of every kind,	15	16½
Hemp,	100 cts. p. cwt.	105⅗
Hides, raw,	free.	free.
Indigo,	25 cents p. lb.	27½
Iron and teutenague wire,	free.	free.
——caſt, ſlit and rolled,	15	16½
——or ſteel locks, hinges, hoes, anvils and vices,	10	11
All other manufactures of iron, ſteel or braſs, not being otherwiſe particularly enumerated,	15 p. ct. ad val.	16½
Jewellery and paſte-work,	15	16½
Laces and lawns,	10	11
Lampblack,	10	11
Lapis calaminaris,	free.	free.
Leather, tanned and tawed, and all manufactures of leather, or of which leather is the article of chief value, not otherwiſe particularly enumerated,	15	16½
Lead and musket ball,	free.	free.
All other manufactures of lead,	1	1$\frac{1}{10}$
Linen, or cotton manufactures, or of both, printed, ſtained, or coloured,	12½ p. ct. ad val.	13¾
——not printed, ſtained or coloured,	10	11

Additional duty on unstained cotton goods, 2½ cents.

Mats and floor cloths,	15 p. ct. ad val.	16½
Malt,	10 cents p. buſ.	11
Marble, ſlate and other ſtone, bricks, tiles, tables, mortars, and other utenſils of marble and ſlate, and generally all ſtone and earthen ware,	15 p. ct. ad val.	16½
Mace and nutmegs,	15	16½
Merchandize, goods and wares imported directly from China or India, in ſhips or veſſels not of the U. States, except teas, China ware, & all other articles liable to higher rates of duties,	—	12½
Merchandize, goods and wares intended to be re-exported to a foreign port or place in the ſame ſhip or veſſel in which they ſhall be imported, and all articles of the growth, product or manufacture of the United States, ſpirits excepted,	free.	free.
Merchandize, goods & wares not herein otherwiſe particularly enumerated and deſcribed,	10	11
Millinary, ready made,	15	16½
Molaſſes,	3 cents p. gal.	3⅛
Muſkets and firelocks, with bayonets fixed to the ſame, and muſket ball,	free.	free.
Muſtard in flower,	15	16½
Nails,	2 cents per lb.	2½
Nankeens,	12½ p. ct. ad val.	
Paper-hangings,	15 p. ct. ad val.	
—— writing and wrapping,	10	11
—— ſheathing and cartridge,	15	16½
Painters' colours, whether dry or ground in oil, except thoſe commonly uſed in dying,	15	16½
Paſteboards, archment, & vellum,	10	11

Plaister of Paris,	free.	free.
Pewter manufactures,	15	$16\frac{1}{2}$
——— old,	free.	free.
Pepper,	6 cents per lb.	$6\frac{3}{5}$
Pictures and prints,	10 p. ct. ad val.	11
Printing types,	10	11
Pimento,	4 cents per lb.	$4\frac{2}{5}$
Pickles of all sorts,	15 p. ct. ad val.	$16\frac{1}{2}$
Powder for the hair,	15	$16\frac{1}{2}$
Powders, pastes, balls, balsams, ointments, oils, waters, washes, tinctures, essences, or other prèparations or compositions commonly called sweet scents, odours, perfumes, or cosmetics, and all powders or preparations for the teeth or gums,	15	$16\frac{1}{2}$
Powder, gun,	free.	free.
Salt, (see note.)	12 cents p. bu.	$13\frac{1}{5}$
Sat-petre,	free.	free.
Starch,	15 p. ct. ad val.	$16\frac{1}{2}$
Sail cloth,	10	11
Saddles,	10	11
Slate stone, or stone ware,	15	$16\frac{1}{2}$
Sattins, and other wrought silks,	10	11
Steel,	100 cts. p. cwt.	110
—— iron or brass locks, hinges, hoes, anvils, and vices,	10 p. ct. ad val.	11
—— all other manufactures of steel or brass,	15	$16\frac{1}{2}$
Sea-stores of ships or vessels,	free.	free.
Spermaceti candles,	6 cents. per lb.	$6\frac{3}{5}$
Spirits distilled in foreign countries, viz.		
From grain, First proof,	28 cts. per gal.	[illegible]
Second do.	29	[illegible]
Third do.	31	[illegible]
Fourth do.	34	[illegible]
Fifth do.	40	44
Sixth do.	50	55
From other materials.		
First proof,	25	[illegible]
Second do.	25	[illegible]

Third do.	28	30 4/5
Fourth do.	32	35 1/5
Fifth do.	38	41 4/5
Sixth do.	46	50 3/5
Spirits distilled in the U. States, imported after the 5th day of June, 1794, in the same ship or vessel in which they had been previously exported from the United States, viz.		
From molasses,		
First proof,	13 cents p. gal.	13
Second do.	14	14
Third do.	15	15
Fourth do.	17	17
Fifth do.	21	21
Sixth do.	28	28
From materials of the growth or produce of the United States.		
First proof,	7	7
Second do.	8	8
Third do.	9	9
Fourth do.	11	11
Fifth do.	13	13
Sixth do.	18	18
Spikes,	1 cent per lb.	1 1/10
Shoes and slippers of silk,	25 cts. per pr.	27 1/2
—— other shoes and slippers for men and women, clogs and goloshoes,	15 p. ct. ad. val.	16 1/2
—— other shoes and slippers for children,	10	11
Stockings,	15 p. ct. ad val.	16 1/2
Soap,	2 cents per lb.	2 1/5
Sulphur,	free.	free.
Sugars, brown,	1 1/2	[illegible]
Clayed,	3	3 3/10
Lump,	6 1/2	[illegible]
Loaf,	9	9 9/10
Other refined,	6 1/2	[illegible]
Sugar candy,	10 p. ct. ad val.	11
Snuff,	22	24 1/5

Teas, from China and India.
 Bohea,   10 cents per lb. 15
 Souchong and other black
  teas,   18   27
 Hyson,   32   50
 Other green teas,   20   30
From Europe.
 Bohea,   12   15
 Souchong and other black
  teas,   21   27
 Imperial, Green-Hyson, or
  Gomee,   40   50
 Other green teas,   24   30
From any other place.
 Bohea,   15 $16\frac{1}{2}$
 Souchong and other black teas, 27 $29\frac{7}{10}$
 Hyson and gunpowder, 50   55
 Other green teas,   30   33
Twine and pack-thread,   400 cts. p. cwt. 440
Tin manufactures,   15 p. ct. ad val. $16\frac{1}{2}$
—— in pigs and plates,   free.   free.
Toys, not otherwise enumerated, 10   11
Tobacco, manufactured,   10 cents per lb. 11
Velvets and velverets,   10 p. ct. ad val. 11
Wafers,   15 $16\frac{1}{2}$
Watches and clocks, or parts of
 either,   15 p. ct. ad val. $16\frac{1}{2}$
Wine, London particular Madaira, 56 cts. per gal. $61\frac{3}{5}$
—— London market do. 49 $53\frac{9}{10}$
—— Other do.   40   44
—— Sherry,   33 $36\frac{3}{10}$
—— St. Lucar,   30   33
—— Lisbon and Oporto, 25 $27\frac{1}{2}$
—— Teneriffe, Fayal and Ma-
 laga,   20   22
—— Burgundy & Champaign, 40   44
—— All other wines (not to
 exceed 30 cents per gallon in
 American vessels, or 33 cents
 per gallon in foreign vessels) 40 p. ct. ad val. 44
Wool, unmanufactured,   free.   free.
Wood, unmanufactured,   free.   free.

Wood, manufactured, (exclusive of cabinet wares)	12½	13¾
Yarn, untarred,	225 cents p.cwt.	247½
All other goods not before particularly enumerated and described,	10 p. ct. ad val.	11

NOTE—The duties on Salt are to be estimated at the rate of twelve cents per bushel, weighing fifty six pounds or less; but the additional duties on Salt imported in foreign vessels, will result from the quantity by measurement only; thus:

Suppose a cargo of salt to contain by measurement 4000 bushels, and that the same cargo weighs 280,000lbs. the duties will be as follow, viz.

If imported in an American vessel, 280,000lbs. at 12 cents per 56lbs. is Dols.	600
If imported in a foreign vessel, 280,000lbs. at 12 cents per 56 lbs. is Dols.	600
Additional duty on 4000 bushels, at 1 1-5 cent per bushel,	48
Dollars,	648

BOUNTY.

On every barrel of pickled fish exported, of the fisheries of the United States, 18 cents.

On every barrel of salted provisions exported, salted within the United States, 15 cents.

And since the first day of January, 1793, an addition of twenty per centum to the allowances respectively granted to the ships or vessels employed in the Bank or other cod fisheries.

TONNAGE.

By act of July 20, 1790, to be paid in ten days after entry, and before clearance.

	Cents per ton.
On vessels of the United States, from foreign ports,	6
On vessels built in the United States, since the 20th of July, 1789, but owned in part or wholly by foreigners—duly recorded,	30
All other vessels,	50
Every vessel employed in transporting goods, coast-ways, except such vessel be built in, and belong to citizens, on each entry;	50

Veſſels built in and belonging to citizens of the United States, in coaſting-trade or fiſhery, pay, once a year, if licenſed,   6

If not licenſed, pay, with goods taken in one ſtate to be delivered in another, except the adjoining ſtate, on each entry,   6

Drawback on merchandize exported, payable by debenture, in not leſs than three months, and at the time the bonds for the duty ſhall be payable.

Bounty on ſalted proviſions and fiſh, not payable until ſix months after exportation, nor until a certificate in writing is produced, by the exporter, from two reputable merchants at the foreign-port or place where landed, together with the oath of the maſter and mate, certifying the delivery thereof: except diſtilled ſpirits, in which caſe a certificate from an American conſul, if ſuch there be, or from two American merchants, reſiding at ſuch foreign port; or if there be neither, then a certificate from two reputable merchants of the place, and the oath of the maſter and mate as above: and an oath is further required, that on diligent ſearch no ſuch conſul or American merchants could be found reſident there.

FEES.

To the Collector and Naval Officer.   D.   C.

	D.	C.
Entry of a veſſel of 100 tons or upwards.	2	50
Clearance do. do.	2	50
Entry of a veſſel under 100 tons,	1	50
Clearance do. do.	1	50
Permit to land goods.	0	20
Every bond taken officially,	0	40
Permit to load goods, for exportation, for drawback,	0	30
Every other official document (regiſter excepted)	0	20

Fees to Surveyor.

	D.	C.
For meaſurement of a veſſel 100 tons and under, per ton,	0	1
For do. 100 to 200 tons,	1	5
For do. above 200 tons,	2	

On each vessel of 100 tons and upwards,
  with goods subject to duty,   3   0
On each vessel under 100 tons, with do. 1 50
All vessels not having goods subject to duty, 0 66¾

No Vessel not wholly belonging to a Citizen or Citizens of the United States, shall be admitted to unload at any Port or Place, except the following, to wit:

NEW-HAMPSHIRE—*Portsmouth.* MASSACHUSETTS—*Portland, Ipswich, Falmouth. New-Bedford,* Dighton, *Berkley, Taunton,* Salem, *Beverly, Gloucester, Newbury-Port,* Marblehead, Sherburn, *Boston* and *Charlestown, Bath, Frenchman's Bay,* Plymouth, Wiscasset, Machias, Penobscot. RHODE-ISLAND—*Newport* and *Providence.* CONNECTICUT—*New-London, New-Haven.* NEW-YORK—*New-York, Hudson.* NEW-JERSEY—*Perth-Amboy,* Tuckerton, Burlington. PENNSYLVANIA—*Philadelphia.* DELAWARE—*Wilmington,* Newcastle, Port-Penn. MARYLAND—*Baltimore, Annapolis, Havre de Grace, Newbury,* Vienna. Oxford, *George-Town* or *Pitowmack,* Chester-Town, *Nottingham,* Town-Creek, Nanjemoy, Digge's Landing, Snow-Hill, Carrollsborough. VIRGINIA—*Alexandria,* Kinsale, Newport, Tappahannock, Port-Royal, Fredericksburgh, Urbanna, York-town, West-Point, Hampton, Bermuda Hundred, City-Point, Rocket's Landing, *Norfolk, Portsmouth.* NORTH-CAROLINA—*Wilmington, Newbern, Washington,* Edenton, and *Plankbridge.* SOUTH-CAROLINA—*Charleston,* Georgetown, *Beaufort.* GEORGIA—*Savannah, Sunbury,* Brunswick, St. Mary, and *Frederica.*

Nor shall any vessel from the Cape of Good Hope, or beyond the same, be admitted to enter, except at the ports in the above list which are distinguished by *Italics.*

Mode of transacting business at the Custom-house of the United States for the port of New-York, and extracts from the Revenue Acts, for the direction of merchants, masters of vessels, and others concerned.

NO goods are to be imported, in any vessel owned in the whole or part by citizens of the United States, from any foreign port, unless the master shall have on board a manifest or written list, containing the names of the ports or places where such goods were received, and the port where consigned or destined to, and the name and built of the vessel, and true tonnage by register, with the name of the master and place to which such vessel belongs, and particular account of all the cargo in packages, or loose, with the marks and numbers, and description of each, by usual denominations in words at length.

For any goods not included in the manifest as above, the master is to forfeit a sum equal to their value, unless it is made to appear to the collector, naval officer and surveyor, or to a court on trial, that no part of the cargo was unshipped, except what is mentioned in the report, or that the manifest has been lost or mislaid without fraud, or defaced by accident, or incorrect by mistake.

The master of any vessel, bound to any port in the United States, on arrival within four leagues of the coast, or within any bays or harbours, ports, rivers, creeks, or inlets thereof, on demand, to produce such manifests to the officer of the customs first coming on board, and deliver him a copy thereof, subscribed by the master, and the officer to certify on the original, that the same was so produced, and a copy delivered him, and the master to produce the original so certified to the officer first coming on board, on his arrival in the district where the cargo is intended to be landed, and deliver to such officer a copy thereof, to be provided and subscribed by the master, the delivery of which to be certified by the said officer on the original manifest, and the original manifest to be delivered afterwards to the collector.

The penalty for not producing such manifests, and delivering copies thereof, or for not informing such officer of the destination of such vessel, or giving false account of destination, is five hundred dollars for each offence.

Any vessel within four leagues of the coast, or within the limits of a district, unloading goods without authority from proper officers, the master and the mate forfeit one thousand dollars, and the goods forfeited, except in case of accident, necessity, or stress of weather, which shall be proved before the collector.

Masters of vessels receiving goods so unladen, (except as before excepted) to forfeit treble the value of such goods, and the ship, boat, or vessel, receiving them forfeited.

If any vessel, arriving within a district, shall depart or attempt to depart from the same (unless to some more interior port, or by stress of weather) without report made to the collector, the master forfeits four hundred dollars.

Any vessel arriving from a foreign port, the master is to report to the collector within twenty-four hours after his arrival; and within forty-eight hours further to report the name, burthen, and loading of such ship, whether in packages or loose, and of the marks, numbers, and contents of each package, and place or places, person or persons, to or for whom they are respectively consigned or unlined, also the places where she took in her loading, what country built, from what foreign port she last sailed, who was master during the voyage, and is at the time of the report, and (if a vessel of the United States) who are owners.

Masters neglecting to make such reports, forfeit 1000 dollars.

Ships of war or packets of any prince or state, and not permitted by such prince or state to carry goods in way of trade, are not required to make such report.

Masters of vessels, after arrival and entry, may proceed to foreign ports, with goods reported for such foreign port, without paying duty thereon, on giving bond; and bonds are not required when vessels put in in distress.

Duties only to be paid where goods are landed (on giving bonds if such vessel proceeds to another district.)

Collector to furnish the master, bound to another district, with a copy of his report, which he is to show to the collector of that district within twenty-four hours after his arrival, on penalty of five hundred dollars.

Owners or consignees of goods imported, are, within fifteen days after the master's report, to make entry with the collector of the marks, numbers, and contents of each package, or quantity and quality in bulk, with the neat prime cost thereof, and produce the original invoice, documents and bills of lading, and declare all the party knows on oath or affirmation, and subscribe the same.

Sea-stores to be specified by masters, and exempted from duty, if not more than the principal officers of the customs think are necessary, but are not to be landed.

Cloaths, books, household furniture, tools or implements of trade or profession of persons arriving in the United States to settle, exempted from duty on due proof.

No goods from foreign parts to be unloaded but between sunrise and sun-set, without special licence for that purpose, nor without a permit, under penalty of four hundred dollars, disability from holding office for seven years, and being advertised in the gazettes, and forfeiture of goods; and if above the value of four hundred dollars, of vessel and apparel.

Goods removed before gauged or weighed, without permission, are forfeited.

Inspectors and officers of revenue cutters may go on board, examine, and search vessels, have free access to the cabbin, and to all packages, and, after sun-set, secure hatches and communications.

Persons in charge of vessels, for breaking fastenings before sunrise and presence of officer, forfeit two hundred dollars.

Goods not entered in fifteen days, to be delivered to the collector to store, &c. except salt or coal, which may remain one for they are paying inspectors.

Packages wanting, or goods not agreeing with manifest, to make forfeits five hundred dollars, unless made appear to the satisfaction of the principal officers of the customs or courts, that such disagreement arises from accident or mistake.

Allowance on draught on   1 cwt. or 112lb. at 1lb.

     1 to 2 cwt. 2

     3   7

	3	10	4
	10	13	7
	Above	1S.	9
Tare on chest bohea tea,			70
Half chest,			36
Quarter chest,		—	20

Chests of hyson or green, weighing 70lb.
and upwards,   20
    Gunpowder,   20
    Other chests of tea, 50 to 70lb.   23
    All others according to invoice.

Coffee in bags,	2 per cent.
Coffee in bales,	3 per cent.
casks,	12 per cent.
Pepper in bales,	5 per cent.
casks,	12 per cent.
Sugars (other than loaf) in casks,	12 per cent.
boxes,	15 per cent.

All other goods according to the invoice thereof.
Leakage, 2 per cent. on liquors in casks.
    Goods damaged in the voyage to be appraised by persons named by the collector and owner, and allowance made for duty.
    Goods without invoice to be stored by the collector or appraised.
    Ships arriving in distress to make protest before a notary, or other person authorised, or before the collector, within twenty-four hours; and within forty-eight hours to report of vessel and cargo to the collector, as in other cases. Goods may be stored, and so much as necessary for repairs sold on payment of duties.
    Duties to be paid before permit, unless they exceed fifty dollars, in which case they may be secured by bond, with one or more securities, payable, viz. salt in nine months, West-India produce (except salt) three and six months, wines twelve months, teas from China twelve months, and if stored under care of the inspector, two years; all other in eight, ten and twelve months; or the importer may deposit double the value of duties in the goods to secure payment of duties, which, on failure of payment, are to be sold.
    Teas from China may be deposited with the collector, and delivered on payment of duties, for such part as is delivered within eighteen months, and then sold for duties if not paid.
    Officers may seize within or without their districts. Persons resisting or impeding them forfeit four hundred dollars.
    In cases of drawback, notice to be given to the collector by the exporter, at least twenty-four hours before shipping the goods; all which are to be inspected and shipped in presence of an officer. Drawbacks are allowed at the place of entry only, on all goods exported to any country without the United States, within twelve months after payment made or security given for the duties inwards, and excepting where the duties do not amount to twenty dollars, or distilled spirits to one hundred gallons at least; retaining one per cent. of the duties, and half a cent per gallon for the charge of entry, &c.

Bonds, with one or more sufficient securities, to be given, that such goods shall not be re-landed in the United States.

In case of vessel cast away, or other accident, to produce protest in due form, or in case such protest cannot be had, the oath or affirmation of the exporter, or other proof to the satisfaction of the collector.

Goods exported for drawback, and re-landed, subject to seizure, together with the vessel, boats, &c. and persons concerned suffer six months imprisonment; but if the voyage is altered, the collector may give permit for re-landing.

Salt fish and salted provisions to be shipped under the same restriction as in case of drawbacks, and the bounty to be paid without abatement; but no drawback to be allowed unless it amount to twenty dollars, nor bounty unless to three dollars.

Persons giving or offering a bribe, forfeit from two hundred to two thousand dollars.

Captains or owners making false entry, forfeit not exceeding one thousand dollars, and suffer not more than twelve months imprisonment.

No goods of foreign growth or manufacture to be brought into the United States unless by sea, and not in vessels under thirty tons, on forfeiture of goods and vessel, (except to Louisville on the Ohio) except household furniture and clothing of persons removing to the United States.

Vessels bound to foreign ports, the master is to deliver a true manifest, on oath, and take clearance, (but without specifying particulars, unless required) under penalty of two hundred dollars.

All permits granted by the collector, for wines and distilled spirits, shall, prior to the landing of such goods, be produced to the inspector of the port, who shall, by indorsement, signify the same. Wines or spirits landed contrary to the above directions, are subjected to forfeiture.

Spirits imported (except gin in cases and cordials) in casks under fifty gallons, are forfeited, and the vessel also, until the 30th day of April, 1793; after which no distilled spirits, except arrack and sweet cordials, can be imported in casks or vessels of less capacity than ninety gallons, on pain of forfeiture: and after the last day of December, 1792, beer, ale or porter, imported in casks less than forty gallons, or, if in bottles, in packages less than six dozen, are forfeited, together with the ship or vessel.

Sureties on all bonds given at the custom-house for duties, shall, in case of insolvency in the principal, have and enjoy the advantages, priority, and preference for the recovery of the monies so bonded, out of the estate and effects of such insolvent, as are reserved and secured to the United States by the 45th section of the act for the collection of duties, &c.

No ship or vessel from foreign ports, or coming by sea from any port in the United States, shall be permitted to report, make entry, or break bulk, till the master shall deliver to the postmaster all letters under his care, or within his power, other than such as are directed to the owner or consignee: the collector to require an oath or affirmation from every maker of such delivery: masters of vessels to receive two cents for every letter so delivered.

☞ The exportation of brass cannon, muskets and firelocks, with bayonets suited to the same, pistols, swords, cutlasses, musket balls, lead and gunpowder, salt-petre, and sulphur, is prohibited under the penalty of forfeiture of vessel and tackle, and the Captain liable to indictment.

☞ For forms of manifests, oaths, entries, &c. &c. see last year's Directory, page 35.

☞ For list of duties payable in the French Leeward Islands, see last year's Directory, page 15.

Extract of an Act of Congress, passed 3d March, 1797, to take place the first of April following.

THE weighmasters shall mark on each cask, bag or package, the weight thereof, where the same is not less than 800 pounds, if thereunto required by the owner, at the time of weighing.

Hours of doing Business at the Custom-house.

From ten till two, and from four till six o'clock; but no business is done in the afternoon, except clearing of vessels and cancelling bonds.

Officers of the Customs for the District of New-York.
Joshua Sands, Collector.
Richard Rogers, Naval Officer.
John Lasher, Surveyor.
Inspectors of the Customs.
John Stephens, Samuel Scudder, Ralph Hedge, James Paine, William Leaycraft, William Lasher, Jedediah Waterman, John Banks, William Hurtin, William Forbes, Peter Kinnan, John King, John Boerum. Walter Heyer.
David Burger, supernumerary.
Coopers.
James Bingham, John Herttell, William Strachan.
Weighers.
John Banker, Charles Duryee, James Cebrea, Walter Picker, Daniel Kemper, Jonas Addoms.
Measurers.
Richard Norwood, Aaron Gilbert, Andrew No-

wood, Jacob Van Waggenen, William Degrove, Gerard Sickels, William Walmiley, Luke C. Quick, William Dodge.

Measurers of Lime.

William Van Gelder, William Heyer, J. Stanton, James Wessels, ——— Campbell.

Post Days at New York for the Year 1798.

SOUTHERN MAIL—*Throughout the year.*

ARRIVES.		DEPARTS.	
Monday,	9 A. M.	Monday,	1 P. M.
Tuesday,	9 A. M.	Tuesday,	1 P. M.
Wednesday,	9 A. M.	Wednesday,	1 P. M.
Thursday,	9 A. M.	Thursday,	1 P. M.
Friday,	9 A. M.	Friday,	1 P. M.
Saturday,	9 A. M.	Saturday,	1 P. M.

EASTERN MAIL—*Throughout the year.*

ARRIVES.		DEPARTS.	
Tuesday,	12 M.	Monday,	11 A. M.
Thursday,	12 M.	Wednesday,	11 A. M.
Saturday,	12 M.	Friday,	11 A. M.

NORTHERN MAIL—*From May to October.*

ARRIVES.		DEPARTS.	
Sunday,	11 A. M.	Monday,	2 P. M.
Tuesday,	11 A. M.	Wednesday,	2 P. M.
Thursday,	11 A. M.	Friday,	2 P. M.

From October to May.

ARRIVES.		DEPARTS.	
Sunday,	2 P. M.	Monday,	9 A. M.
Tuesday,	2 P. M.	Wednesday,	9 A. M.
Thursday,	2 P. M.	Friday,	9 A. M.

The Rhode-Island mail, by way of New-Haven, Guilford, Killingworth, Saybrook, Lyme, New-London, Norwich, Plainfield, Providence, Newport, and Easton, will leave New-York every Tuesday, Thursday and Saturday, at 9 A. M. and return Wednesday, Friday and Sunday, at noon.

The mail for Bennington, in Vermont, by way of White-Plains, Bedford, South-East, Franklin, Dover, Sharon, Sheffield, Great-Barrington, Stockbridge, Pittsfield, and Williamstown, will leave New-York every Monday, Wednesday and Friday, at 7 A. M. and return Tuesday, Thursday and Saturday, at 6 P. M.

The mail for Hartford, by way of Ridgefield, New-Milford, Danbury, and Lichfield, arrives every Thursday, at 8 A. M. and departs at 4 P. M. the same day.

The mail for Morristown, Boonetown, Rockaway, Suffex, Ward's Bridge, and Goshen, arrives every Monday, at 9 A. M. and departs every Tuesday at noon.

The mail for Hackinsack, Paramus, New-Antrim, Chester, and Goshen, arrives every Wednesday, at 6 P. M. and departs at 6 A. M. on Friday.

The mail for Sag-Harbour, on Long-Island, by way of Jamaica, Queen's county court-house, Huntington, Smithtown, Corum, Suffolk, Southampton, and Bridgehampton, arrives every Wednesday, at 4 P. M. and departs next day at 10 A. M.

Notice.—All letters must be lodged one hour before the time fixed for the departure of the mail, or they will lie over until the next post.

As there are several places of the same name in the United States, the merchants and others are requested to be very particular in the direction of their letters; distinguishing the states, and, where it would otherwise be doubtful, the counties in which those places are situated. And when letters are not for a post-town, the nearest post-town to the place ought to be mentioned.

All letters which are lodged to go by the British Packets, should be distinguished by writing *per Packet*, for there are places of the same name in the United States, similar to those in Europe.

S. BAUMAN, *Deputy-Postmaster.*

☞ The mails which arrive on Sunday are not opened till Monday morning.

General Post-Office.

Jacob Habersham, Post-master-general.
Charles Purrall, Assistant.

For the rates of postage, see last year's Directory p. 46, 47.

New-York Fire Engineers.

Wm. Hardenbrook, Thomas Hazard, John Stagg, Ahasuerus Turk, John Post, James Tylee, Thomas Brown.

Fire Wardens.

John Remsen, Thomas Ludlow, 1st Ward.
George Harsen, John Titus, 2d Ward.
Jeronemus Alstine, Wm. Hardenbrook, 3d Ward.
Jacob Abramse, John Bogart, 4th Ward.
Benjamin Egbert, Archibald Kerly, 5th Ward.
Jacob Harsen, Jacobus Vervelan, 6th Ward.
Nathaniel Fanning, Robert Fox, 7th Ward.

Fire Department.

Daniel Hitchcock, President.
———— ———— Vice-President.
James Parsons, jun. Secretary.

Fire Department Fund for the Relief of Firemen and their Families who may be disabled in the discharge of their Duties as Firemen.

Christopher Halstead, President.
Nicholas Van Antwerp, Treasurer.
Benjamin Strong, Secretary.
Martin Morrison, Collector.

Stephen Smith, James Tylee, Jacob Sherred, Thomas Brown, Frederick Devou, John Striker, and James Stuart, *Trustees.*

Firemen.

Attlee, Henry
Astin, Isaac
Allen, Stephen
Ashfield, John
Alstine, John
Allen, William
Albertus, William
Aubick, Henry
Abeel, Garrit
Anderson, Israel
Aubick, Ernest
Allen, Robert
Annely, John
Acker, Jacob

Andriese, John
Brown, John
Brown, jun. Edmund
Bruen, Thomas
Brevoort, Abraham
Bond, Abraham
Banyhier, Henry
Baehr, Christian
Bushfield, Thomas
Brooks, Michael
Balm, Peter
Brown, John
Brown, William
Bloodgood, Abraham

Burling, Samuel
Brufter, Samuel
Beekman, Richard
Brower, Abraham
Brower, Jacob
Blauvelt, Herman
Barrow, John T.
Ball, John
Bowie, Daniel
Bufh, Evert
Bertine, James
Baker, William
Brown, Robert
Buckmafter, George
Barton, William
Baudouine, Abraham,
Baptift, John
Bud, Mathew
Bunce, Mathew
Buchanan, Philip
Brinckerhoff, Cornelius
Berry, Jacob
Burdge, Uriah
Breath, John
Brinckerhoff, Sebe
Barker, Joshua
Brown, William
Blanck, Jacob
Carvey, Matthias
Cromwell, Oliver
Colvill, John
Coles, Willet
Chadwick, Abraham
Crocheron, Jacob
Cafting, Gideon
Cregier, John
Cock, Andrew
Cunningham, Richard
Carmer, Henry
Coddington, Mofes
Carter, Robert
Corey, Abraham

Child, Francis
Collet, John
Carpenter, Jacob
Collard, Thomas
Cornell, Gilliam
Covenhoven, Henry
Clapp, Alien
Coddington, Uzziah
Cook, William
Cregier, Cornelius
Conftantine, John
Cooper, Francis
Coddington, Abraham
Concklin, David
Cunningham, David
Coutant, John
Coutant, Gilbert
Clark, John
Cox, Lewis
Cornell, Thomas
Donaldfon, Jeffe
Dominick, Francis I.
Dufenbury, Barzilla
Doughty, Samuel
Duflie, John
Duyckinck, Evert
Dafh, John B.
Degrove, William
Drake, James
Demilt, Thomas
Dominick, George F.
Demareft, Simon
Devou, Frederick
Drake, Thomas
Dally, George
De Bow, Garrit
De Bow, Robert
Dieterich, George
Doty, Jacob
De Groot, Richard
Dobbs, John
Dufenbury, Amaziah

Dominick, John
Day, William
Drake, John
Eckert, Frederick
Earle, Joseph
Embury, Peter
Evans, Jacob
Evans, John
Fowler, David
Fisher, Leonard
Franklin, Thomas
Franklin, Anthony
Fenton, Peter
Fosbrook, William
Fox, George
Furman, Wood
Franklin, jun. John
Franklin, Walter
Ferdon, Thomas
Farrington, John
Ferguson, William
Fullam, J.
Gosman, George
Gosman, Robert
Gosman, James
George, Joseph
Garrebrants, Peter
Gibson, Alexander
Groshong, John P.
Gale, Marinus
Gedney, Samuel
Grainger, John
Graham, Joseph
Goodman, Mathew
Heckel, David
Hardenbrook, John A.
Hubbert, James
Hadley, Isaac
Hunt, Joshua
Hardenbrook, Abel
Haviland, Israel
Hitchcock, Daniel

Hitchcock, Miles
Heyer, John
Hawxhurst, Nathaniel
Hallet, Richard
Hunt, Alsop
Hicks, Smith
Hardenbrook, Wm. A.
Haviland, Caleb
Hunter, William
Halstead, Christopher
Halstead, John
Halstead, Daniel
Helms, Obadiah
Herttell, Adam
Hone, Samuel
Hopson, James
Howell, Mathew
Hennegar, John
Horton, Nathaniel
Houseman, Jacob
Hatfield, Isaac
Heekle, Thomas
Halstead, David
Hardenbrook, John W.
Hatfield, Elias
Helter, Abraham
Ham, Richard
Hilliker, John
Haller, Samuel
Journeay, William
Johnston, Robert
Jarvis, Mathew
Johnston, John
Johnson, Thomas
Jagger, Jehiel
Johnson, Francis
Johnson, John R.
Jacobs, David
Jordan, Matthias
Killam, Peter
Kessen, John
Kaylor, George

E

Lord, Samuel
Lord, George
Lawrence, Daniel
Lent, James W.
Lent, John
Lawrence, Peter
Lamplin, George
Lozier, Nicholas
Lockwood, Philip
Lorten, Lewis
Lewis, Evan
L'Hommedieu, William
Lawrence, Richard
Lord, William
Livingston, Edmund
Lynch, Francis
Lorillard, Peter
Moore, William
Moore, Jacob
Mooney, William
Minuse, John
Morris, Andrew
M'Cullen, Robert
Morrison, Martin
Morris, Jacob
Murray, John
Ming, John
Many, Francis
Motley, John
Mildenberger, John
Miller, Frederick
Maghee, John
Mildenberger, Adam
M'Comb, John
Maverick, Peter
Mount, Mathew
M'Carty, Charles
Mowatt, Alexander
Mowatt, jun. John
M'Dowl, Robert
Meserve, William
M'guire, Mathew

Mott, Jacob
Myers, John D.
M'Eachen, John
M'Kennedy, William
Moore, Baltus
Marschalk, Francis A.
M'Dougall, Hugh
Minuse, Andrew
Marvin, John
Marshall, Joseph
Myers, Martin
Mabie, Cornelius
Mabie, Peter
Mercereau, John
Mott, William
Marsh, David
Myer, Hazael
M'Evers, James
Newton, Joseph
North, Benjamin
Nack, Matthias
Ogden, Benjamin
Odell, John
Oakley, James
Parks, Peter
Pick, George
Post, jun. John
Pell, Aaron
Perrin, John
Pannill, Hayes
Peterson, William
Pritchet, James
Pasman, Francis
Parsons, jun. James
Prall, Abraham
Pell, John
Post, William
Phillips, James
Pentz, Frederick
Pentz, Adam
Parker, Michael
Peterson, Garrit

Pritchet, John
Pearsock, David
Pancoast, Solomon
Pinckney, Elijah
Powell, Joseph
Purdy, John
Pell, John
Palmer, William
Quackenbos, James
Quick, William
Quick, Tunis
Roome, Jacob P.
Rose, John
Riker, Mathew
Robinson, James
Rankin, William
Roome, John
Roome, John P.
Roome, William P.
Riker, Samuel
Rose, Stephen
Ronalds, James
Ritter, Peter
Russel, Abraham
Ryckman, Albert
Ritchie, John I.
Rydeback, Henry
Robins, Ezekiel
Rawlinson, Wilson
Rogers, Henry
Russel, Richard
Robertson, William
Rich, Abraham
Roome, Nicholas
Rogers, Leonard
Ross, Alexander
Rollinson, William
Rich. Thomas
Riker, George
Riker, Gerard
Riker, James
Ryckman, James

Reaker, Frederick
Romaine, jun. Nicholas
Skaats, David
Steenbergh, Anthony
Smith, John
Skaats, Bartholomew
Sneden, Samuel
Sneden, Robert
Smith, jun. Joseph
Shotwell, Abraham
Smith, Jacob
Stuart, James
Sherred, Jacob
Smith, Moses
Smith, Stephen
Stagg, Isaac T.
Seaman, John
Seal, George
Stevenson, Thomas
Strong, Benjamin
Stanton, Jesse
Somerindike, Jacob
Skinner, Thomas
Scott, James
Smith, Charles
Sharpless, Isaac
Smith, Thomas
Smith, George
Smith, Arthur
Skillin, Simeon
Skaats, Jacob
Shotwell, James
Stansbury, Daniel
Smith, John
Scherrack, Christian
Stickler, John
Sterling, James
Smith, John
Stillwell, Stephen
Striker, John
Stevenson, John
Shaw, James

Stephens, John
Smith, Gamaliel
Smith, John
Sharp, William
Townsend, Thomas
Ten Eyck, Andrew
Teller, James
Ten Eyck, Abraham
Tier, Jacob
Tom, Thomas
Timpson, Thomas
Taylor, John
Townsend, George
Targee, John
Tiebout, Alexander
Tier, Cornelius
Torbofs, Isaac
Thompson, John
Thorne, Isaac
Taylor, Henry
Throckmorton, John
Thomas, Abraham
Taylor, Thomas
Utt, John
Utt, Jonas
Vervelan, Henry
Van Wart, William
Van Antwerp, Daniel
Van Antwerp, Nicholas
Van Dyke, Isaac
Van Norden, Abraham
Van Norden, John
Van Norden, Mathew
Vanderbeck, Coenrad
Van Dyke, James
Vernon, John
Van Zandt, Mathew
Verian, Isaac
Vandervoort, Paul
Van Pelt, Tunis
Vandewater, Henry
Van Woenen, jun. Jacob

Valentine, Jacob
Van Buskirk, Luke
Vermillie, William D.
Vail, Enos
Valentine, Abraham
Vark, John
Wynkoop, Peter
Wright, William
Williamson, Richard
Woodhull, James
Woodhull, Gilbert
Waldron, Daniel
Warner, Cornelius
Warner, Charles
Westervelt, Andrew
Warner, George J.
Williams, Andrew
Wardell, Robert
White, Aaron
White, jun. Thomas
Woodward, Nathaniel
Webb, Joseph
Wendover, Peter H.
Wright, Augustus
Whitlaw, Thomas
West, Mathew,
Wood, Jeremiah
Wheeler, Richard
Whitehand, John
Williams, Joseph
West, Andrew
Wilson, Nevin
Wilson, William
Wenman, Richard
White, Charles
Witherspoon, John N.
Weeks, Ezra
Witter, Thomas
Wade, Robert
Youle, George
Young, John
Zelverton, Andrew

(45)

LIST OF CARTMEN.

FIRST CLASS.
1 Daniel Thorpe,
2 James Myer,
3 Abraham E. Day,
4 Alexander Trembly,
5 I. G. Van Houten,
6 Peter Cutler,
7 Abm. Coddington,
8 Nicholas Lawrence,
9 Martin Ame,
10 Jacob D. Demarest,
11 Charles M'Cown,
12 William Conrey,
13 Robert Stewart,
14 Albert Amerman,
15 David Demarest,
16 Elias Day,
17 Peter D. Demarest,
18 Edward Harbert,
19 John De Grauw,
20 Uzal Word,
21 John Brower,
22 Horton Magie,
23 Andrew Myer,
24 Nathaniel Kilmaster,
25 Vincent Carter,
26 Thomas Forbes,
27 Hugh Moore,
28 Henry Scott,
29 Robert De Grusie,
30 Benj. M'Cloughen,
31 Abraham Moore,
32 William Lawrence,
33 Thomas Richey,
34 William Pinkney,
35 John Day,
36 Andrew Romaine,
37 Increase Green,
38 John Lamoreux,

39 Nathan Campbell,
40 Isaac Kip,
41 John Mead,
42 George Hall,
43 Cornelius Polhemus,
44 Eldad Porter,
45 Fred. Dickeman,
46 Alexander Dugan,
47 David Waldron,
48 Jacob Rapp,
49 John Sharp,
50 Isaac Wilfey.

SECOND CLASS.
51 Andrew Losye,
52 Joseph Ely,
53 John Letson,
54 Abraham Day,
55 John Leonard,
56 Benjamin Oakley,
57 David C. Demarest,
58 Jacob Smith,
59 Samuel Riker,
60 Joseph Demarest,
61 Thomas M'Guire,
62 Benjamin Leshure,
63 Mathew M'Guire,
64 John M'Donald,
65 Maurice Smith,
66 Joseph Stevens,
67 Jacob Ame,
68 John Concklin,
69 Isaac Pangburn,
70 John Hill,
71 Peter Mabee,
72 John I. Demarest,
73 Andrew Hamilton,
74 Philip Fea,
75 George Van Alst,

D 9

76 Wm. Somerindyck,
77 Daniel Shotwell,
78 Joseph Fictor,
79 Isaac Paul,
80 Henry Taylor,
81 Abraham Vermylia,
82 Thomas Gardiner,
83 George Shade,
84 Isaac Allin,
85 Edmund Taylor,
86 John Henning,
87 Andrew Mather,
88 James Ryckman,
89 Cornelius Maby,
90 David Coddington,
91 Daniel Thorpe,
92 Michael Valentine,
93 Jonathan Frazee,
94 Conrad Jordan,
95 James Biles,
96 Evan Lewis,
97 Peter Parks,
98 John Edwards,
99 James Ryckman,
100 John Vanderhoff.

THIRD CLASS.

101 Waters Furman,
102 Corn. Vradenburgh,
103 James White,
104 Samuel Romine,
105 Charles Coleman.
106 Corn. Vandenhoven,
107 Nicholas Concklin,
108 Alex. Buchanan,
109 Adam Bready,
110 Frederick Devoe,
111 Jonathan Wade,
112 Isaac See,
113 Mat. Cunningham,
114 John Berwick,
115 Valentine Tier,

116 David Davis,
117 Edward Briggs,
118 Charles Jillard,
119 Ebenezer Bishop,
120 George Bechteel,
121 John Bayard,
122 Moses Ely,
123 Isaac Halfey,
124 Nathan Keeler,
125 Matthias Kerby,
126 John Wilson,
127 Isaac Bogert,
128 Philip Ruckel,
129 Walter De Graw,
130 Martin Ritter,
131 Stephen Platt,
132 Richard Anderson,
133 Benjamin Downing,
134 James Pike,
135 Richardson Parcels,
136 David Taylor,
137 Conrad Row,
138 William M'Murdy,
139 Thomas Skaats,
140 Abraham Campbell,
141 Francis Lewis,
142 Henry Nicholas,
143 James M'Keown,
144 Jacob Acker,
145 Andrew Simmons,
146 John Everitt,
147 Thomas Buys,
148 Joseph Devoe,
149 Arthur Orr,
150 Joshua Bloodgood.

FOURTH CLASS.

151 Corn. Van Horne,
152 Philip Jordan,
153 Mic. Van Beuren,
154 William Sargeant,
155 Christian Brower,

156 James Anderson,
157 George Williams,
158 Henry Bloom,
159 Edward Sheals,
160 Monson Force,
161 James M'Clour,
162 Robert Sneden,
163 John Turner,
164 Albert G. Bogert,
165 Joseph Hull,
166 Abraham Stagg,
167 Andrew Jennings,
168 Gilbert Appleby,
169 Abm. Chadwick,
170 Nicholas Brower,
171 Joseph Overy,
172 Abijah Wells,
173 John Wood,
174 Augustin Goebell,
175 Nathaniel Palmer,
176 John Van Norden,
177 Gilbert Dean,
178 Jonathan Wheeler,
179 Ezekiel Knap,
180 John Feres,
181 Barnes Bennet,
182 John Lamson,
183 William Anderson,
184 Edward Fowler,
185 Josiah Brown,
186 William Andem,
187 William Crum,
188 Cornelius Van Cott,
189 James Welsh,
190 Nicholas A. Jacobus,
191 John Shaver,
192 Robert Giles,
193 David J. Demarest,
194 Jacob Evans,
195 William Kelley,
196 William Shields,
197 Peter A. Brower,

198 Thomas Gibson,
199 Peter Brewer,
200 William Castle.

FIFTH CLASS:
201 John Webster,
202 James Couenhoven,
203 John Bowman,
204 John Hosier,
205 John Purdy,
206 Hugh M'Dermot,
207 Clarkson Manning,
208 Herman Beekman,
209 William Inslee,
210 John Gaffis,
211 George Vroom,
212 Sam. Cunningham,
213 Samuel Sneden,
214 Jacob Lawrence,
215 Tobias Weygant,
216 Henry Darby,
217 Abraham Riker,
218 Mathew Riker,
219 John W. Trip,
220 Peter Pulis,
221 Casparus Romine,
222 Peter Bogart,
223 Lewis Pangburn,
224 William Van Wart,
225 Moses Egbert,
226 John P. Westman,
227 Andrew Van Alen,
228 Thomas Bridges,
229 Jacob I. Brower,
230 Jacob Simonson,
231 Joseph Sutton,
232 Frederick Long,
233 Abraham Phillips,
234 John Giles,
235 William Davison,
236 Matthias Mount,
237 Isaac Morehead,

238 David Lyons,
239 David Young,
240 George Tankard,
241 John Scudder,
242 Lawrence Buskirk,
243 Mathew M'Dowall,
244 John Markins,
245 Nicholas Pitt,
246 Peter Coculet,
247 John Parker,
248 Jacobus Bogart,
249 William Robinson,
250 Joseph Russel.

SIXTH CLASS.
251 James Snow,
252 Charles Stewart,
253 John Owen,
254 Cornelius Tharp,
255 John Wetzell,
256 Daniel Slott,
257 John Turner,
258 Jacob Thorn,
259 Peter Hendrickson,
260 Joseph Haning,
261 Jabez Shire,
262 Conrad Carr,
263 John Fritz,
264 Lewis Gordon,
265 John Bogardus, jun.
266 Jacob Hopper,
267 Joseph M'Kibbon,
268 John Ernst,
269 Daniel Megie,
270 Angus Sutherland,
271 Stephen Sands,
272 Caspar L. Sander,
273 Peter Du Bois,
274 Samuel Hutchins,
275 Stephen Wood,
276 C. Van Horne, jun.
277 Reuben Coonly,

278 Edmund Butler,
279 James Bartholf,
280 James Winton,
281 Andrew Eddey,
282 Jacob Shurt, jun.
283 George King,
284 Philip Queareau,
285 Benjamin Halsey,
286 Francis Haugedorp,
287 Timothy Bloomfield,
288 Christopher Sanders,
289 John Evans,
290 J. E. Schoonmaker,
291 Daniel Magie,
292 John Ackerman,
293 Peter Lawson,
294 Garret Steymets,
295 John Walters,
296 William Evans,
297 Lawrence Brower,
298 Conrad Vanderbeek,
299 Silas Smith,
300 John Valentine.

SEVENTH CLASS.
301 Thomas Duffield,
302 Daniel Hewlett,
303 James Caldwell,
304 William Butler,
305 John Vandenbergh,
306 Lewis Kniffen,
307 Moses Coddington,
308 Richard Lewis,
309 Waters Higgins,
310 Benj. Westervelt,
311 Richard Wheeler,
312 James M'Gown,
313 Valentine Vaughan,
314 John Devoe,
315 Peter P. M'Guire,
316 John Stagg,
317 John Meeks,

318 Joseph Reynolds,
319 James Bussing,
320 Abraham Brower,
321 Lewis Ackerman,
322 James Cottle,
323 Michael Gates,
324 William Tilford,
325 John Payne,
326 William White,
327 Edmund Coffee,
328 Wm. D. Vermyllia,
329 Peter Ferguson,
330 William Anderson,
331 Ezekiel Sneed,
332 Abraham Young,
333 James Sargeant,
334 Charles Dailey,
335 Michael Sandford,
336 William Bussing,
337 Jacob Sherman,
338 John Smith,
339 William Purdy,
340 Thomas Bloomfield,
341 Peter Lyons,
342 Harmanus Blauvelt,
343 Samuel Arnet,
344 Jesse Donaldson,
345 Henry Sanders,
346 Isaac Stagg,
347 John Dusenberry,
348 Christian Rider,
349 John Outen Bogert,
350 Abraham Jansen.

EIGHTH CLASS.
351 Jacob Day,
352 Robert Watts,
353 Christian Smack,
354 George Johnson,
355 Abraham A. Brower,
356 Frederick Fowler,
357 Silas White,
358 Godfrey Warner,
360 William Terbos
361 Hugh Rose,
362 William Post,
363 Moses Bishop,
364 John Vark,
365 Shepherd Johnson,
366 John Bumstead,
367 James Gritman,
368 John Myers,
369 Ralph Thomson,
370 Paul Green,
371 Enos Tompkins,
372 Herm. Gardineer,
373 Francis Post,
374 Abner Wade,
375 Nathaniel Mourison,
376 John Johnson,
377 Henry Lines,
378 Henry Dow,
379 Is. De la Montanye,
380 Jn. De la Montanye,
381 David Skaats,
382 Ezekiel De Camp,
383 William Todd, jun.
384 James Moore,
385 Michael Cook,
386 John Bisset,
387 Joshua Hunt,
388 John Myer,
389 Jacob Demarest,
390 Charles Alexander,
391 Samuel Vaileau,
392 James Targay,
393 Benjamin Corts,
394 Benjamin Smith,
395 Henry Stanton,
396 John Dennison,
397 Samuel Pierce,
398 William Hammond,
399 Lambert Anderson,
400 Jacob Brower.

NINTH CLASS.

401 William Needham,
402 Charles Dougherty,
403 James Sirrine,
404 John E. Bogert,
405 John Vermyllia,
406 John Post,
407 John Clark,
408 Simon Demareft,
409 Silas Coleman,
410 J. A. Van Norden,
411 Barnet Simonson,
412 Eliphalet Barnum,
413 Jacob Hylaman,
414 William Morrison,
415 Corn. Westervelt,
416 Matthias Nack,
417 George Beekman,
418 Richard Wenman,
419 Richard Robertson,
420 Barzillia Ranson,
421 William Reyer,
422 David Brower,
423 William Darby,
424 John Retan,
425 William K. Parker,
426 Isaac Brower,
427 Richard Berrien,
428 Thomas Jaycocks,
429 Christian Brill,
430 Conrad Rawba,
431 John Leacock,
432 Cornelius Myer, jun.
433 John West,
434 John Sloot,
435 James Thompson,
436 Frederick Truelight,
437 John A. Gilbert,
438 And. Zimmerman,
439 William Broom,
440 William Deaty,
441 E. S. V. Bunfchoten,
442 John Mace,
443 Benjamin Parrimore,
444 Francis A. Marfchalk
445 John Banta,
446 Duncan Frazer,
447 James Van Gelder,
448 James Riley,
449 Peter Hageman,
450 John Van Dolfon.

TENTH CLASS.

451 Henry Bartholf,
452 William Day,
453 John Torrey,
454 Jacob Blank,
455 John Pritchet,
456 John Devoe,
457 Henry Stine,
458 John Veele,
459 Amaziah Dufenbury
460 Abraham DeRiemer
461 Robert Caffel,
462 John Wheeler,
463 Anthony M'Clung,
464 Daniel Parker,
465 John Hifield,
466 Frederick Hoffman,
467 John De Revere,
468 John A. Haring,
469 Jacob Ashley,
470 John Fife,
471 Peter King,
472 William Cooper,
473 James Berrian.
474 Thomas Patterson,
475 Patrick Dearing,
476 Daniel Fargo,
477 John Hardie,
478 Patrick Fox,
479 Daniel Concklin,
480 Samuel Hall,
481 Walter M'Bride,

482 Nathaniel Foster,
483 James Van Zile,
484 Peter Leroy,
485 Adam C. Van Horne
486 Archib. Thompson,
487 Charles Liddel,
488 Jeremiah Dob,
489 Tobias Dob,
490 Lewis Shinnet,
491 William Collins,
492 John Burger,
493 Joseph Craft,
494 Garrit Benson,
495 William Harris,
496 John Minard,
497 Baruck Wright,
498 Maurice Kellinger,
499 Gilbert Smith,
500 Dedrick Grofs.

ELEVENTH CLASS.

501 James Black,
502 Abraham Van Zile,
503 Henry Myers,
504 Poules Powlefe,
505 Henry Singer,
506 Daniel Thorpe,
507 Benjamin Hoogland,
508 Matthew Van Orden,
509 Corn. Hulfart, jun.
510 John Rikeman,
511 Alex. Porterfield,
512 John. All,
513 John Hoffer,
514 Schuk. Goonichalk,
515 Jacob Skaats,
516 Samuel Freeman,
517 Joseph Robinson,
518 Peter Peterson,
519 Anthony Gelber,
520 Henry Billing,
521 Nicholas Whitty,

522 Richard Deremer,
523 James Dougherty,
524 Gershom Dunn,
525 John Vermyllia,
526 Nich. Wetherfhien,
527 William Berrian,
528 John Foster,
529 Jacob. Demareft, jun.
530 James Eddey,
531 Abraham Collard,
532 Thomas Waters,
533 Joseph Washburn,
534 Stephen Johnson,
535 Caleb Hall,
536 Nathaniel Bailey,
537 Jacob Brunn,
538 John Harrington,
539 Abraham Couvert,
540 Stephen Huftace,
541 John Creyton,
542 Michael Devoy,
543 Peter Grofs,
544 Jacob Corfa,
545 Richard Davis,
546 Peter Tom,
547 Martin Hill,
548 William Cleary,
549 Peter Prink.
550 Isaac Blanch, jun.

TWELFTH CLASS.

551 William Smith,
552 Paul Friday,
553 Isaac Valentine, jun.
554 John Fisher,
555 Gilbert Sering,
556 Jacob Weeks,
557 John Voorhees,
558 James Downie,
559 John Brown,
560 Henry Hulfot,
561 Isaac Pearlee,

562 Robert Weeks,
563 James Howell,
564 John Newbury,
565 Thomas Bagley,
566 Jonas Tompkins,
567 Henry Luther,
568 Isaac Wm. Hadley,
569 Jonathan Allen,
570 Daniel Ravo,
571 Hendrick Sherman,
572 Samuel Elfworth,
573 Lewis Dixon,
574 A. D. Van Bufkirk,
575 Gerfhom Anfon,
576 Mofes Ofborn,
577 Henry Foreman,
578 Chrif. Hennegar,
579 Samuel M'Kinley,
580 James Johnfon,
581 Dennis M'Guire, jun.
582 Andrew Fech,
583 John Potts,
584 Walter Middleton,
585 John Bonta,
586 Jean Marie Varet,
587 Abraham Pulis,
588 Garret Van Noftrand
589 John Andariefe,
590 Levi James,
591 Richard Salmon,
592 Abraham Rofs,
593 Thomas Hunt,
594 Wright Gilderfleeve,
595 Lewis Ofborn,
596 Henry Anderfon,
597 Leffert Bogert,
598 John Innefs,
599 Petrus Bantz,
600 Joshua Archer.

602 John Smith,
603 Adam Helm,
604 James Voorhees,
605 Henry Orr,
606 William Vafs,
607 John Myer,
608 Hellebrant Lozier,
609 Patrick M'Kew,
610 Peter Van Blarcum,
611 John Little,
612 William Miller,
613 David Beck,
614 Cornel. Bennet, jun.
615 John M'Bride,
616 Jacob I. Vreland,
617 John Hall,
618 Alexander Turner,
619 John Hays,
620 William Hadley,
621 Peter Baufner,
622 William Schureman
623 David Enney,
624 Diederick Lancanao,
625 Ifaac Dean,
626 Thomas Myers,
627 Jehiel Sherwood,
628 Charles Dobbs,
629 Ifaac Jones,
630 Cornelius Henaion,
631 John Smith,
632 David Plumb,
633 Lawrence Myer,
634 John Gould,
635 Cornelius Williams,
636 Æneas Roberts,
637 Ifaac Williams,
638 William Wandle,
639 John Ackerman,
640 Jonathan Dunn,
641 Chriftian Trace,
642 John D. Ackerman,
643 John Valentine,

THIRTEENTH CLASS.
601 Abraham Ely,

NEW-YORK REGISTER. 51

644 John Van Taffel,
645 Michael Brennan,
646 John Johnson,
647 Richard Baker,
648 Isaac Brower,
649 E. W. Somerindike,
650 Fred. Woortendyke.

FOURTEENTH CLASS.

651 Thomas Amerman,
652 Samuel Lewis,
653 David Le Roy,
654 Richardson Fowler,
655 J. A. C. Hotzen,
656 Benj. Van Keuren,
657 William Chatfield,
658 William Holmes,
659 James Van Dyke,
660 Joel Rose,
661 Peter Post,
662 William Elsworth,
663 James Boner,
664 Garret Neefie,
665 Charles Van Orden,
666 John Flock,
667 David Mersereau,
668 Benjamin Westervelt
669 Conrad Pulis,
670 Patrick Larking,
671 Morris Ackerman,
672 Obadiah Wade,
673 Jonathan Archer,
674 James Craft,
675 Joseph Ogden,
676 John P. Bogert,
677 Israel Post,
678 George Mount,
679 Isaac Lopes,
680 Oswald Detchun,
681 James Shotwell,
682 John Garbutt,
683 Henry Moser,

684 Isaac Jezup,
685 William Herbert,
686 Richard White,
687 John Briggs,
688 Peter Hegeman,
689 William Letts,
690 Cornelius Smock,
691 Samuel Freeman,
692 Francis Anderson,
693 Cornelius Ryan,
694 Richard Oliver,
695 Thomas Tuthill,
696 John Turner,
697 James Thompson,
698 Enoch Moore,
699 Henry Baker,
700 John M'Gee.

FIFTEENTH CLASS.

701 Jacob Morris,
702 Joseph Hayatt,
703 Henry Van Taffel,
704 John Vander Beek,
705 Thomas Martin,
706 Stephen Johnson, jun
707 James Bailey,
708 James Appleby,
709 Andrew Gamble,
710 Henry Shombergh,
711 Jeremiah Brown,
712 William Dusenberry
713 Abraham VanOrden,
714 William Force,
715 James Penny,
716 William Marshall,
717 Edward Thalls,
718 John Dunn,
719 Christian Dederer,
720 Stephen Gould,
721 Henry Campbell,
722 Thomas I. Stagg,
723 Henry Hardgrave,

F

724 Lucas Van Buskirk,
725 Charles Theall,
726 Cornelius Vervalen,
727 Peter Sanders.
728 William Nelson,
729 John Sleight,
730 Lawrence Steafel,
731 John C. Rapp,
732 Daniel Noorstrant,
733 Timothy Jarvis,
734 David Morgan,
735 John Conroy,
736 John Purdy,
737 Daniel Lamoreux,
738 Dennis M'Donald,
739 Peter Fisher,
740 Benj. Coddington,
741 John Dobbs,
742 Joseph Braiden,
743 William Ferdon,
744 John Bogardus,
745 Edward Edwards,
746 Peter Lawrence,
747 Goodheart Archer,
748 Walter Braiden,
749 David Hains,
750 Charles Hunt.

—

SIXTEENTH CLASS.

751 Nathaniel Guion,
752 Joseph Frost,
753 Asa Wood,
754 Stephen Travis,
755 David Love,
756 Isaac Hunt,
757 Frederick Ambach,
758 Martin Myers,
759 Henry Pulis,
760 Jacob Romine,
761 David Lennox,
762 Peter Banta,
763 David Van Horn,
764 Mathew Granger,
765 James Van Curan,
766 Peter Cole,
767 Benjamin Guion,
768 John Anderson,
769 Gideon Swanzer,
770 John Carloch,
771 Jacob Hart,
772 James Frazee,
773 Jesse Heustis,
774 John Garrison,
775 William Parcells,
776 David Van Gelder,
777 George Britt,
778 George Tippet,
779 Dudley Wood,
780 Albert Kennar,
781 Andrew Braden,
782 James Nelson,
783 J. B. Van Kleeck,
784 Mathew Wilkey,
785 Gerardus Riker,
786 Jacob King,
787 Gilbert Honeywell,
788 George Weeks,
789 Levy Johnson,
790 John Westfield,
791 John Cairns.
792 Halmigh Garrison,
793 William Hoff, jun.
794 James Coddington,
795 James M'Evers,
796 Benjamin Dunham,
797 James Bunn,
798 Francis Smiley,
799 Ezekiel Green,
800 David R. Bogert.

—

SEVENTEENTH CLASS.

801 John Neel Johnson,
802 Andrew M'Mullen,
803 Alexander M'Bain,

804 L. Commardinger,
805 Daniel Canniff,
806 Joseph Brooks,
807 James Morgan,
808 And. Champenois,
809 Jacob Powlese,
810 Jacob Van Pelt,
811 Garret I. Ackerson,
812 Michael Ryer,
813 William Bafsford,
814 Samuel Burtis,
815 Thomas Moore,
816 James Gordon,
817 Robert Bocock,
818 Mark M'Manus,
819 Peter Totten,
820 Smith Mead,
821 Charles Keyes,
822 George Patch,
823 William Harrison,
824 Robert Lewis,
825 William Ludlam,
826 Nathaniel Hunt,
827 William Clark,
828 Joseph Cafs,
829 George Gordon,
830 James Buchanan,
831 Cornelius Gordon,
832 John Bennet,
833 Bryan Rosfetter,
834 David Brockway,
835 Adam Henegar,
836 Elias Tucker,
837 Benjamin Berrian,
838 Affel Pelsner,
839 James Bready,
840 Abraham De Reviere
841 Gerret Van Dyne,
842 Henry Valentine,
843 Daniel Strain,
844 James Precho,
845 John Lely,

846 Henry Flock,
847 Wm. Southerland,
848 George Snedgrafs,
849 William Welsh,
850 John Smith.

—

EIGHTEENTH CLASS.

851 Isaac Hadley,
852 Nevers Perry,
853 Walter Carpenter,
854 John Angevine,
855 Bernardus Rider,
856 John Hunt,
857 Samuel Spragg,
858 Garrit Nooftrant,
859 Philip Hunt,
860 Joseph Brafs,
861 Matthias Van Wyck,
862 John Ludlum,
863 Frazee Connet,
864 John Joice,
865 Eleazer Read,
866 Henry Hofier,
867 Patrick Gallihan,
868 Robert Coles,
869 John Campbell,
870 James Edgar,
871 Matthias Baldwin,
872 James Powers,
873 Benjamin VanCuran,
874 James Howie,
875 Philip Smith,
876 Stephen Weeks,
877 John Hurly,
878 David Haffy,
879 Peter Wefterfield,
880 Henry Hunfan,
881 William Wright,
882 George Seifferth,
883 Robert Perrine,
884 Abraham Potts,
885 Peter Mirielus,

886 David Braambos,
887 Richard Shute,
888 George Snyder,
889 John Grant,
890 Jacob Lent,
891 Thomas Green,
892 John Toers,
893 John Loder,
894 John Crawford,
895 Calvin Robinson,
896 John Blauvelt,
897 John Van Buskirk,
898 Francis Martin,
899 Martin Post,
900 John M'Mullen.

Record of Inspectors of Hay.

8 Nicholas Lawrence,
47 David Waldron,
102 Corn. Vradenburgh,
107 Nicholas Concklin,
115 Valentine Tier,
162 Robert Sneden,
178 Jonathan Wheeler,
187 William Crum,
232 Frederick Long,
240 George Tankard,
372 Herm. Gardineer,
381 David Skaats,
395 Henry Stanton,
396 John Dennison,
409 Silas Coleman,
438 And. Zimmerman,
553 Isaac Valentine, jun.
634 John Gould,
643 John Valentine,
681 James Shotwell,
685 William Herbert,
751 Nathaniel Guion,
801 John Neel Johnston,
813 William Bassford.

Record of Porters in the City of New-York.

1 Jeremiah Dolloway,
2 James Tremble,
3 Frederick Leverge,
4 Tertullian Quin,
5 George Maul,
6 Hermanus Rutan,
7 John Bogert,
8 William Bingley,
[The foregoing stand at the Fly market.

9 Anthony Railey,
10 John Shreder,
11 William Jones,
12 ———,
[Stand at the Oswego market.

13 George Cole,
14 Gideon Arden,
15 John Prowe,
16 William Mills,
22 Mathew Mahny,
[Hudson market.

17 Timothy Wade,
18 Patrick Flinn,
[Exchange market.

19 Jacob Rhinehart,
21 Charles Menteng,
[Catharine-slip market.

20 John Shudy.
[Cortlandt-street &c.

Officers of the State of New-York.

John Jay, Governor.
Stephen Van Renffelaer, Lieutenant-Governor.
Daniel Hale, Secretary of State.
Jofiah O. Hoffman, Attorney-General.
Cadwallader D. Colden, Affiftant do.
———— ————, Treafurer.
Samuel Jones, Comptroller.
Simeon De Witt, Surveyor-General.
Jafper Hopper, Deputy Secretary of State.
Robert Hunter, Commiffioner of Military Stores.
Alexander Lamb, Keeper of the State Prifon.

Commiffioners of the Land Office.

The Governor, Lieutenant-Governor, Speaker of the Affembly, Secretary of State, Attorney-General, Treafurer and Comptroller.

Council of Appointment.

His Excellency the Governor, *ex officio*.
Jofeph White, Weftern Diftrict.
Mofes Vail, Eaftern Diftrict.
William Thompfon, Middle Diftrict.
Ezra L'Hommedieu, Southern Diftrict.

Court of Impeachment and Errors.

The Prefident of Senate and Senators.
The Chancellor and Judges of Supreme Court.
Abraham B. Bancker, Clerk.

Council of Revifion.

The Governor, Chancellor, and Judges of the Supreme Court.

Officers in Chancery.

Robert R. Livingfton, Chancellor.
Peter R. Livingfton, Regifter.
Gilb. Livingfton, Jer. Lanfing, Abm. B. Bancker, James M. Hughes, Garrit Wendell, and Thomas Cooper, Matters in Chancery.
Abraham G. Lanfing, Gabriel V. Ludlow, and Edward W. Laight, Examiners.
Richard S. Treat, Ifaac L. Kip, Thomas Smith, and James Van Ingen, Clerks in Chancery.
Peter Cole, Sergeant at Arms.

Supreme Court.

Morgan Lewis, Egbert Benson, and James Kent, Puisne Judges.

James Fairlie, New-York, } Clerks.
Francis Bloodgood, Albany,

Court of Exchequer.
Egbert Benson, Judge.
William Popham, Clerk.

Court of Probates.
Peter Ogilvie, Judge.
William Ogilvie, Clerk.

Notaries Public.
John Keefe, James M. Hughes, Charles Bridgen, Isaac Van Vleeck, John Wilkes, John F. Roorbach, Isaac L. Kip, Tunis Wortman, Charles Adams, John S. Hunn, Francis Lynch, William Bleecker, John H. Remsen, Edward Dunscomb, Abraham Skinner, Jasper Hopper, William Bache.

Justices for preserving the Peace and executing the business of the Police Office.

Theophilus Beekman, and Jacob De la Montagnie.
Bernard O'Blenis, Clerk.

Justices appointed under the new ten pound act of Feb. 16, 1797.

Jacob Morton, James Morris, and William Johnson.
Washington Morton, Clerk.

Port Officers.
Christopher Miller, Harbour-master.
William Heyer, Jonathan Lawrence, Anthony Rutgers, and James Farquhar, Wardens of the Port.
Richard Bayley, Health-Officer.
John Oothout, Jacob Abramse, and Ezekiel Robins, Commissioners of the Health Office.

List of Branch and Deputy Pilots now acting to and from Sandy-Hook.

David Morris, Mathew Daniel, John Callahan, John Funk, Nathaniel Funk, Edward Wilkie, John Minugh, Thomas Gray, Zachariah Rusler, James Daniel, William Minugh, Jacob Buffoloree, branch pilots.—James Flinn, Charles Penny, Christopher Seward, Robert Mitchell, Robert Bennett, John Carter, John Kidder, Michael Bloomer, David Thomson, ———— Wilkie, deputy pilots.

Pilots for the Sound.

Willet Leaycraft, Hoystead Hacker, Thomas Hunt, Daniel Lawrence, and Samuel Harrold.

Inspectors.

Henry H. Kip, Jonathan Lawrence, John H. Kip, and ———— Brower, of pot and pearl ashes.

John Titus, of flour.

Thomas Ivers, of hemp.

Robert Newson, Jeremy Marshall, Thomas Ogilvie, William Carmer, Silas White, Joseph Pierson, Joshua Mills, and George Peek, of lumber.

Robert Towt and James Tylee, of leather.

Jacob Morris, John Post, Thomas Post, Samuel Page, William Baker, Matt Cannon, John Hillyer, and Jacob Skaats, of beef and pork.

Michael Sickles, William Dean, Abraham Anderson, Garrit Walgrove, Gideon Harpur, Francis Johnson, Gilbert Thornton, Zachariah Sickles, John O. Bogardus, John Morris, John Hadley, and Robert M'Dowell, cullers of staves and heading.

Officers of the City and County of New-York.

Richard Varick, Mayor.
Richard Harison, Recorder.
Jacob John Lansing, Sheriff.
Robert Benson, Clerk.
Daniel Phœnix, Chamberlain.
Charles Dickinson, Coroner.
David Gelston, Surrogate.
William W. Gilbert, Commissioner of Excise.
James Culbertson, High Constable, and Deputy Clerk of the Market.
John W. Gilbert, Under Sheriff.
Thomas Hazard, Deputy Sheriff, and Keeper of the Goal.
Arnout Cannon, Zadock Hedden, William W. Parker, Simon Fleet, John Shute, and Ebenezer Merritt, Deputy Sheriffs.

Aldermen and their Assistants.

First Ward.—Gabriel Furman, Alderman.—Thomas Storm, Assistant.—John Remsen and James Van

Dyk, Assessors.—William G. Forbes, Collector.—Charles Handasyde and Philip Fulkerson, Constables.

Second Ward.—John B. Coles, Alderman.—Garrit Harsin, Assistant.—Abraham Varick and Josiah Shippey, Assessors.—Cornelius C. Wynkoop, Collector.—Barnet Newkerk and Henry Borisell, Constables.

Third Ward.—Theophilus Beekman, Alderman.—Nicholas Carmer, Assistant.—David Wolfe and John I. Glover, Assessors.—Hugh Montgomery, Collector.—Samuel Stockwell and Robert Johnson, Constables.

Fourth Ward.—Anthony Post, Aldermen.—John Bogert, Assistant.—Isaac Jones and Benjamin Romayne, Assessors.—Thomas Le Foy, Collector.—John Ackerman and John Reins, Constables.

Fifth Ward.—Jotham Post, Alderman.—Philip I. Arcularius, Assistant.—Nicholas N. Anthony and Andrew Marcein, Assessors.—David Harriot, Collector.—Joseph Dunkley and Samuel Montgomery, Constables.

Sixth Ward.—Jacob De la Montagnie, Alderman.—Anthony Brown, Assistant.—James Riker and Joseph Watkins, Assessors.—John Fox, Collector.—William Campbell and Henry Bogardus, Constables.

Seventh Ward.—Richard Furman, Alderman.—Mangle Minthorne, Assistant.—Henry Rutgers and William W. Gilbert, Assessors.—Martin Morrison, Collector.—John M'Laughlin and Lewis Smith, Constables.

Harlaem Division.—Jonathan Randall and John Delaney, Assessors.—John Busting, Collector.—Aaron Busting and Adolphus Busting, Constables.

Record of Marshals in the City of New York.

1. Rinier Skaats, and Cryer of the Courts.
2. William Thompson.
3. Hugh Gobel, and a Deputy Clerk of the Market.
4. Richard Smith, and Turnkey of the Goal.
5. Peter Cole, Keeper of the Bridewell.
6. David Burgher, Deputy Water Bailiff.
7. George Webster.   8. Melancton Baylis.
9. Abraham Walker.   10. William Cumming.
11. John S. Delamater.   12. Henry Gandy.

13. James Conning. 14. Alexander Wiley.
15. Luke Kip. 16. William Chevers.
17. Charles Thompson. 18. Barnet Bush.
19. Abraham Manning. 20. Joseph Gilmore.
21. Robert Fletcher. 22. John R. Ross.
23. Winard Mitchell. 24. Jonathan Porter.
25. Thomas Blank. 26. Joseph Brotherton.
27. John Michael, Assistant Keeper of the Bridewell.
28. John Farrington. 29. Asa Hall.
30. Henry Hyde. 31. James Thompson.
32. William Humphryes. 33. Adam Parker.
34. Levi Munson. 35. Abraham G. Forbes.
36. James Green. 37. John Richardson.

Commissioners of the Alms-House and Bridewell.
William Hardenbrook, William Depeyster, Willet Seaman, Elijah Cock, and Richard Lawrence.

Samuel Dodge, Keeper of the Alms-House.

William Hardenbrook, and Jeremiah Wool, Sealers and Markers of Weights and Measures.

Circuits and Courts of Oyer and Terminer for 1798, are to be held as follows.

Onondaga—At the house of Seth Phelps, in the town of Scipio, on the second Tuesday in June.
Ontario—At the court-house, third Tuesday in June.
Steuben—At the court-house, fourth Tuesday in June.
Tioga—At the court-house, first Tuesday in July.
Chenango—At the academy, in the town of Oxford, second Tuesday in July.
Montgomery—At the court-house, last Tuesday in August.
Herkemer—At the court-house, first Tuesday in September.
Oneida—At the school-house, near Fort-Stanwix, in the town of Rome, second Tuesday in September.
Otsego—At the court-house, third Tuesday in September.
Schoharie—At the house of Johannis Ingold, in the town of Schoharie, fourth Tuesday in September.
Albany—At the court-house, second Tuesday in October.
Rensselaer—At the court-house, first Tuesday in June.
Saratoga—At the court-house, second Tuesday in June.
Washington—At the court-house, third Tuesday in June.
Clinton—At the block-house, in the town of Willsburgh, the fourth day of July.
Rockland—At the court-house, the 17th day of August.
Orange—At the court-house, third Tuesday in August.
Dutchess—At the court-house, fourth Tuesday in August.
Columbia—At the court-house, first Tuesday in September.

Ulster—At the court-house, second Tuesday in September.
Delaware—At the house of Gideon Frisbie, in the town of Kortright, the 21st day of September.
Richmond—At the court-house, last Monday in August.
Kings—At the court-house, the 31st day of August.
Queens—At the court-house, first Tuesday in September.
Suffolk—At the court-house, second Tuesday in September.
Westchester—At the court-house, third Tuesday in September.
New-York—At the city-hall, the 19th day of July.

A sitting for the trial of issues, &c. to commence at the city-hall of the city of New-York, on Monday the 13th day of August next.

Government of the United States.

JOHN ADAMS, President of the United States, Commander in Chief of the Army and Navy thereof.

THOMAS JEFFERSON, Vice-President, and President of the Senate.

Department of State.
Timothy Pickering, Secretary of State.

Department of War.
James M'Henry, Secretary.—William Simmons, Accountant.

Treasury Department.
Oliver Wolcott, Secretary.—John Davis, Comptroller.—Richard Harrison, Auditor.—Joseph Nourse, Register.—Samuel Meredith, Treasurer.

Naval Department.
George Cabot, Secretary.

Judiciary of the United States.
Oliver Ellsworth, of Connecticut, Chief Justice.

William Cushing, of Massachusetts; James Wilson, of Pennsylvania; James Iredell, and William Patterson, of North-Carolina; and Samuel Chase, Associate Judges.

Charles Lee, Attorney-General.

New-York District.
John Sloss Hobart, Judge.—Richard Harison, Attorney.—Edward Dunscomb, Clerk.—Aquila Giles, Marshal.

Place and Time of holding the Circuit Court of the United States.

In the State of *New-York*, at the city of *New-York*, on the first days of April and September.

Ministerial and Consular Appointments by the United States.

In France and its Dominions.

Fulwar Skipwith, Consul-General.—Joseph Fenwick, Consul at Bordeaux.—P. F. Dobree, Consul at Nantz.—S. Cathalan, Vice-Consul at Marseilles.—Nathaniel Cutting, Vice-Consul at Havre-de-Grace.—William M'Carty, Consul at the Isle of France.—Isaac Cox Barnet, Consul at the port of Brest.—Frederick Folger, Consul for the port and district of Aux-Cayes, St. Domingo.

In Spain.

William Short, Minister Resident.—Moses Young, Consul at Madrid.—Edward Church, at Bilboa.—Joseph Yznardi, Cadiz.—Robert Montgomery, Alicant.—Michael Murphy, Malaga.—Procopio Jacinto Pollock, New-Orleans.

In the Batavian Republic.

William Vans Murray, Minister Plenipotentiary.—Sylvanus Bourne, Consul-General.—Charles W. F. Dumas, Agent at the Hague.—John Beeldernaker, Consul at Rotterdam.—Ebenezer Brush, Consul at Surinam.—David M. Clarkson, Consul at St. Eustatia.—Benjamin H. Phillips, Consul at Curracoa.—Samuel H. Johonet, Consul at Demarara.

In Great-Britain and Ireland.

Rufus King, Minister Plenipotentiary.—Samuel Williams, Consul at London.—James Maury, Consul at Liverpool.—Thomas Auldjo, Vice Consul at Poole.—Edward Fox, Consul at Falmouth.—Joseph Wilson, Consul at Dublin.—John Gavins, Consul at Gibralter.—David Lenox, Agent to reside in the Kingdom of Great-Britain, for the relief and protection of American seamen.

In the Dominions of Portugal.

David Humphreys, Minister Resident.—John M.

Pintard, Conful at Madeira.—John Street, Vice-Conful at Fayal.—John Culhan, Conful at Teneriffe.

In the Dominions of Pruſſia.

John Quincy Adams, Miniſter Plenipotentiary, and Commiſſioner to negociate a Treaty of Amity and Commerce with Sweden.

In the Dominions of Sweden.

Elias Bachman, Conful at Gottenburg.

In the Dominions of Denmark.

Henry Cooper, Conful at St. Croix.

In the City of Hamburgh.

Joſeph Pitcairn, Vice-Conful at Hamburgh.

In Germany.

Arnold Delius, Conful at Bremen.—Philip Mark, Conful at Franconia.

In China.

Samuel Shaw, Conful at Canton.

In Morocco.

Joel Barlow, Conful-General for the city and kingdom of Algiers.

James Simpſon, Conful at Morocco.—Guiſeppe Chiappe, Agent at Magador.

In Italy.

Conrad Frederick Wagner, Conful at Trieſte.—Peter Fellecky, Conful at Leghorn.

In Aſia.

Benjamin Joy, Conful at Calcutta, and other ports on the Coaſt of India.

Miniſterial and Conſular Appointments, by foreign Powers, to the United States.

By the French Republic.

Le Tombe, Conful-General.—Mozard, Conful for N. Hampſhire.—Arcambal, Vice-Conful for Rhode-Iſland.—Rozier, Vice-Conful for New-York.—Duhail, Vice-Conful for Maryland.—Dupont, Vice-Conful for North-Carolina.—Liet, Conful par interim, for Pennſylvania.—Rey, Vice-Conful for Virginia.

By Spain.

Don Carlos Martinez Yrujo, Miniſter Plenipotentiary.—Don Juan Stoughton, Conful for New-H...

shire, Massachusetts, Connecticut, Vermont, and Rhode-Island.—Don J. Wiseman, Vice-Consul for the same states.—Don Thomas Stoughton, Consul for New-York.—Don Juan B. Bernabeu, Consul for Maryland.—Don Antonio Argotee Villalobos, Consul for Virginia and Kentucky.—James Morphy, Consul for North and South-Carolina, and Georgia.

By Portugal.

Don Friere, Minister Resident.—Don Ignatius Playart, Consul-General.—Don Richard Codman, Vice-Consul for Massachusetts.—Don John Abrams, Vice-Consul for New-York.—Don James Barry, Vice-Consul for Maryland and Virginia.—Don Francis Vercknock, Vice-Consul for South-Carolina.

By Great-Britain.

Robert Liston, Minister Plenipotentiary.—Sir John Temple, Bart. Consul-General for the eastern states.—J. Hamilton, Consul for Virginia.—T. M'Donogh, Consul for New-Hampshire and Massachusetts.—Phineas Bond, Consul-General for the southern states.—George Miller, Consul for North and South-Carolina, and Georgia.—David Thornton, Secretary of Legation.

By the Batavian Republic.

G. Van Polanen, Minister Resident.—Adrian Valck, Consul for Maryland and Virginia.—Jan. H. C. Heineker, Consul for Pennsylvania and Delaware.—Jan. B. Graves, Consul for North and South-Carolina, and Georgia.—Diederick Larrouwer, Consul for New-Hampshire and Massachusetts.

By Sweden.

Richard Soderstrom, Consul for Boston and the eastern states.—Charles Nelstadt, Consul for Philadelphia and the southern states.

By Genoa.

Joseph Ravara, Consul-General.

By Prussia.

Charles G. Poleski, Consul-General.

Bank of New-York.
Gulian Verplanck, President.

Samuel Jones, (as Comptroller, ex officio) Charles Smith, Nicholas Governeur, Richard Varick, Daniel M'Cormick, William Seton, John B. Coles, J. H. Thompson, John M'Vicker, Archibald Gracie, Peter Schermerhorn, William Denning, and Harman Le Roy, Directors.—Charles Wilkes, Cashier.

United States Bank, New-York Branch.
Cornelius Ray, President.
Thomas Buchanan, Gerard Bancker, William Laight, Nicholas Low, Mathew Clarkson, Robert Lenox, John Murray, John Atkinson, Gabriel W. Ludlow, Philip Livingston, William Minturn, John I. Glover, Directors.—Jonathan Burrall, Cashier.

The interest for discounts in the Banks in this city is fixed at six per cent. per annum upon notes or bills not having more than thirty days to run; three days of grace are allowed, and the discount taken for the same.

☞ *The Branch Bank discount notes at 60 days.*

Discounts are done on Tuesdays and Thursdays in every week; and every bill or note offered for discount, must be delivered on the day preceding the day of discount, enclosed under a sealed cover, directed to the cashier, advising the name of the person on whose account it is offered.

Money lodged at the banks may be re-drawn at pleasure, free of expence; but no draft to be paid beyond the balance of accounts.

Bills or notes left at the banks for collection, will be noticed for payment, and the money collected free of expence; in case of non-payment and protest, the charge of protest must be paid by the person lodging the bill.

Payments made at the banks are to be examined at the time, as no deficiency, afterwards suggested, can be admitted.

Gold coins of England and Portugal are received and paid at the banks, at the rates established by an act of congress which became a law in July, 1795, viz. 89 cents per pennyweight; and those of France and Spain, and the dominions of Spain, are rated at 87 cents the pennyweight.

Silver coins are received at the banks as follows:
For 1 crown, 110 cents, For 1 piftareen, 20 cents,
1 dollar, 100 do. 1 Eng. fhill. 22 do.

Weight of the Federal Coins.

	dwt.	gr.		dwt.	gr.
1 eagle	11	6	½ dollar	4	8
½ eagle	5	15	1 dime	1	17¾
¼ eagle	2	19½	½ dime	0	20¼
1 dollar	17	8	1 cent	11 of copper
½ dollar	8	16	½ cent	5	12

Bank of the United States.
Thomas Willing, Prefident.

Elias Boudinot, Samuel Breck, Joseph Anthony, Archibald M'Call, Henry Hill, William Bingham, Robert Smith, Isaac S. Cox, Thomas Ewing, James C. Fisher, Abijah Dawes, Joseph Sims, John G. Wachfmuth, Ellifton Perot, Jacob Downing, John Lawrence, Abijah Hammond, Thomas Pearfall, Gerard Walton, John G. Leake, William Henderfon, Jacob Read, Harrifon G. Otis, Directors.

Bank of Albany.
Abraham Ten Broeck, Prefident.

Stephen Van Renffelaer, Jeremiah Van Renffelaer, Abraham Van Vechten, Jacob Vander Heyden, Barent Bleecker, Stephen Luth, Robert M'Callen, Elifha Kane, Dudley Walfh, George Pearfon, John C. Cuyler, and Simeon De Witt, Directors.—Garrit Van Schaick, Cafhier.

New-York Chamber of Commerce.
John Murray, Prefident.
Geo. Barnewall & John B. Coles, Vice-Prefidents.
Cornelius Ray, Treafurer.
William W. Woolfey, Secretary.

New-York Insurance Company.
Archibald Gracie, President.
John Broome, John H. Thompson, David M. Clarkson, George Barnewall, James Scott, Ebenezer Stevens, Wynant Van Zandt, Moses Rogers, Edmund Seaman, Samuel Ward, David Smith, William Neilson, Pascal N. Smith, John P. Mumford, John Blagge, J. C. Vandenheuvel, Elisha Colt, William W. Ludlow, William Denning, Charles M'Evers, Directors.
Daniel Phœnix, Secretary.

United Insurance Company.
Nicholas Low, President.
John Delafield, Daniel Ludlow, John Shaw, William Henderson, Thomas Buchanan, Cornelius Ray, Daniel M'Cormick, Robert Lenox, John B. Coles, Charles Smith, Edward Goold, William M. Seton, William Laight, John Murray, William Minturn, and Nicholas Governeur, Directors.
Joseph Stansbury, Secretary.

New-York Western and Northern Canal Company.
Philip Schuyler, President.
Gerard Walton, Vice-President.
John Murray, Robert Bowne, Edmund Prior, William Henderson, Mathew Clarkson, Cornelius Ray, John Atkinson, Peter Curtenius, Nicholas Governeur, William T. Robinson, and John Rogers, Directors.

University of the State of New-York.
The Governor and Lieutenant-Governor for the time being are, ex officio, together with the following persons, instituted perpetual Regents of the University.
The Governor, Chancellor.
Rev. John Rodgers, Vice-Chancellor.
Philip Schuyler, Egbert Benson, James Livingston, Ezra L'Hommedieu, Rev. Nathan Kerr, Peter Sylvester, James Cochran, Ebenezer Russel, Mathew Clarkson, Rev. Benjamin Moore, Zephaniah Platt, Rev. Andrew King, Rev. William Linn, Jonathan G. Tompkins, Gulian Verplanck, James Watson, Rev. Thomas Ellison, and Simeon De Witt.

Gerard Banker, Treasurer.
De Witt Clinton, Secretary.

Columbia College.

Samuel Provoost, D. D. John H. Livingston, D. D. Richard Varick, Alexander Hamilton, Brockholst Livingston, Abraham Beach, D. D. John Lawrence, Morgan Lewis, Rev. Gersham Seixas, Thomas Jones, Samuel Bard, M. D. William Moore, M. D. William S. Johnson, L. L. D. John Watts, Richard Harison, Edward Dunscomb, Rev. John M. Mason, George Anthon, M. D. John Cozine, Cornelius I. Bogert, and Edward Livingston, Trustees.

Abraham Beach, Clerk of the Corporation.
Brockholst Livingston, Treasurer.

Faculty of Arts.

William S. Johnson, L. L. D. President.
John Kemp, L. L. D. Professor of Mathematics. Natural Philosophy, Chronology, and Geography.
Rev. John C. Kunze, D. D. Professor of Oriental Languages.
Elijah D. Ratoone, A. M. Professor of the Greek and Latin Languages.
Samuel L. Mitchill, M. D. Professor of Natural History and Agriculture.
A. V. Marcellin, Professor of the French Language.
James Kent, L. L. D. Professor of Law.
John M'Knight, D. D. Professor of Logic and Moral Philosophy.
John Bisset, A. M. Professor of Rhetoric and Belles Lettres.

Faculty of Physic.

Samuel Bard, Dean.
Richard Bayley, Professor of Surgery.
Wright Post, Professor of Anatomy.
David Hosack, Professor of Botany and Materia Medica.
John R. B. Rodgers, Professor of Midwifery, and Clinical Lecturer of the New-York Hospital.
Samuel L. Mitchill, Professor of Chemistry.
William Hammersley, Professor of the Practice and Institutes of Medicine.

Agricultural Society.

Robert R. Livingston, President.
Ezra L'Hommedieu, Vice-President.
John Taylor, Treasurer.
Samuel L. Mitchill, } Secretaries.
Benjamin De Witt, }

Robert R. Livingston, William S. Johnson, Samuel L. Mitchill, Stephen Lush, and Simeon De Witt, Committee of Publications.

Society for the Relief of distressed Prisoners.

Rev. John Rodgers, President.
Rev. Abraham Beach, Vice-President.
John Murray, jun. Treasurer.
James Bleecker, Secretary.

City Dispensary.

Rev. John Rodgers, President.
Moses Rogers, Treasurer.
Anthony Bleecker, Secretary.
Hugh M'Lean, Physician and Surgeon.

Rev. Abraham Beach, John Broome, John Charlton, Mathew Clarkson, John Cozine, Rev. William Linn, Jacob Morton, Samuel Osgood, Edmund Prior, Moses Rogers, Rev. John Rodgers, James Watson, and John Watts, Trustees.

New-York Hospital.

Gerard Walton, President.
Mathew Clarkson, Vice-President.
John Murray, Treasurer.
Thomas Eddy, Secretary.

Governors.

Thomas Franklin, Samuel Bowne, John B. Coles, William Edgar, William Minturn, Hugh Gaine, Thomas Buchanan, Henry Rutgers, Robert Bowne, Moses Rogers, John Murray, jun. James Watson, Peter Schermerhorn, John Barrow, Edmund Prior, John I. Glover, J. C. Kunze, Henry Haydock, jun. John Tharston, William T. Robinson, William Jauncey, and Jacob De la Montagnie.

Physicians.
John R. B. Rodgers, Samuel L. Mitchill, Elihu H. Smith, and David Hosack.

Surgeons.
Richard Bayley, Wright Post, Richard S. Kissam, Samuel Borrowe, and Valentine Seaman.

J. Boyd, Apothecary.
Samuel Barnum, House-Surgeon.
Mary Smith, Matron.

The New-York Hospital affords one of the best practical Medical Schools in the United States. Physic and surgery are here taught with care and attention, and Clinical Lectures are given, during the winter season, on the most important and best selected cases that occur.

Annual meetings the 17th of May, and stated meetings on the 4th of every month.

New-York Manumission Society.
Mathew Clarkson, President.
William W. Woolsey, } Vice-Presidents.
William Johnson,   }
John Murray, jun. Treasurer.
Elihu H. Smith, Secretary.
Jacob Doty, Assistant Secretary.
George M. Woolsey, Register.

Standing Committee.
Willet Seaman, Chairman.
William Dunlap, Secretary.

Trustees of the School.
Samuel Bowne, Chairman.
James Robertson, Secretary.

Committee of Correspondence.
Thomas Eddy, Chairman.
Valentine Seaman, Secretary.

Marine Society.
James Farquhar, President.
Paschal N. Smith, first Vice-President.
Thomas Farmer, second Vice-President.

William Heyer, Treasurer.
William Newton, Secretary.
Francis Lynch, Attorney.
Thomas P. Smith, Collector.

Paschal N. Smith, Thomas Farmer, Hoysted Hacker, John Willson, Thomas Hooke, Elisha Coit, Thomas Carpenter, John Newson, Nicholas Duff, John Thurston, William Lovett, William Newton, and Thomas P. Smith, standing Committee.

Annual meeting, second Monday in March.

Friary.

Bernard Hart, Father.
Charles Buxton, Chancellor.
John Marschalk, Treasurer.
B. P. Melick, Secretary.

Walter Bowne, Jacob Bradford, and John Motley, Priors.

William Hartshorne, Andrew Smyth, Robert Murray, John Marschalk, Anthony Pell, Nathaniel Gardiner, William Richardson, Nicholas G. Carmer, William Parker, John Motley, John Banks, Isaac L. Kip, standing Committee.

The stated meetings are on the first and third Tuesdays in each month, at No. 50 Pine-street; and annual meeting, for the appointment of officers, November 10.

St. Cecilia Society.

Lewis Ogden, President.
Frederick Rausch, Vice-President.
Andrew Smyth, Treasurer.
Robert M'Mennomy, Secretary.

Joseph Fitch, John M. Bradford, and George L. Caliment, Committee.

Benjamin Skaats, Doorkeeper.

Meet every Saturday, and elect on St. Cecilia's day.

This Society was instituted with a view to cultivate the science of Music, and a good taste in its execution.

Harmonical Society.

John R. Conine, President.

Fortefcue Cuming, Vice-Prefident.
Solomon Roe, Treafurer.
John Bleecker, Secretary.
Nathaniel Paulding, fecond Secretary.
This Society was inftituted March 17th, 1796, for the purpofe of cultivating the Knowledge of Vocal and Inftrumental Mufic.

Columbian Anacreontic Society.
John Hodgkinfon, Prefident.
John C. Shaw, firft Vice-Prefident.
Aquila Giles, fecond Vice-Prefident.
John Bleecker, Secretary.
John Ferrers, Treafurer.
Alexander Bleecker, Alexander L. M'Donald, Harman G. Rutgers, William Ricketts, Thomas Cooper, John K. Beekman, Harmonics.
George Pollock, B. Winthrop, Jofeph Stanfbury, Edward Moore, A. Giles, William Richardfon, and John Ferrers, ftanding Committee.

Uranian Mufical Society.
Jofeph Kimball, Prefident.
———— Prince, Vice Prefident.
Hugh Taylor, Treafurer.
J. C. Totten, Secretary.

General Society of Mechanics and Tradefmen.
James Tylee, Prefident,
Thomas Timpfon, Vice-Prefident.
Cornelius Crygier, fecond Vice-Prefident.
John Striker, Treafurer.
William Whitehead, Secretary.
Paft Mafters.
 Edward Watkeys,
 Jacob Sherred,
 Anthony Brown,
 Abraham Labagh.

New-York Coopers Society.
John Utt, Chairman.
George Seal, Deputy Chairman.

Jacob M. Morris, Treasurer.
James Cock, Secretary.

New-York Mariners Friendly Society.
William Goodman, President.
Alexander Cooley, Vice-President.
Thomas Lasley, Treasurer.
Moses Jarvis, Secretary.

Annual meeting first Wednesday in October; stated meeting, first Wednesday in every month.

Society of Associated Teachers.
John Woods, President.
James Gibbon, Vice President.
Jonathan Fisk, Secretary.
Gad Ely, Treasurer.
Jacob Brown, Steward.

Associated Body of House Carpenters.
Hugh Torrence, President.
Anthony Brown, Vice-President.
John Maghe, Secretary.
Samuel Holmes,
Lewis Lorton, } Treasurers.
Henry B. Earl,

Committee for the Relief of sick Members
Jacob Parsells, Messenger.

John Craig, Daniel Halstead, Alexander Walker, Eleazer Ball, Joseph Young, Thomas Whitchurch, John King, John Targay, Jeremiah B. Taylor, Caleb Fordham.

Cincinnati.
George Washington, President-General of the Society.
Thomas Mifflin, Vice-President General.
Henry Knox, Secretary-General.
William Macpherson, Assistant Secretary General.
William Jackson, Treasurer-General.

☞ New-York Society Cincinnati elect 4th July.

St. George's Society.
Theophylact Bache, President.
Miles Sherbrook, Vice-President.
Frederick Philips, Affistant Vice-President.
John Ferrers, Treafurer.
William Bache, Secretary.
D. Badcock, Samuel March, Henry White, and John Ellis, Stewards.
Rev. Benjamin Moore, Samuel Corp, John Atkinfon, Samuel March, Thomas Roberts, and Benjamin Winthrop, Charitable Committee.

St. Andrew's Society.
Walter Ruthurfurde, President.
Peter M'Dougall, Vice-President.
George Turnbull, fecond Vice-President.
George Douglafs, Treafurer.
George Johnfon, Secretary.
John Munro, Affiftant Secretary.
Rev. John M. Mafon, } Chaplains.
Rev. John Biffet,
Dr. James Tillary, Phyfician.
William Renwick,
James Stuart,
John Knox, } Managers.
Alexander Thomfon,
Andrew D. Barclay,
John M'Gregor,

St. Patrick's Society.
Daniel M'Cormick, President.
James Conftable, Vice-President.
John M'Vickar, fecond Vice-President.
William Hill, Treafurer.
R. R. Waddell, Secretary.

German Society.
David Grim, President.
Leonard Fifher, Vice-President.
David Lydig, Treafurer.
John Speyer, Secretary.
Henry Heyfer, Solicitor.

Godfrey Kant, Jacob Schieffelin, George Gilfert, Christian Baehr, John Peter Ritter, and John Miller, standing Committee.

Caledonian Society.
George Knox, President.
Malcolm Campbell, Vice-President.
John M'Intire, Treasurer.
——— Wiley, Secretary.

A List of the Officers of the Grand Lodge of the State of New-York.

The Most Worshipful the Hon. R. R. Livingston, Grand Master.

The Right Worshipful Jacob Morton, Deputy Grand Master.

The R. W. James Scott, Senior Grand Warden.
The R. W. De Witt Clinton, Jun. Grand Warden.
The R. W. John Abrams, Grand Secretary.
The R. W. Martin Hoffman, Grand Treasurer.
The R. W. the Rev. Dr. Beach, Grand Chaplain.
The R. W. the Rev. John Bisset, Assistant do.

Brothers Cuyler, Clapp, Adams, } Grand Deacons.

Brothers Graham, Barclay, Bache, Horton, } Grand Stewards.

Brother Adamson, Grand Pursuivant.
Brother Benjamin Jones, Grand Tiler.

Grand Lodge meets on the first Wednesday in March, June, September and December; the Grand Stewards Lodge on the last Wednesday in February, May, August and November, at No 66 Liberty-street.

The officers of the Grand Lodge are elected at the yearly meeting in June, and the officers of the private Lodges at the regular meetings in December, previous to the Festival of St. John.

Grand Chapter of Royal Arch Masons.
Right Worshipful Abraham Skinner, High Priest.
Francis Lynch, King.
Jonathan Perry, Scribe.
Ralph Hodge, Secretary.
John Moore, Treasurer.
Ezra Weeks, Zerubbabel.
John Taylor, first Grand Master.
John Pray, second Grand Master.
George Graham, third Grand Master.
John Martin, Architect.
Isaac Delamater, Clothier.
Philip Buchanan, Herald and Tiler.
Meet the 4th Friday in every month, No. 87 Fair-street.

Washington Chapter of Royal Arch Masons.
John Abrams, High Priest.
John C. Ludlow, King.
William Richardson, Scribe.
John Burt, Zerubbabel.
Garret N. Bleecker, Royal Arch Captain.
William Bache, first Grand Master.
Peter Irving, Second Grand Master.
Andrew D. Barclay, third Grand Master.
Andrew Smyth, Treasurer.
Nicholas G. Carmer, Secretary.
Doctor John Onderdonk, Architect.
William Mooney, Clothier.
Benjamin Jones, Tiler.
Meet on the second Friday in January, March, May, July, September and November, at No. 66 Liberty str.

Encampment of Knights Templar.
Jacob Morton, Grand Master.
John Abrams, Generalissimo.
Andrew Smyth, Captain General.
Stated meetings on the fourth Friday of March, June, September and December. Annual meetings on Trinity Sunday; on which day, between the hours of twelve and one o'clock, a moral discourse is delivered by the Grand Master, or by a Sir Knight, deputed by him for that purpose, at the Holland

Lodge Room, No. 66 Liberty-ſtreet; at which diſcourſe all maſter maſons are permitted to attend.

St. John's Lodge, No. 1.

Abraham Skinner, Maſter.
John Henry, Senior Warden.
——— Woods, Junior Warden.
Ezra Weeks, Treaſurer.
John Buel, Secretary.
Stated meetings on the ſecond and fourth Thurſdays in every month, at No. 90 William-ſtreet.

Independent Royal Arch, No. 2.

Francis Lynch, Maſter.
Ralph Hodge, Senior Warden.
Robert Adams, Junior Warden.
John Burt, Secretary.
Abraham B. Martling, Treaſurer.
David Henry, Tiler.
Stated meetings on the firſt and third Tueſdays in every month, at No. 87 Naſſau-ſtreet.

Mark Lodge, annexed to No. 2.

Ralph Hodge, Maſter.
Peter Black, Senior Warden.
Philip Buchanan, Junior Warden.
John Bud, Secretary.
Abraham B. Martling, Treaſurer.
David Henry, Tiler.

St. Andrew's Lodge, No. 3.

Martin Hoffman, Maſter.
William Howell, Senior Warden.
Andrew D. Barclay, Junior Warden.
James Maitland, Secretary.
John Knox, Treaſurer.
Stated meetings on the ſecond and fourth Tueſdays in every month, at No. 90 William-ſtreet.

St. John's Lodge, No. 6.

(No return of Officers.)
Stated meetings on the ſecond and fourth Thurſdays in every month, at No. 51 Whitehall.

Hiram Lodge, No. 7.

Samuel Clark, Master.
James M'Kay, Senior Warden.
John Hyslop, Junior Warden.
Thomas Warren, Secretary.
James Allen, Treasurer.
Benjamin C. Stevenson, Senior Deacon.
William Hays, Junior Deacon.
Thomas Gibson, } Stewards.
—— Douglass, }
Gabriel Legget, Tiler.
Stated meetings first Wednesday in every month.

Holland Lodge, No. 8.

John Jacob Astor, Master.
William Irving, jun. Senior Warden.
John Moore, Junior Warden.
Alexander Robertson, Secretary.
Andrew Smyth, Treasurer.
John M'D. Lawrence, } Masters of Ceremony.
John Rodman, }
Benjamin Onderdonk, Senior Deacon.
John Henry, Junior Deacon.
Thomas R. Smith, and Michael Brooks, Stewards.
Meet the first and third Fridays in every Month, at No. 66 Liberty-street.

Howard Lodge, No. 9.

Samuel Jones, jun. Master.
John H. Remsen, Senior Warden.
Nicholas G. Carmer, Junior Warden.
Edward W. Laight, Secretary.
Robert J. Thurston, Treasurer.
Peter Irving, Senior Master of Ceremonies.
J. W. Mulligan, Junior Master of Ceremonies.
Samuel Hake, Senior Deacon.
Jasper D. Blagge, Junior Deacon.
William Cutting,
Peter Irving,
John W. Mulligan, } Standing Committee.
Daniel Van Voorhis,
John T. Bainbridge,
Baltus P. Melick, and Richard Ellis, Secretaries.

Stated meetings on the second and fourth Thursdays in every month, from November to May, and from May to November, on the first Thursday in every month, at No. 66 Liberty-street, except the City Assemblies interfere on either of these times; in which case the meetings are deferred to the Thursday following.

Trinity Lodge, No. 10.

John Taylor, Master.
Joseph Pierson, Senior Warden.
Peter Clark, Junior Warden.
John Marvin, Treasurer.
Benjamin Cutler, } Deacons.
Jacob Bedell,
William Sands, } Stewards.
William Totten,
James B. Moore, } Masters of Ceremony.
William Shipman,
Benjamin Jones, Tiler.

Stated meetings on the second Monday in every month, at No. 89 Fair-street.

Mark Lodge, annexed to No. 10.

The officers the same as before.

Stated meetings on the fourth Mondays in January, April, July and October.

Phœnix Lodge, No. 11.

John Fitzpatrick, Master.
Alexander Gordon, Senior Warden.
John Slidell, Junior Warden.
Nathaniel Bell, Secretary.
Mark Tier, Treasurer.
John Black, Tiler.

Stated meetings on the second and fourth Wednesdays in every month, at No. 26 South-street.

Mark Lodge, annexed to No. 11.

David Dunham, Master.
M. Myers, Senior Warden.
D. Conchlin, Junior Warden.

Regular meetings on the first Monday in every month.

Le Unite Americaine, No. 12.
Pierre Daniel Biddetronoulleau, Master.
John B. Fauvée Sablon, Senior Warden.
A. C. Poitenin Deveyriere, Junior Warden.
Joseph Marcadier, Secretary.
H. Garcin, Treasurer.
John Mouchon, Orator.
G. Beuze, Master of Ceremonies.
John Lemaire, Tiler.
Stated meetings on the first Monday in every month.

Temple Lodge, No. 13.
Isaac Delamater, Master.
Abraham Walker, Senior Warden.
William Milns, Junior Warden.
William Carroll, Secretary.
Michael Robson, Treasurer.
Michael Gough, Senior Deacon.
John R. Ress, Junior Deacon.
Nicholas Ellion, } Stewards.
Solomon Gadman, }
Stated meetings on the second and fourth Tuesdays in every month, at the corner of Oliver and Water-streets.

☞ For a list of all the Lodges under the Jurisdiction of the Grand Lodge of the State of New-York, see last year's Directory, page 87.

Brigade of Militia of the City and County of New-York.
James Miles Hughes, Brigadier General.
Garret N. Bleecker, Inspector and Major of Brigade.

First Regiment.
Gerard Steddiford, Lieut. Col. Commandant.
William I. Vredenburgh, first Major.
James Morris, second Major.
Captains.
Cornelius N. Bogart, Isaac H. Kip, Jacob De la

Montague, Garret N. Bleecker, Richard Duryee, J. H. Hulett, Francis Arden, John Tabele, John L. Broome, John Mercereau.

Lieutenants.

John M'Kenzie, Cornelius Herttell, Thomas Herttell, John T. Duryee, H. G. Stoutenburgh, John Watts, jun. Peter Utt, Richard M. Lawrence, Oliver L. Cozine, Thomas T. Gaston.

Ensigns.

Daniel R. Durning, John Marschalk, William De Forest, Peter C. Schuyler, Thomas Phœnix, John G. Bogert, David Morgan, Isaac A. Van Hook, John Barbarie, George Campbell.

Richard Furman, Pay-master.
John Elsworth, Quarter-master.
Thomas T. Gaston, Adjutant.
Daniel M. Hitchcock, Surgeon's mate.

Second Regiment.

William Boyd, Lieut. Col. Commandant.
Walter W. Heyer, first Major.
Peter Van Zandt, second Major.

Captains.

Elbert Roosevelt, Archibald M'Cullum, Alexander Mowatt, John Divine, Isaac Torbos, Leonard Kip, jun. Theunis Dey, John B. Miller, Charles Smith, Nathan Furman.

Lieutenants.

Peter Kettletas, George I. Eacker, John Wheeler, Joel Davis, James B. Kortright, William Whitehead, John M'Keison, jun. Robert Whiting, Isaac Pierson.

Ensigns.

Joseph Constant, Robert C. Degrove, Richard Riker, Joseph Strang, Alexander Phœnix, Joseph Simpson, Daniel Coe, Andrew Sitcher, John E. Brooks.

George I. Eacker, Adjutant.
George Campbell, Pay-master.
Charles F. Thomas, Quarter-master.
Charles Buxton, Surgeon.
John B. Jones, Surgeon's mate.

NEW-YORK REGISTER. 81

Third Regiment.
Jacob Morton, Lieut. Col. Commandant.
James L. Bogert, first Major.
Robert Rutgers, second Major.
Captains.
Isaac Heyer, Henry I. Wyckoff, John Eiting, John Wells, William Richardson, John Crawford, William Cocks, John Childs, Nathaniel Bloodgood, John Graham.
Lieutenants.
William Hosack, Peter Hawes, Andrew Anderson, Henry Sickles, Edward W. Laight, Henry Sands, Richard M. Malcom, George Clarke Morton, Peter A. Jay, John R. Cozine.
Ensigns.
Henry A. Livingston, Benjamin R. Seaman, George F. Harison, William Paulding, Henry Cruger, jun. Joseph Blackwell, jun. Gerard De Peyster, Thomas Uttick, Alexander L. M'Donald, David S. Jones, Juan F. Lewis.

Nicholas Depeyster, jun. Pay-master.
Bernard Hart, Quarter-master.
John Neilson, Surgeon's mate.

Fourth Regiment.
Benjamin North, Lieut. Col. Commandant.
Gabriel Furman, first Major.
Thomas Campbell, second Major.
Captains.
John A. Wolfe, John I. Staples, John P. Pearss, Abraham Riker, Henry Post, Charles Watkins, Caleb Boyle, Ezekiel Dodge, Elias Hicks, Theo. Polhemus.
Lieutenants.
Daniel Dodge, John Chessman, Edward Meeks, jun. Thomas Ammerman, William L. Nott, Henry Hunt, Jasper Ward, Jabez Pell, Beekman Van Beuren, Nicholas Anthony.
Ensigns.
Jonathan Weeder, James M'Kay, Elbert Herring, ——— Tom, Charles Adams, William Cutting, Isaac Houseman, John G. Lockwood, William Chambers, Nicholas Bogert, William Pollix, John P. Anthony.

Frederick Jay, Pay-master.
Jonathan Weeden, Quarter-master.
Daniel Dodge, Adjutant.
John Onderdonk, Surgeon.

Fifth Regiment.

Bernardus Swartwout, jun. Lieut. Col. Commandant.
Whitehead Fish, first Major.
John Morton, second Major.

Captains.

James Striker, Jacob Bradford, Samuel B. Waldron, Francis Childs, Gasherie Brasher, John C. Freeckes, Robert Bogardus, Jasper Hopper, Washington Morton, Samuel Jones, jun.

Lieutenants.

Benjamin Thurston, Cornelius Brinckerhoff, Anthony Pell, John Schenck, Jonas Mapes, Robert Pettit, Anthony Ernest, Thomas Salter, Samuel Hake, Nicholas W. Stuyvesant, Peter G. Stuyvesant, John W. Mulligan.

Ensigns.

Isaac F. Roe, Benjamin Pomeroy, Francis Saltus, Robert I. Thurston, Samuel S. Brush, Henry Norton, John Millan, Samuel Henshaw, John Buntin, Thomas Van Zandt.

James Bailey, Pay-master.
Anthony Ernest, Quarter-master.
Jonas Mapes, Adjutant.
Anthony Anderson, Surgeon.

NEW-YORK REGIMENT OF ARTILLERY.

Field and Staff.

Ebenezer Stevens, Lieut. Col. Commandant.
Peter Curtenius, first Major Commandant.
De Witt Clinton, second Major.
Anthony Lamb, Adjutant.
John Delamater, Pay-master.
Peter Irving, Surgeon.

Captains.

George Snowdon, Nicholas Roosevelt, John Swartwout, John C. Ludlow.

Captain Lieutenants.
Nicholas N. Depeyster, J. Speyer, Libeus Loomis, Augustus Sacket.

First Lieutenants.
John Suydam, Jonathan Lawrence, jun. Anthony Lamb, James Manning.

Brigade Company of Artillery.
John Ten Eyck, Captain.
————— —————, Lieutenant.
John Grenzebach, second Lieutenant.

First Troop of Horse.
John Lovell, Captain.
Edward Patten, Captain Lieutenant.
James Hearn, Lieutenant.
John Fink, Cornet.
James Warner, Quarter-master.

Second Troop.
Nicholas Lawrence, Captain.
William Beekman, first Lieutenant.
David Waldron, second Lieutenant.
James Bartholf, Cornet.
David Waldron, Quarter-master.

New-York Rangers.
————— —————, Captain.
Edward W. Laight, Lieutenant Commandant.
Benjamin R. Seaman, Ensign.

Washington Military Society.
Brigadier-General James M. Hughes, President.
Lieut. Colonel Jacob Morton, Vice-President.
Lieut. Col. B. Swartwout, jun. 2d. Vice-President.
————— —————, Inspector.
Ensign Francis Saltar, Paymaster.
Ensign John G. Bogert, Secretary.
————— —————, Adjutant.

New-York Society for promoting Christian Knowledge and Piety.
Rev. John Rodgers, President.

Rev. John C. Kunze, Vice-President.
Garrit H. Van Waggenen, Treasurer.
John M. Mason, Secretary.
Rev. William Phœbus, Rev. William Linn, Thomas Storm, George Warner, and Rev. James Birkby, Assistants.

Annual meetings, 4th Monday in June. Stated meetings, quarterly, on the 4th Monday in March, June, September, and December.

New-York Missionary Society.
Rev. John Rodgers, President.
Rev. William Linn, Vice-President.
Divie Bethune, Treasurer.
Rev. John M. Mason, Secretary.
Rev. John N. Abeel, Clerk.
Rev. John M'Knight, Rev. Benjamin Foster, Rev. Gerardus A. H. Kuypers, Rev. Samuel Miller, Leonard Bleecker, John Broome, T. Mackaness, Thomas Storm, George Lindsay, John Bingham, and Peter Wilson, Directors.

This society was instituted, in 1796, for the purpose of propagating the gospel in such places as are destitute of it, or of the means of obtaining it.—Annual meetings, first Tuesday in November. Stated meetings, first Monday in February, May, August, and November.

Rates of Storage per Month, as established in the City of New-York.

	Dols.	Cts.
Hogsheads of sugar, 12 cwt. or under,		37
Do. do. 12 cwt. or upwards,		50
Do. of tobacco,		50
Puncheons of rum, &c.		37
Hogsheads molasses,		43
Pipes of wine, gin, &c. from 100 to 140 gals.		50
Half pipes do.		25
Butts do. 140 gallons and upwards,		62
Quarter casks do.		12
Tierces of rice,		25
Do. of flaxseed, &c.		30

Do. molasses, sugar, paint, and other wet articles,	28
Do. oil,	31
Barrels provisions, fish, &c.	9
Do. flour, meal, and other dry articles,	6
Bags containing 100lbs. coffee, pepper, cocoa, &c.	4
Do. do. larger, in proportion.	
Cases gin, &c.	4
Do. do. larger in proportion.	
Chests tea, largest size,	25
Do. smaller, in proportion.	
Boxes soap, candles, &c.	4
Do. glass containing 100 feet,	4
Firkins of butter, lard, &c.	4
Hides, dry,	3
Leather, per side,	$1\frac{1}{2}$
Duck, Russia, per bolt,	2
Do. Ravens, per piece,	1
Grain, per bushel,	2
Salt,	$2\frac{1}{2}$
Iron, steel, lead, &c. per ton,	75
Cordage, per ton,	1 25
Cotton in bales of 300lbs.	31
Others in proportion.	
Earthenware, per crate,	37
Sheathing paper,	3
Boxes of tin,	$1\frac{1}{2}$
Dye-wood, per ton,	75
Dry fish, per quintal,	9

The owner of the goods to pay the porterage, &c.
—Goods remaining in store one or more days over a month, are to pay a month's additional storage—All goods unpacked while in store to pay double storage.

STAGES.

The Old Line leaves New-York Mondays, Wednesdays, and Fridays, at 2 o'clock, until December; then every day till the first of April.

A number of Stages for Philadelphia leave this city at different hours every day. Also Stages for Boston, Morristown, Newark, Hackensack, &c. ply regularly. [For the different stage-offices, see Philadelphia, Albany, &c. &c. in Directory.]

Hand in Hand Fire Company.

Instituted in this city, in November, 1780, for the purpose of averting, as much as possible, the ruinous consequences which may occasionally happen by fire.

The officers for the present year are—
John Murray, Esq. President.
Peter M'Dougall, Vice-President.
Nicholas G. Carmer, Secretary.

The company consists of fifty members, who are provided with bags for the removal of effects at a fire.

ERRATA.

The following names are to be substituted for those of the same numbers in the list of Cartmen.

51 Peter Bogart,	547 Charles Suydam,
130 William Dennison,	657 Any. Dougherty,
133 Henry Lowther,	671 Abraham Hopper,
138 William Ketchum,	675 John M'Gowan,
140 Oliver Crane,	692 Henry Adams,
153 Peter Brass,	812 Isaac Fountain,
222 Andrew Losye,	852 Willian Long,
301 Michael Ryer,	880 James Gilbert.
326 John Graham,	

☞ The continuation of the roll of Attornies at Law could not be obtained in time from Albany for this year's Register.

☞ For an alphabetical list of all the streets, lanes, alleys, wharves, public buildings, &c. in the city of New-York, with their situations in respect to each other, and references for finding them on LONGWORTH's Plan of New-York; see last year's Directory, page 100.

☞ Paintings, Drawings, Prints, Needle-workings, &c. framed in a neat and elegant manner, by D. Longworth, Printseller, No. 66 Nassau-street. Books, stationary, maps, drawing paper, glass, &c. &c. sold at the same place.

THE NEW-YORK DIRECTORY.

A

AARON, Henry, merchant, No. 74 Maiden-lane.
Abanaths, Anson, grocer, Henry-street.
Abbot, Samuel, grocer, 29 Broad do.
Abbot, Richard, taylor, 66 James do.
Abeel, Rev. John N. 29 Fair do.
Abeel, Garrit, merchant, 13 Pine do.
Abeel, James, land-broker, 55 Broad do.
Abeel, Garrit B. ironmonger, 85 Cherry do.
Abel, John, 49 Division do.
Abernethy, George, shoemaker, 33 Barclay do.
Ablin, John, shipmaster, 58 John do.
Abraham, Hyman, tobacconist, 24 Water do.
Abraham, Isaac, trader, 433 Pearl do.
Abraham, Isaac, merchant, 209 Greenwich do.
Abrams, John, merchant, 178 do.
Abramse, Jacob, 83 Liberty do.
Acker, Jacob, cartman, Greenwich-road.
Ackerman, Adam, shoemaker, 21 Skinner-street.
Ackerman, Richard, 65 Partition do.
Ackerman, William, 249 Greenwich do.
Ackerman, John, constable, 2 Ann do.
Ackerman, Lewis, cartman, Winne do.
Ackerman, John, cartman, 97 Reed do.
Ackerman, Samuel, butcher, Second do.
Ackerman, David, ropemaker, Winne do.
Ackerman, David, wheelwright, First do.
Ackerman, Abraham, sugarboiler, 7 Thomas do.
Ackerman, David, harness-maker, 27 Chapel do.
Ackerman, John, chairmaker, 119 Bowery-lane.
Ackerman, Morris, boarding-house, 66 Partition-st.
Ackerman, John, flour-store, 66 do.
Ackerman, John, baker, Upper Reed do.
Ackerman, Henry, mason, Magazine do.

NEW-YORK DIRECTORY.

Ackerman, James, ropemaker, Winne-street.
Ackerson, Garrit, cartman, Barclay do.
Ackisa, Andrew, labourer, 21 Batavia-lane.
Ackley, John, 72 Gold-street.
Ackley, Anthony, merchant, 48 Broad do.
Ackley, Francis M. silversmith, 29 Bowery-lane.
Acton, George, gold-beater, Pearl, corner of Hague-str.
Adam, Robert, mason, 63 Murray do.
Adam, C. fruiterer, 43 Chatham do.
Adams, John, mariner, 43 Banker do.
Adams, Margaret, 6 Moore do.
Adams, ——, mariner, Eagle do.
Adams, William, druggist, 193 Pearl do.
Adams, William, painter and gilder, 63 do.
Adams, Francis, mason, 4 Murray do.
Adams, widow, seamstress, Mulberry do.
Adams, John, mason, 98 Reed do.
Adams, widow, 3 New do.
Adams, Charles, counsellor at law, 27 Beaver do.
Adams, John, merchant, 97 Beekman do.
Adams, William, rigger, 20 Harman do.
Adams, Peter, cartman, 21 Bancker do.
Adams, widow, grocer, 82 Catharine do.
Adams, George, shipwright, Charlotte do.
Adams, Henry, cartman, 52 E. George do.
Adams, John, mason, Little Catharine do.
Adamson, Alexander, merchant, 179 Pearl do.
Addoms, Jonas, weigher, 49 Beekman do.
Adee, David, dry goods store, 59 James do.
Adley, Simon, dry goods store, 235 Broadway.
Adriance, Abraham I. 61 Front and 35 John-street.
Adriance, Samuel P. merchant-taylor, 93 Pearl do.
Affleck, Robert, merchant, 108 William do.
Agar, William, mariner, 8 Frankfort do.
Agnel, Hyacinth, French teacher, 137 William do.
Agnew, John, tobacconist, 308 Water do.
Agnew, Andrew, carpenter, Greenwich-road.
Aikins, Alexander, rigger, 6 Harman-street.
Aikman, John, shipcarpenter, 50 James do.
Aime, Jacob, cartman, 6 Robinson do.
Aime, Martin, cartman, 14 George do.
Aime, Robert, Magazine, corner of Augustus do.

Air-furnace, Curtenius's, Greenwich-road.
Air-furnace, Industry,   do.   do.
Air-furnace, Union, upper end of Broadway.
Air-furnace, Youle's, Corlaer's-hook.
Akeley, Joshua, Bowery-lane.
Akerly, Jacamiah, blacksmith, 133 Cherry-street.
Akerly, Samuel, shipwright, E. Rutger do.
Albany stage-office, 1 and 5 Cortlandt do.
Albert, widow, 6 Augustus do.
Albert, Rev. M. 67 Maiden-lane.
Albertson, Sarah, grocer, Oliver-street.
Aldworth, Sarah, grocer, 47 Gold do.
Alexander, Alexander, harness-maker, 44 Chatham do.
Alexander, Hugh, cooper, 58 Pearl do.
Alexander, ———, taylor, 33 Bancker do.
Alexander, Robert, insurance-broker, 59 Stone do.
Alexander, William, attorney at law, 287 Broadway.
Alexander, Andrew, grocer, 60 Murray-street.
Alhart, Morris, blacksmith, 89 Nassau do.
Alibur, Stephen, grocer, 101 Division do.
Alix, Charles L. confectioner, 7 Chatham-row.
Alizou, George, 48 Chapel-street.
All, Michael, grocer, 25 Fayette do.
Allaire, Peter A. livery stabler, 29 John do.
Allan, Robert, grocer, 300 Broadway.
Allan, William, shoemaker, 80 Wall-street.
Allan, James A. shoemaker, Chapel do.
Allan, John, cooper, 40 James do.
Allan, Richard, porter-bottler, 48 Catharine do.
Allen, James, carpenter and shipjoiner, 67 Liberty do.
Allen, John, carpenter, 51 Harman do.
Allen, John, cooper, Fisher do.
Allen, Peter, Church do.
Allen, Mrs. callender of silk stockings, 67 Liberty do.
Allen, Nehemiah, grocer, 22 Oliver do.
Allen, William, 135 Greenwich do.
Allen Stephen, 38 Rutger do. loft Jackson's wharf.
Allen, John, cooper, Cherry, corner of E. George-str.
Allen, John, clockmaker, E. Washington do.
Allen, ———, mariner, 63 Catharine do.
Allen, Jolly, mariner, 81 James do.
Allen, Stephen, mason, 24 Reed do.

Allen, Thomas, bookseller and stationer, 186 Pearl-str.
Allen, William, gunsmith, 108 Maiden-lane.
Allen, Henry, do. 34 do.
Allen, Jonathan, cartman, 87 Warren-street.
Allen, Henry, mariner, 27 Chesnut do.
Alley, James, rigger, Charlotte do.
Alley, Enos, shoe-store, 99 Maiden-lane.
Allien, Lawrence, 95 Bowery-lane.
Allison, Peter, gold and silversmith, 156 Broadway.
Allison, Peter, tavern, Warren-street.
Alner, Gen. James, 171 William do.
Alner, Charity, 62 Cherry do.
Alston, Isaac, tavern, 85 Murray do.
Alstyne, John, 15 Liberty do.
Alstyne, Abraham, cabinetmaker, 174 William do.
Alstyne, John, cooper, Little Ann do.
Alstyne, Jeronymus, blacksmith, 15 Liberty do.
Altenus, Jacob, coachmaker, 185 Broadway.
Altgilt, John, cabinetmaker, 29 Nassau-street.
Altgilt, Jacobus, 93 Reed do.
Always, Obadiah, weaver, 1 Fayette do.
Always, John, windsor chairmaker, 42 James do.
Always, James, chairmaker, 38 do.
Ambler, Silas, carpenter, Third do.
Ambrose, William, mason, Harman do.
Ammerman, Thomas, cartman, 11 Vandewater do.
Ammerman, Albert, cartman, 27 do.
Ammerman, Peter, shoemaker, 69 Chatham do.
Amory, James, whipmaker, 71 Water do.
Amory, John, whipmaker, Lumber do.
Anderiese, Nicholas, shoemaker, 29 Chatham do.
Anderson, John, grocer, 4 Front do.
Anderson, widow, 41 Chapel do.
Anderson, Mary, 94 Catharine do.
Anderson, ——, cartman, 2 Moore's-row.
Anderson, Hutton, ladies seminary, 47 Whitehall-str.
Anderson, William, cartman, 50 Chatham do.
Anderson, Andrew, grocer, 138 do.
Anderson, Hannah, 29 William do.
Anderson, John, cartman, 12 Barclay do.
Anderson, jun. John, attorney at law, 129 Front do.
Anderson, John B. carver and gilder, 409 Pearl do.

Anderson, John, carpenter, 23 Murray-street.
Anderson, Abraham, culler, 86 Front do.
Anderson, Anthony L. physician, 461 Pearl do.
Anderson, David, boarding-house, 18 Cooper do.
Anderson, John, carpenter, 49 Cliff do.
Anderson, Berthrong, leathercutter, 180 William do.
Anderson, James, shopkeeper, 144 Broadway.
Anderson, John, auctioneer, 77 Wall-street.
Anderson, Henry, housecarpenter, 22 Thames do.
Anderson, Elbert, cabinetmaker, 3 Cortlandt, and 7 Barley do.
Anderson, Andrew, chairmaker, 50 Beekman do.
Anderson, Alexander, M. D. 27 Liberty do.
Anderson, James, cutler, 63 Cherry do.
Anderson, John, mariner, 88 John do.
Anderson, Lambert, cartman, 17 Warren do.
Anderson, Israel, grocer, Chamber, corner Greenwich.
Anderson, David, carpenter, 60 Chapel do.
Anderson, Asa, carpenter, Barley do.
Anderson, Henry, labourer, E. George do.
Anderson, Robert, mason, 16 do.
Anderson, Peter, M. D. 206 Broadway.
Anderson, Richard, cartman, 17 Thomas-street.
Anderson, Alexander, cabinetmaker, 35 Beekman do.
Anderson, Francis, cartman, 26 Roosevelt do.
Anderson, James, shoemaker, Eagle do.
Andras, William, jeweller, 166 Broadway.
Andre, Bartholomew, merchant, 150 William-street.
Andre, Elizabeth, 17 Rutger do.
Andres, Jonathan, 72 Vesey do.
Andrews, Charles, mariner, Hester do.
Andrews, Geo. composition manufac. 51 Barclay do.
Andrews, Peter, carpenter, 88 Bowery-lane.
Andrews, C. surgeon, 203 Water-street.
Andrews, John, cartman, Bowery.
Andrews, Isaac, shipmaster, 124 Cherry-street.
Angevine, John, grocer, 29 Reed do.
Angevine, Gilbert, grocer, 429 Pearl do.
Angevine, Peter, carpenter, Pump do.
Angevine and Hoagland, grocers, 2 Oliver do.
Annely, John, gunsmith, 57 Water do.
Anspack, Frederick, cartman, First do.

Anthon, George, M. D. 11 Broad-street.
Anthoine, Andrew, merchant, 48 Whitehall do.
Anthony, Ann, boarding-house, 222 Water do.
Anthony, Nic. N. tanner & currier, 34 Frankfort do.
Anthony, John, blockmaker, 12 do.
Anthony, Nic. tanner & currier, 18 Vandewater do.
Anthony, John P. tanner & currier, 64 Frankfort do.
Assy, David, cartman, 32 Moore do.
Apple, John, shipmaster, 50 Catharine do.
Apple, Conrad, surgeon, 9 Murray do.
Appleby, Gilbert, cartman, 47 Barley do.
Appleby, James, cartman, 94 Chatham do.
Appleby, Mary, washer, 22 Vesey do.
Applegate, John, manufactory of ground coffee and boarding-house, 194 Water do.
Appley, Jacob, butcher, Pell do.
Apthorp, George, 73 Liberty do.
Apthorp, Charles, 103 do.
Archer, Annanias, taylor, 22 Nassau do.
Archer, Goodheart, cartman, Third do.
Archer, Moses, shoemaker, 345 Broadway.
Archer, Joshua, labourer, Division-street.
Archer, Ezekiel, shoe-store, 364 Pearl do.
Archer, Dupoy, and Co. store, Stevens' wharf.
Archer, Jonathan, 53 Reed street.
Arcularius, George, baker, 37 Dey do.
Arcularius, Philip, tanner, 11 Frankfort do.
Arcularius, widow, 1 Skinner do.
Arden, John, carpenter, 438 Pearl do.
Arden, Germain, 8 Murray do.
Arden, Thomas, 162 Greenwich do.
Arden, Francis, cabinetmaker, 49 Rose do.
Arden and Co. John, shipchandlers, 78 Front do.
Arden, widow Catharine, 28 Frankfort do.
Arden, James, merchant, 64 Broadway.
Arden, Thomas, Mulberry-street.
Arden, Francis, butcher, 207 William do.
Arden, Francis, attorney at law, 207 do.
Arden, John, ropemaker, Bayard do.
Arding, Charles, M. D. 75 Beekman do.
Arell, Peter, 35 Chamber do.
Arents, Stephen, cedarcooper, 27 Chapel do.

Arkels, John, tavern, Robinson-street.
Armstrong, John W. merchant, 126 Broadway.
Armstrong, Simon, carpenter, 26 Skinner-street.
Armstrong, Mrs. 6 Duane do.
Armstrong, John, blacksmith, Washington do.
Armstrong, Nathan, shoemaker, 17 Thomas do.
Armstrong and Barnewall, merchants, 129 Water do.
Armstrong, William, grocer, 8 Broadway.
Armstrong, William, merchant, 89 Liberty-street.
Armour, Samuel, shipmaster, 83 Beekman do.
Armour, John, shipmaster, 75 Gold do.
Arnold, George, merchant, 134 Greenwich do.
Arnold, John, rigger, 27 Rutger do.
Arnold, Valentine, inspector of wood, 26 James do.
Arnold and Ramsay's counting-house, 20 William do.
Arnold widow, corner of First and Pump do.
Arnold, John, Cherry, near E. George do.
Arnold, Joseph, shipmaster, 43 Catharine do.
Arnold, Jacob, currier, 26 James do.
Arnold, J. Hobuck ferry-house, 175 Washington do.
Arnold, Moses, ropemaker, Mulberry do.
Arnet, Samuel, measurer, 13 Stone do.
Arthur, Peter, carpenter, 83 Warren do.
Ash, William, windsor chairmaker, 17 Cedar do.
Ash, Thomas, windsor chairmaker, 43 John do.
Ashfield, John, baker, 194 William do.
Ashley and Collard, shopkeepers, 348 Water do.
Ashley, Robert, mariner, 84 Harman do.
Ashman, Richard, grocer, Cherry do.
Ashmore, John, distiller, Bowery-lane.
Ask, Samuel, mason, Charlotte-street.
Askins, Caleb, mariner, 4 Chamber do.
Askins, John, mason, 56 Barclay do.
Askins, John, 52 New do.
Aspin, Thomas, mariner, 66 Cliff do.
Aspinwall, Gilbert and John, merchants, 207 Pearl do.
Asque, Mary, Bedlow-row.
Astin, Isaac, shoemaker, 73 Chamber-street.
Astor, Jacob John, fur-merchant, 149 Broadway.
Astor, Henry, butcher, 94 Bowery-lane.
Atherton, Otis, clockmaker, 109 Harman-street.
Atkins, Isaac, baker, 13 E. George do.

NEW-YORK DIRECTORY.

Atkinson, John, merchant, 20 Cortlandt, and store 4 Fletcher-street.
Atkinson, Edward, mariner, 342 Water do.
Atkinson, John W. 227 Pearl do.
ATTORNEY General's office, 33 Broad do.
Aubick, Earnest, tanner and currier, 78 Gold do.
Aubry, Peter, merchant, 37 George do.
Auchinvole, David, merchant, 141 Pearl do.
Auge, Fanny, 28 Frankfort do.
Auld, Isaac, Magazine do.
Austin and Adams, tayloresses, 62 Harman do.
Austin, Nathaniel, accountant, Cross do.
Avery, John, mariner, 73 Division do.
Avery, John, Elysian boarding-house, Broadway.
Avery, Sarah, shopkeeper, 157 Water-street.
Avery, Ann, dry goods store, 67 Maiden-lane.
Avis, John, taylor, 331 Water-street.
Ayerigg, Benjamin, painter and glazier, 97 Cherry do.
Aymar, John D. block & pumpmaker, Bache's wharf.
Aymar, widow of James, 557 Broadway.
Aymar, widow Jane, grocer, 100 Nassau-street.
Aymar, John, grocer, 55 do.
Aymar, James, grocer, 1 Chatham-row.
Aymar, Peter, grocer, 128 Broad-street.
Ayres, Camp, mason, 79 Vesey do.

B

Baalman, John, accountant, Magazine-street.
Babb, James, carpenter, 32 Barclay do.
Babcock, John, mariner, 28 Oliver do.
Babcock, Frederick, merchant, 100 Front do.
Babcock, Cortlandt, merchant, 170 Water do.
Bach, Henry, boarding-house, 55 Pine do.
Bache, Theophylact, merchant, 122 Pearl do.
Bache, Paul and Andrew, merchants, 86 Water do. and store Slote-lane.
Bache, William, attorney at law, 91 Front-street.
Bachman, John N. labourer, First do.
Backhouse, William, shipmaster, 80 Roosevelt do.
Backus, Ebenezer, merchant, 133 Water do.
Bacon, William, cutler, 235 Water do.
Bacon, John, cutler, 206 Broadway.
Bacon, Thomas, butcher, Eagle-street.

Bacque, John B. 19 New-street.
Badcock, Daniel, merchant, 120 Water do.
Badger, Rich. & Nath. merchants, 117 William do.
Badgley, Isaac, 52 Barley do.
Badgley, Jacob, mason, 52 do.
Badollet, Paul, clock and watchmaker, 101 Pearl do.
Baehr, Christian & Daniel, merchant-taylors, 151 do.
Baehr, Daniel, 52 Beaver do.
Baehr, Frederick, baker, 8 do.
Baenum, Eliphalet, grocer, Fayette, corner of Henry do.
Bagley, Rachel, 16 Fayette do.
Bagley, Martha & Eliz. mantau-makers, 36 Dey do.
Bagot, Lewis, carpenter, Bowery-lane.
Bailey, Abraham, bricklayer, 86 Roosevelt-street.
Bailey, William and James, store, 56 Front do.
Bailey and Bogert, 115 Front do.
Bailey, James, merchant, 12 Stone do.
Bailey, John, ironmonger and founder, 60 Water do.
Bailey, Benjamin, merchant, 402 Pearl do.
Bailey, Joseph, tavern, 57 Chatham do.
Bailey, Mr. 107 Liberty do.
Bailey, John, mason, Mott do.
Bailey, James, cartman, Hester, corner of Elizabeth do.
Bailey, Simeon C. watchmaker, 56 Stone do.
Baillie, James, hair-dresser, Cherry do. Ship-yards.
Bain, widow, 4 George-street.
Bain, John, mariner, 46 Ferry do.
Bainbridge, Absalom, physician, 58 Pine do.
Bainbridge, John T. attorney at law, 134 Pearl do.
Baisley, John, butcher, Elizabeth do.
Baisley, Harman, ropemaker, Winne do.
Baker, James, mason, First do.
Baker, Peter, shipwright, Bedlow do.
Baker, Charles, shoemaker, Mott do.
Baker, Daniel, carpenter, 41 Barley do.
Baker, Phoebe, seamstress, First do.
Baker, John, tavern, Cherry do. Ship-yards.
Baker, Eliza, grocer, 22 Peck-slip.
Baker, David, shoemaker, 255 Water-street.
Baker, William, cooper, 54 Cherry do.
Baker, William, coppersmith, 68 Ann do.
Baker, Robert, shipwright, Birmingham-row.

Baker, Daniel, carpenter, 40 Lumber-street.
Baker, Richard, cartman, Pump do.
Baker, William, shoemaker, 106 Division do.
Baker, Gardiner, keeper and proprietor of the Museum, in the Exchange, Broad-street.
Baker, Thomas, mariner, 40 Warren do.
Baker, Allen, mason, 115 Reed do.
Baker, Henry, smith, 31 James do.
Baker, William, taylor, Bedlow do.
Baker, Stephen, grocer, 119 Greenwich do.
Baker, George, coachmaker, 17 Barclay do.
Baker, Phœbe, seamstress, 36 Augustus do.
Baker, George, tavern, 7 New-slip.
Bakewell, Benjamin, merchant, Washington-street.
Bakewell, Joseph, grocer and joiner, 61 Ann do.
Baldwin, Elizabeth, 177 William do.
Baldwin, Charles, counsellor at law, 1 Nassau do.
Baldwin, Aaron, carpenter, 2 Theatre-alley.
Baldwin, Sylvester, shipmaster, Charlotte-street.
Baldwin, John, grocer, 153 Front do.
Baldwin, Moses, boarding-house, Charlotte do.
Baldwin, Matthias, cartman, Henry do.
Baldwin, Daniel, 49 Rose do.
Ball, Eleazer, carpenter, 4 Chapel do.
Ball & Largin, young ladies teachers, 38 Partition do.
Ball, John, mason, 3 Moore do.
Ball, Elizabeth, Barley do.
Ball, Elizabeth, seamstress, 8 Augustus do.
Ball, Flamen, counsellor at law, 35 & 38 Cherry do.
Ball, Archibald, mason, 40 Reed do.
Ball, Isaac, physician, 40 Chamber do.
Ball, Edward John, 59 Murray do.
Ball, John, accountant, 16 Dutch do.
Ball, John, comb-manufactory, Bowery-lane.
Ball, William, shipwright, 6 Lumber-street.
Ballard, William, measurer of grain, 5 Dutch do.
Balor, John, painter, Orange do.
Balts, Jacob P. labourer, 120 Cherry do.
Bancker, Elizabeth, 43 Oliver do.
Bancker, Gerard, 39 Pearl do.
Bancker, Ann, corner Cherry and Clinton streets.
Bancker, jun. Evert, city-surveyor, 46 Vesey-street.

Bancker, John, shoemaker, 57 Ann-street.
Bancker, Henry, mason, 34 Vandewater do.
Bancker, Christopher, accountant, 12 Lombard do.
Bancker, Abraham, mason, 25 Warren do.
Bancker, John, weigher, 97 Cherry do.
Bancker, Gerard I. 97 do.
Bancker, John K. merchant, 119 Front do.
Bancker, Margaret, 41 Warren do.
Bancker, Evert, loan-officer, &c. 58 Cedar do.
Bancker, Abraham, shoemaker, 1 Dutch do.
Bangs, Eliakim, shoemaker, 49 Chapel do.
BANK of New-York, 32 Wall do.
BANK, United States Branch, 38 do.
Banks, John, 10 Cortlandt do.
Banks, Mary, boarding-house, 56 Chamber do.
Banks, James, rigger and stivadore, Lumber do.
Banks, John, inspector of the customs, 134 Front do.
Banks, Daniel, boatman, Third do.
Banner, Peter, carpenter & builder, 81 Greenwich do.
Bannerman, Alexander, taylor, 32 Broad do.
Bannerman, widow, 45 Robinson do.
Bannon, John, shipwright, Birmingham-row.
Banta, Jane, shopkeeper, 27 Chatham-street.
Banta, John, grocer, Thomas, corner of Chapel do.
Banta, Peter, cartman, 249 Greenwich do.
Banta, John carpenter, Cross do.
Banta, John, cartman, 53 Harman do.
Banta, Jacob, gardener, Bowery-lane.
Banta, widow, do.
Banta, Peter, cartman, Cross-street.
Barber, Oliver, Jay do.
Barber, Robert, carpenter, 10 Beaver do.
Barber and Griffin, grocery & flour-store, 49 Front do.
Barber, Thomas, rigger, 62 Gold do.
Barber, Silas, 39 Robinson do.
Barbarie and Co. John, dry-goods store, 131 Front do.
Barclay, Andrew D. merchant, 127 Water do.
Barclay, Elizabeth, 306 Broadway.
Bard, jun. John, 157 Pearl, and 41 Vesey streets.
Bard, Henry, 73 Chamber-street.
Bard, ——, boarding-house, 12 Broadway.
Barker, B. B. clock and watchmaker, 65 Stone-street.

NEW-YORK DIRECTORY.

Barker, George, carpenter, 30 Auguſtus-ſtreet.
Barker, Joſhua, manager airfurnace, Greenwich-ſtr.
Barker, John, carpenter, 76 Warren do.
Barker, Stevenſon & Co. iron-foundery, Greenwich-road.
Barker, Peter, 21 Bowery-lane.
Barley, Caſper, painter, Firſt-ſtreet.
Barlow, William, merchant, 280 Pearl do.
Barnard, widow, corner of Henry and Catharine do.
Barnard, Albert, ſhipmaſter, 25 Bancker do.
Barnes, Robert, brewer, 43 Cheapſide.
Barnes, Charles, 78 Warren-ſtreet.
Barnes, Breſted, ſhip-carpenter, 116 Harman do.
Barnet, Robert, mariner, Charlotte do.
Barnet, John, maſon, 11 Auguſtus do.
Barnewall, George, merchant, 129 Water do.
Barney, Henry, hatter, Auguſtus do.
Barnum, Wheeler, taylor, 25 Oliver do.
Baron, Jacque, 8 Barley do.
Barr, John, butcher, Grand do.
Barrd, John, butcher, Firſt do.
Barrea, Sarah, 19 Cedar do.
Barrett, Francis, 8 Ann do.
Barret, John, hairdreſſer, 15 Burling-ſlip.
Barrett, Joſeph, merchant, 55 Beaver-ſtreet.
Barretto, Francis, merchant, Greenwich-road.
Barrick, widow, milliner, 59 Dey-ſtreet.
Barron, James, merchant, Cherry do. Ship-yards.
Barrow, John T. painter and gilder, 15 New-ſtreet.
Barrow, John, merchant, Corlaer's hook.
Barrow & Co. Thomas, merchants, 31 William-ſtreet.
Barry, John, 60 Naſſau do.
Barry, David, boatman, Henry do.
Barry, Thomas, grocer, 141 Front do.
Bartholf, Henry, cartman, Barley do.
Bartles, Henry, ſugar-refiner, 4 Jacob do.
Bartlet, James, tavern, 512 Water do.
Bartlet, Wm. phyſician and druggiſt, 120 Cherry do.
Bartlet, William, ſhopkeeper, 21 Lumber do.
Bartlet, Joſeph, carpenter, Bayard do.
Bartlet, Benjamin, ſhipjoiner, Harman do.
Bartley, Lewis, ſhoemaker, 18 Diviſion do.
Barton, William, blackſmith, 71 Dey do.

Barton, John, boatman, Second-street.
Barton, William, shoemaker, Mott
Bartow, Andrew A. merchant, 33 Dey
Bartow, Theodosius, druggist, 7 Beekman-slip.
Bartow and Bradley, merchants, 181 Front-street.
Bartow, Thomas, merchant, Magazine
Bartow and Walden, merchants, 172 Front
Bartow, A. & Rob. S. auctioneers, 128 Water
Bartow, Anthony, merchant, 128 do.
Bartram, Benjamin, 28 Church
Bartram, John, carpenter, Winne
Bass, Barnabus, labourer, 15 E. George
Bass, Joseph, carpenter, Elizabeth
Bassery, Jane, confectioner, 36 John
Basset, Frederick, plumber & pewterer, 218 Pearl
Basset, Francis,   do.   213 do.
Basset, John, 49 Church
Batchelor, John, smith, 5 Barley, and 53 Cortlandt
Batchelor, William, Brushmaker, Bowery-lane.
Bateman, Elias, labourer, 227 William-street.
Bates, James, labourer, 29 Cliff
Bates, John, dry-good store, 72 Maiden-lane.
Bates, John G. hatter, 71 Murray-street.
Bates, Abraham, merchant, 21 Wall
Bates, Sarah, 71 Murray
Batts, Robert B. grocer, 122 Greenwich
Baudouine, Abraham, hatter, 140 Front
Baudouine and Jagger, hatters, 158 Water
Baum, George, grocer, Barley
Bauman, Sebastian, postmaster, 30 Wall
Bausher, Henry, smith, 77 Nassau
Bausher, jun, Henry, smith, 77 do.
Bawky, Lucretia, cook, 47 Ann
Baxter, Schuyler, taylor, 29 Cooper
Baxter, James, coachmaker, 197 Broadway.
Bayard, Nicholas, M. D. 85 Liberty-street.
Bayard, William, merchant, 49 Wall
Bayley, Richard, health-officer, 5 State
Bayley & Douglass, gold & silversmiths, 136 Broadway.
Baylis, Melancton, marshall, 3 Banker-street.
Baylis, Nathaniel, carpenter, Henry
Beach, Samuel, shoemaker, 11 Reed

b

Beach, Daniel, lumber merchant, 14 Washington-str.
Beach, Rev. Abraham, D. D. 88 Beekman
Beach, Israel, grocer, 66 Dey
Beach, William, carpenter, 63 Chapel
Beadle, Mordecai, carpenter, E. Rutger
Beakley, Christopher, tavern, 128 Fly-market.
Beam, John C. shoemaker, 7 Thomas-street.
Bear, Robert, mariner, Bedlow
Beard, John, sailmaker, 48 E. George
Bearin, Wm. cartman, Chapel, corner of Thomas
Beaty, Robert, taylor, 38 Cherry
Beaumont, Arthur C. attorney at law, 135 Broadway,
Beaumont, Gabriel, 7 Murray-street.
Becanon, Philip, porter-house, 87 Fair
Beck, David, cartman, 6 Chamber
Beck, John, shipjoiner, Lumber
Beck, Leopold, baker, 8 Barclay
Beck, Margaret, mantuamaker, 45 John
Beckett, Thomas, butcher, Bowery-lane.
Becketts, George, 46 Cedar-street.
Becquet, Lewis, taylor, 11 Rutger
Bedell, William, shipmaster, 51 Harman
Bedell, Jacob, grocer, 141 Fly-market.
Bedell, Israel, merchant, 13 Pearl-street.
Bedient, Kimberly and Co's. store, 17 Beekman-Sip.
Bedient, John, merchant, 17   do.
Bedlow, Wm. & Henry, Charlotte, corner Cherry-str.
Beebee, Lester, mariner, Henry
Beebee, Samuel, broker, 18 Pine
Beebee, Edward, shipwright, Lumber
Beekman, Theophilus, alderman, 64 Beekman
Beekman, William, Oliver
Beekman, Nicholas, hairdresser, 32 Rutger
Beekman, Magnus, shoemaker, 3 Bowery-lane.
Beekman, widow of Gerard, &c   do.
Beekman, John, druggist, 161 Broadway.
Beekman, widow of James I. 57 Maiden-lane,
Beekman, W. livery stabler, 13 Partition-street.
Beekman, George, cartman, 9 Reed
Beekman, widow, Mott
Beekman and Burtus, merchants, Front, corner of
  Taylor's wharf.

Beekman, Henry, wood inspector, 13 Oliver-street.
Beekman, Henry, carpenter, Charlotte
Belden, Rich. book & jewellery store, 151 Broadway.
Bell, Andrew, sho maker, 65 Chatham-street.
Bell and Poillon, merchants, 87 Maiden-lane.
Bell, Andrew, merchant, 36 Partition-street.
Bell, Thomas, labourer, 8 Moore
Bell, John, mason, 34 Rutger
Bell, Thomas, cooper, Sixth
Bell, Joseph, near airfurnace, Greenwich
Bell, John, tavern, 10 Peck-slip.
Bell, Robert, smith, 47 James-street.
Bell, Thomas, rigger, 63 E. George
Bell, John, packer, 53 Ann
Bell, Nath. bookbinder & stationer, 94 Chatham
Belnap, Elizabeth, 2 Garden
Belvidere, Mrs. 43 Water
Bement, George, grocer, 50 do.
Ben Ali, Ibrahim A. physician, 212 Greenwich
Benfield, widow, Eagle
Benford, William, carpenter, 70 Chamber
Benham, John, brewer, Greenwich
Bennet, Jacob, shoemaker, 54 Rutger
Bennet, Benjamin and Job, grocers, 222 Front
Bennet, James, accountant, 264 Greenwich
Bennet, James, merchant-taylor, 99 Cherry
Bennet, Robert, pilot, 83 Fair
Bennet, widow, 72 Warren
Bennet, Agnus, mantuamaker, 104 Liberty
Bennett, Thomas, cabinetmaker, 63 Beekman
Bennett, C. and J. merchant-taylors, 156 Front-street.
Bennett, James, coppersmith, 9 Peck-slip.
Bennie, John, accountant, 32 Lombard-street.
Benschoten, Elias, cartman, Winne
Benson, Gerrit, cartman, Greenwich-road.
Benson, Johannes, do.
Benson, William H. merchant, 89 Water-street.
Benson, Robert, clerk city & county N. Y. 21 Pine
Benson, John, lapidary and optician, 147 Pearl
Benson, Jonas, leather-dresser, 76 Bowery-lane.
Benson, Benjamin, carpenter, 10 Frankfort-street.
Benson, Benjamin, cooper, Bowery-Lane.

Benter, Godfrey, tobacconist, Pump-street.
Berard, Catharine, 92 Warren
Berdan, David, 14 Maiden-lane.
Bergh, Adam, grocer, 10 Dutch-street.
Bergh, Christian, shipwright, Charlotte
Berian, Benjamin, cartman, Eagle
Berian, Richard, grocer, do.
Berien, Eleanor, 97 Fair
Berman, Jacob, baker, 38 Dey
Berry, James, bookseller, 191 Washington
Berry, Judith, 92 Gold
Berry, Daniel, slopshop, 213 Water
Berry, Jacob, grocer & flour dealer, 192 Greenwich
Berryhill, Arthur, grocer, 143 Cherry
Berryman, Isaac, mariner, 57 do.
Bertruc, Francis, starchmaker, Broadway, near furnace.
Berwick, widow, 262 Greenwich-street.
Berwick, John, cartman, 12 Vesey
Berwick, William, pilot, 17 Chapel
Besh, Charles, dry good store, 313 Broadway.
Bessonett, John, watchmaker, 34 Maiden-lane.
Best, William, teacher, 95 Greenwich-street.
Bethell, William, brewer, 11 James
Bethune, Divie, merchant, 11 Liberty
Betts, William, grocer, 18 Read
Betts, Daniel, carpenter, 45 Catharine
Betts, Aaron, cooper, 47 Harman
Betts, John, corner of Division and First streets.
Betts, widow Ann, Chapel-street.
Beyea, Isaac, butcher, Elizabeth
Bice, Isaac, cordwainer, Mulberry
Bicker, Walter, weigher, 69 Cedar
Bidetrenoulleau, P. Daniel, merchant, 129 William
Bierfield, Henry, taylor, 265 Broadway.
Bijotat, Silvian, goldsmith & jeweller, 14 James-street.
Billings, Henry, grocer, Greenwich-road.
Billington, Elias, carpenter, 59 Barclay-street.
Billop, Thomas, merchant, 150 Water
Binckes, John, carpenter, 8 Roosevelt
Bincon, Joseph, merchant, 150 Broadway.
Bing, Moses, labourer, 5 Lumber-street
Bingham, James, gauger, 390 Pearl

Bingham, John, 148 William-street.
Bingham, Martha, 13 Ferry
Bingham, James, labourer, Division
Bingley, William, taylor, 15 Dutch-street.
Binninger, Abraham, grocer, Oswego-market.
Binninger, John, accountant, 76 Fair-street.
Birch, Thomas, labourer, 26 Chatham
Bird, Mathew, carpenter, 77 Harman
Bird, Charles, Elizabeth
Bird, William, shoemaker, 41 Chatham
Bird, Henry, rigger, 59 Catharine
Birdsall, Abigail, boarding-house, 44 Rutger
Birkby, Rev. James, 44 Fair
Bishop, John, hairdresser, 90 Chatham
Bishop, Joanna, tavern, 76 Pine
Bishop, Ezekiel, grocer, Winne
Bishop, Ebenezar, cartman, 22 Division
Bisset, James D. cabinetmaker, 93 Beekman
Bisset, John, cartman, 29 E. George
Bisset, James, merchant-taylor, 160 Pearl
Black, John, merchant, 17 Broad
Black, John, bookbinder, 5 Cedar
Black, Peter, tavern, 304 Water
Black, James, cartman, 95 Beekman
Black, William, cabinetmaker, 34 Bancker
Black, Isaac, cook, 15 Ann
Black, William, mariner, 58 E. George
Black, Richard, mariner, 2 Rose
Blackberry, John, smith, Eagle
Blackburn, ———, carpenter, 52 E. George
Blackford, and Co. Edward, store 15 Burling-slip.
Blackledge, Corn. carp. Chapel, corner Barley-street.
Blackman, Thomas, muffin-baker, 3 Ferry
Blackwell, Joseph, merchant, 9 Beaver
Blackwell, and Co. Josiah, iron store, 104 Front
Blackwell, Robert, sawyer, 34 George
Blackwell and M'Farlane, merchants, 6 and 41 Water
Blagge, John, merchant, 42 John, and store 182 Front
Blagge, Jasper, merchant, 42 John
Blair, Daniel, stivadore, 20 Ferry
Blair, J. A. grocer, 294 Water
Blair, widow, 60 Pearl

Blake, Margaret, 318 Broadway.
Blake, Elizabeth, shopkeeper, 14 Nassau-street.
Blake, Robert, stonecutter, 45 Ann
Blake, Samuel, carpenter, Pump-street.
Blake, Peter, baker, 52 Ann
Blakeley, Josiah, merchant, 50 Broad
Blakeley, Charles, grocer, 24 Harman
Blakeney, Thomas, mason, 2 Chamber
Blakeney, Davis, blockmaker, 33 Rose
Blakeney, Jacob, carp. corner Chapel & Barley streets.
Blakeley, David, mason, First-street.
Blakeslee, Archibald, boarding-house, 68 John
Blanchard, John, cooper, 54 do.
Blanchard, Andrew, rigger, Bedlow
Blanchard, Francis, mason, 46 Barley
Blanck, Isaac, cartman, Chapel, corner Barley street.
Blanck, Richard, carpenter, do.
Blanck, Jacob, cartman, Little Ann
Blanck, Thomas, 13 Skinner
Blanck, Francis currier, Hague
Blandin, John, rigger, 47 Skinner
Blauvelt Harman, cartman, 83 Reed
Blauvelt, John, cartman, 45 Barley
Blauvelt, Jesse, blockmaker, Reed
Bleecker, Anthony L. & Sons, auctioneers, 178 Pearl
Bleecker, James, merchant, 29 do.
Bleecker, William, 66 Pine
Bleecker, Rutger, measurer, 29 Cheapside.
Bleecker, Anth. & Wm. attornies at law, 53 Wall-str.
Bleecker, Leonard, stock & insurance broker 5 do.
Bleecker, Rutger, jun. 44 Frankfort
Bleecker, Samuel, measurer, 13 Cheapside.
Bienon, Anthony, druggist, 100 Maiden-lane.
Bliss, Beza E. grocery, 183 Front & 35 Beekman street.
Bloodgood, Abraham, currier, 13 Vandewater
Bloodgood, John, coachmaker, 69 Warren
Bloodgood, Thomas, coachmaker, 48 Reed
Bloodgood, Thomas, merchant, 25 Cherry
Bloodgood, Nathaniel, merchant, 25 Cherry
Bloodgood, Joshua, cartman 62 Vesey
Bloom, Barnet and Peter, grocers, 63 Warren
Bloome, widow, 245 William

Bloome, Peter, mariner, Fisher-street.
Bloomer, Michael, pilot, 18 Cliff
Bloomer, David, labourer, Rutger
Bloomfield, Thomas, cartman, 58 Reed
Bloomfield, Timothy, cartman, 30 Lombard-street.
Blossom, Elijah, shipwright, 147 Harman
Blucke, Stephen, confectioner, 14 Pine
Blunck, John, currier 26 Harman
Board, James, carpenter, 48 Church
Board, Joseph, carpenter, Thomas
Boardman, Daniel, merchant, 245 Pearl
Boardman, widow, boarding-house, 230 Greenwich
Boardman and Hunt's store, 184 Water
Bockhorst, Harman, baker, 25 Cheapside.
Bocking, John, Pump-street.
Bockover, Peter, smith, Bowery-lane.
Bocock, John, carpenter, 11 E. George-street.
Boden, Omar, turner and canemaker, 61 James
Boerum, Jacob, dry-good store, 2 Coenties-slip.
Boerum, John, custom-house officer, 59 Murray-street.
Boerum and Wynkoop, grocers, 7 Coenties-slip.
Bogardus, Robert, attorney at law, 60 Cherry-street.
Bogardus, John, cartman, Thomas
Bogardus, Henry, cartman, 33 Barley
Bogardus, Henry, labourer, 90 Catharine
Bogart, Roelef, 159 Greenwich
Bogart, Catharine, shopkeeper, 165 William
Bogart, Catharine, 226 do.
Bogart, Gilbert, shoemaker, 229 Water
Bogart, Joseph, butcher, Pell
Bogart, Jacob, cartman, 24 Cooper
Bogart, Adrian, weaver, 49 Augustus
Bogart, widow, 65 Ann
Bogart, John, labourer, Rose
Bogart, John O. cooper, 33 do.
Bogart, Abraham O. butcher, 47 do.
Bogart, Albert, cartman, First
Bogart, Adrian, blockmaker, Barclay
Bogart, James, cartman, 41 Rose
Bogart and Leton, grocers, 74 Catharine
Bogart, Daniel, mariner, 51 Harman
Bogart, Peter, cartman, 57 Cedar

Bogart, Catharine, midwife, 57 Cedar-street.
Bogart, Andrew, carpenter, 82 Liberty
Bogatch, Frederick, grocer, 55 Chatham
Bogert, Leffert, labourer, Barley
Bogert, Mary, 71 William
Bogert, John, cartman, Greenwich-road.
Bogert, John P. cartman, 6 Thomas-street.
Bogert, David, cartman, Greenwich
Bogert, Jacobus, baker, 171 Broadway.
Bogert, James L. shopkeeper, 185 Greenwich-street.
Bogert, John, merchant, 171 Broadway.
Bogert, Corn. I. counsellor at law, 18 Beekman-street.
Bogert, Cornelius, attorney at law, 83 Pearl
Bogert, Peter, merchant, 162 William
Bogert, James, 419 Pearl
Bogert, jun. James, merchant, 419 do.
Bogert, Rudolphus, merchant, 239 Pearl
Bogert and Hopkins' store, 168 Front
Bogert, Nicholas, grocer, 55 Barclay
Boggs, James, shipjoiner, Division
Boggs, William, taylor, 70 Broad-street.
Bokee, John, carver, 31 John
Bokee, William, carpenter, 31 do.
Bokee, Abraham, cabinet-maker, 34 Rose
Bokee, Isaac, cooper, 7 Cliff
Bokee, Abraham, cooper, 5 do.
Bollis, widow Ann, Orchard
Bolmer, Mathew, granary-store, 94 Chatham
Bolmer, Peter, smith, 146 do.
Bolmer, Jacob, shoemaker, First
Bolton, Anthony, shoemaker, 20 Broadway.
Bolton, Thomas, carpenter, Charlotte-street.
Bomel, widow, Harmen
Bond, Abraham, grocer, 16 Front
Bond, Joseph, 49 Barclay
Bond, James, smith, Elizabeth
Bond, Peter, mason, Henry
Bonger, Albert, boarding-house, 90 Catharine
Bonham, Blathwaite, shipwright, 79 Cherry
Bonham, Michael, labourer, 11 Moore's-row.
Bonker, Oliver, livery-stabler, 16 Cherry-street.
Bonker, W. livery-stabler, 35 Cherry & 30 Roosevelt

Bonnett, Peter, tanner, & currier, 22 Frankfort-street.
Bonnett, Daniel, do. do.
Bonnett, Peter, 19 Bowery-lane.
Bonfall, John, lumber-merchant, 159 Washington-str.
Bonfoll, Samuel W. 69 Dey
Bockless, John, taylor, 440 Pearl
Bool, Henry W. shipmaster, 3 E. Rutger
Boorman, Mrs. 10 William
Boos, Wendell, baker, 60 Bowery-lane.
Borduzat, Anthony M. 88 Chatham-street.
Borhar, Christian, taylor, 18 Chamber
Borris, John, tavern, 9 Wall
Borrowe, Samuel, M. D. 77 Water
Borrowe, Samuel, sailmaker, 65 Front
BOSTON stage-office, 1 and 5 Cortlandt
Bostwick, James, carpenter, 75 William
Bostwick, Mary, tea-store, 75 do.
Bourdett, Benjamin, bricklayer, Greenwich-road.
Bourdett, Stephen, grocer, 121 Harman-street.
Bourdett, Abraham, mason, 3 Lombard
Boutier, John, merchant, 174 Chatham
Bourne, John, smith, 84 Fair
Bouvier, Julien, physician, 293 Broadway.
Bowering, C. B. merchant, 316 Pearl-street.
Bowcot, John, mariner, 21 Lumber
Bowers, Henry, merchant, 35 Pine
Bowers, widow, Charlotte
Bowers, Jesse, shipmaster, 10 Dutch
Bowie, Thomas, labourer, 60 Broad
Bowie, James, 53 Reed
Bowie, Daniel, grocer, 60 Partition
Bowie, Ann, 55 do.
Bowles, Catharine, 59 Liberty
Bowman, George, mariner, 50 E. George
Bowman, George, mason, 43 Barclay
Bowman, John, cartman, 45 Augustus
Bowman, George, carpenter, 40 Bowery-lane.
Bowman, Abigail, boarding-house, 188 Water-street.
Bowne, George, merchant, 254 Pearl
Bowne and Embree, shipchandlers, 228 Water
Bowne, Walter, merchant, 280 Pearl
Bowne, Cornelius, 28 Church

NEW YORK DIRECTORY.

Bowne, Hannah, boarding-house, 37 Beekman-street.
Bowne, William, merchant, 265 Pearl
Bowne, Robert, merchant, 256 do.
Bowne, Robert L. and Samuel S. merchants, 252 do.
Bowne, Obadiah & Andrew, merchants, 7 William
Bowne, Samuel, merchant, 267 Pearl
Bowne, Conway, merchant, 25 Rutger
Bowne, Elizabeth, boarding-house, 51 Cliff.
Boyce, Abraham, baker, 87 Bowery-lane.
Boyce, Isaac, butcher,   do.
Boyce, Peter, Little Catharine-street.
Boyd, John, hairdresser, 135 Cherry
Boyd, Robert G. 105 Liberty
Boyd, Joseph, smith, Washington-str. near the furnace.
Boyd, Samuel, counsellor at law, 19 Cedar-street.
Boyd, William, 225 Cherry
Boyd, James, 22 Pearl
Boyer, Anthony, glover, 41 Chatham
Boyer, John, rigger, 26 Division
Boyle, Caleb, coach-painter, 8 John
Bradberry, Wimond, shipmaster, 67 James
Bradberry, James, shoemaker, Fisher
Bradford, William, cloathing store, 12 Beekman-slip.
Bradford, Catharine, 38 Cortlandt
Bradford, Jacob, merchant, 38 do.
Bradhurst, Samuel, physician, 82 Water
Bradhurst and Field, druggists, 82 do.
Bradley, William, labourer, Eagle
Bradley, James, boarding-house, 1 Gold
Bradley, James, 3 Reed
Bradshaw, Dolly, tayloress, 252 Water
Brady, Thomas, labourer, 34 Ferry
Brady, Adam, cartman, 90 Warren
Brady, George, taylor, 22 Stone
Brady, Joseph, cartman, Bow
Brady, Walter, do.   do.
Braley, George, 4 Maiden-lane.
Brailsford, Samuel, merchant, 7 Murray-street.
Brain, Daniel H. shipmaster, 68 Beekman
Brain, Charles, labourer, 3 Rider
Brain, William, corner of Lumber & L. Rutger streets.
Branneyson, Charles, tavern, 263 Broadway.

Brannon, Mrs. 8 Cortlandt-street.
Branson, Ware, cabinetmaker, Elizabeth
Branthwaite, Sarah, 76 Fair
Brantingham, Thomas H. merchant, 35 Warren
Brard, James, carpenter, 24 Robinson
Brasher, Ephraim, gold and silversmith, 5 Cherry
Brasher, Elizabeth, boarding-house, 72 William
Brasher, Philander, store, 92 do.
Brasher, Philip, attorney at law, 92 do.
Brasher, widow of Abraham, 72 Broadway.
Brasher, Gasherie, merchant, 13 Pine-street.
Brasher, John G. 19 Chamber
Brasher, James C. 3 Ann
Brass, Joseph, cartman, Eagle
Brass, Peter, cartman, 18 Chapel
Brass, John, smith, 18 do.
Brauer, Ded. Con. merchant, 55 Stone
Bray, John, labourer, 21 Rutger
Bray, James, labourer, E. Rutger
Braymer, George, shoemaker, 453 Pearl
Brazier, Daniel, shipmaster, 55 Whitehall
Brazier, John, shipmaster, South
Breasch, John, baker, 324 Broadway.
Breath, John, 29 Beekman-street.
Breedy, George, taylor, 24 Stone
Bremner, Colin, taylor, 342 Pearl
Brett and Bunn, merchants, 66 Front
Brett, Elizabeth, mantuamaker, 4 New
Brett, John, joiner, 17 Batavia-lane.
Brett, George, cartman, 3 Moore-street.
Brevoort, Abraham, porter house, 26 Chatham
Brevoort, John V. 36 Maiden-lane.
Brevoort, Elias, merchant, 80 William-street.
Brewer, Peter, cartman, 55 Bowery-lane.
Brewerton, Henry, attorney at law, 27 Oliver-street.
Brewster, Samuel, 59 Cherry
Bridgen, Charles, 5 Nassau, and office 12 Pine
Bridges, Thomas, 57 Rutger
Briggs, John, cartman, corner of Eagle & Third streets.
Briggs, Gabriel, grocer, 64 Read-street.
Briggs, Ebenezer, 60 Chamber
Bright, Jennet, mantuamaker, 66 Ann

Brinckerhoff, Peter & A. jun. merchants, 67 Stone-st.
Brinckerhoff, S. carpenter, 44 Barley
Brinckerhoff, Henry, tavern, 229 Greenwich
Brinckerhoff, Abraham, merchant, 73 Pearl
Brinckerhoff, Cornelius, brass-founder, 187 Water
Brinckley, Catharine, 12 Cortlandt
Brinckerhoff, Harman, 6 Barley
Brird, Mathew, stonecutter, 7 Augustus
Briskoa, John, brushmaker, 84 Maiden-lane.
Briss, widow Sarah, 71 James-street.
Bristowe, Samuel, accountant, 79 Beekman
Britten, Christopher, stonecutter, 17 Thames
Britten, widow, midwife, First
Britten, Robert, sawyer, 36 Vesey
Britten, Abigail, seamstress, 61 Pine
Britten, James, labourer, Greenwich-road.
Britten, John C. mason, 22 Thomas-street.
Broadwell, Abigail, 147 Chatham
Brogan, James, mariner, 4 Moore's-row.
Bronson, Laban, merchant, 1 Beekman-street.
Broodie, John, grocer, 104 Chatham
Brooks, Richard, 245 William
Brooks, John Wallis, surgeon, 44 Dey
Brooks, Mrs. young ladies seminary, 44 do.
Brooks, William, shoemaker, Division
Brooks, Samuel, currier, 7 Chatham
Brooks, Joseph, labourer, 42 Chapel
Brooks, Henry S. grocer, 127 Cherry
Brooks, Michael, painter and glazier, 66 Liberty
Brooks, Henry, tanner and currier, Magazine
Brooks, Daniel I. mason, 170 Division
Brooks, ———, mariner, 23 Bancker
Broome and son, John, merchants, 75 Stone
Broome, William T. attorney at law, 3 William
Broome, William, cartman, 8 Augustus
Brothers, Coster, and Co. merchants, 59 Water
Brotherton, Philip, 111 Front
Brotherton, Joseph, marshall, Upper Reed
Brott, Andrew, merchant, Provost
Brouwer, Abraham, taylor, 142 Broadway.
Brouwer, jun. Jacob, cabinetmaker, 17 Beaver-street.
Brower, Jacob, cartman, 76 Reed

Brower, Abraham E. hatter, 28 Maiden-lane.
Brower and Gallatian, upholsterers, 65 Broad-street.
Brower, Abraham, physician, 31 Frankfort
Brower, David, wheelwright, 49 Warren
Brower, Nicholas, cartman, 73 Reed
Brower, John, carpenter, Upper Reed
Brower, Cornelia, boarding-house, Harman
Brower, Abraham I. grocer, Washington
Brower, David, smith, 55 Harman
Brower, Christeard, cartman 7 Division
Brower, Jacob, cartman, 69 Church
Brower, Jacob, cartman, 91 Reed
Brower, James, coachmaker, 13 Partition
Brower, John, inspector of pot-ash, 26 Water
Brower, David, cartman, 18 Division
Brower, Jeremiah, merchant, 200 Front
Brower, David, shoemaker, 200 Broadway.
Brower, Abraham, cartman, Hester-street.
Brower, Samuel, carpenter, 74 Chatham
Brower, David, buttonmaker, 53 Warren
Brower, Abraham, cartman, 65 Partition
Brower, Lawrence, cartman, 32 Barley
Brower, Isaac, cartman, Hester
Brower, John, 50 Warren
Brower, Theophilus, merchant, 9 Burling-slip.
Brower, Abraham, smith, 5 Partition-street.
Brower, Mary, 41 Broad
Brown, Mary Ann, mantuamaker, 74 Gold
Brown, Catharine, 188 William
Brown, Thomas, teacher, end of Reed
Brown, Thomas, mariner, 43 Rose
Brown, Richard, shipmaster, 71 Roosevelt
Brown, William, mariner, 106 Division
Brown, Talbot & Co. commiss. merchts. Murray's whf.
Brown, J. H. merchant, Whitehall, corner of Water-str.
Brown, Catharine, 4) Bowery-lane.
Brown and Stanbury, booksellers, 114 Water-street.
Brown, Thomas, store Front, corner Crane wharf.
Brown, John, grocer, 19 Beekman-slip.
Brown, John, copper plate printer, 29 Gold-street.
Brown, Andrew, merchant, 38 Stone
Brown, Kimberly and Co. merchants, 169 Front

C

Brown, William, mariner, 54 Chatham-street.
Brown, James, labourer, Mulberry
Brown, Joseph, taylor, 42 Chamber
Brown, James, printer, 32 Lombard
Brown, Charles, shipwright, Henry
Brown, William, merchant, 20 Pearl
Brown, Thomas, sailmaker, 20 Pearl
Brown, jun. Samuel, sailmaker, Peck-slip.
Brown, George, grocer, 74 Vesey-street.
Brown, Jacob, shoemaker, 67 Water
Brown, Andrew, merchant, 93 William
Brown, Ths. boatbuilder, 265 Water, & 6 Roosevelt
Brown, William, earthen and grocery store, 53 Broad
Brown, and Co. James, brewers, 534 Broadway.
Brown, Anthony, brewer, 338   do.
Brown, Wm. sexton St. Paul's church, 1 Church strt.
Brown, John, baker, 123 Chatham
Brown, Benjamin, stivadore, 27 Bancker
Brown, Josiah, cartman, 74 Catharine
Brown, Alexander, cooper, 198 Front
Brown, Thomas, shipmaster, 10 Chesnut
Brown, John, mariner, Magazine
Brown, John, bellows-maker, 21 Cheapside.
Brown, Thomas, brass-founder, Henry-street.
Brown, Gilbert, tallow-chandler, 41 E. George
Brown, Thomas, brewer, 5 Lumber
Brown, Samuel, cooper, 78 Murray
Brown, John, shipmaster, 58 Chamber
Brown, Robert, coachman, 40 Vandewater
Brown, John, granary store, First
Brown, Edmund, carpenter, Division
Brown, Thomas, smith, 16 Cliff
Brown, Peter, labourer, 130 Chatham
Brown, Nathaniel, hatter, 215 Water
Brown, John, hair-dresser, 16 Burling-slip.
Brown, William, mariner, 24 Bancker-street
Brown, Frank, tavern, Lumber
Brown, George, grocer, 84 Bowery-lane.
Brown, Paul, shoemaker, Essex-street.
Brown, Walter, shipwright, Gibbs' alley.
Brown, Adam, shipwright, 62 Harman-street
Brown, Noah, shipwright, 62 Harman

Brown, John, boatman, 21 Lumber-street.
Brown, Margaret, boarding-house, 146 Water
Brown, John, physician, 23 Cliff
Brown, Peter, baker, 54 Vesey
Brown, Alexander, carpenter, 7 Robinson
Brownin, Thomas, shoemaker, 66 Harman
Brownjohn, Elizabeth, 90 Liberty
Browse and Brown, shipchandlers, Catharine-slip.
Bruce, widow of Peter, 120 Front-street.
Bruce, widow of Robert, 125 Water
Bruce, William, grocer, 129 Front
Bruce, widow, 42 Barley
Bruce, Judith, 12 Broadway.
Bruce and Morison, merchants, 120 Front-street.
Bruck, Francis, mason, 24 Harman
Bruen, Thomas, lastmaker & leathercutter, 65 Nassau
Brunel's, ——, manufactory, 38 George
Brunn, Jacob, cartman, First
Brunn, Andrew, baker, 450 Pearl
Brunson, Isaac, merchant, 32 Cortlandt
Brush, Thomas, boarding-house, 71 Division
Brush, Caleb, boatman, 83 Reed
Brush, Ebenezer, merchant, 144 Washington
Brush, Edward, smith, Elizabeth
Bryan, John, mariner, 27 Lumber
Bryan, Joseph, baker, First
Bryar, James, tobacconist, 114 Front
Bryar, William, tobacconist, 104 Water
Bryson, Eleanor, slopshop, 330 Water
Bryson, James, merchant, 289 Pearl
Buchan, Robert, lumber-merchant, Greenwich-road.
Buchanan, Walter, merchant, 88 Liberty-street.
Buchanan, William, Thomas
Buchanan and Mabie's store, 206 Pearl
Buchanan, Thomas, merchant, 41 Wall
Buchanan, Archibald, shopkeeper, 64 L. George
Buchanan, Alexander, cartman, Mulberry
Buchanan, John, merchant, 206 Pearl
Buchanan, James, cartman, Mulberry
Buchanan, William, merchant, 206 Pearl
Buchey, Peter, jeweller, 5 Broad
Buck, widow of Richard, 10 Jacob

Buckbee, Stephen, shoemaker, saw-pits, Greenwich.
Buckbee, Doctor, Pump-street.
Buckland, William, grocer, 182 William.
Buckle, William, merchant, 145 Chatham
Buckler, John, shoemaker, Church
Buckley, Dennis, rigger, 43 Rutger
Buckley and Underhill's store, Front, near Peck-slip.
Buckley, Thomas, merchant, 263 Water-street.
Buckley, Abel, merchant, 174 Water
Buckley, James, mason, 3 Ferry
Buckley, James, shipwright, Mulberry
Buckmaster, George, boat-builder, 194 Cherry
Buckmaster, Sarah, sick-nurse, 51 Roosevelt
Budd, Elizabeth, 3 Chesnut
Buel, John, printer and bookseller, 2 Cedar
Buffet, George, perfumer, 76 Pearl
Buffaloree, Jacob, pilot, 43 George
Bull, Francis, merchant, above airfurnace, Greenwich.
Bull, William, rigger, 21 Baucker-street.
Bull, Michael, merchant, 181 William
Bull, Rachel, 10 Fair
Bull, Joseph, mariner, Pump
Bull, Michael and Thomas, merchants, 165 Front
Bull, Joseph, hatter, Hester
Bumstead, William, grocer, Henry
Bumstead, Jacob, milkman, Second
Bunce, Eve, 54 Oliver
Bunce, Matnew, boat-builder, 37 Oliver
Bunker, George, merchant, 99 Greenwich
Bunker, Abel, shipmaster, 11 Chesnut
Bunn, Reuben, ladies' shoemaker, 60 William
Bunn, Mary, midwife, 64 Barclay
Bunn, William, shoemaker, 93 Chamber
Bunn, John, Broadway, near Union furnace.
Bunnell, Doctor, bricklayer, 30 Catharine-street.
Bunting, Samuel, taylor, 205 Broadway.
Bunting, William, distiller, 87 Murray-street.
Burbank, James, porter-house, 107 Oliver
Burchill, George, grocer, 184 Front
Burden, Samuel, carpenter, Bayard
Burdge, Uriah, grocer, 55 Gold-street.
Burdge, Uriah, labourer, Winne

Burdges, Samuel, grocer, Hester, corner of Winne-str.
Burgen, George, cordwainer, 126 Chatham
Burgen, Hannah, mantuamaker, 61 Ann
Burger, Elias, dockbuilder, 76 Barclay
Burger, jun. Elias, dockbuilder, 260 Greenwich
Burger, Daniel, blockmaker, 35 Frankfort, & 59 Front
Burger, John, gold and silversmith, 62 James
Burger, jun. John, copperplate-printer, 192 William
Burger, David, water-bailiff, 76 John
Burger, jun. David, inspector of customs, 26 Liberty
Burgess, Abraham, smith, 35 Church
Burjeau, James, shoemaker, 10 Bancker
Burk, Mary, 45 Bowery-lane.
Burk, William, block & pumpmaker, 14 Chesnut-str.
Burk, William, mariner, 36 Harman
Burk, Rev. ——, 7 Reed
Burk, Miles, mariner, 19 Batavia-lane.
Burl, John, shipmaster, Winne-street.
Burling, Ebenezer S. 33 Oliver
Burling, Lancaster, 12 Cherry
Burling and Co. William, merchants, 291 Pearl
Burling, Samuel, cabinetmaker, 38 Beckman
Burling & son, Thomas, cabinetmakers, 25 Beckman
Burling, jun. Thomas, printer, 33 Oliver
Burlock, Thomas, grocer, Charlotte, corner of Harman.
Burnet, Joseph, carpenter, Hester
Burnham, John, smith, 32 Bowery-lane.
Burns, widow, 74 Warren-street.
Burns, Thomas, carpenter, 249 Broadway.
Burns, ——, 95 Liberty-street.
Burnton, Catharine, 28 Cedar
Burr, William, 327 Broadway.
Burr, Hare, merchant, 87 Beckman-street.
Burr, Aaron, counsellor at law, 55 William
Burr, ——, shoemaker, 458 Pearl
Burrall, Jonathan, cashier branch bank, 4 State
Burras, William, merchant-taylor, 93 Water
Burras, John, rush bottom chairmaker, 2 Nassau
Burras, Thomas, rigger, Bedlow
Burras, Lawrence, hairdresser, Greenwich
Burras, George G. ladies shoemaker, 7 Will
Burrell, Doctor, 60 Maiden-lane.

Buristy, Samuel C. mariner, 42 Harman-street.
Burt, John, custom-house clerk, 60 Warren
Burtis, Samuel, cartman, Henry
Burtis and Woodward, coachmakers, 4 Fair
Burton, Thomas, baker, Bayard
Burton, Thomas, shipmaster, 28 Church
Burton, William, livery-stabler, 53 Maiden-lane.
Burtsell, David, shipwright, Henry-street.
Burtsell, Peter, book-binder, 95 Beekman
Burtsell, Henry, constable, 11 Cedar
Bush, Charles, tavern, 19 Chatham-row.
Bush, John, broker, 50 Pine-street.
Bush, Evert, boatbuilder, 317 Water
Bush, ———, shipmaster, 68 James
Bush, William, merchant, Barley
Bush, James, shipwright, Orchard
Bustiat, Mary, tavern and boarding-house, 30 Moore
Bushfield, Thomas, grocer, 18 Stone
Bushnell, James, shipmaster, 205 William
Buskerk, Sylvester, livery-stabler, 209 Broadway.
Buskerk, John, milkman, 21 Chapel-street.
Bussing, William, cartman, 92 Liberty
Bussing, Aaron, cartman, 92 Liberty
Bussing, Abraham, merchant, 59 Cortlandt
Bussy, J. L. chancellor French consulate, 22 Pearl
Butler, John, blockmaker, above New-slip, Water
Butler, William, cartman, 175 Division
Butler, John, blockmaker, Charlotte
Butler, Nicholas, labourer, 16 Rose
Butler, Thomas, shipmaster, 30 Gold
Butler, Edmund, cartman, 201 Greenwich
Butler, James, sailmaker, 1 Chesnut
Butler, John, boot and shoemaker, 91 Pearl
Butler, Thomas C. merchant, 60 Cherry
Butler, John, oyster-man, 57 Catharine
Butler, George, taylor, 10 Harman
Butler, Daniel, shoemaker, Chapel, corner of Barley
Butler, Daniel, mason, Chapel
Butler and Baker, taylors, 429 Pearl
Putman, Edward, livery-stables, 74 Nassau, & Theatre-
    alley.

Butterworth, James, oil silk manufact. 144 Division-str.
Buxton, Enoch, shoemaker, 56 Chatham
Buxton, Charles, physician, 216 Broadway.
Byrd and Barrow's store, 294 Pearl-street.
Byrd, James, merchant, 270 Pearl
Byrd, Joseph, merchant, 294 Pearl
Byrne, John, keeper old coffee-house, 115 Water
Byrne, James, gold and silversmith, 126 Fly-market.
Byrne, Lawrence, grocer, 320 Water-street.
Byrne, Bernard, porter-house, 249 Water
Byrne, Simon, 40 Warren
Byrne, Patrick, bricklayer, Charlotte
Byrnes, Simon, grocer, 52 E. George
Byrnes, Henry, grocer, 22 George
Byrnes, John, mariner, 90 Cherry.
Byron, William, 341 Broadway.
Byvanck, Mrs. 309 Pearl-street.
Byvanck, William, shipwright, 35 Harman

C

Cable, widow, boardinghouse, 13 Burling-slip.
Cable, Denbou, shipmaster, 98 Catharine-street.
Cadle, Thomas, merchant, 119 William
Cadle and Cammann, merchants, 101 Front
Caignet, Armand, 125 Greenwich
Cain, Ann, 78 Cherry
Cairns, Frears, and Co. merchants, 24 Beekman
Cairns, Douglass, 195 Broadway.
Cairon, Peter, 45 Beekman-street.
Calder, Andrew, 23 Murray
Caldwell, Tilit, carpenter, Corlaer's hook.
Caldwell, Jacob, accountant, 21 Cheapside.
Caldwell, Alexander, merchant, 200 Water-street.
Caldwell, James, cartman, 23 Moore
Caldwell, John, chairmaker, 78 Nassau
Caldwell, John, merchant, 138 Pearl
Caldwell, Joshua, 45 Robinson
Callahan, John, branch-pilot, 88 Fair
Callender, William, grocer, 52 Fair
Collier, Gabriel, hairdresser, Elizabeth
Callige, Samuel, carpenter, 42 Lumber
Callige, J. P. bookseller, 139 William
Callow, James, upholsterer, 140 Broadway.

NEW-YORK DIRECTORY.

Callow and Van Winkle, upholsterers, 140 Broadway.
Cameron, Allen, measurer, 224 William-street.
Cameron, Abigail, mantuamaker, 97 Fair
Cameron, John, grocer, 136 Front
Cameron, Donald, taylor, 40 Vesey
Cameron, Margaret, 50 Chatham
Cammann, Charles L. merchant, 58 Broad
Cammerdenner, Ludowick, First
Cammerdenner, Jacob, rigger, 18 Harman
Cammeyer, William, baker, 7 Bridge
Campbell, William, taylor, 354 Water
Campbell, Samuel, bookseller & stationer, 124 Pearl
Campbell, John, teacher of languages, 4 Pine
Campbell, Malcolm, A. M. 66 Cortlandt
Campbell, Thomas I. potter, 297 Broadway.
Campbell, John T. 297 Broadway.
Campbell, Alex. stonecutter, 92 Greenwich-street.
Campbell, James, butcher, Elizabeth
Campbell, Aaron, grocer, Eagle
Campbell, Jacob, mason, Greenwich-road.
Campbell, William, constable, 71 Reed-street.
Campbell, Duncan, carpenter, Greenwich-road.
Campbell, David, attorney at law, 396 Pearl-street.
Campbell, Thomas, mason, Division
Campbell, Jared, carpenter, Greenwich-road.
Campbell, James, shipmaster, Henry-street.
Campbell, Nathan, cartman, 4 E. George
Campbell, William, mariner, 22 Oliver
Campbell, Patrick, labourer, 21 E. George
Campbell, John, teacher, 15 Rose
Campbell, Mrs. 114 Liberty
Campbell, Gen. 80 Barclay
Campbell, Thomas, labourer, Sixth
Campbell, Thomas B. merchant, 7 Maiden-lane.
Campbell, Daniel, mariner, 47 Beaver-street.

Cannon, Mott, cooper and repacker, 5 Mulberry-str.
Cannon, Abraham, shoemaker, 63 Fair
Cannon, Abraham, tavern, Corlaer's hook.
Cannon, Robert, taylor, 386 Pearl-street.
Cannon, Peter, inspector of revenue, 51 Liberty
Canschat, Michael, instrument maker, Second
Canton, George, grocer, 355 Water
Capes, Richard, commission-merchant, 26 Old-slip.
Carberry, Thomas, shipmaster, 144 Front-street.
Carberry, John, tavern, 77 Pine.
Carberry, Daniel, hair dresser, 44 Cedar
Card, Elisha, caulker, corner Harman & E. George
Card Manufactory, 24 Cheapside.
Carew, Dyer, mariner, 6 Oliver-street.
Carsrae, and Co. William, grocers, 65 Cedar
Cargill, William, grocer, 431 Pearl
Cargill, David, 5 Coenties-slip.
Caritat. H. circulating library, 153 Broadway.
Carle, Thomas, grocer, Magazine-street.
Carll, Solomon, merchant, 53 Gold
Carlock, John, grocer, Rose-street.
Carlton, John, boatman, 1 Pearl
Carman, William, measurer of lumber, 90 James.
Carman, Samuel, boarding-house, 64 E. George
Carman, widow, 215 William
Carman, John, sadler, 36 Barclay
Carmer, Nicholas, merchant, 101 Maiden-lane.
Carmer. Nicholas G. & H. store, 216 Pearl-street.
Carmer, Nicholas, sailmaker, 35 Rose
Carmer, Frederick, taylor, Cherry-street, Ship-yards.
Carmer, Nicholas, shoemaker, 207 Greenwich-street.
Carne, John, mariner, 27 Garden
Carnes, John, cartman, Winne
Carnes, James, labourer, 17 Harman
Carnes, George, gardener, Bowery-lane.
Carnley, Robert, starchmaker, 150 Division-street.
Carpenter, Catharine, 20 Division
Carpenter, Benjamin, carpenter, 10 Bancker
Carpenter, Thomas, painter, 50 John
Carpenter, Jacob, shipwright, Henry
Carpenter, Stephen, leadbuilder, 27 Cherry
Carpenter, Thorn, merchant, 7 Peck-slip.

Carpenter, Sam. grocer, Broadway, corner Barley-str.
Carpenter, Eleanor, 150 Harman
Carpenter, and Co. Thomas, merchants, 209 Water
Carr, Robert, mason, 225 William
Carr, James, Philadelphia stage directer, 1 Cortlandt
Carr, Joshua, grocer, 1 Ferry
Carr, Andrew, mason, 21 Barclay
Carr, Cæsar, labourer, Grand
Carr, Coenrad, cartman, 21 Bancker
Carr, Joshua, accountant 45 John
Carrer, Mathew, 41 Church
Carroll, William, teacher, 172 William
Carroll, widow, 12 George
Carrow, widow, 8 Dey
Carse, James, mariner, 3 Chesnut
Carsin, William, grocer, 28 Broad
Carson, George, shoemaker, 29 Cheapside
Carstang, Gideon, ropemaker, Eagle-street
Carstang, Gideon, ropemaker, Mulberry
Carter, James, merchant, 144 Front
Carter, John, pilot, 88 Fair
Carter, Robert, cabinetmaker, 43 Fair, and 40 Ann
Carter, Jonathan, shoemaker, 29 Cherry
Carter and Burling, looking-glass store, 65 Beekman
Carter, John, cabinetmaker, 19 Rose
Carter, Adolph, shipwright, 69 James
Carter, Mary, 98 Pearl
Carter, Edward, mason, 40 Barley
Carter, Enoch, painter and glazier, 36 Church
Carter, James, cartman, 10 Beaver
Carton, Thomas, carpenter, 115 Liberty
Carver, William, smith, 67 Liberty
Carver, William, farrier, 42 Chatham
Carver and Doorplace, smith & farrier, 38 Cedar
Cary, Isaac, turner, 23 Bancker
Cary, John, labourer, 10 Beaver
Casey, James, merchant, 84 John, and store 164 Front
Casey, James, baker, 15 Chesnut
Casey, John, shoemaker, 34 Augustus
Cason, Michael, grocer, 14 Ferry
Cass, Joseph, cartman, 45 Barley
Cassaday, James, labourer, 25 Augustus

Cassady, Dennis, shoemaker, 120 Broadway.
Cashn, Peter, shipmaster, 10 George-street.
Cassella and Corti, printshop, 47 Barclay
Cassidy, John, teacher, 43 Chapel
Cassil, Arnell, brushmaker, 305 Pearl
Cassiliar, widow, 36 Augustus
Cassils, Robert, cartman, Eagle
Cassin, Lewis C. tavern, 160 Fly-market.
Castelli, Piettro, staymaker, 146 Broadway.
Caster, Anthony, labourer, Henry-street.
Casterline, Silas, smith, 58 and 60 Gold
Casterline, David, smith, 54 E. George
Castine, Jacob, hair-dresser, 210 Greenwich
Castle, William, grocer, 40 Lombard
Caswell, widow, 6 George
Caswell, John, mariner, 31 Lumber
Cator and Co. T. soap & candle manufact. 33 Partition
Catlin, L. teller in the U. S. bank, 105 Greenwich
Catin, John, smith, Charlotte
Cation, Archibald, grocer, 284 Water
Cauchois, John, hardware store, 110 Maiden-lane.
Causy, Andrew, hatter, 103 Chatham-street.
Cave, James, carpenter, 74 James
Caven, John, grocer, 189 Washington
Cavenagh, William, coppersmith, Charlotte
Cavenagh, Thomas, grocer, 82 Wall
Cavenagh, Stephen, labourer, Bedlow
Cavenagh, James, shipwright, Charlotte
Cavenagh, Charles, nailor, 36 Barclay
Caverly, William, merchant, 17 Broad
Cazenove and Blanchereau, merchants, 8 James
Cebra, James, weigher, 66 Wall
Ceron, Madam, 44 Greenwich
Chadd, Mary, 22 Church
Chadeayne, David, shipmaster, 39 Bancker
Charles, Mrs. 80 Pearl
Chadwick, Joseph, rigger, 16 Harman
Chadwick, James, carpenter, 82 Chamber
Chadwick, William, 8 Depeyster
Chadwick, Reuben, tavern, 146 Bowery-lane.
Chaffers, James, tavern, 283 Water-street.
Chalk, Richard, grocer, 45 Cortlandt

Chalon, De Ayral, 16 James-street.
Chambers, Mary, Rose
Chambers, Mary, 88 Division
Champenoy, Thomas, Little Catharine
Champenoy, William, Little Catharine
Champlin John T. merchant, 308 Pearl
Champlin, Seabury, 49 Beekman
Chanlen, Wm. fancy chairmaker, 116 Chatham
Chapman, John, merchant, 26 Maiden-lane.
Chapman, George W. physician 307 Washington-strt.
Chapman, John, trader, 384 Pearl
Chapman and Co. John, merchants, 170 Front
Chapman, Mary, 35 Lumber
Chapman, James, painter, 46 Barclay
Chapman, Henry, merchant, 120 Water
Chappell, Roswell, labourer, 6 Moore
Chardavoyne, Isaac, inspector, of wood, 8 Dutch
Charles, Eleanor, mantuamaker, Birmingham-row.
Charlote, Samuel, chairmaker, 30 Church-street.
Charleton, John, physician, 34 Broadway.
Charters, John, mason, 19 Barclay-street.
Charters, John, cabinetmaker, 33 Barclay
Chase, John, boatbuilder, 69 James
Chase, William, shoemaker, Mott
Chase, Ammie, shipwright, Division
Chase and Carter, boatbuilders, 302 Water
Chatfield, William, cartman, 75 Reed
Chatterton, Sarah, 75 Maiden-lane.
Cheesebrough & Cairn's store, 182 Broadway.
Cheesebrough, Robert, merchant, 53 Vesey-street.
Cheeseman, Samuel, carpenter, Gibb's alley.
Cheeseman, John, mason, 16 Fayette-street.
Cheeseman, widow, 262 William
Cheeseman, Furman, shipwright, Lumber
Cheetham, J. and B. hat manufactory, 456 Pearl
Cheetham, John, 215 Broadway.
Cheetham, James, hatter, 16 Warren-street.
Cheriot, Henry, merchant, 84 Pearl
Cheris, David, mariner, Bayard
Chevalier, James, merchant, 263 Pearl
Chevallie, Mrs. 40 Rutger
Chevallie & Rainteaux, merchants, 100 Murray's wharf.

Chevee, James B. merchant, 159 William-street.
Chevers, William, grocer, 82 Cherry
Chevers, William, marshall, 37 Harman
Chickering, D. physician, 44 Ferry
Child, William, grocer, 219 William
Child, Francis, conveyancer, 15 Chatham
Child, Abraham, merchant-taylor, 24 William
Child, Evander, 19 Chatham-row.
Chiney, William, shipwright, 137 Cherry-street.
Chisholm, John, 98 Broad
Chisholm, George, mariner, 15 Fayette
Choate, Seth, grocer, Cherry
Chopin, John, Little Catharine
Christian, Zach. 76 Warren
Christian, Charles, cabinet-maker, 61 New
Christie, Richard, glass-store, 3 Albany bason.
Christie, William, smith, 7 John-street.
Christie, Mary, china and glass store, 37 Maiden-lane.
Christie, James, smith, 19 Robinson-street.
Christie, Alexander, bookbinder, 3 Rider
Christie, George, cooper, 201 Front
Church, John B. 52 Broadway.
Church, Alexander, tavern, 125 Fly-market.
Church, George, labourer, Mott-street.
Church and Haven's store, 161 Front
Church, John, merchant, 164 William
Church, Thomas C. mariner, 25 Roosevelt
Church, John, shipmaster, 164 William
Church, Benjamin, shipmaster, 25 Roosevelt
Clabby, Richard, grocer, 36 Harman
Claelly, George, shoemaker, 6 Frankfort
Claghorn, Joseph, sailmaker, Mulberry
Clake, widow, 22 Dey
Clapp, John, lawyer, 9 Moore's-row.
Clapp, Thomas, tallow-chandler, 240 Greenwich-st.
Clapp, John, merchant, 21 Vandewater, and store, Clark's wharf.
Clapp, Samuel, shipmaster, 26 Oliver-street.
Clare, Conrad, 28 Division
Clark, Sime., washer, 11 George
Clark, Hugh, labourer, 67 Roosevelt
Clark, John, shoemaker, 26 Harman

Clark and Co. grocers, 137 Cherry-street.
Clark, Samuel, mariner, 43 Gold
Clark, Alexander, Broadway, corner of Reed
Clark, James, Phila. stage direct. 78 Cortlandt-street.
Clark, Ebenezer, coachmaker, 202 Broadway.
Clark, John, Fisher-street.
Clark and sons, Nathaniel, lumber-yard, Clark's wharf.
Clark, Nathaniel, merchant, 68 Cherry-street.
Clark, John, druggist, 66 Maiden-lane.
Clark, Jacob, carpenter, 130 William-street.
Clark, Thomas, merchant, 40 Roosevelt
Clark, John, boatbuilder, 343 Water
Clark, George, shipmaster, 15 Stone
Clark, John, dry goods store, 13 Maiden-lane.
Clark, Alexander, merchant, Lumber-street.
Clark, Samuel, labourer, 9 Rose
Clark, Robert, shoemaker, 61 Harman
Clark, Benjamin, shoemaker, 82 John
Clark, John, carpenter, 39 Reed
Clark, Richard, rigger, 11 Chesnut
Clark, Amos, cooper, Essex
Clark, William, grocer, 36 Roosevelt
Clark, Sarah, Magazine
Clarke, James B. attorney at law, enquire at 144 Pearl
Clarke and son, druggists, 210 Broadway.
Clarke, Scott L. merchant, 168 William-street.
Clarke, James, physician, 2 Vesey
Clarke, Peter, druggist, 138 Pearl
Clarke, Mary, milliner, 332 Water
Clarkson, Levinus, merchant, 460 Pearl
Clarkson, General Mathew, 26 Pearl
Clarkson, S. & L. merchants, Stone, corner of Mill
Clarkson, David M. merchant, 25 Cortlandt
Clarkson, Charles, merchant, 25 Dey
Clarkson, Mathew M. accountant, 8 Lombard
Clarkson, Freeman, merchant, 29 William
Clarkson, Elizabeth, 29 William
Clason, Isaac, merchant, 61 Broadway.
Claus, Christ. musical instrument-maker, 4 Dover-str.
Clay, Stephen, shipmaster, 4 Rutger
Clayton, John C. broker and conveyancer, 4 George
Clayton, Thomas, merchant, 16 and 66 Beekman

Clement, Jane, boarding-house, 14 Peck-slip.
Clement, Henry, 300 Greenwich-street.
Clement, Henry, ironmonger, 193 Greenwich
Clendining and M'Laren's store, 209 Pearl
Clendining, John, merchant, 209 Pearl
Clifford, James, labourer, Division
Clifford, Thomas, boarding-house, 54 Pearl
Cliland, George, ironmonger, 33 Maiden-lane.
Cliland, Mrs. midwife, 95 Chatham-street.
Climson, William, tea-waterman, Bayard
Clinch, Jacob, accountant, 61 Pine
Clinch, John, carpenter, Division
Cling, Henry, labourer, First
Clinton, George, late governor, at Greenwich.
Clinton, De Witt, 9 Cherry-street.
Clinton, George, attorney at law, 34 Liberty
Clinton, widow, 16 Bancker
Clipincork, Jedediah, 23 Batavia-lane.
Clitz, John, hairdresser, 31 Cedar-street.
Clopper, Peter, merchant, 23 William
Close, David, huckster, 25 Harman
Clossey, Miles F. merchant, 31 Greenwich
Clough, Capt. John, 51 Cedar
Cluet, John, conveyancer, 3 Barclay
Coats, John H. merchant, 444 Pearl
Coats, John, tinplate-worker, 157 Water
Cobb, widow, 80 Warren
Cobb, William, 80 Warren
Cobby, John, carpenter, 31 James
Cochran, Patrick, hairdresser, 26 Front
Cochran, John, painter and glazier, 34 Church
Cochran, John, tobacconist, 1 Cheapside.
Cochran, Michael, mariner, 10 Chesnut-street.
Cock, Phœbe, milliner, 266 William
Cock, Joshua, merchant, 11 Peck-slip.
Cock, James, printer, 12 Garden-street.
Cock, Isaac, merchant, 5 and 26 Peck-slip.
Cock, and Co. Andrew, store, 15 Peck-slip.
Cock, George, merchant, 104 Cherry-street.
Cock, James, cutter of staves, &c. 50 Bedlow
Cock, John, merchant, 7 Peck-slip.
Cock, Andrew, merchant, 15 Peck-slip.

Cock and Frost's store, 258 Water-street.
Cock, Charles, merchant, 76 Catharine-street.
Cock, Elijah, merchant, 230 Water
Cockcraft, Lydia, 15 Bowery-lane.
Cockrem, Philip, 56 Whitehall.
Cocks, Robert, merchant-taylor, 100 Water-street.
Cocks, jun. Robert, merchant, 100 Water
Coddington, John, cartman, 41 Barclay
Coddington, John, taylor, 176 Greenwich
Coddington, James, cartman, Crofs
Coddington, Uziah, cartman, 62 Vesey
Coddington, jun. Uziah, mason, Barley
Coddington, David, cartman, 92 Chamber
Coddington, Benjamin, cartman, Bowery-lane.
Coddington, Moses, cartman, 298 Greenwich-street.
Codman, William, merchant, 30 William
Codwise, George, merchant, 341 Pearl
Codwise, jun. George, merchant, 75 Beekman
Codwise, Christopher, merchant, 341 Pearl
Codwise, Ludlow, and Co.'s store, 226 Pearl
Coe, Moses, Barley
Coen, George, labourer, Henry
Coen, Daniel, gold and silversmith, 95 Maiden-lane.
Coffey, William, hairdresser, 74 William-street.
Coffey, Edward, cartman, Sixth
Coffin, John, A. M. teacher, 91 Beekman
Cogen, John, labourer, 28 Barclay
Cogswell, William, combmaker, 51 Division
Cohen, Charity, 48 Beaver
Coit, Levy, merchant, 33 Greenwich, and 90 Wall
Coit, David, shoemaker, 92 Harman
Coit, Elisha, merchant, 91 Cherry
Coit, Elisha and William, store 16 Crane-wharf.
Colbreth, John, mariner, 24 Banker-street.
Colourn, George, mariner, Bayard
Colden, H. M. 15 Dey
Colden, Cadwallader D. Assistant Att. Gen. 47 Wall
Cole, Abraham, smith, 11 Division
Cole, John, smith, 11 Division
Cole, Peter, keeper of the bridewell, and county jail
Cole, Peter, cartman, 11 Barclay-street.
Cole, Henry, cooper, Henry.

Coleman & Southerland, grocers, 303 Washington-st.
Coleman, John, grocer, 271 Greenwich-street.
Coleman, William, 39 Pine
Coleman, Charles, carpenter, Second
Coles, James, merchant, 11 Peck-slip.
Coles, Caleb, cordwainer, 90 Chatham-street.
Coles, Robert, cartman, Cross
Coles, and Co. Jordon, store 25 Beekman-slip.
Coles, and son's, Stephen, distillery, 26 Ferry-street.
Coles, Willet, distiller, 45 Ferry
Coles, John B. merchant, 82 Pearl, and store 1 South
Collard, James, 20 Chesnut
Collard, Abraham, taylor, 16 Reed
Collard, Thomas, slopshop, 27 Banker
Collard, James, taylor, 52 E. George
Collard, Isaac, shoemaker, 12 Frankfort
Collard, Jeremiah, shipwright, 16 Reed
Collell, Bentura, 217 Greenwich
Colles, John, paper-hanging manufactory, 42 Pearl.
Colles, Richard, paper-stainer, 38 Church
Collet, William, shipwright, 19 Lumber
Collett, John, blockmaker, 342 Water
Colley, Mary, boarding-house, 25 Partition
Collier, Thomas, 20 Rose
Collier, Richard, grocer, 22 Rose
Collier, Mathew, labourer, 178 Division
Collier, Benjamin, carpenter, 29 Reed
Collins, Thomas, tavern, 73 Wall
Collins, Joseph, grocer, 101 Catharine
Collins, Thomas, smith, Henry
Collins, William, hairdresser, 70 Pine
Collins, Mary, 3 Rider
Collins, Isaac and Charles, merchants, 189 Pearl
Collins, Samuel, boarding-house, 4 Cedar
Collins, Elizabeth, shopkeeper, 49 John
Collins, William, tobacconist, 31 Front
Collins, Mark, shipmaster, 41 Pine
Collins, John, rigger, 27 Chesnut
Collins, John, grocer, 26 Vesey
Collins, Lawrence, grocer, 124 Chatham
Collins, John, rigger, 55 Rutger
Collins, William, cartman, 37 Chapel

Collis, George, smith, 8 Chesnut-street.
Collishaw, Joseph, cabinetmaker, 16 Chapel
Collister, Thos. sexton Trinity church, 84 Beekman
Colman, Mary, washer, 12 E. George
Colon, Jonas, chairmaker, 6 Murray
Colon, David, chairmaker, 14 Robinson
Colpoys, Mrs. 19 Thames
Colt, Elisha, merchant, 230 Pearl
Colter, James, boarding, 26 Front
Colter, Mark, porter-vaults, 22 Pearl
Colvil, John, grocer, 49 Maiden-lane.
Colwell, Isaac, boarding-house, 314 Water-street.
Comber, D. labourer, 16 Bancker
Combs, Sarah, milliner, 63 Broad
Commerford, Bernard, grocer, 18 Banker
Compton, Cornelius, shoemaker, 46 Gold
Compton, Ebenezer, shipwright, 107 Oliver
Compton, Cornelius, shipwright, Birmingham-row
Conard, Nicholas, cabinetmaker, 21 Barley-street.
Concklin, John C. grocer, New-slip.
Concklin, Nathan, 261 Water-street.
Conckline, James, shoemaker, 11 William
Conckline, David, 27 Moore
Conckline, Titus, shipmaster, 74 Roosevelt
Conckline, David, cartman, 25 Reed
Conckline, Matthias, carpenter, 39 Partition
Conckline, Lewis, livery stabler, 24 James
Conckline, Jacob, grocer, Water-street, New-slip.
Congar, Obadiah, shipmaster, 227 Water-street.
Congar, Jos. shoe warehouse, Front
Congar, Matilda, 45 Cliff
Conley, Mrs. Upper Barley
Conley, Jeremiah, tavern, 30 Rutger
Connell, James, tavern, Bruce's-wharf.
Connell, John, mason, Orange-street.
Connolly, James, tavern, Theatre-alley.
Connolly, Thomas, shipwright, 29 Cheapside
Connolly, John, shoemaker, Pell-street.
Connor, James, carpenter, 9 Moore's-row.
Connor, Samuel, mason, Elizabeth-street.
Connor, Richard, hairdresser, 23 Augustus
Connor, James, mariner, 34 Vandewater

Connor, Daniel, grocer, 92 Broadway.
Connor, Aaron, labourer, 10 Augustus-street.
Connor, John, taylor, 207 Greenwich
Conrad, Peter, carpenter, 18 Ccamber
Conrey, William, cartman, 34 Rutger
Conrey, Abraham, shoemaker, 72 James
Conrey, Thomas, cabinetmaker, Cross
Conrey, Peter, cabinetmaker, 11 Roosevelt
Conrey, Jonathan, grocer, 15 Chesnut
Constable, James, sadler, 78 James, and 153 Water
Constable, W. and J. counting-house, 51 William
Constable, William, merchant, 223 Broadway.
Constable, James, merchant, 41 Pine-street.
Constant, Joseph, attorney at law, 19 Broad
Constantine, John, smith, 10 New, and 1 Wall
Conver, John, 39 Greenwich
Cook, William, grocer, 23 Peck-slip.
Cook, Asher, shipmaster, 36 Whitehall.
Cook, John, 261 Greenwich-street.
Cook, Mrs. 3 Wall
Cook, James, mariner, 20 Lumber
Cook, and Co. John, jewellers, &c. 133 William
Cook, Daniel, sawyer, 33 Oliver
Cook, John, carpenter, 36 Beaver
Cook, Micheal, cartman, 51 Church
Cook, Sisel, pastry cook, 57 Lumber
Cook, Nicholas, labourer, Eagle
Cook, Peter, cedar cooper, 22 Vesey
Cook, John G. mercht. Front-st. corner Crane-wharf.
Cook, Charles, Cross-street.
Cook, David, eating-house, 354 Water
Cook, Joseph, mariner, Mulberry
Cooley, Alexander, mariner, 19 Batavia-lane.
Coon, Godfrey, tavern, 14 John-street.
Coon, widow, 229 William
Cooper, Nathaniel, merchant, 21 Albany-pier.
Cooper, Stephen, builder, 20 Thomas-street.
Cooper, Cornelius, merchant, 29 Vandewater
Cooper, Francis, coppersmith, 36 Water
Cooper, Thomas, counsellor at law, 55 Wall-street.
Cooper, Albert, taylor, 48 Church
Cooper, William, wheelwright, 144 Chatham

Cooper, James, merchant, 91 Maiden-lane.
Cooper, Joseph, tavern, 11 Cliff-street.
Cooper, Susannah, Bowery-lane.
Cooper, Thomas, labourer, Greenwich-road.
Cooper, Albert, 60 Chapel-street.
Cooper, Joseph, Chapel
Cooper, Thomas, comedian, 1 George
Cooper, Thomas, shoemaker, 8 Rose
Cooper, William, cartman, 45 Division
Copland, George, grocer, 72 Water
Coppin, John, carpenter, 29 Roosevelt
Corbit, Catharine, 60 Broad
Corbit, Sarah, shopkeeper, 195 William
Corey, Timothy, carpenter, 101 Harman
Corey, Abraham, cabinetmaker, Reed
Cork, Margaret, dry goods store, 7 Maiden-lane.
Corkhill, John, mariner, 28 Roosevelt-street.
Corleys, George, mason, 1 Hague
Corleys, widow, market-woman, 23 Harman
Cornell, Aspinwall, grocer, E. Rutger
Cornell, Elizabeth, 304 Pearl
Cornell and Gordon, merchants, 82 William
Cornell, Charles, merchant, 23 Liberty
Cornell, Thomas, cabinetmaker, First
Cornell, Gilliam, merchant, 131 Fly-market.
Corner, Richard, physician, 56 Water-street.
Corning, Amos, carpenter, &c. saw-pits, Greenwich.
Cornock, widow, 22 William-street.
Cornwall, & Co. Jas. shipchandlers, 15 Beekman-slip.
Cornwell, William H. 135 Broadway.
Cornwell, John J. butcher, 19 Barley-street.
Cornwell, widow, First
Corp, Samuel, merchant, 171 Pearl
Corre, Joseph, ice ____ ____, 9 State
Cortelyou, ____ ____ ____, 57 Whitehall.
Cortlandt, P. ____, Cedar-street.
Cortlandt, Elizabeth, 9 Broadway.
Coruth, John, smith, 192 Division-street.
Corwin, George, teacher, Birmingham-row.
Corwin, Martin L. carpenter, 2 Birmingham-row.
Corwin, William, shipmaster, 8 Front-street.
Corwin, Luther, carpenter, Birmingham-row.

Corwin, James, carpenter, Birmingham row.
Corwin, Benjamin, carpenter, Birmingham-row.
Cosart, Benjamin, carpenter, 74 Bowery-lane.
Cosborough, Robert W. accountant, First-street.
Cossar, Peter, rigger, Moore's-row.
Cossen, Cornelius, shoemaker, Essex-street.
Coster, John G. merchant, 26 William
Coster, Henry A. merchant, 59 Water
Costigan, Lewis I. boarding-house, 126 Front
Cotter, Timothy, smith, Little Catharine
Cottle, Peter, cartman, Pump
Cottle, Samuel, mariner, 52 James
Cottle, Sarah, 1 Roosevelt
Cottle, Grant, upholsterer, Barley
Cottle, James, cartman, E. Washington
Cotton, James, mercht. 47 Beekman str. & 30 Old-slip.
Cotton, Daniel, merchant, 36 Cherry-street.
Cotton, John, 55 Warren
Cotton, Rowland, composer of music, Charlotte
Cottrel, Thomas, shipmaster, 19 James
Cottrel, Eleazer, shipmaster, Henry, corner Charlotte
Cottrel, Richard, cooper, 1 Pearl
Cottrel, Samuel, oysterman, 51 Broad
Couilie, Peter, labourer, 11 Moore's-row.
Coulthard, Isaac, tanner and currier, Cross-street.
Courbe, Doctor, 54 Cortlandt
Courtney, John, mason, 24 Harman
Courtney, Anna H. Cherry-street, Ship-yards.
Courtney, Lawrence, drayman, Mott-street.
Coutant, Daniel, shoemaker, 79 Chatham
Coutant, John, grocer, Bowery-lane.
Couzens, Mathew, shoemaker, Little Catharine-street.
Covenhoven, Elizabeth, tayloress, 59 Water
Covenhoven, Francis, grocer, airfurnace, Greenwich
Covenhoven, Henry, taylor, 4 Cortlandt
Covenhoven, Catharine, 60 Vesey
Covenhoven, James, cartman, Magazine
Covenhoven, Francis, taylor, Magazine
Coventry, I. H. physician, 69 Greenwich
Coventry, Elizabeth, 55 Wall
Covert, William, shoemaker, 3 E. George
Covert, widow, 3 Division

Covert, Abraham, tea-waterman, Third-street.
Covil, John, bellows-maker, 23 Cheapside.
Cowan, John, labourer, E. Rutger-street.
Cowan and Carer, merchants, 179 Broadway.
Cowan, John Nevill, physician, 44 Vesey-street.
Cowan, widow, boarding-house, 37 Nassau
Cowan, Barnet, physician, 5 Thames
Cowdry, Benjamin, hatter, 5 E. George
Cowdry, Jonathan, 1 E. Rutger
Cowley, William and Joseph, store, 233 Pearl
Cowley, Joseph, merchant, 78 John
Cowley, William, merchant, 78 John
Cowley, George, sexton, 32 John
Cox, Thomas, shoemaker, 21 Rose
Cox, Ralph, labourer, 5 Harman
Cox, Gabriel, carpenter, 27 Roosevelt
Cox, John, shipwright, Charlotte
Cox, Henry, Bowery-lane.
Cox, Whitehead and Co. merchants, 272 Pearl-street
Cox, Catharine, 35 Pearl
Cox, William, Second
Cox, Jamison, 214 William
Cox, Charles, store 96 Bowery-lane.
Cox, John W. hairdresser, 62 John-street.
Cox, Thomas, shoemaker, 6 George
Cox, Nicholas, hatter, 56 Partition
Cox, Moses, oysterman, Grand
Cozine, John, counsellor at law, 42 Beekman
Crabb, Thomas, tea-merchant, 123 Front
Craboch, Godfrey, butcher, Bowery-lane.
Craboch, Peter, butcher, Bowery-lane.
Craft, Joseph, grocer, Charlotte-street.
Craft, James, cartman, Little Catharine
Craft, John B. labourer, 20 Ferry
Craig, Alexander, cabinetmaker, 82 Reed
Craig, James, taylor, 15 Dutch
Craig, Mary, 17 New
Craig, John, carpenter and builder, 42 Greenwich
Craig, William, labourer, Batavia-lane.
Cral, Thomas, carpenter, 6 Lumber
Crane, Isaac B. carpenter, 35 Barley
Crane, Martha, teacheress, 54 Beaver

Crane, Sarah, teacheress, 91 Beekman-street.
Crane, Reuben, mariner, Beaver-lane.
Crank, Robert, boatman, 79 Reed
Cranse, William, shoemaker, Third
Craton, John, cartman, Mulberry
Craven, widow, 60 Warren
Craufurd, Gov. James, 168 Greenwich
Crawford, John, carpenter, Mulberry
Crawford, Alexander, carpenter, 92 John
Crawford, William, mason, First
Crawford, John, merchant, Cherry-street, Ship-yards.
Crawford, Peter, rigger, Fisher-street.
Crawley, Dewsbury, tin-plate-worker, 28 Nassau
Creed, Conrad, grocer, corner of E. Rutger
Cregier, Martin, wood inspector, 67 Nassau
Cregier, Jacob, painter, 102 Liberty
Cregier, John, carpenter, 10 Barclay
Creighton, James, attorney at law, 43 Stone
Creighton, Elizabeth, midwife, 36 Beaver
Creland, William, shipwright, Birmingham-row.
Crendall, Abraham, labourer, Charlotte-street.
Cripps, James, cooper, 5 Ferry
Crocheron, Jacob, grocer, 53 Whitehall-street.
Crolius, sen. John, stone-ware potter, 215 Greenwich
Crolius, Clarkson, potter, Potter's-hill.
Crolius, jun. John, stone-ware-potter, 78 Chatham-str.
Crolius, George, stone-ware-potter, 46 Augustus
Crolius, William, potter, Little-Ann
Crommelin, widow, corner of Garden and Broad-strs.
Cromwell, Oliver, grocer, 26 Maiden-lane.
Cromwell, Daniel, merchant, 232 Water-street.
Cromwell, John, grocer, 34 Warren
Cromwell, Jacob, oysterman, 57 Catharine
Crone, David, 64 James
Crook, Joseph, collector of the revenue, 259 William
Crook, Mrs. wet, 48 Dey
Crooks, Andrew, smith, 17 Division
Crooker, James, tavern, Water-street, above New-slip.
Crooks, John, printer of the Diary, 41 Liberty-street.
Crookshank, Benjamin, cabinetmaker, 151 William
Crookshank, William, carpenter, 100 Greenwich
Cropsey, Jasper, boatman, 65 Ann-street.

Crosbie, Alexander, Greenwich-road.
Crosbie, William, grocer, 61 E. George-street.
Crosbie, Cornelius, shipwright, 17 Fayette
Cross, jun. John, 61 Fair
Cross, William, labourer, Ferry
Croswaite, Peter, mariner, 66 Harman
Crow, Simon, shoemaker, 33 Chatham
Crowell, Jen. grocer, Cherry
Crowley, Florence, accountant, 59 Cherry
Cruger, Nicholas, merchant, 78 and 80 Broad
Cruger, Henry, merchant, 87 Greenwich
Cruger, John, 50 Greenwich
Crumb, Henry, cartman, 45 Barley
Crumpton, John, grocer, New-slip.
Crygier, Peter, livery-stabler, 13 Dey-street.
Crygier, widow, 1 Warren
Crygier's & Collis's paper manufactory, 3 Warren do.
Crygier, Aaron, shipjoiner, Winne
Crygier, Simon, 35 Murray
Crygier, Corneilus and John, upholsterers, 84 Water
Crygier, Augustus, mason, 27 Barclay
Cudmore, Paul, trunkmaker, 94 Cherry
Culberhouse, William, Orange
Culbert, Hugh, grocer, Mulberry
Culbertson, James, high constable, 1 Broad
Culbertson, James, carpenter, 17 Thomas
Cullen, Elizabeth, boarding-house, 13 Wall
Cullum, George, harness-maker, 45 Barclay
Cumberland, John, looking-glass manuf. 100 William
Cuming, and Co. F. merchants, 97 Front
Cumming, William, marshall, 45 Rutger
Cummings, James, 160 Broadway, & 77 Liberty-str.
Cummings, John, carpenter, 72 E. George-street.
Cummings, Patrick, coachman, 1 Oliver
Cunning, William, printer, 61 Chatham
Cunningham, William, slopshop, 146 Front
Cunningham, Richard, tanner and currier, 47 Ferry
Cunningham, Eleanor, tavern, 82 Catharine
Cunningham, David, brewer, 60 Catharine
Cunningham, Andrew, mariner, 10 Harman
Cunningham, Mathew, cartman, Division
Cunningham, Samuel, cartman, 15 Division

Cunningham, John, grocer, 144 William-street.
Cunningham, James, taylor, 38 Beaver
Cunningham, Paul, tanner, near Cross
Curin, Anthony, taylor, 8 Fair
Curley, Michael, 94 Greenwich
Curran, ———, mariner, 51 Rutger
Currie, John, labourer, E. Rutger
Currie, widow, 53 Chatham
Currie, Archibald, merchant, 17 Liberty
Currie, John, merchant, 41 Stone-street.
Currie, John, smith, 41 Whitehall.
Currie, John, carpenter, 8 Pine-street.
Currie, Francis, constable, 30 Rutger
Curtenius, Peter, merchant, 122 Liberty
Curtis, Robert, salesman, 62 Maiden-lane.
Curtis, Joel, grocer, 211 Greenwich-street.
Curtis, widow, 8 Robinson
Curtis, Richard, grocer, 56 Catharine
Curtis, Charles, merchant, 32 Cherry
Curtis, John, 195 William
Curtis, John, carpenter, 61 Chapel
Curtis, Hannah, 2 Jacob
Curtis, Theodora, seamstress, 168 William
Curtis, Thomas, labourer, Bowery-lane.
Cutch, George, rigger, Birmingham-row.
Cuthill, Alexander, taylor, 68 John-street.
Cutler, Benjamin, tavern, 162 Fly-market.
Cutler, Ebenezer, smith, 12 Harman-street.
Cutter, Mitchell, shipmaster, 46 Fair
Cuyler, ———, shipmaster, 121 William
Cuyler, Jane, boarding-house, 58 Wall

D

Daams, Henry, taylor, 296 Broadway.
Dailey, Patrick, Little Catharine-street.
Dale, Robert, accountant, 237 Greenwich
Dally, Philip, smith, 45 Chatham
Dally, George, smith, 93 Chatham
Dally, Philip, sailmaker, 55 Lumber
Dally, Joseph, shipwright, 95 Harman
Dalmas, Doctor, 2 Robinson
Dalrymple, Paul, shoemaker, 35 Nassau
Daly, William, 47 Ferry

Dalziel, John, clockmaker, 72 Broad-street.
Damaret and Co. confectioners, 99 Beekman
Dando, Stephen, hat store, 3 Maiden-lane.
Dando, Mary, 3 Maiden-lane.
Danforth, Rachel, boarding-house, 79 Fair-street.
Dangel, Beat, professor of languages, 34 Dey
Danham, Joseph, 6 Moore's-row.
Daniel, David, tavern, 3 New-slip.
Daniel, James, tavern, 145 Front-street.
Daniel, Ephraim, carpenter, 201 William
Daniel, Mathew, pilot, 49 Beaver
Daniel, Henry, glass engraver, 61 New
Daniel, James, pilot, 3 Hague
Daniel, John, segar manufactory, 64 Cherry
Daniels, John, tavern, 8 Broad
Darby, John, 75 Warren
Darby, Henry, cartman, Norfolk
Darg, John, baker, Upper Reed
Darley, Arthur, marble & stonecutter, 90 Greenwich
Darling, Thomas, boatman, Rope-walk.
Darling, Thomas, tavern, 27 Moore-street.
Darracq, Cloid, Eagle
Darracq, Bernard, merchant, 68 Chamber
Darrah, John, shipmaster, 25 Rutger
Darnion, Madam, 96 John
Dash, jun. John B. ironmonger, 147 Broadway.
Dash, John B. tin and coppersmith, 138 Broadway.
Daubeney, Mary, boarding-house, 52 Wall-street.
Davenport, Rufus, hatter, 327 Pearl
David, John, grocer, Little-Catharine
Davidson, William, cartman, Chamber
Davidson, James, shipchandler, 173 Washington
Davidson, John, shipwright, Orchard
Davidson, John, stonecutter, Upper-Reed
Davidson, widow, 59 Church
Davidson, Margaret, mantuamaker, 59 Church
Davie and McKillop, slopshop, 273 Water
Davis, Cornelius, bookseller and stationer, 94 Water
Davis, Phœbe, boarding-house, 3 South
Davis, Mathew L. & William A. printers, 26 Moore
Davis, James, mariner, 26 Oliver
Davis, Richard, carver and gilder, 25 Vesey-street.

Davis, John and Joseph, merchants, Jackson's wharf.
Davis, John, carpenter, 1 Henry-street.
Davis, Samuel, carpenter, Little Catharine
Davis, John, mason, First
Davis, William, labourer, 14 Moore
Davis, William, accountant, 45 Catharine
Davis, Robert, taylor, 80 Beckman
Davis, Thomas, caulker, 21 Bancker
Davis, widow, 36 Division
Davis, George, shoemaker, 52 Cedar
Davis, Francis, taylor, 11 Vandewater
Davis, Charles, boatman, 51 Church
Davis, Joel, carpenter, 32 Oliver
Davis, John, labourer, 18 James
Davis, John, mariner, 14 Bancker
Davis, Mrs. 78 Liberty
Davis, Mrs. 180 Greenwich
Davis, John, merchant, 6 William
Davis, widow, taylorels, 59 John
Davis, Abraham, tavern, Broadway, near Bayard's-lane.
Davoue, Fred. 52 Beckman-str. & store 24 Peck-slip.
Daws, Caleb, grocer, 39 Greenwich-street.
Dawson, John, hairdresser, 30 Cortlandt
Dawson, Thomas, umbrella-maker, Division
Dawson, Thomas, mariner, 79 James
Dawson, Francis, boarding-house, 42 Stone
Dawson, Abraham, mariner, 78 Cherry
Dawson, Sarah, seamstress, 55 Ann
Dawson, John, porter vaults, 41 William
Day, widow, 92 Chamber
Day, William, taylor 40 Warren
Day, John, carpenter, 18 Roosevelt
Day, Abraham, labourer, 55 Chamber
Day, A. sicknurse, 7 Chapel
Day, John, sailmaker, Mulberry
Day, Jacob, cartman, 32 Vesey
Day, Abraham, cartman, Greenwich-road.
Day, widow, 56 Chatham-street
Day, Michael, carpenter, 46 Warren
Day, John, cartman, Little Ann
Day, Jacob, carpenter, 42 Warren
Day, Cornelius, mason, Winne

Day, Samuel, carpenter, 44 Rutger-street.
Deal, William, tea-waterman, Winne
Dealing, Maria, shopkeeper, 199 Broadway.
Dealy, James, carpenter and joiner, 43 Cliff-street.
Dean, Sarah, teacheress, Provost
Dean, Evans, grocer, 93 Division
Dean, Moses, labourer, 54 E. George
Dean, Joseph, labourer, 16 Moore
Dean, Isaac, labourer, Little Catharine
Dean, James, shipmaster, Winne
Dean, John, grocer and porter-house, 73 James
Dearman, Justice, Greenwich-road.
Deary, James, cartman, Little Catharine-street.
Deas, David, shipmaster, 70 Bowery-lane.
Deas, James, First-street.
Debow, William, surgeon, &c. 50 Cherry
Debow, Garrit, shoemaker, 132 Front
Debow, Garrit, grocer, Greenwich, corner Thames-st.
Debevoise, Charles, smith, 91 Reed
De Camp, Ezekiel, cartman, Eagle
De Camp, Moses, carpenter, Little-Catharine
De Camp, John, mason, Greenwich-road.
Declue, Margaret, 6 John-street.
Declue, John, confectioner, 6 Nassau
Decoto, Anthony, mariner, 18 Chesnut
Decou, Francis, Chapel
Dederer, Christian, cartman, 6 Duane
Dederer, Joseph, carpenter, 185 Greenwich
De Forest, Theodorus, grocer, 149 Fly-market.
De Forest, John, shoemaker, Winne-street.
De Forest, Isaac, carpenter, 303 Washington
De Forest, William, merchant, 11 Nassau
De Forest, Gerard, shipwright, corner of Harison
Degarmo, William, grocer, 78 Vesey
Degraw, Nicholas, Little Catharine
Degraw, Isaac, smith, 1 Augustus
Degraw, Abraham, taylor, 92 John
Degray, John, hairdresser, 122 Broad
Degray, Michael, physician, 8 Catharine
Degremont, Simon, hairdresser, 1 Murray
Degrooat, Susannah, 8 Liberty
Degroodt, John, smith, 72 Harman

Degroodt, Samuel, shoe warehouse, 152 William-str.
Degroodt, John, shipwright, 69 E. George
Degroodt, Richard, shipwright, Fisher
Degroodt, Peter, shipwright, Pump
Degrove, William, measurer, 124 Cherry
Degrove, Robert C. and A. hatters, 338 Pearl
Degrove, Walter, cartman, 17 Chapel
Degrove, widow, 8 Roosevelt
Degrove, Adolphus, hatter, 51 Roosevelt
Degrove, sen. Walter, 25 Chapel
Degrushe, Robert, cartman, 51 Partition
Degrushe, John, upholsterer, 54 John
Deiguin, William, tavern, 46 Water
Dekay, George, shipmaker, 29 Liberty
Dekline, Barnet, baker, 171 Greenwich
Delabarre, Marin, Upper Reed
Delacroix, Jos. confectioner & distiller, 112 Broadway.
Delacroix, Francis, 10 Murray-street.
Delafield, John, merchant, 25 Wall
Delafite, ——, 87 Nassau
Delafond, John, merchant, 4 Roosevelt
Delagarde, Monsieur, 8 Murray
Delamater, William, smith, 20 Ferry
Delamater, John, 13 Chapel
Delamater, widow, 21 Chamber
Delamater, Isaac, tavern, Chatham-row.
Delamater, Isaac, shoemaker, 49 Pearl-street.
Delamater, John S. marshall, 112 Broad
Delamater, Duggan & Co. tanners & curriers, 18 Dey
Delamater, John, carpenter, 75 Chatham
De la Montagnie, Jacob, alderman, 38 Chamber
Delamontanye, Catharine, Hester
Delamontanye, Isaac, 249 Greenwich
Delamontanye, John, taylor, 55 Barclay
Delancey, John, 34 Cherry
Delap, Richard, smith, 41 Rutger
Delap, John, mariner, 30 Henry
De la Pierre, coach lacemaker, 101 Beekman
Delaplane, Samuel, 136 Bowery-lane.
Delaplane, Joseph, grocer, 303 Pearl-street.
Delaplane, jun. Joseph, 263 Pearl
Delaplane, James K. porter-house, 18 Burling slip.

Delarue, Bauduin, smith, 3 Murray-street.
Delarue, William, Eagle
Delavigne and Co. Casimir, 13 Cortlandt
Dellinger, Joseph, wafermaker, Theatre-alley.
Delmes, William Alexis, 1 Eagle-street.
Deloffre, John B. tavern, 134 Fly-market.
Delonguemar, N. merchant, 39 Broad-street,
Delves and Thompson, store 133 Front
Delves, Thomas, merchant, 56 Wall
Demande, Robinet, 396 Pearl
Demarest, David, shoemaker, 38 Reed
Demarest, David, grocer, Thomas, corner of Chapel
Demarest, Jacob, shoemaker, Chapel
Demarest, David T. grocer, 68 Cortlandt
Demarest, Jacob, cartman, 76 Murray
Demarest, David C. cartman, Leonard
Demarest, John, 47 Chapel
Demarest, Thomas, grocer, 13 Murray.
Demarest, John, shoemaker, 38 Reed
Demarest, Albert, mason, 60 Chapel
Demarest, Samuel, cartman, 14 Thomas.
Demarest, Roelof, carpenter, 46 Barley
Demarest, Daniel, cartman, 73 Reed
Demarest, widow, 28 Lombard.
Demarest, James, cartman, saw-pits, Greenwich.
Demill, Peter, accountant, 186 Water-street.
Demilt, Benjamin, shipwright, Eagle
Demilt, Isaac, carpenter, 48 Gold
Demilt, Peter, taylor, 17 Cliff
Demilt, Isaac, hatter, 13 Murray
Demilt, Thomas, watchmaker, 156 Water
Deming, Simeon, cabinetmaker, 373 Pearl
Dempsey, Elizabeth, 62 Cortlandt
Dempsey, John, shoemaker, Gibbs' alley
Deno, Per, James, shoemaker, 259 Broadway.
Denew, ———, mason, 22 E. George-street.
Denham, widow, 60 Broad
Denning, William, merchant, 42 Wall
Denning, jun. William, merchant, 44 Wall
Dennis, Jonathan, cabinetmaker, 133 Chatham
Dennison, John, cartman, 15 Oliver
Dennison, William, cartman, 36 Catharine-street.

Dennison, Alexander, boarding-house, 29 Lumber-str.
Denny, Henry, tavern, 210 Greenwich
De Noil, Paul, carpenter, Broadway, near the furnace.
Denton, Samuel, dry goods store, 81 Maiden-lane.
Denton, Samuel, merchant, 38 Pine
Denton, Peter, shoemaker, 40 Barclay
Depeyster, William, merchant, 297 Pearl
Depeyster, Ab. B. merchant, Clinton, corner Cherry
Depeyster, Sarah, 16 Beaver
Depeyster, Pierre, shipmaster, 43 Vesey
Depeyster, John, 95 Liberty
Depeyster, Frederick, merchant, 71 Stone
Depeyster, jun. Nicholas, 297 Pearl
Depeyster, Gerard, merchant, 6 Cherry
Depeyster, John and Gerard, store Rose's wharf.
Depeyster, John, merchant, 297 Pearl-street.
Deriemer, Peter, hay-weigher, 36 Whitehall.
Deriemer, Abraham, cartman, 10 Fayette-street.
Deriemer, John, carpenter, Bedlow
Deriemer, Margaret, 64 Gold
Deriemer, Isaac, smith, Hester
Desbrosses, James, merchant, 174 Pearl
Deschent, Peter, grocer, 9 Chatham-row.
Desdoity, John B. 74 Front, and 69 Water-street.
Deseze, John, music-teacher, 86 Nassau
Deshay, David D. painter, First
Despret, Antoine Ignace, 7 Bridge
Devenport, James, colour-maker, 37 Warren
Devenport, jun. John, butcher, Bowery-lane.
Devenport, Thomas, cabinetmaker, 71 Warren-street.
Devenport, John, cartman, Bunker-hill.
Devillers, Auguste, 32 Church-street.
Devoe, Joseph, inspector of wood, 24 Garden
Devoe, Charles, cooper, 123 Cherry
Devou, Joseph, shoemaker, 38 Warren.
Devou, Peter, stonecutter, 29 Oliver
Devou, John, cartman, Mott
Devou, John, carpenter, Second
Devou, Joseph, cartman, 93 Greenwich
Devou, Frederick, shoemaker, 38 Warren
Devou, Sarah, midwife, Frankfort
Devou, Lewis, 172 Division-street.

Devou, John, cartman, 85 Chamber-street.
Devoy, Michael, cartman, 71 Harman
Dewitt, Peter, 17 George
Dewitt, John, windsor chairmaker, 442 Pearl
Dey, Theunis, attorney at law, 105 Liberty
Dick, Thomas, grocer, 23 Ferry
Dickey, George, shipmaster, 6 Harman
Dickinson, John, tavern, 122 Fly-market.
Dickinson, Charles, 57 Liberty-street.
Dickinson, David, lumber merchant, 1 Hague
Dickinson, Charles, 13 Oliver
Dickinson, John, boatman, 74 Chamber
Dickinson, and Co's. David, flourstore, 220 Front
Dickison, Abraham, shipwright, Bedlow
Dickson, John, stivadore, Henry
Dickson, Daniel, Belvidere-house.
Dickson, John, shoemaker, 115 Cherry-street.
Dickson, Peter, distiller, 27 Ferry
Dickson, Ellen, 303 Pearl
Dickson, Thomas, tallow-chandler, 22 Church
Dickson, John, ironmonger, 56 Chatham
Dickson, John, leather-dresser, 43 Augustus
Dieterich, George, baker, 351 Pearl
Dietz, John, skinner & leather-dresser, 7 Catharine
Diggins, Codwise, & Co. ironmongers, 212 Pearl
Diggins, Augustus, merchant, 212 Pearl
Dikeman, William, mariner, 270 Water
Dikeman, William, shoemaker, 13 Nassau
Dikeman, Mathew, block & pumpmaker, Oliver
Dikeman, John, grocer, Bowery-lane.
Dikeman, Tunis, 57 Catharine-street.
Dikeman, Richard, ropemaker, 146 Division
Dilford, George, Fisher
Dilks, Thomas, shoemaker, 33 Augustus
Dillen, William, mariner, 3 Moere's-row.
Dillon, Bartholomew, shoemaker, Bowery-lane.
Dillon, John, boatman, 34 Oliver-street.
Dillon, Edward, rigger, 1 Augustus
Dillon, Bartholomew, shoemaker, 7 Broad
Dills, Vincent, 6 Dutch
Dimelo, Joseph, sashmaker, 22 Lombard
Dingley, Amasa, physician and surgeon, 26 Nassau

Dinfdon, Thomas, mariner, 31 Lumber-ftreet.
Dinwoodie, James, teacher, 2 Cedar
Difbrow, Henry G. fhoemaker, 54 Chamber
Difbrow, John, taylor, 18 Thames
Difofway, Ifrael and Mark, merchants 12 Front
DISPENSARY, corner of Beekman & Naffau-ftreets.
Divine, John, 10 Beaver
Divine, Jane, 61 Ann
Divine, John, fhoemaker, 102 Liberty
Diweeds, John, mariner, 23 Fayette
Dixon, Lewis, cartman, 78 Bowery
Dixon, Sarah, 52 Partition
Dixon, Robert, porter-houfe, 16 Harman
Dixon, Jofeph, fhipmafter, 67 Harman
Dob, Jeremiah, cartman, 61 Chapel
Dob, Peter, dockbuilder, 266 Greenwich
Dobbin, James, grocer, 3 Catharine
Dobbs, Benjamin, tobacconift, 54 Warren
Dobbs, Henry M. watchmaker, 8 Cliff and 64 Wall
Dobbs, John, cooper, 28 Vandewater
Dobbs, John, cartman, 22 Catharine
Dobbs, Jeremiah, cooper, Divifion
Dobbs, Tobias, cartman, Barclay
Dobbs, Elias, carpenter, Chapel
Dobbs, John, mafon, 84 Murray
Dobbs, Thomas, boatman, 44 Reed
Dobbs, John, boatman, 100 Warren
Dobin, Alexander, 75 Warren
Dobfon, Jofeph, mariner, 27 Bowery-lane
Dobfon, John, gunfmith, 80 Cherry-ftreet.
Dodds, Robert, filk dyer & china ftore, 178 Broadway
Dodds, Thomas, fhoemaker, 41 Auguftus-ftreet.
Dodge, Daniel, carpenter, 40 Lumber
Dodge, Daniel, carpenter, 156 William
Dodge, John, carpenter, Corlaer's-hook.
Dodge, Samuel, keeper of the Alms-houfe.
Dodge, Ifaac, fhipwright, 360 Pearl-ftreet.
Dodge, William, ftate-meafurer, 32 George
Dodge, Jeremiah, fhipwright, Bedlow
Dodge, Amos, taylor, 47 Roofevelt
Dodge, widow of Thomas, 98 Catharine
Dodge, Capt. Duane

Dodge, widow, E. George-street.
Dodge, widow, 45 Roosevelt
Dohrman, A. H. merch. 278 Broadway, store 32 Front
Dolbeer, Ely, carpenter, Henry-street.
Dolives, William, and Co. merchants, 30 Pearl
Dollaway, Jeremiah, porter 50 Barley
Dolphen, Swan, grocer, 16 Robinson
Dominick, George F. carpenter, 30 Harman
Dominick, Francis, lumber merchant, 16 Cherry
Dominick, Francis J. butcher, 43 Bowery-lane.
Dominick, George, lumber-yard, upper end Cherry-str.
Dominick, John, lumber merchant, 66 Beekman
Don, Alexander, mariner, 71 Roosevelt
Donahgy, John, rigger, Division
Donaldson, Jesse, cartman, 27 Harman
Donaldson, John, drayman, 11 E. George
Donaldson, William, coachmaker, 7 John
Donaldson, James, lumber merch. saw-pits, Greenwich
Donaldson, James, labourer, Charlotte-street.
Donlevy, Gregory, grocer, 14 Augustus
Donnally, Thomas, boatman, Greenwich-road.
Donnoker, Henry, labourer, Mott street.
Donovan, T. tobacconist, 68 Catharine
Donovan, William, grocer, 77 Cherry
Donovan, William, tobacconist 249 Water
Doolett, George, architect, 34 Beaver
Doolittle, E. soap & candlemaker. 69 Frankfort
Dorgan, Andrew, shipmaster, 352 Water
Dorgan, Timothy, shipmaster, 62 Cherry
Dorn, James, mariner, 20 Batavia-lane.
Dorn, James, tavern, 83 James-street.
Dorsey, James, labourer, 100 Gold
Doty, Joseph, smith, 30 Warren
Doty and Franklin, merchants, 269 Pearl
Doty, Jacob, merchant, 304 Pearl
Doty, Isaac, hardware store. 295 Pearl
Doubleday, John, printer, 74 John
Dougall, Walter, 24 Robinson
Dougall, Hugh, cabinetmaker, 14 Chamber
Dougall, William, wheelwright, 27 Bowery-lane.
Dougan, Richard, shipwright, Henry-street.
Dougharty, John, 47 Warren

Dougharty, Anthony, labourer, 31 Lumber-street.
Dougharty, Charles, cartman, 35 Bancker
Dougharty, John, cooper, 41 E. George
Dougharty, widow, 16 Chamber
Doughty, William, merchant, 305 Pearl
Doughty, Samuel, lumber merchant, 58 Catharine
Doughty, Isaac, carpenter, Bedlow
Douglas, jun. George, merchant, 173 Pearl
Douglass, George, labourer, 21 E. George
Douglass and Lawrence, merchants, 173 Pearl
Douglass, John, tavern, Slote-lane.
Douglass, widow, teacherels, 14 Broad-street.
Douglass, James, merchant, 63 Maiden-lane.
Douglass, C. accountant, 51 Partition-street.
Douviel, John, carpenter, Birmingham-row.
Dove, William, cabinetmaker, 161 William-street.
Dover, John, merchant, 164 Broadway.
Dowe, Adrian, chairmaker, 35 Bowery-lane.
Down, William, baker, 10 Ruiger-street.
Downey, James, cartman, 42 Chamber
Downey, widow, Moore's-row.
Downing, John, accountant, 12 Augustus-street.
Downing, John, merchant, 379 Pearl
Downing, Moses, carpenter, 4 Lumber
Downing, Benjamin, cartman, Lumber
Downing, Samuel, 49 Partition
Dowtreep, Henry, tavern, 43 E. George
Doyer, Henry, merchant & distiller, 156 Chatham
Doyl, widow, 47 Lumber
Drake, Gilbert, grocer, Washington
Drake, Oliver, boarding-house, 44 Front
Drake, John, and Jacob, grocers, 195 Front
Drake, Samuel, shoemaker, 43 Partition
Drake, Rufus I. grocer, Catharine
Drake, Edward, labourer, Mott
Drake, Thomas, grocer, 156 Cherry
Drake, James, merchant, 125 Cherry
Drake, Capt. at Mrs. Cheeleman's, Ship-yards.
Drake, widow, boarding-house, 275 Pearl-street.
Drake, Francis, Colden
Draper, James, mariner, 46 Harman
Dremer, Henry, Pump

Drenan, John, cotton manufacturer, 52 Pearl-street.
Driskel, Jacob, mason, 16 Chesnut
Drummond, William, slopshop, 6 Peck-slip.
Drummond, Arch. 53 Pine, & store 132 Water-street.
Drummond, James, grocer, Henry
Drummond, Robert, carpenter, 25 Division
Dublayn, Henry, mariner, 36 Barclay
Dubois, Tunis, gold and silversmith, 111 Pearl
Dubois, Francis, intelligence-office, 9 Broad
Dubois, Joseph, gold and silversmith, 81 John
Dubois, Peter, cartman, Chamber
Dubuar, Mrs. staymaker, 2 Fair
Dubue, Marentille, 274 Greenwich
Duche, ———, gold and silversmith, 62 Nassau
Duchesne, Monsieur, 42 Division
Duclos, I. B. merchant, 27 James
Dudley, William, carpenter, 44 Maiden-lane.
Duer, Col. William, 37 Cortlandt-street.
Daesch, Henry, teacher, 53 Division
Duff, James, taylor, First
Duff, Nicholas, shipmaster, 29 Partition
Duffie, James, grocer, 6 Front
Duffie, John, store 20 Old-slip, & house 30 Water-str.
Duffie, Barbara, teacheress, 25 Cedar-street.
Duffie, James, mason, 25 Chamber
Duffie, William, taylor, 29 Chatham
Duffie, Hugh, taylor, 14 Augustus
Duffiel, Edward, labourer, 18 Harman
Duggan, Thomas, tanner, near Union furnace.
Duggan, Alexander, shoemaker, Chapel-street.
Duggan, Alexander, cartman, Elizabeth
Dumas, Madam, 2 Robinson
Dumont, Peter, physician, 66 Water
Dunbar, Daniel, merchant, 176 Water
Dunbar, James, merchant, 120 Water
Dunbar, George, 91 William
Duncan, Hugh, letter-carrier, 26 Cedar
Duncan, Alexander, confectioner, 158 William
Duncan, Henry, teacher, near airfurnace, Greenwich
Duncan, Thomas, 20 Broadway.
Dunham, Mathew, Washington-street.
Dunham, John, mariner, Lumber

Dunham, John, carpenter, 22 Division-street.
Dunham, David, merchant, 26 Moore
Dunham, Benjamin, cartman, 22 Division
Dunkley, Joseph, street inspector, 30 Cherry
Dunlap and Grant, merchants, 69 Stone
Dunlap, Alexander, merchant, 69 Stone
Dunlap, Miſs, 74 Gold
Dunlap, James, merchant, 163 Greenwich
Dunlap, William, merchant, 41 John
Dunlap, Margaret, 8 Lumber
Dunlap & Judah, looking-glaſs, &c. store, 189 Water
Dunlap, William, labourer, 6 Moore's-row.
Dunlap, James, grocer, Washington-street.
Dunlap, Archibald, pumpmaker, 90 John
Dunmore, widow, 7 Moore's-row.
Dunn, S. mason, corner of Thomas and Chapel streets.
Dunn, John, mariner, 1 Fayette-street.
Dunn, Michael, labourer, Oliver
Dunn, widow, 65 Division
Dunn, Jonathan, cartman, 12 Chapel
Dunn, E. and M. ladies store, 76 Broadway.
Dunn, Robert, mariner, 40 Pearl-street.
Dunn and Clark, grocers, 24 Moore
Dunn, Samuel, cooper, Magazine
Dunn, Benjamin, corner Harman & E. George
Dunn and Bowering, merchants, 241 Pearl
Dunn, Joel, mariner, 243 William
Dunn, Suſannah, grocer, 20 Fayette
Dunn, Richard, accountant, 25 New
Dunn, Thomas, merchant, 316 Pearl
Dunn, Joseph, 6 Barley
Dunn, Gersham, cartman, Barley
Dunning, Patrick, tobacconist, 5 Water
Dunscomb, Eliza, teacheress, 28 Marketfield
Dunscomb, Daniel, grocer, 58 Pearl
Dunscomb, Edward, notarial office, &c. 49 Dey
Dunscomb, Samuel, 52 Fair
Dunscomb, jun. Daniel, ironmonger, 301 Pearl

Dupont, J. 37 Church-street.
Dupuy, Lewis, musician, 345 Broadway.
Dupy, Nicholas, shoemaker, 244 Broadway.
Dura, Joseph, hairdresser, 3 Lombard-street.
Durand, Anthony, merchant, Bayard
Durando, Stephen, merchant-taylor, 714 Cherry
Durell, Jonathan, potter, 12 Roosevelt
Durham, Andrew, carpenter, 220 William
Durking, Capt. 264 Greenwich
Durie, Thomas, merchant, 12 Wall
Durning, Daniel R. ironmonger, &c. 96 Water
Durry, Thomas, shipmaster, 53 Fair
Duryee, John T. store 74 Pearl, and house 75 Broad
Duryee, Charles, weigher, 18 Marketfield
Duryee, Pratt, dry goods store, 377 Pearl
Duryee, Richard, merchant, 48 Water
Duryee and Heyer's store, 48 Water
Duryee, Mrs. 55 Wall
Duryee and Smith, merchant-taylors, 200 Water
Duryee, Peter, grocer, 58 Bowery-lane.
Dusenberry, Arnsey, cartman, 42 Chapel-street.
Dusenbury, William, cartman, 85 Reed
Dusenbury, John, carpenter, 43 Chamber
Dusenbury, Barzillai, coachmaker, 54 Chatham
Dusenbury, John, cartman, 52 Chamber
Dustan, Peter, grocer, 46 Front
Dustan, William, grocer, 63 Chamber
Dustan, James, grocer, 14 Coenties-slip, & 48 Front-str.
Dutcher, Peter, mason, Magazine-street.
Dutcher, David, mason, Magazine
Dutfield, Catharine, mantuamaker, 56 Ann
Duvall, William, taylor, 19 Partition
Duvivier, Charles, 29 James
Duyckinck, widow of Gerardus, 65 William
Duyckinck and Co. Evert, booksellers, &c. 110 Pearl
Duyckinck, jun. Gerardus, merchant, 120 Liberty
Duyckinck, sen. Christopher, sailmaker, 45 Gold
Duyckinck, jun. Christopher, sailmaker, 30 Fair
Duyckinck, Elizabeth, milliner, 72 Stone
Duyckinck, Daniel, silversmith, 75 Fair
Dupuy, James, merchant, 1 Cedar
Dye, Vincent, mill-wright, First

Dyer, James, mason, Mulberry-street.
Dyett, Joshua, merchant, 81 Broad
Dyke, Daniel, boat-builder, Pump
Dykes, Alexander, dry goods store, 174 Broadway.

E

Eacker, George I. attorney at law, 125 Water-street.
Eagan, John, grocer, 50 Cheapside.
Eagles and Morris, jewellers, 83 Nassau-street.
Eagles, John, carpenter, Orange
Eagles, William, baker, 81 Reed
Eagles, Thomas, wood inspector, 5 Chamber
Eagles, Christiana, milliner, 403 Pearl
Eagles, Thomas W. tinman and brazier, 9 Old-slip.
Eames, Henry, tanner, 7 Magazine-street.
Earland, Harman, baker, 13 Murray
Earle, William, hatter, 60 Vesey
Earle, Henry B. grocer, 28 Murray
Earle, Morris, painter and glazier, 34 Rose
Earle, Joseph, measurer, 30 Church
Earle, Samuel, carpenter, 3 Barley
Earle, Robert, carpenter, 41 Roosevelt
Earle, Thomas, shopkeeper, 197 Broadway.
Earle, James, mariner, 36 Harman-street.
Eastburn, John, shipwright, Henry
Easterly, John, labourer, 21 Marketfield
Eaton, William, baker, 14 Broad
Ebbets and Gale, china, &c. store, 71 Pearl
Ebbets, Daniel, 26 Beaver
Ebbets, Daniel I. merchant, 71 Pearl
Ebert, Philip, 37 Bowery-lane.
Eckert, Frederick, carpenter, 24 Warren-street.
Eddy, Thomas, merchant, office 1 Beekman-slip.
Eddy, John, grocer, 95 James-street.
Eden, Medcef, brewer, 28 Gold
Edgar, William, merchant, 50 Broadway.
Edwards, William C. taylor, 29 George-street.
Edwards, Edward, cartman, 21 Rose
Edwards, Cath. calender of silk stockings, 43 Nassau
Edwards, John, rigger, 96 Catharine
Edwards, Ruth, 23 Gold
Edwards, George, labourer, 2 Garden
Egbert, widow, Eagle

Egbert and son's store, 31 Peck-slip.
Egbert, John, carpenter, 176 Division-street.
Egbert, Benjamin, merchant, 54 Fair
Ehrnfreit, Conrad, taylor, 74 Bowery-lane.
Eichell, Henry, blacksmith, 26 Fair-street.
Elder, William, milkman, Harman
Eldridge, Joseph, mason, 80 Warren
Eldridge, widow, 4 Fair
Eldridge, Eli. cabinetmaker, 20 Augustus
Elliot, John, merchant-taylor, 133 Pearl
Ellis, Henry, merchant, 191 Water
Ellis, Catharine, milliner, 383 Pearl
Ellis, William, cutler, 99 Chatham
Ellis, John, tavern and boarding-house, 9 Dover
Ellis, Josiah, trader, 24 New
Ellis, John, merchant, 219 Pearl
Ellis, Richard, grocer, 170 Water
Ellis, James, smith, 5 Cherry
Ellis, Samuel, butcher, 7 Jacob
Ellison, Thomas, 42 Broadway.
Ellison, Eleanor, 39 Dey-street.
Elmes, Thomas, merchant, 234 Pearl
Elmore, James, boarding-house, 46 John
Elsworth, Francis, brass-founder, 54 Bancker
Elsworth, Verdine, 24 Vesey
Elsworth, Samuel, cartman, 103 Reed
Elsworth, John, boarding-house, 93 Front
Elsworth, Theophilus, 69 John
Elsworth, William, cartman, Little Catharine
Elsworth, Esther, 14 Beekman
Elsworth, widow, 75 John
Elsworth, John, hatter, 23 Broad
Elting, Peter, merchant, 164 Greenwich
Elting, jun. and Co. Peter, store 58 Water
Elting, John and Edward, merchants, 54 Water
Ely, Gad, young ladies' seminary, 91 Beekman
Ely, Moses, cartman, 37 Barley
Ely, John, shoemaker, 28 Murray
Ely, Abraham, cartman, 59 Cedar
Emberson, William, mariner, 56 Rutger
Embury, Peter, grocer, 54 Nassau
Enthuff, Amos, labourer, 231 William

Emmet, widow, 20 Lombard-street.
Emmet, James, cordwainer, near Union furnace.
Emmet, James, cartman, Mulberry-street.
Emmons, Isaac, grocer, Mulberry
Emmons, James, shoemaker, Chapel
Emmons, Elizabeth, seamstress, 94 Catharine
Englehart, Martin, baker, Mulberry
English, Mary, grocer, 16 Pine
Ennerton, widow, 71 Chatham
Ennis, widow, 52 Broad
Ennis, John, cartman, First
Ensley, William, nailor, Gibbs' alley.
Ensley, Daniel, butcher, 5 Reed-street.
Entiman, Christopher, tea-waterman, Mulberry
Erben, Peter, grocer, 29 Division
Ernest, John, cartman, Mulberry
Errickson, ——, grocer, Chapel, corner of Barley
Eshbock, Martin, carpenter, Magazine
Esquirol, J. upholsterer 235 William
Evans, Owen, mariner, 360 Broadway.
Evans, Charles, hardware store, 108 Maiden-lane.
Evans, Jesse, taylor, 104 Reed-street.
Evans, John, carpenter, 62 Barclay
Evans, Lewis, shipwright, 70 E. George
Evans, Jacob, Upper Reed
Evans, William, mariner, Henry
Evans, John, cartman, 41 Barclay
Evans, William, cartman, Third
Evans, William, taylor, 71 Cortlandt
Eveard, Lewis, cabinetmaker, 247 Broadway.
Everdell, James, musician, 34 Cedar-street.
Everet, John, cartman, 25 Thames
Everet, Ely, carpenter, Pump
Everingham, Gilbert, merchant, 159 Water
Everson, George, tanner and currier, 46 Ferry
Everson, Nicholas, attorney at law, 25 Pine
Everson, Barnet, mason, 109 Harman
Eves, Thomas, tavern, above airfurnace, Greenwich
Ewen, John, 47 Rutger
Ewen, Benjamin, shipwright, Third
Ewen, Duncan, shoemaker, 233 Greenwich
Eyres, Sarah, boarding-house, 350 Water-street.

F

Faber, George, porter to branch bank, 46 Cedar-strt.
Fach, John, mason, 52 Chatham
Faganham, John, rigger, 7 Lumber
Fairbairn and Richardson, merchants, 209 Broadway.
Fairchild, Robert, baker, Second-street.
Fairchild, Samuel, shipmaster, E. Rutger
Fairchild, Thomas, carpenter, Division
Fairchild, jun. Thomas, porterhouse, 11 Fair
Fairchild, Benjamin, taylor, 352 Water
Fairclo, George, rigger, 26 Fayette
Fairlie, James, clerk supreme court, 22 Cortlandt
Fairlie, Joseph, cartman, E. Washington
Fairlie, widow, Greenwich-road.
Falconer, Samuel, shoemaker, 69 Murray-street.
Falconer, William, bookseller, 124 Pearl
Falconer, Joseph, boarding-house, 34 Dey
Fanning, Thomas, carpenter, 53 Barcley
Faniworth, Jonathan, carpenter, Greenwich-road.
Far, John, ladies shoemaker, 134 William-street.
Fardon, Abraham, sailmaker, 75 Fair
Fardon, Thomas, taylor and clothier, 353 Water
Fardon & Van Wagganen, sailmakers, Stevens'-wharf
Fardon, William, cartman, 14 Barclay
Fargeson, David, tavern, lower end of Oliver
Fargo, Daniel, boatman, Bedlow
Fargue, John, brewer, 93 Greenwich
Farmar and Co. Thomas, store, 75 Front
Farmar, Nancy, confectioner, 14 Frankfort
Farmar, Thomas, merchant, 46 Broadway
Farquhar, James, wine-merchant, 150 Pearl-street.
Farquharson, Lewis, merchant, 51 Cortlandt
Farran, William, teacher, 69 George
Farrell, Peter, mariner, Birmingham-row.
Farrell, James, 27 James-street.
Farrell, Patrick, mariner, 10 Moore's-row.
Farrell, William, taylor, 289 Water-street.
Farrier, John, shipmaster, 113 Harman
Farrier, John, ropemaker, Greenwich-road.
Farrington, John, marshall, 10 Warren-street.
Farrington, James, 1 Eagle

Farthing, Abraham, carpenter, 5 Tryon-row.
Farrow, Daniel, chimney-office, Bedlow-street.
Fash, widow, milkwoman, 76 Bowery-lane.
Fash, Andrew, cartman, 51 Division street.
Fash, Elizabeth, 455 Pearl
Fashur, Henry, painter, 323 Broadway.
Fasly, Andrew, 12 Murray-street.
Fatin, Thomas, merchant, 54 Dey
Faugeres, Lewis, physician & druggist, 79 John
Faugeres, Peter, surgeon and physician, 19 Rose
Faulkner, Archibald, carpenter, 42 Partition
Faulkner, Patrick, tavern, 34 E. George
Fawpel, John, hairdresser, 5 Warren
Fay, Joseph, 6 Stone
Fay, Jacob, shoemaker, Mulberry
Fee, Philip, cartman, Upper Barley
Feely, John, labourer, 14 Moore's-row.
Feeyetta, Mrs. 153 Chatham-street.
Feitner, Peter, bookseller, 15 Warren
Fellows, John, bookseller, 68 Pine
Felter, John, shoemaker, 23 Reed
Fendine, Garrit, cartman, Harman
Fenton, Peter, cooper, 25 Reed
Fenton, John, hairdresser, 68 Gold
Ferch, M. musician, 24 Church
Ferdon, Thomas, attorney at law, 9 Water
Ferguson, James, grocer, 2 Bowery-lane.
Ferguson, Duncan, slopshop, 127 Fly-market.
Ferguson, William, turner, 13 Bowery-lane.
Ferguson, William, rigger, 12 Harman-street.
Ferguson, James, mason and grocer, Mulberry
Ferguson, James, biscuit-baker, 45 Rose
Ferguson, David, shoemaker, 55 Oliver
Ferguson, Hugh, mason, 12 Harman
Ferguson, Ebenezer, carpenter, 44 George
Ferguson, Philip, porter, 3 Pearl
Ferguson, Robert, lawyer, saw-pits, Greenwich
Ferguson, John, mariner, Mulberry-street.
Ferguson, Peter, labourer, saw-pits, Greenwich
Ferguson, William, labourer, Greenwich
Ferguson, James, grocer, Greenwich
Ferguson, Daniel, grocer, 355 Pearl

Ferguson, John, coachman, 65 Cliff-street.
Ferguson, George, leather-store, 33 Vandewater
Ferguson, James, hair-dresser, 15 Dutch
Ferguson and Sloley, porter-vaults, 278 Water
Ferrers, John, merchant, 103 Water
Ferris, Benjamin, attorney at law, 13 Fair
Ferris, Joseph, cartman, Upper Reed
Ferris, Edward, grocer, 60 Roosevelt
Ferris, jun. David, labourer, E. Rutger
Ferris and Son, John, merchants, 256 Water
Ferris, Elijah, merchant, 430 Pearl
Ferris and Oakley, dry goods store, 464 Pearl
Ferris, David, baker, Charlotte
Ferris, Thomas and George, merchants, 218 Water
Ferris, Jacob, cartman, Mutual
Ferris, Isaac, waterman, E. Rutger
Ferris, Curren, shipmaster, 22 Rutger
Ferris, Thomas, merchant, 63 James
Ferris, Cornul, & Sands, merchts. Front, near Crane-wf.
Ferry, James, hairdresser, 67 Barclay-street.
Fictor, Joseph, cartman, Upper Reed
Fief, John, cartman, 29 Barclay
Field, Charles J. joiner, Upper Reed
Fields, Oliver, grocer, 25 Division
Fields, William, tallow-chandler, 32 Lombard
Fields, Samuel, carpenter, 5 Rector
Finch, Jeremiah, taylor, 36 Barclay
Finch, Samuel, 431 Pearl
Finchett, John, tavern, Bruce's-wharf.
Fine, Jacobus, merchant, 117 Fly-market.
Fine, J. grocer, 264 Greenwich, & 169 Washington-st.
Finegan, John, merchant, 54 Front
Finglass, Susannah, 32 Beekman
Fink, Alexander, butcher, 39 Chatham
Fink, John, butcher, 23 Bowery-lane.
Fink, Philip, butcher, 39 Chatham-street.
Fink, jun. Alex. butcher, corner First and Grand
Fink, jun. Adam, tavern, 194 Greenwich
Finlay, Stephen, 45 Fair
Finn, George, taylor, 96 Warren
Finnay, Elizabeth, confectioner, 17 Water
Finnever, Alexander, labourer, 29 Cheapside.

Finraper, Cornelius, labourer, Henry-street.
Finton, James, labourer, Henry
Firth, Miss, milliner, 42 William
Fish, Nichs. supervisor, 52 Wall, & office 16 Nassau
Fisher, John, carpenter, 14 Frankfort
Fisher, Henry, labourer, First
Fisher, John, 54 New
Fisher, Peter, taylor, Leonard
Fisher, Leonard, surgeon-dentist, 451 Pearl
Fisher, George, weaver, Winne
Fisher, Albert, tea-waterman, Winne
Fisher, John, cartman, Leonard
Fisher, widow, Eagle
Fisher, John, grocer, 19 Maiden-lane.
Fisher, Alexander, tavern, 107 Front-street.
Fisher, Moses, labourer, First
Fisher, John, labourer, 85 Chamber
Fisk, Jonathan, teacher, 91 Beckman
Fitch, Wm. merch. 536 Pearl, & store Fitch's wharf.
Fitch and Taylor's shoe store, 79 William-street.
Fitch, Stephen, schoolmaster, 51 Cliff
Fitch, Mrs. E. 16 Broadway.
Fitner, Francis, grocer, 15 Warren-street.
Fitten, Alexander, optician, &c. 210 Water
Fitz, Ezekiel, sadler, 36 Bowery-lane.
Fitz, Nathaniel, leather-cutter, 78 Vesey-street.
Fitzgerald, John, butcher, Orange
Fitzpatrick, James, carpenter, 69 Chamber
Fitzpatrick, James, grocer, 74 E. George
Fitzpatrick, ——, carpenter, Bedlow
Fitzrandolph, John, carpenter, 246 William
Fladung, Frederick William, First
Flanagan, widow, 3 Pearl
Flanagan, Owen, grocer, 205 Greenwich
Flanagan, Thomas, grocer, 113 Cherry
Flavel, Anthony, carpenter, Hester
Fleet, Simon, deputy sheriff, 322 Broadway.
Fletcher, George, coachmaker, 16 Murray-street
Fletcher, Robert, city marshal, Mulberry
Fletcher, Nicholas, shipmaster, 5 Rutger
Fletcher, John, baker, 94 Catharine
Flick, widow, Mulberry

Flinn, Patrick, carpenter, Charlotte-street.
Flinn, James, grocer, 47 E. George
Flinn, James, baker, Henry, corner of Catharine
Flinn, Lewis D. merchant, 110 Water
Flinn, James, pilot, 93 Gold
Flint, William, labourer, 48 Roosevelt
Flood and Co. John, grocers, 45 E. George
Flood, Thomas, labourer, Greenwich-road.
Florentine, Thomas, cartman, Thomas-street.
Flowers, John, labourer, Greenwich-road.
Fogall, William, smith, 10 Chamber-street.
Fogarty, Elizabeth, boarding-house, 12 Broad
Foley, Marianne, milliner, 80 Roosevelt
Foley, Walter, carpenter, Lumber
Fonds, John, shoemaker, 89 Reed
Fontaine, C. G. merchant, 5 Pearl
Foord, William, shoemaker, 213 Water
Foord, John, currier, Little Catharine
Foorvit, Mathew, 10 Division
Foos, George, musician, Little Ann
Foott, Thomas, plaisterer, 394 Pearl
Forbes, widow of Duncan, shopkeeper, 28 Cliff
Forbes, Gitty, milliner, 30 Fair
Forbes, William G. gold & silversmith, 90 Broadway.
Forbes, Abraham G. marshal, 9 Rose-street.
Forbes, Thomas, cartman, Mulberry
Forbes, M. milliner, 157 William
Forbes, Sarah, 23 Rutger
Forbes, Peter, baker, 27 Dey
Forbes, John, 16 Nassau
Forbes, William A. inspector of customs, 96 Gold
Forbes, Collin V. G. watchmaker, 90 Broadway.
Forbes, John & Bennett, merchants, 111 Water-street.
Forbes, James, merchant, 122 Front
Forbus, Alexander, shoemaker, 55 Augustus
Forbus, Christopher, shoemaker, Winne
Force, William, cartman, Greenwich-road.
Force, ———, labourer, Greenwich-road.
Ford and Lockwood, merchants, 360 Water-street.
Ford, Eliakim, merchant, 360 Water
Ford, widow of George, 60 Catharine
Ford, Benjamin, shipwright, 90 James

Ford, Lewis, carpenter, 31 Reed-street.
Ford, Lewis, gardener, Third
Fordham, George, carpenter and grocer, Lumber
Fordham, Caleb, carpenter, 14 L. George
Fordham, Robert, cooper, 70 William
Foreman, Henry, cartman, 59 Chapel
Forman, George, printer, 64 Water
Forman, Lewis, merchant, 12 Division
Forman & Co. Lewis, merchants, 106 Murray's wharf.
Forrest, David, grocer, 96 Warren-street.
Forrest, James, accountant, 15 Partition
Forrestel, Thomas, soapboiler, Charlotte
Forrester, John, merchant, 9 Chatham-row.
Forshee, James, 150 Chatham-street.
Forsyth, Jacob, hat coverer, 24 Pearl-street.
Forsyth, John, merchant-taylor, 108 Water
Fortin, Claude, merchant, 286 Pearl
Fortune, Euphemia, boarding-house, Chatham-row.
Fosbrook, Wm. surgeon's inst. maker, 5 Beekman-str.
Foster, Joseph, sawyer, 83 Chamber
Foster, Henry, mariner, 43 Rutger
Foster, the Rev. Benjamin, D. D. 37 Gold
Foster, Charles, teacher, 77 Murray
Foster, Andrew, mariner, 38 George
Foster, Nathaniel, cartman, South
Foster, George, carver, 4 Hague
Foster & Giraud, merchs. Front, corner Taylor's whf.
Fotheringham, Thomas, stonecutter, 5 Barclay-street.
Fought, Jacob, baker, 67 Chatham
Fouillolle, Louis, 9 Roosevelt
Foules, John, cabinetmaker, 60 Barclay
Fountaine, Margaret, 58 Barclay
Fountaine, John, mason, 58 Barclay
Fountaine, widow, Charlotte
Fountaine, Garrit, grocer, South
Fournequet, Lewis, gold and silversmith, 53 Ann
Fowler, Frederick, cartman, 12 Reed
Fowler, David, mason, Magazine
Fowler, Thomas, hatter, 250 William
Fowler, Richardson, cartman, 3 Herman
Fowler, Mrs. 43 Robinson
Fowler, Daniel, labourer, 44 Reed

Fowler, Willsey, mariner, 441 Pearl-street.
Fowler, widow, Birmingham-row.
Fowler, ———, mariner, 43 Robinson-street.
Fowler, David, mason, Cross
Fox, Patrick, cartman, 67 Church
Fox, George, taylor, 171 Water
Fox, Mathew, butcher, Winne
Fox, John, grocer, 251 Broadway.
Fox, Robert, grocer, 90 Water-street.
Fram, George, mariner, 45 Cortlandt
Frame, and Co. Jesse, leather store, 33 Vandewater
Francis, Elizabeth, 12 Water
Francis, Joseph, caulker, 46 Harman
Francis, Lewis, sexton, 47 Chatham
Franklin, and Co. Anthony, store 255 Pearl
Franklin, Mary, 16 Cooper
Franklin, Gideon, coasting-pilot, 8 Ferry
Franklin, and Co. Henry, merchants, 173 Water
Franklin, John, merchant, 105 Cherry
Franklin, Walter, flour merchant, 103 Cherry
Franklin, Robinson, & Co's. counting house 279 Pearl
Franklin, Samuel, merchant, 279 Pearl
Franklin, Thomas, merchant, 282 Pearl
Franklin, Abraham, merchant, 279 Pearl
Franklin, Mathew, merchant, 161 Water
Franklin, jun. John, merchant, 327 Pearl
Franks, William, miniature painter, 167 William
Fraser, William, merchant, 38 Beaver
Fraser, Christian, teacher, Hester
Fraser, Donald, teacher, 178 William
Fraser, Duncan, cartman, 8 Batavia-lane.
Fraser, Josiah, carpenter, 58 Rutger-street.
Fraser, William, inspector of lumber, 12 Oliver
Fraser, Alexander, grocer, Lumber
Fraser, Daniel, cowkeeper, 146 William
Fraw, Madam, 142 Pearl
Frazer, Jonathan, 42 Reed
Frazer, William, grocer, 61 Chamber
Frazer, Robert, shoemaker, 67 Chatham
Frazer, John, carpenter, 24 George
Frazer, Samuel, shipwright, Henry

NEW-YORK DIRECTORY.

Frazer and Larit, bakers, 10 Barclay-ſtreet.
Frazer, Thomas, ſawyer, ſaw-pits, Greenwich.
Frazer, John, carpenter, 82 Liberty-ſtreet.
Frazer, William, carpenter, 36 Lombard
Frederick, Adam, 45 Bowery-lane.
Frederick, Henry, maſon, 27 Barclay-ſtreet.
Frederick, Henry, breeches-maker, 50 Maiden-lane.
Frederick, James, carpenter, 96 Harman-ſtreet.
Frederick, John, ſhoemaker, Mott
Freeborn, Robert, grocer, Lumber
Freeckes, John C. ſtore 157 Fly-market.
Freeland, John, ſhoemaker, 37 Chapel-ſtreet.
Freeton, Abraham, fan-light-maker, 110 Pearl
Freeman, Samuel, cartman, 246 William
Freeman, Amos, grocer, Greenwich-road.
Freeman, Samuel, 69 Warren-ſtreet.
Freeman, Thomas, carpenter, 91 Diviſion
Freeman, Judah, Corlaer's-hook.
FREEMASON Lodge rooms, 66 Liberty, 90 William, 87 Naſſau, 2 George, 3 South, 89 Fair, 31 Ann, corner of Water and Oliver, &c.
French, Benjamin, Firſt
Frend, John, tavern, 18 Bowery-lane.
Friday, Jacob, grocer, 276 Water-ſtreet.
Friday, Paul, cartman, 31 Auguſtus
Fries, Thomas, mariner, 3 Rutger
Friſk, John, cooper, Charlotte
Fritkeey, Sarah, milliner, 32 Beaver
Fritot, Charles Euſtache, 37 Barclay
Fritz, Elias, dealer, Charlotte
Fritz, John, labourer, 3 Reed
Fritz, Henry, ſadler, &c. 98 Chatham
Frizell, Charles, mariner, 28 Rooſevelt
Froſt, Ezra, ſhoemaker, Birmingham-row.
Frod, E. hairdreſſer, 62 Maiden-lane.
Froſt and Ward, merchants, 302 Pearl ſtreet
Froſt and Sober, dry goods ſtore, 136 Chatham.
Froſt, Jacob, merchant, 302 Pearl
Froſt and Cock, merchants, 5 Peck-ſlip.
Froſt, William, merchant, 226 William-ſtreet.
Froſt, Joſeph, cartman, 13 Stone
Fueter, Daniel, goldſmith, 126 Cherry

Fullam, Michael, grocer, 37 Catharine-street.
Fullam, John, grocer, 239 William
Fuller, John, carpenter, 13 Thomas
Fuller, Benjamin, painter, 25 Chapel
Fuller, James, shoemaker, 445 Pearl
Fuller, Joseph, cabinetmaker, 5 Robinson
Fulmer, widow of John, Sixth
Funk, Nathaniel, pilot, 70 Gold
Funk, John, pilot, 74 Fair
Furman, Gabriel, alderman, 106 Broadway.
Furman, J. painter & glazier, Chatham-square.
Furman, Woods, carpenter, Orchard-street.
Furman, George, painter and glazier, 17 Division
Furman, Richard, alderman, Division
Furman, Walter, cartman, 39 Division
Furman, Job, carpenter, 53 Division
Furman and Mapes, merchant-taylors, 245 Water
Furman, Nathan, 245 Water
Furman, Samuel, shoemaker, 53 Division
Furtado, Jacob, merchant, 95 Fair

G

Gabel, Augustus, 35 Church-street.
Gabel, Henry, musician, Bayard, corner of Winne
Gaffet, John, cartman, 52 Vesey
Gahn and Mumford's counting-house, 51 Pine
Gahn, Henry, merchant, 51 Pine
Gaill, William, carpenter, 2 Temple
Gaine, Hugh, bookseller and stationer, 148 Pearl
Gaine and Ten Eyck's book-store, 148 Pearl
Gains, George W. sailmaker, 14 Barclay
Galatian, William W. upholsterer, 65 Broad
Galbreath and Elmes' store, 234 Pearl
Gale, W. W. porter-house, 139 Cherry
Gale, Marinus, book-binder, 36 Lombard
Gale, Reuben, mason, Harman
Gale and Campbell, grocers, 122 Broad
Gale, Samuel, china-store, 71 Pearl
Gallahar, Patrick, shoemaker, 4 New
Gallahar, Benjamin, carpenter, 253 William
Gallalee, Mathew, baker, 3 Cliff
Gallaudet, Paul, hairdresser, 141 Chatham
Gallop, Benjamin, 27 Broadway.
Gallop, Mrs. 15 Partition-street.

Galloway, James, rigger, Pump-street.
Gamage, John, physician, 20 John
Gamble, Ambrose, cartman, Hester
Gamble, Andrew, cartman, Hester
Ganly, Henry, taylor, 12 Barclay
Gantley, Sarah, teacher, Lumber
Gantz, Gabriel, 174 Division
Gantz, Francis, sen. shipwright, Pump
Gantz, jun. Francis, shipwright, Pump
Gantz, Otto, carpenter, Potter's-hill.
Garbrance, Peter, turner, &c. 60 Nassau-street.
Gardere, Alexius, 156 Chatham, store Murray's-whf.
Gardiner, Timothy, nailor, Harman-street.
Gardner, Edward, Greenwich-road.
Gardner, Thomas, cartman, Mott-street.
Gardner, Nathaniel, rigger, 34 Liberty
Gardner, Gaife, 16 Barclay
Gardner, Hiram, ladies shoemaker, 114 Broadway.
Gardner, Charles, porter-house, 77 Fair-street.
Gardner, Solomon, shoemaker, 289 Water
Gardner, James, merchant, 75 William
Gardner, Thomas, merchant, 212 William
Gardner, William, taylor and tavern, 239 William
Garner, Frederick, merchant-taylor, 306 Pearl
Garey, Margaret, widow, Pope's alley.
Garey, widow, Corlaer's-hook.
Garland, widow, 85 Bowery-lane.
Garosey, Enoch, shoemaker, 89 Fair-street.
Garr, Andrew, ship-builder, 118 Cherry
Garret, Michael, smith, Mulberry
Garrick, Mary, Elizabeth
Garrigues, White Thomas, shopkeeper, 6 E. George
Garrison, John, grocer, Greenwich-road.
Garrison, Isaac, Bowery-lane.
Garrison and Lockhart, shoemakers, 285 Water-street.
Garrison, Benjamin, lumber-merchant, 11 Cherry.
Garrison, Peter, labourer, Henry-street.
Garrison, John, cartman, Chamber
Garfan, Thomas, grocer, 46 Cortlandt
Garfan, ——, baker, 33 Ann
Gartler, widow, Charlotte
Gash, Ursula, Pope's alley.

Gaffner, Henry, shoemaker, 91 James-street.
Gaffner, Isaac, mariner, 79 Murray
Gaffner, Peter, grocer, 56 Barclay
Gaffner, John G. sadler & harness maker, 96 Chatham
Gaffner, John, 36 Dey
Gaston, Ide, grocer, Elizabeth, corner Hester
Gaston, Thomas T. accountant, 32 Lumber
Gates, Michael, cartman, 41 Chamber
Gates, Leonard, smith, 77 Chatham
Gatfield, Benjamin, leather-dresser, 231 Pearl
Gatfield, Charles, cutler, Mulberry
Gatter Samuel, hairdresser, 41 Water
Gattey, Henry, math. instrumentmaker, 274 Water
Gaudu, Louis, shipjoiner, 54 E. George
Gauk, James, engraver, 41 Cedar
Gaunt, widow, silk stocking washer, 55 John
Gautier, Samuel, taylor, 61 Gold
Gautier, Lewis A. shoemaker, 37 Augustus
Gautzret, Xaviere, dry goods store, 237 Broadway.
Gay, Luther, grocer, 185 William-street.
Gay and Barnum, grocers, 78 Beekman
Gay, Kirkpatrick, joiner, 42 James
Gedney, Robert, combmaker, 1 Mutual
Gedney and Co. merchants, 59 Maiden-lane.
Gedney, John, mason, 21 Harman-street
Gedney, Elizabeth, 170 Broadway.
Geer, George, tavern, 13 Ann-street.
Geer, Thomas, mariner, 93 Reed
Geer, Ebenezer, shoemaker, 10 Lombard
Geib, John, organbuilder, First
Gelston, M. attorney at law. 34 Liberty
Gelston, John, merch.t 53 Beaver, and store 160 Front
Gelston, David, merchant, 89 Pearl, and 170 Front
Gelston, John, carpenter, 7 Warren
Gelston, William, carpenter, 14 Murray
George, Joseph, currier, 60 Broad, and 44 Tr
George, Ruth, 82 James
Geraud, ——, 26 Harman
Geraerdt, I. P. 58 Partition
German, Jacob, joiner, 19 Dutch
Gerard, William, merchant, 20 Broad
Gervaise, Nicholas, Eagle

Gethan & Son, Ths. skinners & glovers, 35 Frankfort-st.
Geuie, Christian F. taylor, 369 Pearl
Gibbons, James, teacher, 12 Chamber-street.
Gibbons, Margaret, fruiterer, 25 Broad
Gibbs, widow of George, poulterer, Mulberry
Gibbs, Isaac, joiner, 37 James
Gibo, I. J. grocer, Little Ann
Gibson, John, mason, Eagle
Gibson, Alexander, cooper, Batavia-lane.
Gibson, James, shipwright, 21 Batavia-lane.
Gibson, Thomas, shipwright, 58 Bowery-lane.
Gibson, Joseph, labourer, 58 E. George-street.
Gibson, Lewis, carpenter, 37 Augustus
Gibson, Jane, 25 Cedar
Gibson, William, hairdresser, 111 Maiden-lane.
Gibson, James, accountant, 193 William-street.
Gibson, Aaron, taylor, Greenwich-road.
Gibson, Margaret, 59 Chatham-street
Gibson, Thomas, house and sign painter, 27 John
Gibson and M'Farlane, porter-house, 8 Cedar
Gifting, Francis, 21 Liberty
Gifting, William, carpenter, 40 Chapel
Gifting and Herring, porter-house, 21 Liberty
Gifford and Scotland, cabinetmakers, 25 John
Gifford, Alexander, mason, 82 Reed
Gilbert, William W. Greenwich.
Gilbert, Garrit, merchant, 189 Broadway.
Gilbert, Aaron, measurer, 60 Chamber-street.
Gilbert, John W. 21 Partition
Gilbert, Thomas, 94 Greenwich
Gilbert, John, cartman, 46 Reed
Gilberts, James, labourer, Little Catharine
Gilchrist, Robert, grocer, 34 Pearl
Gildersleeve, ——, grocer, William, corner Barley
Giles, John, shoemaker, Winne
Giles, Robert, carpenter, 40 Rose
Giles, Col. Aquila, 54 Broadway.
Gilfert, George, musical magazine, 177 Broadway.
Gilford, Henry, carpenter, 36 Harman-street.
Gilford & Son, Samuel, 122 William & store 76 Front
Gilford, Benjamin, cooper, 10 Cooper
Gill, Thomas, carpenter, 14 Jacob

Gill, James, shoemaker, 2 Ann-street.
Gill, ———, whitewasher, 23 Market
Gillander, ———, shipmaster, 29 Beckman
Gifferd, Charles, cartman, 215 William
Gillies, Alexander, confectioner, Mott
Gillespie, widow, 109 Harman
Gillespie and Co. Colin, merchants, 156 Pearl
Gillespie, Charles, grocer, 17 Bowery-lane.
Gillhope, John, huckster, 8 Cheapside.
Gilliher, Susannah, 12 Chapel-street.
Gillman, Charles, butcher, 34 Church.
Gilmore, Charles, boot and shoemaker, 325 Pearl
Gilmore, Benjamin, boot and shoemaker, 25 Barclay
Gilmore, Joseph, marshal, 441 Pearl
Gilmore, Mary, shopkeeper, 381 Pearl
Gilmore, John, carpenter, Winne
Gilmore, John, cabinetmaker, 43 Augustus
Gilmore, James, shoemaker, 5 Bancker
Giraud, Frederick, cooper, 127 Front
Giraud, James, hatter, 244 Water
Giraud, widow Ann, 4 Cortlandt
Girault, ———, miniature painter, 241 Broadway.
Glass, James, grocer, 34 Pearl-street.
Glass, Alexander S. Nassau, corner of Beckman
Glean, Abraham, painter, &c. Bedlow
Gleeson, Mathew, grocer, 340 Water
Glentworth, Thos. custom-house boatman, 60 Gold
Glover, John I. merchant, 223 Pearl
Glover, John G. merchant, 174 Broadway.
Goater, Thomas, ladies shoemaker, 1 Cedar-street.
Gobert, Charles, merchant, 64 Pearl
Gochee, Garrit, baker, 69 Division
Godby, William, carpenter, 336 Water
Goddard, Thomas, shoemaker, 59 Ann
Godfrey, Ebenezer, shoemaker, 414 Pearl
Godin, Francis, embroiderer, 34 Cedar
Godwin, Elizabeth, widow, 80 Reed
Godwin, widow, 3 Thomas
Goederfoon, Mathys, news-carrier, 295 Broadway.
Goelet, Peter, merchant, 113 and 115 Pearl-street.
Goelet, Peter P. merchant, 65 Pearl
Goelet, Robert Ratsey, merchant, 44 Water

Goerck, Caffimer T. city surveyor, 76 Gold-street.
Goggin, Edward C. merchant, 432 Pearl
Goix and Co. N. merchants, 41 Cortlandt
Gilien, James, carpenter, Winne
Golden, Charles, grocer, Crofs, corner Mulberry
Golder, Margaret, grocer, 1 New-flip.
Goldfmith, Thomas, 33 Lombard-street.
Gollow, Chriftopher, cooper, 51 Roofevelt
Gomes, John, joiner, 71, and fhop 66 Beekman
Gomez, Rebecca, 37 Stone
Gomez, Mofes, fig blue manufactory, 64 Naffau
Gomez, jun. Ifaac, merchant, 109 Water
Gomez, Ben. bookbinder & ftationer, 97 Maiden-lane.
Gomez, Efther, widow, 109 Water-street.
Gomez, jun. Abraham, broker, 29 Ann
Good, William, carpenter, 46 Cherry
Goodberlat, John, taylor, 7 Vandewater
Goodeve, John, foap and candlemaker, 23 Bridge
Goodeve & Brown, foap & candlemakers, 23 Bridge
Goodhart, George, butcher, Bayard
Goodman, W. grocer, Catharine-flip, corner Water-ft.
Goodrich, Charles, merchant, 103 Maiden-lane.
Goodwin, William, waterman, Birmingham-row.
Goodwin and Adams, druggifts, 193 Pearl
Goodwin, Oliver, druggift, 193 Pearl
Goodwin and Clarke, druggifts, 144 Pearl
Goodwin, Peter, cooper, Eagle
Goold, Edward, merchant, 37 Wall
Goold and fon's, Edward, counting-houfe, 39 Wall
Goole, Robert, carpenter, Pump
Gordon, widow, boarding-houfe, 144 Chatham
Gordon, George, mariner, 19 Cheapfide.
Gordon, Alexander, filverfmith, 40 William-street.
Gordon, Lewis, carpenter, Third
Gordon, Thomas, fringe-weaver, 71 James
Gordon, William, labourer, E. Wafhington
Gordon, Samuel, papermaker, 36 Church
Gordon, James, filverfmith, 68 Ann
Gordonear, William, painter, Eagle
Gorman, Patrick, grocer, 300 Water
Gorman, Edward, labourer, 11 Moore
Goffin, John, cabinetmaker, Thomas

Gofman, Jacob, carpenter, 4 Vesey-street.
Gofman, Robert, carpenter and builder, 108 Liberty
Gofman, George, mason and builder, 112 Liberty
Gofman, James, ladies' shoemaker, 104 Pearl
Gofwell, widow, 72 Warren
Gouge, Joseph, blockmaker, 8 Rose
Gould, John, rigger, 49 Augustus
Gould, John, cartman, 4 Warren
Gould, Stephen, shoemaker, Henry
Gould, John, taylor, 17 Peck-slip.
Goulden, Hugh, Charlotte-street.
Gourney, James, shopkeeper, 90 Chatham
Gouverneur and Kemble, Gouverneur's wharf.
Gouverneur, Isaac, merchant, 98 Front-street.
Gouverneur, Nicholas, merchant, 23 Beaver
Gowan, A. portrait-painter, 102 Pearl
Gowan, Joseph, mariner, Charlotte
Gowan, Mrs. M. milliner, 102 Pearl
Goynard, Lewis P. glass and china store, 51 Murray
Grace, Mary, 192 William
Gracie, Archibald, merchant, 110 Broadway.
Grady, John, shoemaker, 62 Barclay-street.
Graff, John, butcher, 35 Bowery-lane.
Graham, Jacob, shipmaster, 51 Lumber-street.
Graham, George, plumber, 30 Augustus
Graham, John C. teacher, 74 Barclay
Graham, Mrs. Misses boarding-school, 91 Liberty
Graham, Mrs. 97 Water
Graham, jun. John, merchant, 111 William
Graham, Elizabeth, 85 Broad
Graham, Archibald, rigger, 17 Bowery-lane.
Graham, John, rigger, 19 Herman-street.
Graham, Peter, cabinetmaker, 19 Robinson
Graham, Andrew, mason, Magazine
Graham, Ebenezer, M. D. 126 Water
Graham, Sarah, boarding-house, 22 Malden-lane.
Graham, John, cartman, Jay, corner of Washington-st
Grandine, John, 65 Fair
Grange, T. porter-vaults, 130 Cherry
Granger, John, shoemaker, 17 Augustus
Granger, Mathew, Third
Grant, John, cartman, Charlotte

Grant, Ann, 15 Cedar-street.
Grant, Ann N. 21 Beaver
Grant, James, 58 Roosevelt
Grant, John, merchant, 69 Stone
Grant, Michael, tavern, 242 Water
Grant, John, tea-waterman, Division
Grant, John, mason, Cherry-street, Ship-yards
Grant, John, baker, 13 Murray
Grant, William, taylor, 45 Division
Grant, Peter, nailor, Gibb's-alley
Grant, Solomon, grocer, Cherry, corner George
Grant, William, pilot, 60 Ann
Grapin, Claude, grocer and pastry-cook, 104 Broad
Graves, Rosewell, grocer, 154 Front
Graves, John B. merchant, 105 Water
Gray, Thomas, pilot, 71 Ann
Gray, Peter, cook, 55 Cortlandt
Gray, John, sawyer, Mulberry
Gray, James, boarding-house, 82 Barclay
Gray, James, taylor, 38 Lombard
Green, Increase, cartman, 17 Thomas
Green, Martha, Barley
Green and Lovett, merchants, 117 Front
Green, Susannah, 46 Fair
Green, John, merchant, 21 Cherry
Green, Thomas, grocer, 275 Greenwich
Green, Abraham, carpenter, 95 Chamber
Green, Paul, cartman, 30 Vandewater
Green and Co. William, tobacconists, 216 Water
Green, William, tobacconist, 7 Rose
Green, William, carpenter, 95 Chamber
Green, Samuel, carpenter, 28 Catharine
Green, widow, 90 Catharine
Green, Thomas, labourer, 32 E. George
Green, William, mariner, 273 Broadway
Green, Henry, mariner, 24 Roosevelt-street
Green, John, physician, 57 E. George
Greenfield, John, shipmaster, 8 Pine
Greenleaf, Thomas, printer and bookseller, 54 Wall
Greenwood, John, dentist, 3 Church
Greenwood, C. mathematical inst. maker, 126 Front
Greig, James, shipwright, Henry

Grellet, Jos. state prison shoe store, 1 Burling-slip.
Grenzebach, John, grocer, 1 Chatham-street.
Gresenhouse, John, farrier, Upper Reed
Grices, John, grocer, 21 Chatham
Griffen, widow, 49 Cherry-street.
Griffen, William, grocer, 19 Beaver
Griffen, Thomas, milkman, 49 Reed
Griffen, Peter, auctioneer, 124 Water
Griffen, Henry, watchmaker, 318 Water, & 49 Cherry
Griffith, Isaac, labourer, 61 Reed
Griffith, jun. John, merchant, 69 Maiden-lane.
Griffith, Hugh M. bookbinder, 238 Greenwich-str.
Griffith, William, silkdyer, 72 Broad
Griffith, John & Nath. merchants, 69 Maiden-lane.
Griffiths, James, labourer, 360 Broadway.
Griffiths, Jas. money &c. broker, 268 Greenwich-str.
Griffiths, widow, 19 Murray
Grigg, John, ironmonger, 87 Cherry
Grigg, Henry, merchant, 23 Partition
Grim, David and Philip, merchants, 23 Cedar
Grim, Jacob, tanner, Magazine
Grim, Henry, tea-waterman, Winne
Grim, Peter, tanner, Magazine
Grim, Charles, taylor, Mulberry
Grimes, Patrick, taylor, 41 Oliver
Grinard, Navenson, carpenter, 12 Oliver
Grinding, William, tavern, 20 Front
Grisdall, Margaret, 8 Pine
Griswold, Jedediah, grocer, 7 Front
Griswold, Joseph, 22 Chatham
Griswold, Thomas, distiller, 43 Oliver
Griswold, Nath. L. & George, flour-store, 169 Front
Groen, Garrit, hatter, Pump
Groshon, John P. brewer, 7 Barley
Gross, Peter, cartman, 46 Reed
Gross, Diederick, cartman, 21 Skinner
Groteclofs, Gilbert, flour-store, 49 Barclay
Grozart, John, merchant, 51 Beekman
Gruber, Nicholas, Second
Gruet, Peter, Bowery-lane.
Grunt, John, tea-waterman, Division-street.
Guarry, E. James, cock, 153 Chatham

Guercy, Dominick, gold & silversmith, 113 William-st.
Guerlain, Lewis H. merchant, 89 Broad
Guerlain and Co's counting-house, 27 Stone
Guest, Lewis, shoemaker, 14 E. George
Guillemat, Jean Baptiste, boarding-house, 2 Cherry
Guinnel, Millison, tavern, Lumber
Guion, Isaac, carpenter, 67 Harman
Guion, Monmouth, grocer, 309 Water
Guion, Elijah, carpenter, Henry
Gunn, Sarah, silk-dyer, 74 Gold
Gunn, William, teacher, Division
Gunn, James, oysterman, 48 Cedar
Gunton, Mark, painter, Little-Catharine
Guppy and Armstrong, merchants, 126 Broadway.
Gurner, Isaac, shoemaker, 98 Reed-street.
Gurner, Phillip, 233 Greenwich.
Guynyard, Nicholas, mariner, 90 Gold-street.

H

Habermel, John, grocer, 121 Greenwich-street.
HACKENSACK stage-office, Hobuck ferry-house
Hacker, Hoystead, pilot for the Sound, 91 Catharine-st.
Hacket, T. G. translator of languages, 18 William
Haddock, widow, 25 Frankfort
Hadley, jun. George, cartman, 97 Harman
Hadley, Isaac, cartman, 64 Murray
Hadley, Abraham, carpenter, 40 Chapel
Hadley, John, inspector of lumber, 21 Roosevelt
Hadley, W. cartman, 26 Barclay
Haff, John P. shoe and bootmaker, 207 & 247 Water
Haff, John, shipmaster, 2 Coenties-slip.
Hagadorn, Francis, cartman, Second-street.
Hagerman, Jacob, ladies hat store, 136 William
Hagerman, Andrew, measurer, 54 Dey
Hague, John, shipwright, 110 Harman
Haight, Benj. sadler & harness-maker, 152 Broadway.
Haight, Thomas, grocer, 88 James-street.
Haight, David, sadler, 169 Broadway.
Haines and Denton's store, 4 South-street.
Hains, Daniel, cartman, Third
Hake, Samuel, merchant, 45 Front, and 71 Stone
Hall, William, mariner, Roosevelt
Hall, John, cartman, Norfolk

Hall, George, cartman, near Union-furnace.
Hall, Thomas, shipwright, Lumber-street.
Hall, Caleb, cartman, Hague, corner of Skinner
Hall, Asa, carpenter, Barley
Hall, Archibald, 94 Catharine-street.
Hall, Luke, mariner, 13 Skinner
Hall, Mary, widow, 96 Catharine
Hall, Margaret, widow, Gibb's-alley.
Hall, Stephen, Eagle
Hall, Samuel, cartman, near Alms-house.
Hall, Peter, pilot, 274 Water-street.
Hall, Drew, silversmith, 45 Gold
Hallam, Lewis, comedian, 18 John
Hallam, M. comedian, 200 William
Hallet and Co. Jer. & A. S. ironmongers, 178 Water
Hallet, Richard S. merchant, 39 John
Hallet, Bowne, and Co. merchants, 182 Water
Hallet, James, coachmaker, 194 Broadway.
Hallet, jun. James, cabinetmaker, 9 Beekman-street.
Hallet, Thomas, grocer, Lumber
Hallet, John, wheelwright, 53 Bowery-lane.
Hallet, Samuel, 53 Division-street.
Hallet, Samuel, grocer, Bowery-lane.
Hallet, Jeremiah, merchant, 221 Pearl-street.
Hallet, widow, 26 Church
Hallet, Samuel, gardener, Bowery-lane.
Halliday, William, grocer, 203 William
Halliday, Catharine, 29 Vesey
Halliday, John, taylor, 204 Greenwich
Hallowell, Samuel, carpenter, 7 Rector
Halsey, John, merchant, 85 Pearl
Halsey, Jacob, carpenter and builder, 80 Chamber
Halsey, Jabez, customhouse-officer, 105 Liberty
Halsey, Susannah, boarding-house 25 Moore
Halsey, Stephen, carpenter, Saw-pits, Greenwich.
Halstead, Benjamin, gold & silversmith, 67 Broad-street
Halstead, Pearton, carpenter, 70 Chatham
Halstead, Cristopher, carpenter and builder, 54 James
Halstead, John, carpenter, 14 Rose
Halstead and Sprong, grocers, 22 Front
Ham, Coenrad W. baker, 45 Broad
Ham, Wandle, baker, 45 Broad

Ham, Richard C. baker, 63 Water-street.
Hamersley, Andrew, 109 Pearl
Hamersley, William, physician, 18 Broadway.
Hamersley, Lewis C. & Ths. ironmongers, 109 Pearl-st.
Hamilton, Alex. I. mercht. and distiller, 286 Water
Hamilton, James, carpenter, 17 Dutch
Hamilton, Andrew, cartman, Hester
Hamilton, John, drayman, 12 Lumber
Hamilton, Alexander, counsellor at law, 26 Broadway.
Hamilton, Robert, mariner, 26 Stone-street.
Hamilton, John, smith, 333 Broadway.
Hamilton, widow, Duane-street.
Hamilton, John, silversmith, 26 Harman
Hamilton, James, 4 Bancker
Hammil, John, printer, 31 Cherry
Hammil, John, labourer, Charlotte
Hammond, Abijah, merchant, 229 Broadway.
Hand, Hannah, mantuamaker, 58 James-street.
Handaside, Charles, tavern, Broad
Handcock, John, mariner, 448 Pearl
Handcock, William, cabinetmaker, Garden
Hannah, Andrew, grocer, 9 Chatham
Hannah, Mary, Upper Reed
Hannan, Henry, shoe and slop store, 11 Old-slip.
Hannan, John D. baker, 19 Augustus
Hannar, John, grocer, 34 Roosevelt
Hannas, Thomas, shoemaker, 36 Vandewater
Hannay, Anna, 20 William
Hannes, Joseph, cooper, 309 Water
Hanrahan, James, trader, 2 Division
Hanson, Mary, 72 Broadway.
Hanton, Jeremiah, mariner, 1 Lumber-street.
Hardcastle, Joshua, printer, 50 James
Hardenbrook, John A. broker, 54 Nassau
Hardenbrook, Gerardus, tavern, 104 Chatham
Hardenbrook, Wm. city sealer & tinman, 293 Pearl
Hardenbrook, Wm. A. merchant, 22 Bowery-lane.
Hardenbrook, Peter, paver, 57 Lumber-street.
Hardenbrook, jun. Wm. brass-founder, 22 Beekman
Hardie, James, A. M. teacher of languages, Ryder
Hardie, James, stonecutter, Beaver-lane.
Hardie, Thomas, silk-dyer, 69 Fair-street.

Harding, Stephen R. shipmaster, 29 Beekman-street.
Harding, Richard, carver and gilder, Cross
Harding, Seth, boarding-house, 147 Water
Harding, John, hatter, 116 Cherry
Harding, widow Elizabeth, 12 Thames
Hardmen, John, cooper, Gibbs'-alley.
Hardy, Joseph, merchant, 7 Thames-street.
Hare, Samuel, carpenter, 26 Barclay
Hare, Jonathan, carpenter, Division
Hargrave, Henry, cartman, Sixth
Hargrave, Robert, Little Catharine
Harky, Dennis, labourer, 5 Harman
Harison, Richard, 227 Broadway, & office 7 Wall-st.
Harlow, Nathaniel, mariner, Colden,
Harman, John D. baker, 19 Augustus
Harmony, Nicholas, 65 Division
Harned, Jonathan, merchant-taylor, 9 William
Harned, David, carpenter, 45 Robinson
Harned, Nathaniel, carpenter, Mulberry
Harned, William, 83 Division
Harper, widow, First
Harper, William, labourer, 12 Moore's-row.
Harper, James, grocer, 154 Fly-market.
Harper, Andrew, carpenter, 63 Chatham-street.
Harper, James, taylor, Essex
Harpur, Gideon, cooper and culler, 50 Gold
Harr, Michael, baker, 1 Skinner
Harrington, John R. attorney at law, 117 Water
Harrington, John, cartman, Lumber
Harrington, John, hairdresser, 10 Wall
Harrington and Bayard, grocers, E. Rutger
Harriott, David, collector, 25 Frankfort
Harriott, Conrad, butcher, Elizabeth
Harris, Moses, taylor, 15 Chapel
Harris, Benjamin, shipmaster, 116 Chatham

Harris, ——, rigger, 72 Ann-street.
Harrison, Edward, labourer, Bedlow
Harrison, Thomas, 33 Barclay
Harrison, John, deputy marshal of U. S. 100 John
Harrison, Mary, 15 Pine
Harrison, Henry, mason, 31 Augustus
Harrison, John, printer and stationer, 3 Peck-slip.
Harsin, George, merchant, 151 Water-street.
Harsin, Garrit, 39 William
Harsin & Caverly, store 27 Albany-pier.
Harsin, Jacob, 142 Chatham-street.
Hart, Bernard, insurance broker, 12 Broad
Hart, Ephraim, auctioneer, 3 New, and 84 Broadway.
Hart, Eleazer, 27 Reed-street.
Hart, Robert, grocer, 8 Charlotte
Hart, widow, 21 Fair
Hart, Jacob, grocer, 29 Chesnut
Hart, Elisha, 447 Pearl
Hart, Jacob, merchant, 63 Ann
Hart, Lewis, hairdresser, 280 Water
Hartman, Lewis, grocer, 238 William
Hartman, widow, Eagle
Hartshorne, Richard, merchant, 16 Dey
Hartshorne and Lindley, merchants, 27 Beekman
Hartshorne, William, merchant, 71 Nassau
Hartung, John Daniel, 83 Maiden-lane.
Harvey, George, lamplighter, 31 Church-street.
Harvey, Thomas, merchant, 134 Front
Harvey, George, labourer, 106 Division
Harvey, David, cooper, Cherry
Harvey, Henry, mariner, 64 Frankfort
Harvey, Samuel, painter and glazier, 58 Chamber
Harvey, John, 1 Rector
Harvey, Lewis, shoemaker, Barley
Harwood, Edward, porter-house, 4 Cherry
Haskin, B. F. commission-merchant, 114 Pearl
Hassall, Hamlet, carpenter, 20 Cherry
Haskin, Thomas, mariner, 77 James
Haskin, Thomas, tallow-chandler, 27 Bridge
Hasselton, John, shipwright, 2 Fayette
Hastier, John, ironmonger, 78 Water
Haswell, Thomas, printer, 30 Fair

Haswell, John, oysterman, 206 Greenwich-street.
Hatch, Thomas, tin plate worker, Cherry
Hatch, Allden, grocer, 8 Water
Hate, widow, upper end Charlotte
Hatfield, Isaac, carpenter, 32 Warren
Hatfield, Peter, 99 Harman
Hatfield, Elias, mason, 237 Broadway.
Hatfield, Mary, washer, First-street.
Hatfield, John, 35 Harman
Hatfield, widow, boarding-house, 60 Dey
Hatfield, Abraham, carpenter, Pump
Hathaway, Johanna, washer, 18 Bancker
Hathaway, Nathaniel, shipmaster, 19 Cherry
Hathaway and Lewin, milliners, 24 Maiden-lane.
Hathaway, E. surgeon, 140 Front-street.
Hattrick, Peter, merchant, 310 Pearl
Hatton, James, hatter, 6 New
Haulthouse, Henry, grocer, 271 Broadway.
Haupt, George, shoemaker, 16 Garden-street.
Hauptman, Jacob, grocer, 121 Chatham
Haviland, Israel, shoemaker, 243 Water
Haviland and Ferris's store, 285 Pearl
Haviland, John, tobacconist, 130 Front
Haviland, Caleb, wine and porter merchant, 77 John
Haviland, Horatio G. 39 Pine
Haviland, Patrick, grocer, 54 Catharine
Haviland, Denis, mason, Magazine
Hawes, Peter, attorney at law, 165 Water
Hawes, Pelatiah, cooper, 18 James
Hawes, Margaret, 13 Robinson
Hawes, George, butcher, 13 Robinson
Hawes, Frederick, butcher, 13 Robinson
Hawkins, Mathew, sashmaker & glazier, 12 E. George
Hawkins, Joseph, shoemaker, Beaver-lane.
Hawxhurst, James, 12 Roger
Hawxhurst, Nathaniel, clockmaker, 227 Pearl
Hawxhurst and Franklin, ironmongers, 161 Water
Hay, David, mason, 38 Lombard
Haycock, William W. accountant, 24 Liberty
Haydock, James and Eden, merchants, 225 Pearl
Haydock and Son, Henry, merchants, 251 Pearl
Haydock, jun. Henry, merchant, 249 Pearl

Haydock, William, grocer, 117 Greenwich-street.
Haydock, John W. merchant, 345, & store 276, Pearl
Hayes, William, carpenter, Division
Hays, Henry, ladies shoemaker, 78 Broadway.
Hays, Rachel, mantuamaker, 18 Pearl-street.
Hays, Thomas, boot and shoemaker, 5 William
Hays, Michael S. curer of rheumatics, 19 Garden
Hays, Sarah, seamstress, 74 Reed
Hays, James, breeches maker, 145 Water
Hays, Thomas, rush bottom chairmaker, 456 Pearl
Hays, James, carpenter, 23 Reed
Hays, Jacob, conveyancer, 63 Chapel
Hayt, Monson, merchant, 142 Water
Hayt, James, merchant, 140 Water
Hazard, James, merchant, 29 Rutger
Hazard, Joseph, baker, 81 Chatham
Hazard, Martha, boarding-house, 62 Fair
Hazard, John, Lumber
Hazen, Joseph, mariner, 13 Robinson
Healy, Edward, tavern, Front, near Crane-wharf.
Healy, Dennis, grocer, Oliver-street.
Heard, James, merchant, 88 William
Heard, Henry, tavern, 41 Oliver
Heard, Loran, mariner, 23 Batavia-lane.
Hearn, James, grocer and measurer, 273 Broadway.
Heath, Hezekiah, carpenter, 54 Pine-street.
Heath, Thomas, carpenter, 39 Ferry
Heaton and Ostrander, grocers, 20 E. George
Hebarts, Albert, taylor, 130 William
Hebbard, Thomas, grocer, 184 Division
Heberton, John, taylor, 6 George
Heburn, James, mason, Essex
Heburn, John, shoemaker, Essex
Heckley, David, mason, 310 Broadway.
Hector, Frederick, labourer, Charlotte-street.
Hedden, Abijah, cabinetmaker, 56 Beekman

Heffernan, Mrs. Misses academy, 105 William-street.
Heffey, John, rigger, Bayard
Hegarty, widow, 41 E. George
Hegeman, Cornelius, tavern, 14 Coenties-slip.
Hegeman, Peter, merchant, 256 Water
Hegeman, Peter A. auctioneer, 204 Greenwich
Hegeman, Peter, cartman, Mulberry
Heiser, Jacob, 446 Pearl
Heiser, Henry, starch-manufacturer, 63 Barclay
Heiser, David, shoemaker, 49 Bowery-lane.
Heister, Andrew, 81 Warren-street.
Helbon, William, mariner, 34 Rutger
Heller, Abraham, grocer, 9 Tryon-row.
Hellyes, Jean M. physician, 22 Dey-street.
Helme, Arthur, merchant, 218 Water
Helme, Obadiah, grocer, 36 Moore
Helme, Richard, carpenter, Henry
Helme, John, hairdresser, 138 Fly-market.
Helmer, Jacob, hairdresser, 151 Greenwich-street.
Helms, John, sadler, 21 Frankfort
Helms, Adam, cartman, 3 Cherry
Henderson, John, grocer, 89 James
Henderson, Robert, cooper, 36 Beaver
Henderson, Alexander, grocer, 90 Fair
Henderson, Sarah, Barclay
Henderson, William, merchant, 52 Wall
Henderson, widow, 38 Lombard
Henderson, Joseph, labourer, 96 Catharine
Henderson, Robert, grocer, 57 E. George
Henderson, J. Fisher
Hendricks, Philip, grocer, Eagle
Hendricks, Uriah, merchant, 112 Pearl
Hendricks, Harman, merchant, 112 Pearl
Hendrickson, Gent, carpenter, Henry
Hendrickson, Nicholas, milkman, Sixth
Hendrickson, Jacob, shoemaker, 25 Chapel
Hendrickson, George R. merchant, 42 Maiden-lane
Henegar, John, sailmaker, 3 Harman-street.
Heregar, Adam, 73 Chatham
Hennegar, Christopher, cartman, Bowery-lane.
Henneghen, John, grocer, 28 Cherry-street.
Henning, Joseph, victualer, 18 Robinson

Henning, Catharine, 20 Robinson-street.
Henning, John C. cartman, 22 Robinson
Henning, John, smith, 275 Greenwich
Henry, Hugh, grocer, 77 George
Henry, William, dry goods store, 126 Cherry
Henry, John, insurance broker & auctioneer, 57 Stone
Henry, Michael D. attorney at law, 14 Stone
Henry, David, rigger, Brown's-wharf, Front-street.
Henry, John, hairdresser, 38 Vandewater, & 374 Pearl
Henry, Capt. William, 25 Garden
Henry, widow Sarah, 25 Garden
Henry, ——, 47 Robinson
Henry, Aaron, merchant, 41 Whitehall
Henshaw, Zacheus, shipmaster, 271 Broadway.
Henshaw, Samual, accountant, 279 Broadway.
Hensley, John, butcher, 26 Church-street.
Herbert, Samuel, merchant, 5 Vanderwater
Herbert, Edward, cartman, 92 Chamber
Herbert, Timothy, carpenter, Magazine
Herbert, William, porter-house, Elizabeth
Herbert, Felix, taylor, 49 Cliff
Herbert, Henry, milkman, 312 Broadway.
Herford & Son, dry goods store, 251 & 217 Water-st.
Herford, John, merchant, 251 Water
Heron, Hercules, tallow-chandler, Thomas-street.
Heron, John, cartman, 51 Chamber
Herring, Abraham, merchant, 192 Pearl
Herring, Cornelius, cartman, 71 Chamber.
Herring, Cornelius D. 22 Vesey
Herron, Thomas, 55 Whitehall.
Herttell, John, gauger, 8 Dover-street.
Herttell, jun. John, 8 Dover
Herttell, Cornelius, 279 Pearl
Herttell, Adam, butcher, Bowery-lane.
Herttell, William, baker, 8 Dover-street.
Hervey, sen. William, 181 Pearl
Hervey, William and John, store, 181 Pearl
Hervey, jun. William, merchant, 8 Cortlandt
Hervey and Tucker, merchants, 123 Front.
Hesketh, Thomas, mason, Upper Reed
Hetfel, John, Bowery-lane.
Heusinfrents, Peter, Corlaers-hook.

Hevrin, Martin, rigger, Bayard-street.
Hewett, Thomas, tavern, 72 Front.
Hewitt, Thomas, carpenter & builder, Chamber
Hewitt, James, music-store, 131 William
Hewitt, John, rigger, 88 James-street.
Hewitt, John, accountant, Bayard
Hewlett, Divine, merchant, 22 Vandewater
Hewlett and Co. Divine, flour store, 31 Beekman-slip.
Heyer, widow of Andrew, 32 Bowery-lane.
Heyer, Andrew, baker, 16 Augustus-street.
Heyer, William, shoemaker, Magazine
Heyer, Garrit, shoemaker, 2 New
Heyer, John, cooper, Roosevelt
Heyer and Gibson, coopers, 241 Water
Heyer, Lawrence, baker, 49 Chatham
Heyer, Walter & Isaac, ironmongers, 38 William
Heyer, Walter, umbrella-maker, Lumber
Heyer, widow, 5 Rector
Heyer, Isaac, merchant, 35 Water
Heyer, John C. boatman, 12 Thames
Heyer, James, taylor 5 Vandewater
Heyer, Walter W. merchant, 17 Pine
Heyer, William, measurer of lime, 92 Liberty
Heyer, Walter, cooper, 47 Maiden-lane.
Heyer, Walter, revenue officer, 18 Pearl-street.
Heyer, William, warden of the port, 38 William
Heyer, Cornelius, 46 Dey
Heyer, Daniel, shoemaker, 239 William
Heyer, Sarah, 5 New
Heyle, Christian, joiner, 11 Warren
Hibberd, John, coach-painter, 9 John
Hick, Paul, plaister Paris manufacturer, 49 Oliver
Hicks, Isaac, 340 Pearl, & store 14 Crane-wharf.
Hicks, Mott, merchant, 297 & 371 Pearl-street.
Hicks, William, merchant, 317 Pearl
Hicks, Willet, merchant, 7 Cherry, & store 308 Pearl
Hicks, A. B. mathematical instrument-maker, 82 Wall
Hicks, John B. physician & surgeon, 69 Beekman
Hicks, Benjamin, physician, 63 Reed
Hicks, and Son, John, physicians, 1 Magazine
Hicks, George, taylor and habitmaker, 341 Water-st.
Hicks, Whitehead, lumber-merchant, Lumber

Hicks, Oliver, carpenter, Crofs-ftreet.
Highey, Cheany C. shipmaster, 15 Henry
Higbey, Henry and John, grocers, 74 James
Higgins, E. widow, 39 Roofevelt
Higgins, Lawrence, labourer, 20 Skinner
Higgins, Edward, painter, &c. 319 Pearl
Higgins, Edward, baker, Rofe
Higgins, Waters, cartman, Lumber
Higgins, Abner, grocer, 23 Roofevelt
Higgins, Benjamin, carpenter, 19 Partition
Higgins, widow, 16 Warren
Highfield, John, cartman, Little Catharine
Hilar, George, ship-borer, Eagle
Hilman, Michael, labourer, Winne
Hillman, Jacob, cartman, Winne
Hill, Peter, merchant, 25 Beaver
Hill, William, merchant, 137 Water
Hill, Thomas H. hat ftore, 7 Maiden-lane.
Hill, John, cartman, 6 Reed
Hill, John, pedlar, 31 Lumber
Hill, Uriah, shoemaker, 8 Barley
Hill, John, mariner, 57 Catharine
Hill, E. and Sarah, widows, 16 Fayette
Hill, Mrs. 60 Broadway.
Hill, James, 23 New-ftreet.
Hilers, John, merchant, 55 Stone
Hilliger, David, mafon, Mott
Hilliger, Jacob, butcher, Mulberry
Hillyer, Benjamin, carpenter, Bedlow
Hillyer, William, grocer, South
Hilton, Benj. china, glafs, &c. ftore, 46 Maiden-lane.
Hinds, widow, 10 James
Hines, Edward, tinman, Little Catharine
Hickman, Prifcilla, feamftrefs, 3 Dutch
Hinsdale, Epaphras, jeweller, 110 Water
Hinton, John, fawyer and grocer, E. Rutger
Hinton, John, curler, 212 Water
Hitchcock, Miles, merchant, 73 Gold
Hitchcock, Daniel, carpenter and builder, 79 Gold
Hitchcock, Stephen, broker, 26 Peckman
Hitchcock, Jofeph, failmaker, 31 Roofevelt
Hitchcock & Co. W. M. wine, &c. vaults, 200 Water

Hitchcock and Hopson, merchants, 206 Water-street.
Hitchcock, Daniel M. physician, 26 Beekman
Hitchings, widow, 25 Cliff
Hobart, Noah, 44 Ferry
Hobart, Nathaniel, timber-merchant, 39 Bancker
Hobbs, Zephaniah, Second
Hodge, Ralph, custom-house officer, 12 Rose
Hodgkinson, John, comedian, 17 Fair
Hoes, John, cabinetmaker, 10 Wall
Hoffman, Charles Augustus, 172 William
Hoffman, James H. musician, 307 Washington
Hoffman, Martin, merchant, 33 Broad
Hoffman, J. Ogden, counsellor at law, 221 Broadway.
Hoffman and Seton's auction room, 67 Wall-street.
Hoffman, Frederick, cartman, Bedlow
Hoffman, Elizabeth, milk-woman, First
Hoffman, Tobias, baker, Magazine
Hoffman, widow, 19 Pine
Hoffman, Ryneer, basketmaker, 23 Warren
Hoffman, Cornelius, painter, gilder, &c. 22 Ferry
Hoffmaster, William, musician, 187 William
Hoffmire, Thomas, mason, 27 Vandewater
Hogan, Thomas, huckster, 53 Roosevelt
Hogan, John, grocer, 109 Cherry
Hogken, Charles, tavern, 284 Water
Hogg, John, comedian, 22 Chapel
Hoghland, widow, 17 Warren
Holcomb, Joseph, mariner, Beaver-lane.
Holden, Thomas, shipmaster, 36 Bancker
Holden, Asa, boarding-house, 397 Pearl
Holdron, John, ferry-house, 71 Cortlandt
Holdron and Meffer, grocers, 71 Cortlandt
Holdup, Thomas, tavern, 165 Fly-market.
Hole, James, labourer, 15 Oliver-street.

Holmes, Samuel, carpenter, 3 Rector-street.
Holmes, widow, 10 Rector
Holmes, Joel, tavern, 120 Cherry
Holmes, Eldad, grocer, 360 Water
Holmes, William, merchant, store 143 Water
Holmes, Jacob, oysterman, 57 Catharine
Holmes, Thomas, merchant, 438 Pearl
Holmes, Eli. shipwright, E. Rutger
Holmes, widow, 25 Harman
Holmes, William, cartman, 233 Greenwich
Hoffman, Mrs. 177 Broadway.
Holt, James, mariner, 36 Oliver-street.
Holt, Peter, labourer, 67 Roosevelt
Holt, James, caulker, Orchard
Holthuysen, I. C. 56 Cortlandt
Honefield, Henry, tavern, 197 Front
Hone, Phillip, cabinetmaker, 62 Ann
Hone, Samuel, baker, 69 Cliff
Hone, John, auctioneer, 61 Wall, house 9 Gold
Honeyford, Jemima, grocer, Front, near Crane-wharf.
Honeywell, James, dry goods store, 412 Pearl-street.
Honeywell, Gilbert, cartman, 73 Harman
Honson, John A. inspector of beef and pork, 51 Front
Hoogland, John, sadler, 363 Pearl
Hooke, Thomas, shipmaster, 40 Cedar
Hoops, William, taylor, 41 Barclay
Hooton, William, grocer, Henry
Hopkins, John, shoemaker, Eagle
Hopkins, James, grocer, Henry
Hopkins, Joseph, merc. 36 Beekman, & store 221 Pearl
Hopkins, George F. printer, 3 Nassau
Hopkins, Mary, Lumber
Hopkins, Benjamin, labourer, 6 Moore's-row.
Hopkins, Joseph, merchant, 121 Water-street.
Hopkins, John, butcher, Winne
Hopkins, James, coppersmith, 13 Hararu
Hoppel, John, baker, 50 Nassau
Hoppel, George, lamp-lighter, 1 Augustus
Hopper, Elizabeth, seamstress, 211 William
Hopper, Jacob, hairdresser, 13 Moore
Hopper, Anna, 5 James
Hopper, John, baker, Little Catharine

Hopper, Garrit, shopkeeper, 67 Partition-street.
Hopper, Andrew, dry goods store, 3 Chatham-row.
Hoppin, Samuel, carpenter, 35 Lumber-street.
Hopping, Ephraim, carpenter, 69 E. George
Hopson, William, butcher, Hester
Hopson, James, grocer, corner of Hague & Pearl
Hopson, George, butcher, 24 Vandewater
Hora, Mathew, mariner, 23 Batavia-lane.
Horn, William, boatman, 121 Harman-street.
Horne, Joseph, carpenter, 93 Chamber
Hornung, Martin, grocer, 346 Broadway.
Horsefield & Nostrandt, ironmongers, 144 Fly-market.
Horseman, Nicholas, tea-waterman, Elizabeth-street.
Horton, Ann, grocer, 130 Front, corner of Fly-market.
Horton, Peter, grocer, 42 E. George-street.
Horton, Gilbert, grocer, 147 Fly-market.
Horton, William, gunsmith, 61 Whitehall.
Hortwick, George, cooper, Magazine-street.
Hosack, Alexander, merchant, 45 Vesey
Hosack, David, physician, 65 Broadway.
Hosack, William, attorney at law, 45 Vesey-street.
Hosier, John, cartman, Winne
Hoskings, John, shipwright, 110 Harman
Hotchkiss, Isaac, mason, 13 Harman
Hotto, Coenrad, grocer, 35 Robinson
Hougland, Benjamin, cartman, 31 Division
Hounam, James, Pump
Hounsfield, Ezra, merchant, 61 Maiden-lane.
House, Seth, mariner, 85 Chamber-street.
House, Elizabeth, washer, 42 Vesey
Houseman, John, merchant, 176 Broadway.
Houseman, Jacob, wire-manufacturer, 93 Broad-street.
Houser, Matthias, shoemaker, 45 Barley
Houseworth, Michael, baker, 15 Chamber
Houston, William, attorney at law, 47 Nassau
Houstoun, Hugh, tin-plate worker, 183 Broadway
HOWARD LODGE, (Freemason's) 66 Liberty
Howard, Jonathan, labourer, 59 Church
Howard, James, mariner, 22 Oliver
Howard, James, labourer, 45 Division
Howard, Rachel, 9 Augustus
Howard, William, potter, Cross

Howe, William, organ-builder, &c. 320 Pearl-street.
Howe, Bazaleel, 50 Cherry
Howe, Joshua, dry goods store, 261 Water
Howe, Briegham, hat-store, 1 Liberty
Howell, William, merchant, 58 Stone
Howell, Aaron, measurer, 32 Chatham
Howell, Mathew, grocer, 222 Front
Howell, James, cartman, 37 Reed
Howell, Frederick, sawyer, Greenwich-road.
Howland, Reuben, mariner, Henry-street.
Howlett, Thomas, shoemaker, 19 Thomas
Hoyt and Tom's store, Crane-wharf.
Hoyt, Samuel, 167 William-street.
Hoyt, Jesse, teacher, E. Rutger
Hoyt, Gilbert, mariner, Harrison
Hoyt, Ennis, shipmaster, 61 James
Hubbard, David G. merchant, 83 Wall, & 147 Water
Hubbs, Robert, taylor, 370 Pearl
Hubby, Joseph, tavern, 6 Bowery-lane.
Hudson, Andrew, cartman, Elizabeth
Hudson, Isaac, tanner, Bowery-lane.
Huestin, Daniel, grocer, Greenwich.
Huestis, Mary, 262 William-street.
Huestis, Garrit, shoemaker, Lombard
Huggins and Hassey, hairdressers, 72 Wall
Hughes, Henry, shipmaster, 31 Cheapside.
Hughes, David, labourer, 109 Division-street.
Hughes, James Miles, counsellor at law, 3 Cedar
Hughes, William, tallow-chandler, 36 Cedar
Hughes, Christopher, grocer, 16 Rose
Hughes, Anthony, mariner, 50 Chatham
Hughes, John, auctioneer, 76 Wall
Hughes, Phelix, smith, 32 Harman
Hughes, John, labourer, 32 E. George
Hughston, James, grocer, 33 Warren
Hulett, John Hamilton, dancing-master, 12 Cedar
Hull, John, smith, 398 Pearl
Hull, John, druggist, 146 Pearl
Hull, Oliver, dry goods store, 43 Frankfort
Hull, Peter, cartman, 27 Moore
Hull, Solomon, smith, 49 Augustus
Hullett, Jacob, drayman, Greenwich-road.

Hulfart, Henry, cartman, First-street.
Hulfart, Cornelius, shoemaker, 52 E. George
Hulfart, William, carpenter, Birmingham-row.
Humbert, Jonas, baker, 30 Pine-street.
Humphreys, William, marshall, 38 Chapel
Humphreys, William, taylor, 29 Water
Hungary, William, shoemaker, 6 Barley
Hunn, John S. notary-public, 51 Murray
Hunt, Nathaniel, cartman, Third
Hunt, Benjamin, grocer, 48 Beekman
Hunt, Philip, cartman, Third
Hunt, Josiah, taylor, 16 Bayard
Hunt, Isaac, boarding-house, 68 Catharine
Hunt, Richard, carpenter, 32 Barclay
Hunt, Walter B. grocer, 143 Fly-market.
Hunt, Morris, carpenter, Bedlow-street.
Hunt, Thomas, 94 Chatham
Hunt, Sarah, boarding-house, 137 Cherry
Hunt, Alsop, leatherdresser and glover, 164 Water
Hunt, Roger, merchant, 262 Pearl
Hunt and Prail, merchants, 168 Water
Hunt, James, merchant, 168 Water
Hunt, Thomas, shipwright, Lumber
Hunt, John, cooper, Lumber
Hunt, James, broker, 65 Pearl
Hunt, Thomas, cabinetmaker, Bridge
Hunt, Joshua, cartman, 39 Robinson
Hunt, Francis, labourer, 20 Robinson
Hunt, John, cartman, Pump
Hunt, Hester, First
Hunter and Co. George, auctioneers, 153 Pearl
Hunter, Robert, merchant, 153 Pearl
Hunter, George, merchant, 6 Garden
Hunter, Robert, hotel, 69 Broadway.
Hunter, George, carpenter, 24 George-street.
Hunter, Joseph, mariner, Birmingham-row.
Hunter, George, grocer, 150 Front-street.
Hunter, William, grocer, Lumber, corner E. Rutger
Hunter, Henry, baker, 27 Barclay
Huntington, Henry, merchant, 62 William
Hurk, Peter, shoemaker, 47 Greenwich
Hurley, John, cartman, First

Harley, James, 2 Augustus-street.
Herpels, Lodowick, butcher, Bowery-lane.
Hurst, widow, 53 Cherry-street.
Hartin, William, revenue officer, 35 Barclay
Hartin and Co. John H. merchants, 84 Front
Hartin, Robert M. printer, 29 Gold
Husbands, William, confectioner, 166 William
Hustace, B. and S. grocers, Old-slip.
Hustace, Charles, carpenter, Lumber
Hustace, James, Winne
Hutchings, Ann, tavern, 28 Moore
Hutchings, David, grocer, Orange, corner Cross
Hutchings, Mary, nurse, 47 Gold
Hutchings, Samuel, grocer, 33 Chamber
Hutchinson, John, boarding-house, 101 Water
Hutchinson, James, carpenter, 285 Broadway.
Hutchinson, Thomas, Elizabeth-street.
Hutchinson, James, oil silk manufacturer, 46 James
Hutchison, Alex. Washington, corner Robinson
Huthwaite, William, watchmaker, 267 William
Hutson, John, chimney-office, 28 Vesey
Hutson, William, perfumer, 8 Nassau
Hutton, William, labourer, 69 Church
Hutton, George, butcher, 20 Church
Hutton, John, shipwright, Henry
Hyatt, Joseph, cartman, Mott
Hyatt, John, milkman, Mott
Hyde, John, keeper, Tontine Coffee-house.
Hyde, Henry, labourer, 86 Reed-street
Hynes, Elizabeth. 262 Greenwich.
Hyler, Abraham, mason, Greenwich-road.
Hyslop, Robert, merchant, 62 Dey-street.
Hyslop, John, baker, 26 John

I

Ihmsen, Thomas, carpenter, Bedlow-street.
Isley, Joseph, sexton of St. Peter's church, 5 Church
Inman, John, shoemaker, Pump
Inderweck, Andrew, baker, 50 Pearl
Ingland, William, dry goods store, 10 Front
Ingle, Rachel, dry goods store, 139 Pearl
Ingle, James, china and glass store, 115 Fly-market.
Ingraham, Nathaniel, merchant, 94 Pearl

Inman, Oliver, cooper, 76 Warren-street.
Insley, William, carpenter, Orange
Ireland, John, merchant, 9 Beaver
Ireland, Joseph, porter & liquor vaults, 123 Water
Ireland, Joseph, carpenter, 21 Cheapside.
Irvin, William & Thos. merchants, 19 Maiden-lane.
Irving, William, merchant, 128 William-street.
Irving, jun. William, ironmonger, 240 Pearl
Irving, Peter, physician, 208 Broadway.
Irving, Edward, boarding-house, 59 John-street.
Irwin, Samuel, carpenter, 42 E. George
Irwine, William, smith, Cherry-street. Ship-yards.
Irwine, James, grocer, 268 William-street.
Irwine, Robert, mariner, 7 Cheapside.
Irwine, John, cartman, E. Washington-street.
Isaac, Sampson, accountant, 32 Barclay
Isaacs, Solomon, 17 Chatham
Isaacs, Joshua, broker, 7 Gold
Isaacs, Moses, broker, 32 Barclay
Isbel, Bishop, carpenter, Henry, corner Catharine.
Isenstein, Matthias, shipwright, Washington
Isidine, widow, 59 Division
Isenbergh and Co. John, grocers, 5 Church
Isherwood, Benjamin, confectioner, 112 William
Israel, widow, 63 Liberty
Iseman, John, smith, 119 Bowery-lane.
Ivers, Mrs. 96 Greenwich-street.
Ivers, Thomas, ropemaker, Corlaer's-hook.
Ivory, Joseph, carpenter, Lumber-street.

J

Jackson, Allen, merchant, 277 Pearl-street.
Jackson, John, labourer, First
Jackson, Gilbert, baker, 69 Roosevelt
Jackson, Daniel, carpenter, 72 Chamber
Jackson, John, merchant, 91 Front
Jackson, Tredwell, merchant, 269 Water
Jackson, James, grocer, 19 E. George
Jackson, James, 62 Chapel
Jackson, Thomas T. 21 Roosevelt
Jackson, ———, carpenter, 68 James
Jackson, Ann, white-washer, 11 Rector
Jackson, Ann, milliner, &c. 306 Pearl-street.

Jackson, Amasa, mercht. 85 Wall, & house 53 Dey-str.
Jacobs, Abraham, shipwright, 95 Division
Jacobs, Joseph, porter-house, 14 Pearl
Jacob, Francis, grocer, 41 William
Jacob, James, shipmaster, 1 Jacob
Jacobs, William, shoemaker, 1 Fair
Jacobs, David, grocer, 20 Augustus
Jacobs, Benjamin, 14 Pearl
Jacobs, widow, 1 Fair
Jacobs and Miller, grocers, 46 William
Jacock, Thomas, cartman, 101 Reed
Jacques, Richard, grocer, corner Orchard & Pump
Jacques, John, shipmaster, Pump
Jaffray, Thomas, grocer, 324 Water
Jagger, Rufus, carpenter, 65 E. George
James, (C.) & R. Hunt, merchants, 262 Pearl
James, George, shipwright, 28 Lumber
James, Thomas, soap-and candlemaker, 21 Warren
James, Robert, merchant, 13 Wall
James, Levi, cartman, Bedlow
James, Chalkley, merchant, 126 William
James and Co. Joseph, merchants, 222 Pearl
James, William, stonecutter, 24 Harman
Janeway, George, 92 Chatham
Janeway, William, merchant, 92 Chatham
Jansen, Thomas B. bookbinder, 344 Water
Jansen, George, accountant, 11 Cheapside
Jappie, Paul, shipmaster, 31 Cheapside.
Jaques, Oliver, grocer, 64 Warren-street.
Jarraslav, Pierre, Washington
Jarvis, Noah and Elijah, shoemaker, 156 Front
Jarvis, Frederick, chairmaker, 11 E. George
Jarvis, James, shoemaker, Second, corner of Fisher
Jarvis, Mathew, porter-house, 12 Garden
Jarvis, Moses, boot and shoe store, 4 Catharine
Jarvis, Andrew, 11 E. George
Jarvis, Noah, shoemaker, 10 Ferry
Jarvis, George, mariner, 11 E. George
Jarvis, John F. 238 Greenwich
Jarvis, Ichabud, filmaker, 78 Vesey
Jarvis, G. shipmaster, Eagle
Jauger, Frederick, labourer, 8 Charlotte

I 2

NEW-YORK DIRECTORY.

Jauncey, widow, 57 Beekman-street.
Jauncey, William, 20 Wall
Jay, Peter A. attorney at law, 32 Broadway.
Jay, Frederick, auctioneer, 136 Water-street.
Jay, James, 177 Washington
Jean, Andrew A. 101 Beekman
Jecobis, Rudolph, shoemaker, 54 Warren
Jecovis, Nicholas, cartman, 84 Chamber
Jeffers, Patrick, 4 Augustus
Jeffery, Mary, 32 Liberty
Jemnnison, Neil, Winne
Jenkins, James, shoemaker, 17 Ferry
Jenkins, Edward, mariner, 7 Hague
Jenkins, John, mason, Charlotte
Jenkins, John, teacher, 62 Partition
Jenkins, James, mason, 36 Robinson
Jenkins, George, accountant, 32 Lombard
Jennings, Jonathan, shoemaker, 1 E. George
Jennings, Salmon, smith, 52 Cheapside.
Jennings, Nathan, smith, 56 Beaver-street.
Jennings, William, grocer, Cross. near the Collect.
Jennings, Richard, tavern, 326 Water-street.
Jennings, Andrew, cartman, 77 Warren
Jennys, William, portrait-painter, 42 Gold
Jeremiah, John, butcher, 14 Water
Jeroleman, Jacob, 10 Maiden-lane.
Jessup, Benjamin, shoemaker, 81 Catharine
Jessup, Oliver, grocer, Lumber
Jessup, Edward, grocer, 83 Chatham
Jewell, William, mason, 46 Chapel
Johns, William, shipmaster, 38 Oliver
Johnson, Ammond, tavern, 66 E. George
Johnson, Abraham, cartman, near Union furnace.
Johnson, Ben. bricklayer, Harman, corner Charlotte-st.
Johnson, Charles, harness-maker, Eden's-alley.
Johnson, Charles, shipmaster, 67 Ann-street.
Johnson, Edward, apothecary, 348 Broadway.
Johnson, Francis, cooper, 26 and 31 Ann-street.
Johnson, George, cartman, 69 Harman
Johnson, Horace, merchant, 111 Liberty
Johnson, Isaac, carpenter, 32 Harman
Johnson, John, labourer, 17 Augustus

Johnson, John, currier, 27 Ferry-street.
Johnson, Jesse, shoemaker, 106 Division.
Johnson, Isaac, mariner, 5 Vandewater.
Johnson, John, grocer, 36 Whitehall.
Johnson, Rachel, seamstress, 50 Chatham-street.
Johnson, Robert, shoemaker, 46 Gold
Johnson, Robert, coachman, 43 Gold
Johnson, sen. Stephen, cartman, Elizabeth
Johnson, Stephen, cartman, Pump
Johnson, Seth, merchant, 165 Greenwich
Johnson, Samuel, brass-founder, 12 Beaver
Johnson, Thomas, grocer, 3 E. George
Johnson, William S. L. L. D. 1 College.
Johnson, William, Third-street.
Johnson, William, dry goods store, &c. 376 Pearl
Johnson, William, hardware store, 59 Pearl
Johnson, William, grocer, Cherry, Ship-yards.
Johnson, William, counsellor at law, 45 Pine-street.
Johnson, William, shoemaker, 29 Rose
Johnson & Co. H. & S. counting-house, 34 William
Johnson, ——, stivadore, 49 Cliff
Johnston, Ann, tea store, 50 Maiden-lane.
Johnston, Catharine, seamstress, 27 Vandewater-street.
Johnston, Dorcas, 25 Bancker
Johnston, David, labourer, 458 Pearl
Johnston, Edmund S. shipmaster, 18 Fayette
Johnston, George, merchant, 112 Front
Johnston, George, carpenter, 27 Chamber
Johnston, Harman, carpenter, 30 Roosevelt
Johnston, John R. 65 Partition
Johnston, John, cartman, 305 Broadway.
Johnston, John, 86 Chatham-street.
Johnston, John, carpenter, Little Catharine
Johnston, John, cooper, 1 Old-slip.
Johnston, John, mariner, Bedlow-street.
Johnston, Robert, carpenter, 6 Vandewater
Johnston, Richard, shoemaker, 364 Pearl
Johnston, Thomas, labourer, 11 Moore's-row.
Johnston, Thomas, shoemaker, 141 Chatham-street.
Johnston, William, mariner, Lumber
Johnston, widow, 364 Pearl
Johnston and Co. Robert, merchants, 51 John

Johnston, ———, mariner, 61 Chatham-street.
Joiceland, David, Orange
Jolly, William, labourer, E. Rutger
Jones, Anthony, mason, 82 William
Jones, Benjamin, oysterman, 13 Chapel
Jones, Elijah, cooper, Cross
Jones, Griffith, baker, 58 Barclay
Jones, Gardiner, physician, 20 Dey
Jones, Hulett, shoemaker, 10 Lumber
Jones, Hugh, labourer, 34 E. George
Jones, John S. merchant, 25 Liberty
Jones, John B. surgeon, 82 William
Jones, John, merchant, 57 Wall
Jones, Joshua, merchant, 48, and store 83 Wall
Jones, Isaac, hairdresser, 70 William
Jones, Isaac, merchant, 205 Broadway.
Jones, James, carpenter, 193 Division-street.
Jones, Isaac, cooper, 83 Harman
Jones, John, labourer, Pump
Jones, John, china and glass store, 50 Fair
Jones, Louis, printer, 67 Pine
Jones, Mrs. ladies boarding-school, 82 William
Jones, Owen, soap and candlemaker, 15 Roosevelt
Jones, Samuel, teacher, 224 William
Jones, jun. Samuel, counsellor at law, 28 Pine
Jones, Thomas, merchant-taylor, 6 Wall
Jones, Thomas, malster and brewer, 15 Cheapside.
Jones, Thomas, physician, 74 Broadway.
Jones, William, shoemaker, 18 Reed-street.
Jones, widow, 129 Division
Jones, widow, 37 Partition
Jones, ———, mariner, Lumber
Jordon, Coenrad, cartman, Second
Jordon, Coenrad, labourer, 54 Warren
Jordan, Mathew, milkman, Bowery-lane.
Journeay, William, grocer, 4 Coenties-slip.
Joyce, Benjamin, dry goods store, 163 William-street.
Joyce, Robert, clock and watchmaker, 145 Pearl
Juard, James, mariner, 195 Division
Judah, Cary, merchant, 1 Old slip.
Judah, Napht. bookbinder & stationer, 47 Water-st.
Judah, Benjamin S. merchant, 1 Old-slip.

NEW-YORK DIRECTORY.

Judah, Bernard S. druggist, 168 Broadway.
Judge, Hugh, 391 Pearl-street.
Judgeson, ———, cartman, Henry
Juhel and Co. John, merchants, 15 Gold.
Jumel, Stephen, merchant, 45 Beekman
June, Jacob, tavern, 15 Front
Justice, John, shoemaker, 202 Broadway.

K

Kallenger, Marraus, cartman, 100 Warren-street.
Kane and Co. John, merchants, 162 Pearl
Kane, Oliver, merchant, 162 Pearl
Kann, Dennis, labourer, 33 Beaver
Kant, Godfrey, upholsterer, 58 Beekman
Karnes and Hazlet, windsor chairmakers, 93 John
Karnes, John, windsor chairmaker, 2 Cliff
Kasmer, John, carpenter, 44 Augustus
Kaven, A. and W. boot and shoemakers, 310 Pearl
Keane, James, tavern, 64 Front
Kearney, Margaret, 249 William
Kearvan, Lawrence, grocer, 73 Division
Keating and Hopkins, grocers, 69 Catharine
Keator, Gideon, taylor, Hester
Keecher, Andrew, labourer, Mott
Keefe, Arthur, labourer, 3 Pearl
Keefe, John, mariner, 17 Cooper
Keefe, Philip, mariner, E. Rutger
Keelers, Nathaniel, grocer, Division
Keeling, Catharine, shopkeeper, 138 Front
Keen, William, shoemaker, 1 Lumber
Keens, Elizabeth, boarding-house, 10 Water
Keersey, Abraham, shoemaker, near the Alms-house.
Keefe, Alexander, shoemaker, 62 Cedar-street
Keefe, John, 17 Wall, and notarial office, 121 Water
Kelly, Lewis, grocer, 4 Water
Kelly, Mary, fickmaker, 23 Cedar
Kelly, Mary, seamstress, 96 Chamber
Kelly, Luke, taylor, 2 Broad
Kelly, William, carpenter, 13 Thomas
Kelly, Mathew, taylor, 51 Chatham
Kelly, Patrick, 333 Broadway.
Kelly, John, 38 Greenwich-street
Kelly, L. boarding-house, 50 Dey

Kelly, James, mason, Mulberry-street.
Kelly, John, painter, &c. 46 Chatham
Kelly, Bernard, 50 Liberty
Kelso, Samuel, calicoe-printer, Little Ann
Kelson, John S. tavern, 34 Chatham
Kemble, Peter, merchant, 17 Whitehall.
Kemble, Robert, merchant, 31 Wall-street.
Kemens, widow, market-woman, 76 Harman
Kemens, Richard, mason, Henry
Kemp, John, L. L. D. in the College.
Kemper, Daniel, labourer, 270 Greenwich-street.
Kemper, Daniel, weigher, 120 Pearl
Kempton, Moses, 110 Front
Kenah and O'Connor, grocers, 21 Peck-slip.
Kenard, Albert, tea-waterman, Mulberry-street.
Kenard, Michael, tea-waterman, Orange
Kendrick, Walter, hat store, 5 Maiden-lane.
Kenley, John, accountant, Eagle-street.
Kennan, Patrick, merchant, 130 Pearl
Kennedy, Robert, taylor, 19 Cherry
Kennedy, Charles, shoemaker, 31 Rutger
Kennedy, widow, 45 Roosevelt
Kennedy, John, mariner, 89 James
Kennedy, Thomas H. merchant, 434 Pearl
Kennedy, Archibald, 1 Broadway.
Kent, Joseph, labourer, 13 Oliver-street.
Kent, William, rigger Hester
Kent, John, gilder, 25 Cedar
Kent, Jacob, smith, 7 Murray
Kenyon, William, merchant, 11 & 13 Beekman
Kerley, Archibald, 37 Cherry
Kernit, Henry, shipmaster, 19 Wall
Kerr, Joseph, cartman, Second
Kesner, John N. merchant, 141 Water
Kershaw, ——, painter, & glazier, 1 Henry
Kervan, Moses, sawyer, Bedlow
Kerwin, Andrew, dealer, 116 Harman
Ketchum, William, cabinetmaker, 55 Church
Ketchum, Hannah, schoolmistress, 56 Beaver
Ketchum, James, shoemaker, Division
Ketchum, Solomon, grocer, 152 Front
Ketchum, Richard, waterman, 6 Charlotte

Ketterer, Jacob, taylor, 23 Division-street.
Kettletas, William, attorney at law, 89 Cherry
Kettletas, Gar. mer. 62 Water, & house 11 Stone
Kettletas, Ph. M. D. 43 Division
Keyes, Charles, cartman, Norfolk
Keyser, Jacob, teacher, 17 Thames
Keyser, Michael, tea-waterman, 115 Division
Keyser, John, First
Keyser, jun. John, coach & chairmaker, 88 Bowery-lane.
Keyser, Jacob, labourer, 29 Chamber-street.
Keyser, John, shoemaker, Upper Reed
Kibbe, Isaac, merchant, 214 Pearl
Kidney, James, shipwright, Bedlow
Kidney, Henry, shoemaker, 12 Barclay
Kidson and Philps, cabinetmakers, 31 Beekman
Kidson, William, cabinetmaker, 31 Beekman
Kiersted, John, hatter, 23 Cortlandt
Kiersted, James, brass-founder, near Alms-house.
Kilby, William, merchant-taylor, 229 Water-street
Kiler, Frederick, 311 Broadway.
Kilburn, Ebenezer C. sailmaker, 4 Broad-street.
Killegrew, John, carpenter, 67 Chatham
Killin, Daniel, carpenter, Charlotte
Kilmaster, Nathaniel, cartman, 55 Chamber
Kilmaster, Ann, 46 Cortlandt
Kimball, Joseph, painter and glazier, Theatre-alley.
Kimberly, Gideon, merchant, 54 Gold-street.
Kimberly, Anson, merchant, 255 Pearl
Kimberly, Nathaniel, taylor, 50 Cherry
Kimmons, John, cooper, 22 Lombard
Kimmons, Hugh, rigger, 22 Lombard
King, John, confectioner, 56 William
King, Peter, taylor, Water-street, above Catharine
King, ———, mariner, 6 Vandewater
King, widow, boarding-house, 47 Cortlandt
King, Nathan, labourer, near Union-furnace.
King, Henry, carpenter, 146 Washington-street.
King, Abraham, 109 Reed
King, Jacob, labourer, Greenwich-road.
King, John, carpenter, 86 Chamber
King, Peter, cartman, 40 Barclay
King, John, revenue-officer, Mulberry

King, Hannah, seamstress, 1 Barley-street.
King Cornelius, butcher, Bayard
King, Kenith, mason, 13 Rose
King, Joseph, boot & shoe warehouse, 331 Pearl
King, William, carpenter, 19 Frankfort
King, Peter, inspector of wood, 20 Rose
King, George, cartman, 24 Roosevelt
King, Lydia, tayloress, 22 Batavia-lane.
King, D. S. clothier, 10 Old-slip.
King, Newton, cook, 94 Warren-street.
King, Joseph, merchant, 25 Murray
King, Richard, shoemaker, 91 Division
King, Hezekiah, carpenter, 125 Division
King, William, mariner, Birmingham-row.
King, David, porter-house, 8 Wall-street.
King, Ann, 152 William
King, Miss, 24 Pine
King, ———, mariner, 57 Liberty
Kinghorn, Martha, shopkeeper, Bayard
Kingon, Benon, mason, Greenwich-road.
Kingsland, Aaron, oysterman, 94 Catharine-street.
Kingsland, Cornelius, carpenter, 40 Partition
Kingsland, Daniel, shipjoiner, 8 Cheapside.
Kingsland, widow, 44 Barclay
Kingsland, John, grocer, 195 Washington
Kngston, John, cartman, Bowery-lane.
Kinnan, Peter, revenue officer, 51 Liberty-street.
Kinnan, Thomas, inspector of wood, 51 Liberty
Kinsey, Mrs. boarding-house, 33 Pearl
Kip, Juliet, 6 Ferry
Kip, James, sailmaker, 1 Bancker
Kip, Isaac A. merchant, 34 Stone
Kip, Thomas F. sailmaker, 3 Division
Kip, Isaac L. notary public & clerk in chancery, 4 Nassau
Kip, Henry H. inspector of pot & pearl ashes, 41 Pine
Kip, John M. merchant, 195 Greenwich
Kip, Thomas, grocer, 74 Vesey
Kip and Dubois's store, 36 Front
Kip, Abraham, dry goods store, 40 Water
Kip, Isaac, cartman, 52 Murray
Kip, James H. merchant, 167 Broadway.
Kip, Ann, upholsterer, 154 Broadway.

Kip, jun. Isaac, 66 Chamber-street.
Kip, Leonard, dry goods store, 179 Washington
Kip, jun. Leonard, merchant, 179 Washington
Kip, Garrit, grocer, 261 Broadway.
Kip, widow, 93 Gold-street.
Kip, John, shoemaker, 99 Harman
Kip, widow of Abraham, grocer, Upper Reed
Kirby, William, china, glass, &c. store, 105 Pearl
Kirby, Peter, 344 Broadway.
Kirk, George, grocer, 183 William-street.
Kirk, Thomas, printer, 112 Chatham
Kirkaldie, David, taylor, 93 Greenwich
Kirkby, Myles, merchant, 113 Water
Kirker, John, tin-plate worker, 248 Water
Kirkpatrick, William, dry goods store, 440 Pearl
Kirkpatrick, James, cabinetmaker, 93 James
Kissam, Peter R. & S. wine-merchants, 144 Water
Kissam, Richard S. surgeon, 10 Fair
Kissam, Benjamin, physician, 159 Broadway.
Kissam, Jacob, labourer, 111 Bowery-lane.
Kitchel, Isaac, windsor chairmaker, 66 John-street
Kitchel, Samuel, cooper and culler, 109 Harman
Klyne, Leonard, baker, 35 Bowery-lane.
Knapp, Eli, shoemaker, 12 Robinson-street.
Knapp, Eben, carpenter, 87 Harman
Knapp, Simeon, teacher, E. George
Knapp, jun. Eben, carpenter, 87 Harman
Knapp, Abraham, shoemaker, 91 Harman
Knapp, Benjamin, boatman, Orange
Knapp, John, tavern, 122 Cherry
Knapp, Gilbert, butcher, 87 Harman
Knapp, jun. Gilbert, butcher, 87 Harman
Knapp, Benjamin, stonecutter, 171 Greenwich
Knapp & Co. Stephen, merchant-taylors, 1 New-slip
Knapp, Margaret, boarding-house, 60 Cherry-street.
Kneeland, Seth, grocer, New Albany-bason.
Knees, Warner, stonecutter, 10 Robinson-street.
Knell, Wandle, smith, 21 Chatham
Kniffin, Lewis, cartman, Charlotte
Knight, John, shoemaker, Moore's-row.
Knott, Thomas, grocer, 199 Greenwich-street.
Knott, John, shoemaker, 19 Barclay

Knowles, William, physician, 41 George-street.
Knowlton, John, livery stabler, 45 Nassau
Knox, Thomas, merchant, 46 Wall
Knox, George, stone and marblecutter, 113 Liberty
Knox, John, merchant, 11 Liberty
Knox, James, grocery store, 90 Cherry
Knox and Bethune, merchants & brokers, 11 Liberty
Knox, George, 23 Broadway.
Kohler, Charles, baker, 10 Bowery-lane.
Kohlwagen, John C. baker, Bedlow-street.
Kool, A. accountant, 55 Whitehall.
Kortright, Nicholas, sailmaker, 21 Frankfort-street.
Kortright, James B. cabinetmaker, 44 Church
Krapff, Caspar, grocer, Warren
Kroneholm, Christian, shoemaker, Magazine
Kroushar, Philip, labourer, Eagle
Kumbel, William, clock and watchmaker, 312 Pearl
Kunze, Rev. John, D. D. 100 Chatham
Kursheidt and Co. Israel B. merchants, 235 Broadway.
Kuypers, Rev. Gerardus A. 27 Fair-street.
Kyde, Alexander, shipmaster, 45 Beaver

L

Labagh, Abraham, stonecutter, 53 Cedar-street.
Labee, ———, ladies hairdresser, 247 Broadway.
Laborey, Joseph, cooper, 31 Cherry-street.
Laboyteaux, Mrs. boarding-house, 13 Front
Laboyteaux, Mrs. William, 69 Fair
Laboyteaux and Fox, grocers, 166 Greenwich
Labuzon, Bartholomew, gardener, Third
Lacey, Richard, tallow-chandler, 18 Ferry
Lacey, Lawrence, shipmaster, 93 James
Lacey, John, shipwright, 6 Cheapside.
Lackey, Robert, mastmaker & shipwright, Lumber-st.
Lackey, jun. Robert, cabinetmaker, Harman
Lacoste, R. french academy, 91 Maiden-lane.
Lacour, Peter, painter, gilder, &c. 31 Partition-street.
Ladrick, John, shoemaker, 51 Chapel
Lafferty, Edward, grocer, 1 Pearl
Lafiteau, Edmond, taylor, 51 Church
Laforgue, John, mariner, 66 Murray
Lafuque, ———, Pump
Lagarenne, Charles, merchant, 291 Greenwich

Lagear, John, cooper, 68 Nassau-street.
Lagrelle, widow Margaret, 53 Roosevelt
Laight, William, merchant, 132 Greenwich
Laight, jun. William, ironmonger, 243 Pearl
Laight, Mrs. 17 Cherry
Laight, Edward W. (& C. D. Colden) masters in
   chancery, 47 Wall
Laing, John, carpenter, Little Catharine
Laing, James, turner, 22 Nassau
Laing, Joseph, carpenter, 54 Vesey
Lake, Joseph, labourer, Upper Barley
Lake, William, shopkeeper, 98 Gold
Lalor, Anastasia, 274 Water
Lalor, John, tavern, 292 Water
Lamb, Peter, mariner, 56 Cherry
Lamb, widow, 34 Mill
Lamb, William, taylor, 11 Rutger
Lamb, Gen. john, 34 Wall
Lamb, John, M. D. 34 Wall
Lamb, Anthony, merchant, 34 Wall
Lamb, Alexander, fruiterer, 65 Cherry
Lamb, David, shoemaker, Little Catharine
Lambe, Thomas, cabinetmaker, 34 Vesey
Lambert, Michael, grocer, 132 Bowery-lane.
Lambert, Edward, hairdresser, 81 Nassau-street.
Lambert, Rene, carpenter, 22 Pearl
Lambson, John, Bedlow
Lamerauk, ——, pastry-cook, 7 Tryon-row.
Lamoreaux, John, cartman, Charlotte-street
Lamoreux, Daniel, cartman, Essex
Lamoreux, Jesse, shipwright, 34 Bancker
Lamplin, George, shoemaker, 80 Nassau
Lanchenau, Richard, cartman, First
Lane, Thomas, labourer, 3 James
Laney, David, shoemaker, 115 Reed
Laney, George, hairdresser, 61 Dey
Lang, Peter, mariner, 258 Pearl
Lang, George, taylor 59 Cedar
Lang, John, printer, 19 Broad
Lang, James, cabinetmaker, 53 Liberty
Langdon, John, merchant, 208 Pearl
Langdon, Thomas, shoemaker, 55 Cherry

Langdon, John, boarding-house, 116 Fly-market.
Langley, William, bricklayer, 81 Murray-street.
Langlois, Vincendus, 109 Bowery-lane.
Lannaham, Dennis, grocer, E. George, cor. Cheapside
Lannuier, Augustus, confectioner, 100 Broadway.
Lansdown, Edward, mariner, 13 Roosevelt-street.
Lansing, Jacob John, sheriff, 40 Broad
Lanuel, Mrs. 11 James
Lapier, ———, 35 Chatham
Lardner, James, grocer, 282 Water
Larabee, Daniel, shoemaker, 40 Maiden-lane.
Laroche, John, merchant, 6 William-street.
Laroza, John, tea-waterman, Orange
Lasher, William, revenue officer, 51 Gold
Lasher, Col. John, surveyor of customs, 1 Whitehall.
Latham, Simon, shipwright, 23 Lumber-street.
Latham, Stanton, teacher, 10 Garden
Latham, Daniel, shipwright, 45 Cherry
Latham, John, shipwright, Division
Latham, John, measurer of grain, 12 Cliff
Latham, Joseph, shipwright, 63 James
Latham, Andrew, inspector of lumber, 3 Chesnut
Latham, David, shipwright, Charlotte
Lathrop, Joseph, sailmaker, 21 Roosevelt
Lattimore, Mathew, merchant-taylor, 16 Reed
Laughlin, John, tavern, 90 E. George
Laughton, James, shipmaster, 54 Cherry
Lavolette, D. 290 Broadway.
Laver, Philip, milkman, 40 Harman-street.
Laverton, Peter, hatter, 123 Chatham
Laverty and Endo, dry goods store, 430 Pearl
Laverty, William, labourer, 440 Pearl
Law, David, shoemaker, 63 Nassau
Law and McPherson, grocer, 36 Reed
Lawrence, James, architect, Mott, corner Bay
Lawrence, Peter, cartman, 90 Reed
Lawrence, Benjamin, labourer, Essex
Lawrence and Whitney, merchants, 178 Front
Lawrence and Van Zandt, merchants, 26 Vesey
Lawrence, John and Isaac, merchants, 154 Water
Lawrence, Thomas, merchant, 83 Cherry
Lawrence, William, physician, 60 Roosevelt

Lawrence & Co. Augustine H. merchants, 40 Wall-str.
Lawrence and Schieffelin, druggists, 195 Pearl
Lawrence, Caleb, merchant, 253 Pearl
Lawrence, Richard, merchant, 201 Pearl
Lawrence, Richard R. merchant, 246 Pearl
Lawrence, Silas, boot and shoemaker, 4 Peck-slip.
Lawrence, Jacob, labourer, Lumber-street.
Lawrence, Richard, merchant, 253 Pearl, & 80 John
Lawrence, Jonathan H. merchant, 83 Greenwich
Lawrence, Robert, shipmaster, Jay
Lawrence, Nicholas, cartman, 44 Chamber
Lawrence, Daniel, taylor, 64 Gold
Lawrence, Jona. insp. of pot-ash, 69 Broad, & 7 Stone
Lawrence, William, merchant, 13 Broadway.
Lawrence, Daniel, shipwright, 45 Catherine-street.
Lawrence, and Dayton, merchants, 86 Wall
Lawrence, Samuel D. flour merchant, 454 Pearl
Lawrence, John, B. druggist, 195 Pearl
Lawrence, Samuel, attorney at law, 69 Broad
Lawrence, Dominick, labourer, Mulberry
Lawrence, Augustus, shoemaker, 30 Chamber
Lawrence, Peter, 47 Chamber
Lawrence, John, grocer, William, corner Barley
Lawrence, Jonathan, mariner, 38 Roosevelt
Lawrence, Nathaniel, shipwright, Charlotte
Lawrence, Benjamin, carpenter, 39 Robinson
Lawrence, William, cartman, Third
Lawrence, James, M. D. Elizabeth, near Bayard
Lawrence, Nathaniel, merchant, 121 Water
Lawrence and Van Sinderen, merchants, 201 Pearl
Lawton, William, grocer, 99 Harman
Lawson, John, shipwright, 20 Lumber
Lawson, Peter P. cartman, Nicholas, corner Winne
Lawson, Isaac, sawyer, Pope's-alley.
Lawson, John, tail. 59 William-street.
Laycock, John, cartman, 11 Reed
Lazarus, Samuel, shopkeeper, 19 William
Lazer, Emanuel, 16 Chapel
Lazer, Lawrence, shipmaster, 33 Oliver
Leabech, John G. baker, 6 Augustus
Leach, Thomas, baker, 217 William
Leach, Archibald, mariner, 5 Cheapside.

K 2

Leader, Henry, shipmaster, 171 William-street.
Leaf, William, bootmaker, 155 Pearl
Leake, John G. 40 Nassau
Leakman, John, rigger, Eagle
Leary, Daniel, taylor, 158 Front
Leavenworth, Elisha, merchant, 32 Catharine
Leavenworth and Co. Elisha, store, Bowne's wharf.
Leaycraft, William & taylor, 132 Chatham-street.
Leaycraft, John, shoemaker, 46 Barley
Leaycraft, William, revenue officer, 109 Liberty
Leaycraft, ———, copperplate-printer, 345 Broadway.
Lebrun, Harin, grocer, 137 Fly-market.
Lebeau, Annale, 16 James-street.
Lecount, John, 47 Dey
Ledet, Josiah L. merchant, 66 William
Ledson, John, mason, 11 Vandewater
Ledyard, Peter V. merchant, 91 Maiden lane.
Ledyard, Mrs. young ladies accademy, 32 Dey-street.
Lee, Robert P. attorney at law, 391 Pearl
Lee and Hatton, hatters, 119 Water
Lee, Edward, mason, Eagle
Lee, Andrew, grocer, 57 Nassau
Lee, Alexander, grocer, 63 Reed
Lee, Peter, hivadore, 15 Fair
Lee, John, soap &c. manufactory, 58 Chatham
Lee, Joseph, perfumery store, 116 William
Leech, James, shipwright & tavern, Corlaer's-hook.
Leech, George, 257 Broadway.
Leechman, John, cabinetmaker, 60 Cedar-street.
Leek, Henry, tanner, Little Ann
Lefevre, Elizabeth, 30 Partition
Lefferts, Dirck, 65 Maiden-lane.
Lefferts, Leffert, merchant, 49 Ferry-street.
Lefferts, Lucretia, 7 Nassau
Leffingwell and Pierpont's counting-house, 63 Pine
Leffingwell, William, merchant, 63 Pine
Leroy, Th. hatter & coll. fourth ward, 200 Broadway.
Lefurge, Amos, 32 Warren
Lefarge, Frederick, 16 Warren
Legget, John, mariner, 69 E. George
Legget, Abraham, merchant, 63 Roosevelt
Legget, Ebenezer and John, merchants, 19 Peck-slip

Legget, Gabriel, windsor chairmaker, 8 Frankfort-str.
Legget, Thomas, merchant, 307 Pearl
Legget, Joseph, merchant, 375 Pearl
Legras, John, merchant-taylor, 22 Liberty
L'Hommidieu, Nathaniel, shipmaster, 31 George
L'Hommidieu, William, grocer, 203 Greenwich
Leivley, John, labourer, Mott
Lemaire, John, carver and gilder, 54 Barclay
Lemaire, Rev. John, 255 Broadway.
Leming, Margaret, sick-nurse, 47 Gold
Lemmon, John, confectioner, 71 Division
Lenes, Powles, 74 Murray
Lenox, Robert, merchant, 175 Pearl
Lenox, David, cartman, Winne, corner Hester
Lenox, (James) and Wm. Maitland, merhts. 4 Wm.
Lent, Margaret, mantuamaker, 56 Beekman
Lent, John, brush manufacturer, 2 Beekman-slip.
Lent, James W. grocer and flour store, South-street.
Lent, Henry, cooper, 8 Cherry
Lente, Christopher Lewis, merchant, 108 Gold
Lentner, John, cabinet-maker, 56 Cliff
Lentz, Lewis, taylor, 3 Broad
Leonard, Peter, 144 Chatham
Leonard, John W. shipmaster, 51 Stone
Leonard, John, cartman, 321 Broadway.
Leonard, William, tavern, 61 Bowery-lane
Leonard, James, lower end Barley-street.
Leonard, Jeffrey, mariner, 22 Church
Leonard, Francis, hair-dresser, 3 Beekman
Leonard, Thomas, boarding house, 23 Water
Leonard, Enoch, mason, Orchard
Leremboore, A. M. merch. 27 Wm. & 342 Broadway.
Lerment, Robert, taylor, 45 Nassau-street.
Le Roy, Jacob, merchant, 39 Cortlandt
Le Roy and Sons, Jacob, counting-house, 5 Wall
Le Roy, Harman, merchant, 66 Broadway.
Le Roy, Robert, merchant, 158 Greenwich-street.
Le Roy, Francis, mariner, 51 E. George
Le Roy, Bayard & M'Evers' counting-house, 117 Pearl
Le Roy, David, cartman, 7 Division
Lesano, John, caulker, Charlotte
Leslie, Thomas, rigger, 129 Harman

Lester, Rebecca, 29 Cheapside.
Lester, Andrew, shipwright, 97 Chamber-street.
Lester & Co. Benj. china, glass, &c. store, New-slip.
Lester, Benjamin, merchant, 87 James-street.
Lester, Richard, shipwright, 111 Cherry
Lester, Samuel S. shipwright, Harman
Letts, William, cartman, Elizabeth
Letts, Lorton, carpenter, 41 Barclay
Letts, Elijah, trader, 22 Cooper
Leuthauser, Henry, German teacher, 204 William
Leveridge, John, shoemaker, 44 James
Levinus, Nathaniel, grocer, Greenwich-road.
Levy, Aaron, merchant, 87 Wall-street.
Levy, Joshua, chocolatemaker, 37 Broad
Levy, Eleazer, merchant, 18 Pearl
Levy, widow Sloe, 85 Pearl
Lewis, John, bookbinder, 60 Fair
Lewis, George and James, merchants, 260 Pearl
Lewis, Richard, cartman, 78 Chamber
Lewis, Eleanor, washer, Division
Lewis, David, grocer, 25 Oliver
Lewis, Thomas, carpenter, 10 Augustus
Lewis, John, rigger, 6 Pump
Lewis, Francis, cartman, Pump
Lewis, widow of John, 283 Broadway.
Lewis, Erasmus, grocer, 52 Maiden-lane.
Lewis, Henry, cartman, 437 Pearl-street
Lewis, Rachel, tayloress, 14 Barclay
Lewis, Francis, 144 Greenwich
Lewis, Richard, sailmaker, 67 Ann
Lewis, Evan, cartman, 28 Catharine
Lewis, Nathaniel, shipmaster, 55 Catharine
Lewis, widow, 9 Moore's-row.
Lewis, Beal N. attorney at law, 66 Cherry-street.
Lewis, John, grocer, 78 John
Lewis, Joseph, mariner, 25 Oliver
Lewis, Stevens I. physician, 48 Maiden-lane
Ley, Eleazer, Cross-street.
Liancourt, Stephen, jeweller, 57 William
Liddell, James, teacher, 13 Bowery-lane.
Lichtman, John, lamplighter, 14 Roosevelt-street.
Lighthauser, William, grocer, Division

Lilly, John, labourer, 99 Division-street,
Linberger, Henry, baker, 54 Vesey
Linbert, George, tavern, 68 Bowery-lane.
Lincoln, Ann, 2 Chapel-street.
Lincoln, Francis, rigger, 37 James
Lincoln, Hosea, carpenter, 86 Fair
Lindley, Ebenezer, mason, 40 Barclay
Lindley and Hartthorne, merchants, 27 Beekman
Lindley, Joseph, merchant, 27 Beekman
Lindsay, George, stone & marble-cutter, 118 Liberty
Lindsey, David, carpenter, Bedlow
Lindyman, John, cooper, 23 Harman
Lines, Henry, cartman, 19 Chapel
Lingo, Cornelius, labourer, 6 E. George
Link, Lewis, tobacconist, 250 William
Linn, Rev. William, D. D. corner of Fair and Nassau
Linnen, John, cooper, 14 Beekman-slip.
Linnen, George, carpenter, Little Catharine-street.
Lint, Jacob, cartman, 33 Barley
Lintz, Frederick, grocer, corner of Ann and Nassau
Lippencot, John, mason, Thomas
Lippencot, widow, nurse, 69 John
Liquer, Abraham, Pump
Lispenard, Anthony, brewer, Greenwich-road.
Lispenard, Leonard, brewer, 20 Cortlandt-street.
Little, Eleazer, carpenter, Magazine
Little, William, carpenter, 272 Broadway.
Little, Jona. & E. merchants, 165 Water, & 10 John
Little, Joseph, mason, 6 Batavia-lane.
Little, Michael, porter & boarding-house, 56 Pine-st.
Little & Co. R. wine and porter vaults, 45 E. George
Little, Charles, mariner, Beaver
Little, Moses, milkman, 40 Barclay
Livesey, William, taylor, Pump
Livingston, Edward, carpenter, 25 Barclay
Livingston, Peter V. 22 Cortlandt
Livingston, Margaret, 284 Pearl
Livingston, Philip, merchant, 50 Broadway.
Livingston, Robert R. chancellor, 5 Broadway.
Livingston, Brockholst, counsellor at law, 37 Broadway.
Livingston, Edward, counsellor at law, 43 Broadway
Livingston, John R. merchant, 67 Broadway.

NEW-YORK DIRECTORY.

Livingston, Peter R. attorney at law, 82 Broadway.
Livingston, Edward & Maturin. office 43 Broadway
Livingston, widow, 48 Maiden-lane.
Livingston, Rev. John H. 52 Vesey-street.
Livingston, Daniel, shoemaker, Mulberry
Lloyd, Joseph, grocer, 22 Moore
Lloyd, Paul B. merchant, 10 Coenties-slip.
Lloyd, Michael, tavern, 3 Maiden-lane.
Lloyd, Richard, upholsterer, 30 Vesey-street.
Lloyd, Edward, taylor, 27 Pine
Lloyd, Richard, shipwright, Magazine
Lloyd, Thomas, grocer, 369 Pearl
Lock, Henry, chairmaker, 146 Chatham
Lockman, Jacob, grocer, 73 Cedar
Lockman, Abraham, baker 93 James
Lockman, Samuel, grocer, 116 Broad
Lockwood, Carey, shoemaker, 13 Nassau
Lockwood, Enoch, shoemaker, 91 James
Lockwood, Philip, carpenter and joiner, 84 James
Lockwood, Ann, boarding-house, 13 Cherry
Lockwood, Jos. boarding-house, New Albany bason
Lockwood, James, silversmith, 56 Lombard
Lodge, William, merchant, 24 Nassau
Lucas, ——, merchant, 433 Pearl
Loder, jun. John, cartman, 347 Broadway.
Loftus, Sarah, 3 Roosevelt
Logan, Thomas, shipmaster, 79 James
Logan, Adam, carpenter, 130 Bowery.
Lombard, Mrs. 33 Warren-street.
Londongreen, C F. 5 Augustus
Long, Michael, mariner, 70 E. George
Long, William, cartman, Bayard's-lane.
Long, John, rigger, 18 Roosevelt-street.
Longman, Thomas, 74 Vesey
Longworth, David, 66 Nassau
Loofborough, John, grocer, 411 Pearl
Lookey, Richard, mariner, Charlotte
Loomis, Libeus, merchant, 46 Greenwich
Loomis and Tillinghast's counting-house, 98 Wall
Lopes, Isaac, cartman, Bayard's-lane.
Lopes, Moses, 342 Washington-street.
Lopes, Lewis, barley

Lord, Daniel, physician, 32 Cherry-street.
Lord, William, carpenter, 18 Division
Lord, Samuel, carpenter, Fisher
Lord, George, carpenter, First
Lorillard, B. I. and J. tanners and curriers, Magazine
Lorillard, P and G. tobacconists, 30 Chatham
Loring, Innocent, boarding-house, 147 Harman
Loring, Mrs. 13 Broadway.
Lorton, Lewis, 7 Chapel-street.
Lorton, Paul, segar-maker, William, corner Barley
Lorton, William carpenter, 56 Vesey
Losee, Nicholas, labourer, Ropewalk.
Losey, Cornelius, grocer, 196 Greenwich
Loss, Christian, music teacher, 69 Dey
Lott, Mary, boarding-house, 22 Cedar
Lott, Peter, carpenter, 12 Harman
Lott, widow of Abraham, 36 Broad
Lott, Henry, carpenter, Magazine
Lott, William, 111 Division
Lott, Charles, carpenter, 24 Moore
Loudon, James, carpenter, 40 Lombard
Loudon, Samuel C. bookbinder, 110 Pearl
Loudon, Abigail, mantuamaker, 67 Murray
Louis, Andrew, grocer, Cross, corner of Mulberry
Loullit, Robert, shipwright, Lumber
Love, John, mariner, 78 Cherry
Love, David, cartman, 30 Bancker
Lovell, John, butcher, 140 Bowery-lane.
Lovett, Capt. Daniel, 97 Beekman-street.
Lovett, William, merchant, 395 Pearl
Lovett, John, grocer and tavern, 74 Cherry
Low, John, deputy cashier, bank of N. Y. 56 Fair
Low, Samuel, first book-keeper, B. N. Y. 9 Dutch
Low, Nicholas, merchant, 21 Broadway.
Low, John, bookseller, 332 Water-street.
Low, William, mason, 30 Bancker
Low, Anthony, mariner, 67 Roosevelt
Lowence, Capt. William, 250 William
Lower, Henry, labourer, 111 Division.
Lowerre, Edward, cooper, 55 John
Lowerre, James, cooper, 6 Vesey
Lowerre, John, taylor, 72 Nassau

NEW-YORK DIRECTORY.

Lowerre, Michael, coachmaker, 6 Fair-street.
Lowle, Peter, cabinetmaker, 335 Broadway.
Lowndes, William, 261 William-street.
Lowndes, Thomas, baker, 100 Liberty
Lowrie, William, carpenter and joiner, 184 William
Lowrie, Peter, livery-stabler, 45 Cedar
Lowry, Francis, fruiterer, 148 Broadway.
Lowther, Henry, labourer, near Union furnace.
Lozier, Nicholas, mason, 44 Chapel-street.
Lozier, Hillebrand, cartman, Division
Lozier, Nicholas, physician, 161 Greenwich
Lucas, Rebecca, 19 Lumber
Lucet and Co's. counting-house, 291 Greenwich
Lucet, Eugene, merchant, 291 Greenwich
Ludlam and Thompson, grocers, 145 Fly-market.
Ludlam, John, cartman, Charlotte-street.
Ludlam, William, cartman, 23 Chapel
Ludlam, James, merchant, 64 Beekman
Ludlam, Stephen, 75 Chatham
Ludlam, ——, painter and gilder, 54 John
Ludlam, Phœbe, tavern, 4 Ryder
Ludlow, Thomas, merchant, 58 Broadway.
Ludlow, Gulian, merchant, 13 Whitehall.
Ludlow, Gabriel V. office 18 Broad-street.
Ludlow, William, grocer, 15 Fayette
Ludlow, Gabriel W. merchant, 18 Wall
Ludlow, Charles, merchant, 18 Wall
Ludlow, Carey, counsellor at law, 7 State
Ludlow, John C. attorney at law, 18 Wall
Ludlow and Co. Daniel, counting-house, Garden
Ludlow, William W. merchant, 40 Pine
Ludlow, the Miller, 60 Pine
Ludlow, Ann, 2 Stone
Ludlow, Daniel, merchant, 62 Broadway.
Ludlow, Peter, merchant, 20 Pearl-street.
Ludlum, Jacob, taylor, 30 Moore
Luff, Philip, gardener, First
Luff, Matthias, grocer, First, corner of Eagle
Loftborough, Thomas, carpenter, 221 William
Loftborough, Isaac, shoemaker, 111 Division
Luker, Peter, marine, 45 Harman
Lumley, widow, washer, 5 Division

Lupton, Lancaster, 28 John-street.
Lupton, William, attorney at law, 28 John
Lustas, Joseph, fruiterer, 19 Peck-slip.
Lyde, Rogers, and Co. ironmongers, 229 Pearl-street.
Lyde, Edward, merchant, 4: Wall
Lydig, David, merch. 55 Beekman, & store 32 Peck-slip.
Lydig, widow, 4 Ferry-street.
Lyell, Fenwick, cabinetmaker, 43 and 46 Beaver
Lyell, Mrs. dry goods store, 4 Bowery-lane.
Lyell, Sarah, Mulberry-street.
Lylburn, Robert, merchant, 8 Garden
Lynch, Dominick, merchant, 35 Broadway.
Lynch, Francis, baker, 83 Fair-street.
Lynch, Fra. couns. at law, & notary-public 5 Cherry
Lynch, Patrick, grocer, 115 Cherry
Lynch, widow, 6 Ferry
Lynch, James, tea-waterman, Mott
Lynch, Hester, seamstress, Mulberry
Lyon and Co. Joseph, store, Front, corner Pine
Lyon, Nicholas, cooper, Mulberry
Lyon, Joseph, merchant, 85 Beekman
Lyon, Susannah, Pump
Lyon, widow, mantuamaker, 10 Barclay
Lyon, Jonathan, grocer, 88 James
Lyon, Matthias C. physician, 64 Cortlandt
Lyon, Joseph, mariner, 93 Chamber
Lyon, Hannah, sick nurse, 17 Division
Lyon, David, shoemaker, E. Rutger
Lyon, Isaac, clothier, 9 Moore
Lyon, Peter, smith, 15 Fair
Lyon, Stephen, slop-store, 287 Water
Lyon, David, cartman, 16 Garden
Lyons, James, porter and wine bottler, 45 L. George
Lyons, Thomas, shoemaker, Upper Reed
Lyons, Joseph, corner, 9 Bowery lane.
Lyons, Elizabeth & Jane, milliners, 22 Maiden-lane.
Lyons, James, 305 Pearl-street.
Lyver, Michael, taylor, 57 Ann

M

M'Adam, Ann, 57 Broadway.
M'Adams, John, grocer, Second street
M'Alpin, John, mariner, 11 Rutger

M'Arthur, Alexander, tavern & grocery, 6 Water-st.
M'Auley, William, mason, Bedlow
M'Bain, John, smith, 9 Cheapside.
M'Beth, Alexander, cartman, Orchard-street.
M'Bride, James, tallow-chandler, 93 Beekman
M'Bride and Watson, tallow-chandlers, 98 Beekman
M'Bride, John, lumber-merchant, 20 E. George
M'Bride, John, cartman, First
M'Bride, Walter, 28 Rutger
M'Cabe, widow, 2 Moore's-row.
M'Cabe, Edward, labourer, 300 Broadway.
M'Caffil, widow, washer, 9 Augustus-street.
M'Caffil, John, grocer, 118 Beekman
M'Call, widow, 92 Reed
M'Call, John, labourer, 92 Reed
M'Callom, Archibald, 7 Warren
M'Camman, widow, 50 Chatham
M'Camman, John, labourer, 50 Chatham
M'Camman, Mark, mason, 45 Chatham
M'Can, John, labourer, E. Rutger
M'Carran, John, grocer, 36 Catharine
M'Carty, Charles, grocer, 47 Cherry
M'Carty, James, labourer, 92 Catharine
M'Carty, Roger, teacher, 26 Vesey
M'Carty, James, labourer, 5 James
M'Carty, J. 23 George
M'Carty, Thomas, Greenwich-road.
M'Carty, Thomas, cooper, 21 Cliff-street.
M'Clarren, James, carpenter, 23 Chapel
M'Clalkin, Dennis, labourer, 2 beaver
M'Claughry, James, carpenter, Second
M'Clave, ——, teacher, 75 Warren
M'Clelan, Hugh, 77 Reed
M'Clenachan, Elizabeth, crockery-store, 27 Broad
M'Clerrin, John, grocer, 36 Catharine
M'Cillies, Woren, shoemaker, 209 Broadway.
M'Clouchan, Daniel, mason, 63 Liberty-street.
M'Clouchan, William, cooper, Gibbs'-alley.
M'Clouchan, Benjamin, cartman, 48 Bancker-street.
M'Clouchan, George, cooper, Gibbs'-alley.
M'Clouchan, John, smith, First-street.
M'Clouchan, Archibald, mariner, 33 Rutger

M'Cloafkey, William, porter bottler, 76 James-street.
M'Clare, James, cartman, 7 Robinson
M'Clare, William, mariner, 27 Broadway.
M'Clare, William, taylor, 16 Barclay-street.
M'Clyment, William, grocer, 50 E. George
M'Colgan, ——, grocer, Greenwich-road.
M'Cullough, Robert, taylor, 66 Murray-street.
M'Comb, Sarah, 146 Greenwich
M'Comb, ——, paver, Duane
M'Comb, jun. John, builder, upper end Washington
M'Connel, James, cooper, 5 Ferry
M'Connel, Jacob, cooper, 5 Ferry
M'Cormick, Daniel, merchant, 57 Wall
M'Cormick, David, cabinetmaker, 68 E. George
M'Cormick, widow, 47 Lumber
M'Cormick, Mrs. 12 Barclay
M'Cowiff, Michael, labourer, 12 Moore
M'Coy, John mariner, Harman
M'Coy, ——, labourer, Henry
M'Coy, Patrick, mason, 17 Augustus
M'Craken, John, carpenter, 43 Chatham
M'Crea, John, tavern, 76 James
M'Cready, Thomas, shoemaker, 57 Pine
M'Cready, William, mason, 18 Division
M'Cready, jun. James, taylor, 227 Water
M'Cready, Andrew, boot & shoemaker, 59 William
M'Cready, James, lamplighter, Henry
M'Cready, Thomas, grocer, 68 Broad
M'Cready, Thomas, Little Ann
M'Cullen and Johnston, grocers, 21 Front
M'Cullen, Robert, cooper, 92 Front
M'Culloch, William, shipmaster, 74 Harman
M'Cullam, Mary, sick nurse, 68 Ann
M'Cullum, Archibald, fuller, 102 Broadway.
M'C——, ——, labourer, 12 Moore's-row.
M'Davis, Dennis, baker, 22 Robinson-street.
M'Dermot, Hugh, baker, 37 Warren
M'Dermot, George, tavern, 26 E. George
M'Dermot, John, carpenter, Sixth
M'Darmuk, Robert, carpenter, 26 Harman
M'Dole, James, mason, Winne
M'Donald, John, brassfounder, 39 Roosevelt

M'Donald, Alexander, carpenter, E. Rutger-ſtreet.
M'Donald, Ann, grocer, 2 Harman
M'Donald, John, rigger, 30 Rutger
M'Donald, Catharine, tayloreſs, 9 Dey
M'Donald, Duncan, grocer & ſawyer, Greenwich-road.
M'Donald, Alexander, merchant, 165 Broadway.
M'Donald, Alexander, printer, 62 John-ſtreet.
M'Donald, Alexander L. attorney at law, 12 Wall
M'Donald, Walter, teacher, 15 Harman
M'Donald, Duncan, wine & porter vaults, 13 George
M'Donald, James, mariner, 1 Jacob
M'Donald, Thomas, cooper, 21 Skinner
M'Donald, William, ſhipwright, 89 Chatham
M'Donald, Alexander, 35 Rutger
M'Donald, John, rigger, E. Rutger
M'Donald, John, cartman, 18 Murray
M'Donald, Donald, hair-dreſſer, 16 Burling-ſlip.
M'Dougall, John, taylor, 82 Greenwich-ſtreet.
M'Dougall, Peter, merchant, 191 Pearl
M'Dougall, Hugh, paint and oil ſtore, 92 Broadway.
M'Dougall, Alexander, ſmith, 50 Barclay-ſtreet.
M'Dougall, Benjamin, ſhoemaker, 42 Rutger
M'Dougall, Robert, cooper, 9 James
M'Dougall, Archibald, gardiner, Third
M'Dougall, John, china mender, Orange
M'Dougall, Archibald, ironmonger, 6 Coenties-ſlip.
M'Dowl, widow, 45 E. George
M'Eacken, Peter, currier, 12 Jacob
M'Elwain, John, grocer, Bedlow
M'Evers, James, merchant, 117 Pearl
M'Evers, John, labourer, 27 Ferry
M'Evers, Gulien, merchant, 140 Greenwich
M'Evers and Barclay, auctioneers, 127 Water
M'Evers, James, cartman, Bowery.
M'Ewen and ..., Malmſey, ..., ... Water-ſt
M'Ewen, Margaret, ..., 62 ...
M'Ewen, David, ſmith, 54 ...
M'Fall, Robert, labourer, Water
M'Fall, Daniel, ſhipmaſter, 20 Gold
M'Fergue, Manus, ſmith, ...
M'Farlane, Henry, ... Coenties-ſlip, & ... Water
M'Farlane, James, ..., Ferry

M'Farlane, Alexander, hatter, 57 Reed-street.
M'Farlane, Robert, smith, 22 Reed
M'Farlane, Isabel, boarding-house, 290 Water
M'Farlane, William, carpenter, 98 James,
M'Farlane, John, shipwright, Eagle
M'Farlane, John, air-furnace, Greenwich.
M'Farlane, Patrick, grocer, 9 Harman-street,
M'Farlane, Dougall, labourer, 70 Liberty
M'Farlane, Monteith, printer, 290 Water
M'Farran, Sarah, tavern, 150 Fly-market.
M'Gahagan, Dennis, teacher, 1 Dover-street.
M'Garrah, James, shipwright, 13 Oliver
M'Garry, Chr. & Ric. labourers, E. Washington
M'Gary, Thomas, painter, gilder, &c. 13 Old-slip.
M'Gavitlon, John, shoemaker, 427 Pearl-street.
M'Gee, John, cartman, Second
M'Gie, Joshua H. cartman, 115 Liberty
M'Ginley, David, shoemaker, 83 William
M'Gilvery, Lydia, 52 Cedar
M'Ginnes, widow, Barley
M'Gogan, John, cooper, 10 Rector
M'Gowan, David, cooper, 22 Bancker
M'Gowan, ——, carpenter, Charlotte
M'Gowan, Christopher, mason, 48 Chatham
M'Gowan, Robert, grocer, Charlotte
M'Graw, Arthur, weaver, Greenwich-road.
M'Gregor, John, teacher, 7 Pine
M'Gregor, Elizabeth, Harman
M'Gregor, Alexander, rigger, 58 E. George
M'Gregor, Collin, merchant, 108 Greenwich
M'Gregor, John and Alexander, 190 Pearl
M'Guire, Thomas, cooper, Broadway, near furnace.
M'Guire, Peter P. measurer, 16 Rector-street.
M'Guire, jun. Bernard, cartman, Greenwich-road.
M'Guire, J. Albany coffee-house, 114 Greenwich-st.
M'Intire, John, taylor, 271 Greenwich
M'Intire, Neal, merchant, 43 Ferry
M'Intosh, James, merchant, 14 Beekman-slip.
M'Intosh, Cornelius, 32 Harman-street.

M'Intyre, Peter, hairdresser, 100 Catharine-street.
M'Intyre, Ronald, grocer, 64 Roosevelt
M'Intyre, Duncan, hairdresser, 14 Rose
M'Kay and Thompson, David, grocers, 504 Broadway.
M'Kay, James, grocer, 21 and 23 Old-slip.
M'Kay, John, fruiterer, 116 Broadway.
M'Kay, William, boatman, 50 Barclay-street.
M'Kay, John, painter and glazier, 10 Warren
M'Kay, Æneas, grocer, 20 Harman
M'Kay, Pompey, sweepmaster, 50 Bancker
M'Kay, George and John, grocers, 114 Beekman
M'Kean, Elizabeth, 20 Chapel
M'Kee, John, grocer, 98 Broad
M'Kenley, John, labourer, Little Catharine
M'Kerzie, John, carpenter, 215 Greenwich
M'Kenzie, ——, store, Greenwich, corner of Cedar.
M'Kenzie, widow, 54 Cedar
M'Kenzie, Alexander, smith, 76 E. George
M'Kenzie, Alexander, watchmaker, 161 Pearl
M'Kenzie, Keneth, painter and glazier, 45 Oliver
M'Kenzie, Mary, schoolmistress, 6 Pine
M'Kenzie, Mary, 21 Harper
M'Keowen, James, mason, 71 Reed
M'Kercey, George, carver and gilder, 302 Pearl.
M'Kesson, John, counsellor at law, 67 Pearl
M'Kesson, jun. John, attorney at law, 67 Pearl
M'Kew, John, labourer, 15 Moore's-row.
M'Kinlay, Peter, china and glass store, 119 Fly-market.
M'Kinney, William, stonecutter, Rector.
M'Kinnon, Neil, 75 Fair
M'Kinnon, Daniel, counsellor at law, 17 Broadway.
M'Kinnon, jun. Neil, grocer, 268 Water-street.
M'Knight, Rev. John, D. D. 160 Broadway.
M'Lachlan & Roberts, brewery, 30 Chatham-str.
M'Lachlan, Michael, merchant, 4 Catharine-slip.
M'Lachlan, Patrick, fruiterer, 51 Pearl-street.
M'Laren, John, merchant, 8 Gold
M'Laren, Daniel, dry goods store, 163 Broadway.
M'Laren, Neil, grocer, Front-street, near Peck-slip.
M'Lean, Ann, corner of Beekman and Nassau streets.
M'Lean, Hugh, M. D. corner of Beekman & Nassau

McLean, Murdoch, tavern, Bruce's wharf.
McLean, Neil, rigger, 62 John-street.
McLean, John, labourer, Colden
McLean, John, 27 Oliver
McLean, (Archibald) & Lang, printers, 116 Pearl
McLean, Charles, cabinetmaker, Greenwich-road.
McLean, ——, shopkeeper, 187 Greenwich-street.
McLean, William, carpenter, 10 Vesey
McLean, Duncan, labourer, 9 Moore
McLean, Jacob, smith, First
McLeod, John, carpenter, 23 Chapel
McLeod, John, merchant, 42 Fair
McLeod, jun. Donald, grocer, Greenwich-road.
McLeod, Donald, merchant, 58 Maiden-lane.
McManus, P. grocer, 26 Robinson-street.
McMaster, James, smith, 44 Gold, and 6 Ryder
McMaster, James, grocer, 1 Catharine
McMenomy, Robert, merchant, 107 William
McMichael, Dougal, carpenter, 94 Catharine
McMillan, James, rigger, 12 Harmon
McMillan, Alexander, shoemaker, 37 Murray
McMullen, John, labourer, 18 Batavia-lane.
McMullen, John, cartman, Upper Reed-street.
McMullen, James, mason, 4 Bancker
McMurray, John, labourer, Upper Reed
McMurray, James, mason, Magazine
McNabb, John, grocer, Cross, corner of Orange
McNair, John, mariner, 50 Roosevelt
McNair, Charles, smith, 22 Church
McNally, Martin, taylor, 47 E. George
McNeil, jun. John, attorney at law, 244 William
McNicholl, Arthur, grocer, Bedlow, corner Charlotte
McNichols, Neil, tavern, 195 Cherry
McPherson, Duncan, shoemaker, 4 Harman
McPherson, John, boardore. and tavern, 2 Dover
McPherson, Andrew, chandler, 5 Pearl
McPirie, A. taylor, 139 Greenwich
McQueen, Ann, 3 Maiden-lane.
McQueen, John, taylor, 12 Ferry-street.
McQuoid, Robert, merchant, Magazine
McReady, John, tobacco & snuff manufac. 26 Old-C.
McSweney, George, mariner, 53 Cherry

M'Swine, John, labourer, 10 Moore's-row.
M'Vickar, John & Nathan, store 2 Burling-slip.
M'Vickar, John, merchant, 228 Pearl-street.
M'William, Archibald, grocer, 70 Barley
Mabie, Peter, merchant, 206 Pearl
Maby, John, tavern, 191 Washington
Maby, Peter, cartman, air-furnace, Greenwich-road.
Maby, Corn. cartman, air-furnace, Greenwich-road.
Maby, Jacob, labourer, Third-street.
Mabye, Frederick, shoemaker, 28 Chatham
Mace, Thomas, milliner, 137 William
Macgill, Robert, booksel. & stationer, 105 Maiden-lane.
Mack, Daniel, 19 George-street.
Mack, Ebenezer, miniature-painter, 144 William
Mackaness, Ths. agent of British packets, 32 Partition
Mackawe, widow, 265 William
Mackie, Alexander, labourer, Charlotte
Mackie, Samuel, sailor, Charlotte
Mackie and Son, Peter, merchants, 61 Water
Mackin, Neil, grocer, 24 E. George
Macklin, William, tavern, 36 E. George
Mackrill, William, carpenter, Henry
Macomb, Alexander, merchant, 47 Broadway.
Macomb, John N. merchant, 11 Cortlandt
Macomb, J. patentee, 75 Catharine
Made, John, cartman, 96 Catharine
Maddin, Thomas, grocer, 4 Catharine
Maddison, Duncan, bookseller, 11 Rector
Maddock, James, grocer, 142 Division
Maghee, Daniel, cartman, 55 Church
Maghee, Safety, shoemaker, 61 Gold
Maghee, Tunis, coachmaker, Mulberry
Maghee, John, carpenter, 40 Murray
Maglone, Hugh, husband, Corn. Bowery-lane.
Magnes, John, Little Ann-street.
Magrath, Patrick, grocer, 25 Peck-slip.
Mahaney, Matthias, smith, 25 Chamber
Maharey, widow, shop keeper, 26 Barclay
Mahard, William, carpenter, Magazine
Mair, John, shoemaker, Upper Read
Main, James, shoemaker, 49 Chapel
Main, Diadema, 57 Frankfort

NEW-YORK DIRECTORY.

Main, Andrew, merchant, 31 Murray-street.
Main, James, taylor, 43 Nassau
Maitland, Howel & Co. ship-chandlers, 21 Beekman-st.
Maitland, William, merchant, 4 William-street.
Major, Samuel, painter, 37 Rutger
Makee, Henry, soap, &c. manufactory 14 Bowery.
Makins, John, mariner, 25 Cheapside.
Malcom, widow, of Gen. William, 3 Whitehall.
Malcom and Co. Richard, store, 141 Water-street.
Malcom, Margaret, midwife, 1 Cooper
Malcom, Duncan, labourer, 3 Moore's-row.
Mallaby, Francis, shipmaster, 63 Partition-street.
Mallabay and Durand, merchants, 93 Maiden-lane.
Mallenbrey, Joseph, physician 334 Water
Mallifs, James, cartman, Greenwich-road.
Malloy, John, mariner, Lumber-street.
Malone, Joseph, tavern, Front-st. near Peck-slip.
Mangin and brothers, architects, 37 Chatham-street.
Manley, Robert, grocer, 13 Chapel
Manley, William, mariner, Gibbs'-alley.
Manley, Cæsar, stivadore, 57 Gold-street.
Manley, John, dry goods store, 187 Broadway.
Manley, Robert, 24 John-street.
Mann, John, shoemaker, 393 Pearl
Mann, David, butcher, Bowery-lane.
Mann, Edward, sailmaker, 130 Greenwich-street.
Mann, Elizabeth, 12 Dey
Mann, Archibald, sailmaker, 23 Roosevelt
Mann, William, merchant, 84 Partition
Manney, Francis, cooper, 73 Nassau
Manney, Catharine, toy-shop, 53 Liberty
Manning, Abraham, constable, 34 Barley
Manning, James, 12 Pearl, & store, 23 Albany-basin.
Manning, Clarkson, cartman, 30 Moore-street.
Mansfield, John, carpenter, 69 Harman
Mansfield, Daniel, mariner, 47 Cliff
Martin and Soulier, merchants, 76 William
Manuel, Mary, washer, 70 Ann
Manuel, William, labourer, 18 Garden
Many, Barnabas, flage-office, &c. 48 Cortlandt
Mapes, Jonas, Water
Miranda, Anthony, confectioner, 34 John

Marcadier, Joseph, 57 Chamber-street.
Marcelis, Peter, cartman, 69 Reed
Marcelis, Deborah, 51 Broad
Marcelis, Jacob, cartman, 46 Chapel-street.
Marcellin, Anthony V. 128 Broadway.
Marcer, John, tavern, 77 Wall
March, Samuel, merchant, 22 Beaver-street.
Marchant, John, cutler, 29 Cliff
Maree, Mary, boarding-house, 89 Beekman
Margarum, James I. accountant, 10 Frankfort
Mark, Jacob, merchant, 75 Greenwich
Mark and Co. Jacob, store, William, corner Stone
Mark and Sterlitz, Philip, merchants, 206 Pearl
Markaway, Frederick, mariner, 29 Oliver
Markin, John, cartman, Essex
Marrenner, Edward, hairdresser, 122 Broadway.
Marrenner, John, hairdresser, 19 Dey-street.
Marschalk, Joseph, shipmaster, 82 James
Marschalk, John, accountant, 3 Wall
Marschalk, Miss, milliner, William, corner John
Marschalk, Francis, cartman, Division
Marschalk, John, china-store, 120 Chatham
Marsh, John, carpenter, E. Rutger
Marsh, Joseph, mason, Greenwich-road.
Marsh, Joseph, grocer, 63 Catharine-street.
Marsh, Gideon, smith, 73 Reed
Marshall, William, stonecutter, Greenwich
Marshall, Jeremiah, inspector of lumber, 20 Beekman
Marshall, Joseph, shipbuilder, 72 E. George
Marshall, William, rigger, 15 Harman
Marshall, Elihu, Sound and coasting-pilot, 14 Bancker
Marshall, A. 197 William
Marshall, Amos, scrivener, 14 Bancker
Marshall, Kingston, shipmaster, 14 Bancker
Marshall, Thomas A. shoemaker, 46 Murray
Marshall, Joseph, coppersmith, 183 Water
Marston and Cuyler's store, New Albany-bason.
Marston and Co. John, store, 83 Water-street.
Martin, John, smith and machinist, 17 Barclay
Martin, William, tavern, 99 Catharine
Martin, Samuel, laborer, 89 Division
Martin, Robert, waterman, 137 Division.

Martin, John, mason, Eagle-street.
Martin, Wm. blockmaker, Cherry, corner, E. George
Martin, Runyon, carpenter, Charlotte, corner Bedlow
Martin, John, copperplate-printer, 236 Greenwich
Martin, Edward, buttonmaker, 197 William
Martin, John J. 28 Frankfort
Martin, Josiah, carpenter, Elizabeth
Martin, Peter, 206 Pearl
Martin, Mary, huckster, 96 Cherry
Martin, James, miniature-painter, 8 Wall
Martin, Francis, cartman, 66 Warren
Martine, William, grocer, Greenwich-road.
Martine, John, carpenter, Greenwich-road.
Martinot, Janett, 198 William-street.
Martlings, Henry, shipjoiner, Pump
Martlings, Abraham B. tavern, 87 Nassau
Martlings, Abraham S. cooper, 21 Marketfield
Marvin, John, grocer, 148 Front
Mason, widow of Dr. John, 27 Cortlandt
Mason, Rev. John M. 27 Cortlandt
Mason, Christopher, hat-store, 380 Pearl
Mason, John, merchant, 84 William
Mason, Mary, 12 Moore's-row.
Massabot, P. tobacconist, 48 James-street.
Masse, Madam, 45 Warren
Masse, John, painter, 68 Warren
Massias, A. commission-store, 108 Front
Masterton, Henry, attorney at law, 147 & 172 Water
Masterton, William, merchant, 172 Water
Masterton, David, merchant, 172 Water
Mathews, William, merchant-taylor, 126 Water
Mathews, Andrew, boarding-house, 22 John
Mathews, John, mariner, 7 Lumber
Mathews, Robert, carpenter, 5 Hague
Mathews, John, oysterman, 59 Catharine
Mathews, John, grocer, Bedlow
Mathews, Charles, mariner, 31 Harman
Mathews, William, merchant, 35 Roosevelt
Mathews, David, mason, 34 Harman
Maule, Thomas, merchant, 155 Pearl
Maurin, Peter, chimney-office, 8 George
Maverick, Peter R. engraver & seal-sinker, 65 Liberty

Maxwell, James H. 1 John, corner of Broadway.
Maxwell, William, shipwright, Henry-street.
Maxwell, William, distiller, 225 Greenwich
Maxwell, William, 52 Dey
Maxwell, Daniel, mason, 52 Barley
Maxwell, Joseph, 15 Rose
Mayby, Peter, cartman, Greenwich-road.
Mayell, William, hat-store, 45 Maiden-lane.
Mayer, widow, 144 Division-street.
Mayo, Benjamin, teacher, 57 Roosevelt
Mayo, John, teacher, Bedlow
MAYOR's OFFICE, 1 Pine,
Mead, William, sadler, 147 Chatham
Mead, Halsey, butcher, 53 Bowery-lane.
Mead, Isaac, carpenter and builder, 14 Fair-street.
Mead, Nicholas, tavern, 59 Nassau
Mead, Smith, cartman, Second
Mead, Jesse, carpenter, Birmingham-row.
Mead, Nathaniel, teacher, 13 Nassau-street.
Mead, Henry, grocer, New-slip.
Mealy, Stephen, shoemaker, 53 Barclay-street.
Mean, James, mariner, Little Catharine
Meance, ——, miniature painter, 62 Broadway.
Meafe, Frances, boarding-house, 41 Catharine-street.
Mechefav, widow, Theatre-alley.
Medcalf, widow, Henry-street.
Meeks, Edward, smith, 29 Cedar
Meeks, jun. Edw. clock & watchmak. 114 Maiden-lane.
Meeks, Thomas, mason, 139 Greenwich-street.
Meeks, John, shoemaker, 8 Fair
Meeks, Joseph, shoemaker, 43 Gold
Meeks, Joseph and Edward, cabinetmakers, 59 Broad
Megie, Joshua Horten, cartman, 115 Liberty
Meldrum, John, carpenter, Henry
Meldrum, Robert, grocer, 87 Greenwich
Melick, Baltus P. merchant, 185 Washington
Mellent, John, gardener, Second
Mellows, David, 320 Broadway.
Melvin, widow, teacheress, 10 Beaver-street.
Memin, Charles St. engraver, 27 Pine
Menus, Leonard, tanner, Little Ann
Menzies, widow, 50 Partition

Mercein and Radan, bakers, 93 Gold-street.
Mercein, Andrew, baker, 93 Gold
Merchand, Charles, Orchard
Merchant, Frederick, tanner, Little Ann
Merrell, Frederick, shoemaker, 62 Barclay
Merrell, William, shoe warehouse, 160 William
Merrick, Richard, grocer, 415 Pearl
Merritt, Michael, flour merchant, 17 Rose
Merritt, James, flour merchant, Jay
Merritt, William, carpenter, 76 Harman
Merritt, Mary, Mulberry
Merritt, Ezekiel, mason, 82 Murray
Merritt, Ebenezer, deputy sheriff, 14 Frankfort
Merritt, John, mason, New-slip.
Merritt, John, 300 Greenwich-street.
Merritt, Ezekiel, 63 Murray
Merritt, James, shoemaker, Henry
Merritt, John and James, flour store, 70 Partition
Merritt & Clapp, M. flour merchts. Dover-str. wharf
Merry, Patrick H. grocer, 88 Roosevelt-street.
Mersereau and Breath's store, 38 Water
Mersey, John, fruiterer, 140 Front
Meservy, William, butcher, Bowery-lane.
Mesier, Peter A. bookbinder & stationer, 107 Pearl-str.
Mesnard, Thomas, shoe store, 35 John
Mess, Peter, grocer, 23 Chatham
Mestayer, Benjamin, framemaker, 28 Liberty
Metzler, Joseph, merchant, 88 Nassau
Michel, Joseph, merchant-taylor, 113 William
Michels, John, marshal, Bridewell.
Middlemas, Peter, 21 Beekman-street.
Middleton, Samuel, shipwright, Lumber
Middleton, William, cabinetmaker, 251 Greenwich
Midwinter, John, smith, 62 Catharine
Mildeberger, John, shoemaker, 35 Reed
Mildeberger, John, soap & candlemaker, 23 Nassau
Mildeberger, Oliver, leatherdresser, 19 Vandewater
Mildeberger, John, leatherdresser, 19 Chatham
Mildenburgh, John A. cabinetmaker, 29 Nassau
Miles, Charles, cooper, 61 Beekman
Miles, James, rigger, 47 Cheapside.
Milledoler, John, tobacconist, 412 Pearl-street.

Milledoler, Rev. Philip, 412 Pearl-street.
Millen, Quintin, grocer, 321 Pearl
Miller, Nicholas, smith, Charlotte
Miller, Henry, trunkmaker, 340 Pearl
Miller, Charles, tin-plate worker, 152 Water
Miller, Walter, carpenter, 92 Reed
Miller, George, gardener and tavern, Corlaer's hook
Miller, William, tavern, 2 Depeyster-street.
Miller, George, grocer, 8 Liberty
Miller, John, bookbinder, 6 Chamber
Miller, John Frederick, cooper, 21 Ann
Miller, Phœbe, shoe store, 67 Maiden-lane.
Miller, Rev. Samuel, 158 Broadway.
Miller, George, merchant, 57 Beekman-street
Miller and Hawxhurst, 41 Bancker
Miller, Jacob, mariner, 111 Harman
Miller, Edward, M. D. 158 Broadway.
Miller, Thomas, fruiterer, 12 Fair-street.
Miller, Nicholas, hairdresser, 34 Vesey
Miller, widow of John, 25 Maiden-lane.
Miller, John, shipwright, First-street.
Miller, Christian, butcher, Bowery-lane.
Miller, John, boarding-house, 102 Front-street.
Miller and Brown, grocers, New-slip.
Miller, Christopher, harbour-master, 53 Wall-street.
Miller and Coates, copper manufactory, 152 Water
Miller, Charles, copper manufactory, 152 Water
Miller, John, shoemaker, 15 Pine
Miller, John D. grocer, 6 Chamber
Miller, William G. baker, 60 John
Miller, Euphemia, boarding-house, 1 Rutger
Miller, William, cartman, 53 Reed
Miller, John, tanner, Elizabeth
Miller, John, hairdresser, 201 Broadway.
Miller and Baker, grocers, 119 Greenwich-street.
Miller, the Misses, 10 Nassau
Miller, Adolph, teacher, 32 Nassau
Miller, Andrew, saw framemaker, Winne
Miller, jun. Andrew, cartman, Winne
Miller, William, rope-maker, Pump
Miller, Elizabeth, market-woman, Eagle
Miller, Margaret, 98 Catharine-street.

NEW-YORK DIRECTORY.

Miller, Andrew R. merchant, 130 William-street.
Miller, Thomas, waiter, Mulberry
Miller, Tobias, grocer, Bayard
Miller, Zephaniah, labourer, Henry
Miller and Co. Zebulon, merchant-taylors, 157 Front
Miller, widow, boarding-house, 26 Garden
Miller, Lawrence, mariner, 96 James
Miller, Alexander, bookbinder, 35 Reed
Miller, John F. merchant, 29 James
Milligan, Lawrence, wheelwright, 27 Catharine
Milligan, Samuel, broker & measurer, 77 Maiden-lane.
Milligan, Gilbert, druggist & apothecary, 146 Water-st.
Mills, William, carpenter, 235 Broadway.
Mills, Hannah, boarding-house, 14 Cliff-street.
Mills, William, labourer, 6 Chapel
Mills, Jothan, inspector of lumber, 82 James
Mills, James, grocer, E. George, corner Division
Mills, John, boot and shoe store, 204 Broadway.
Mills and Deming, cabinetmakers, 374 Pearl-street.
Mills, John, boatbuilder, 21 E. George
Mills and Balharey, grocers, 278 Water
Milne, Thomas, jeweller, 120 Fly-market.
Milne, Robert, clock & watchmaker, 212 Pearl-street.
Milns, William, teacher, 29 Gold
M'Wynters, James, mariner, Bedlow
Minard, Isaac, shoemaker, 36 Barclay
Ming, John, pilot, 27 Roosevelt
Ming, Alexander, printer, 86 Front
Mink, George, tiler, 229 William
Minshull, John, merchant, 21 Maiden-lane.
Minthorn, Mangle, Bowery-lane.
Minthorn, Philip, taylor, Barley-street.
Mintern and Boyne, merchants, 258 Pearl
Minturn and Champlin's store, 215 Pearl
Minturn, Benjamin G. merchant, 215 Pearl
Minturn, William, merchant, 330 Pearl
Minugh, widow, shopkeeper, 71 Ann
Minugh, John, pilot, 91 Gold
Minugh, William, pilot, 28 Stone
M'nufe, Andrew, baker, 9 Chatham
M'nufe, John, milkman, 9 Chatham
M'nufe, George, joiner, 9 Chatham

Minuse, John, currier, 20 Jacob-street.
Minuse, Leonard, tanner, Little Ann
Misnour, Jacob, farrier, Thomas
Misplee, Thomas, coffee-seller, 5 Ryder
Mitililier, Lewis, grocer, 89 Nassau
Mitchell, Napier and Co. merchants, 157 Pearl
Mitchell, James, dancing-master, 278 Greenwich
Mitchell, John, accountant, 81 Roosevelt
Mitchell, William, marshal, 15 Water
Mitchell, John, painter, 19 Dey
Mitchell, John, chairmaker, 110 Chatham
Mitchell, widow, 7 Church
Mitchell, William, cartman, 94 Gold
Mitchell, Thomas, labourer, 47 Beaver
Mitchell, Samuel, currier, 39 Ferry
Mitchell, Walter, boatbuilder, 79 James
Mitchell, Robert, pilot, 16 Cliff
Mitchell, Calvin, carpenter, 75 Catharine
Mitchell, Henry, rigger, E. Rutger
Mitchell, Walter, grocer, 168 Greenwich
Mitchell, Andrew, merchant, 177 Pearl
Mitchelson, David, 93 Bowery-lane.
Mitchill, Samuel Latham, M. D. at his chambers in the College, or at his house, Charlotte-street.
Mitchill, Henry, watchmaker, 248 Pearl
Mitchill and Mott, clock and watchmakers, 247 Pearl
Mode, John, cartman, Greenwich-road.
Moller, John C. professor of music, Washington-strt.
Moloney, John, tavern, 117 Cherry
Moloy, Thomas, taylor, 57 Cherry
Monaque, Madam, Chapel
Monnell, Charles, combmaker, 3 E. George
Monnell, widow, 46 Harman
Monson, Daniel, tobacconist, 129 Division
Montague, Mary, 37 Liberty
Montarand, Mercier, Sixth
Montayne and Candell's cooperage, 11 Cooper
Montayne, Joseph De La, grocer, 73 Vesey
Montayne, widow, 38 Cedar
Montayne, Benjamin, china store, 282 Pearl
Montayne, Mary, 52 Roosevelt
Montayne, Peter, 281 Pearl

Montayne, sen. Isaac, mason, 18 Lombard-street.
Montayne, Isaac, mason, 34 Lombard
Montayne, John J. S. mason, 82 Liberty
Montayne, Harman, carpenter, 46 Cortlandt
Montayne, Isaac, 16 Barclay
Montgomery, Hugh, collector, 32 Ferry
Montgomery, Samuel, constable, Hague
Montgomery, widow, 5 Rutger
Montgomery, William, oysterman, 45 George
Montiero, Joaquim, merchant, 11 Broadway.
Mood, Catharine, shop keeper, 8 Depeyster-street.
Moody, William, grocer, 47 Pearl
Mook, William, sadler, 18 Bowery-lane
Moone, Mrs. boarding-house, 36 Maiden-lane.
Mooney, Wm. upholsterer, 31 & 33 Nassau-street.
Mooney, Hannah, 4 Cliff
Mooney, Edward, butcher, 10 Bowery-lane.
Mooney, William, butcher, 75 Well-street.
Mooney, Michael, mariner, 39 Rutger
Mooney, Barnet, hatter, 8 Vesey
Mooney and Brower, hat-store, 17 Maiden-lane.
Moore, widow, 36 Barclay-street.
Moore, Rev. Benjamin. D. D. 180 Broadway.
Moore, Blase, tobacconist, 182 Broadway.
Moore & Son, John S. dry goods store, 192 Broadway.
Moore, Baltus, soap & candlemaker, 212 Broadway.
Moore, Benjamin I. merchant, 121 William-street.
Moore, William, physician, 21 Nassau
Moore, Michael, grocer, 33 John
Moore, Nicholas, mason and builder, 70 James
Moore, Jacob, dry goods store, 39 Fair
Moore, Richard, cooper, 51 Vesey
Moore, Hugh, cartman, 6 Orange
Moore, George E. fruiterer, 43 Cedar
Moore, Mark, hatter, 2 Moore's-row.
Moore, George, laborer, Rope-walk.
Moore, Edward, 30 Broad-street.
Moore, James, mason, Henry
Moore, Thomas, mariner, Gibbs'-alley.
Moore, James, hawker, Orchard-street.
Moore, Thomas, cartman, 20 Warren.
Moore, widow, 8 Moore's-row.

Moore, James, cartman, 111 Harman-street.
Moore, Abraham, grocer, 72 Division
Moore, sen. Abraham, cartman, 152 Division.
Moore, James, tavern, First
Moore, Martha, teacheress, Mott
Moore, John, merchant, 60 Beekman
Moore, Jane, teacheress, 31 John
Moore, Susannah, washer, 47 Ann
Moore, Thomas, labourer, 47 Ann
Moorehead, Isaac, cartman, Fisher
Moorehouse, ——, shipmaster, 50 Cherry
Moores, William, grocer, 66 Warren
Moran, Edward, merchant-taylor, 25 Old-slip.
Morewood and Ogden, 123 Pearl-street.
Morewood, Thomas, merchant, 123 Pearl
Morgan, David, grocer, 29 Bancker
Morgan, Thomas, shipwright, Henry
Morgan, James, cartman, 16 Robinson
Morgan, Richard, merchant, 39 Stone
Morgan, David, stone-potter, Corlaer's-hook.
Morgan, Benjamin, slopshop, Charlotte-street.
Morgan and Co. Henry, grocers, 50 Peck-slip.
Morison, Peter, 120 Front-street.
Morison, John, tavern, 43 New
Morison, Thomas, shoemaker, 13 Thomas
Morison, William, cabinetmaker, 32 Barclay
Morison, James, merchant, 143 Water
Morison, William, grocer, 88 Harman
Morison, Nathaniel, porter-house, 57 Warren
Morits, Casper, lamplighter, Mott
Morrell, Andrew, mason, 29 Frankfort
Morrell, William, carpenter, 43 Oliver
Morrell, Salyer, mason, 119 Harman
Morrell, Richard, shipwright, Bedlow
Morris and Ludlam, hardware-store, 63 Water
Morris, William, taylor, 121 Cherry
Morris, John, cooper and culler, 15 Rutger
Morris, David, pilot, 102 William
Morris, Jacob, cooper, 34 Broad, and 60 Front
Morris, James, attorney at law, 19 Broadway.
Morris, Abraham, cooper, Magazine-street.
Morris, Jacob, cartman, 11 Barly

Morris, Richard H. merchant, 10 Liberty-street.
Morris, Ann, 60 Broad
Morris, Isaac, carpenter, 41 Chapel
Morris, Sylvester, weigher, 48 Church
Morris and Skinner's soap and candle store, 22 Water
Morris, Andrew, 18 Water
Morris, Sarah, 106 Liberty
Morris, Robert, smith, 9 Robinson
Morris, Benjamin, smith, 12 Chapel
Morris, Benjamin, watchmaker, 118 Fly-market.
Morris and Bontecou, taylors, 52 John-street.
Morrison, James, shipwright, 17 Cheapside
Morrison, Martin, collector, 2 Catharine-street.
Morrison, Joseph, perfumer, 87 Pearl, and 7 Old-slip.
Morrison, John, shoemaker, 75 Pine-street.
Morrison, William, shipmaster, 6 Dover
Morrison, John, cabinetmaker, 89 Fair
MORRISTOWN stage-office, foot of Cortlandt
Morss, John, boatman, 104 Liberty
Morton, Jacob, counsellor at law, 59 Broadway.
Morton, John, merchant, 59 Broadway.
Morton, Washington, 14 Broadway.
Morton, Thomas, merchant, 194 Pearl-street.
Moses & Sons, Isaac, auctioneers, 63 Wall, & 86 Pearl.
Mosely, Catharine, 39 Cheapside.
Mosher, Henry, cartman, Mutual-street.
Mosher, James, cartman, Lumber
Moss, Charles, mariner, 5 Chesnut
Mossell, William, carpenter, 4 Reed
Mothrell and Thompson, grocers, 189 Front
Motley, John, 30 Beekman, and store 183 Front.
Mott, Israel, grocer, 31 Reed
Mott, widow, 7 Bowery-lane.
Mott, Wm. and John, merchants, 240 Water-street.
Mott and Co. Benjamin, merchants, 250 Water
Mott, Jacob S. printer and bookseller, 70 Vesey
Mott, Robert, flour-merchant, 161 Pearl
Mott, Jacob, grocery and flour-store, 27 Peck-slip.
Mott, Sarah, widow, 10 Cliff-street.
Mott, Samuel, grocer, 20 Liberty
Mott, John, Mulberry
Mott, widow, 38 Church

Mott, Jordan, watchmaker, 104 Gold-street.
Mott, Jacob C. currier, 59 Frankfort
Mott, William L. merchant, 73 Catharine
Mott, Jacob S. measurer, 14 Thames
Mott and Co. Thomas, upholsterers, 46 William
Mottheau, Gracian, 50 Division
Moulton, Charles, merchant, 64 Broad
Mount, George, shoemaker, 43 Bancker
Mount, Robert, tin and copper worker, 48 Barclay
Mount, Adam D. baker, 51 Ferry
Mount, Matthias, painter and glazier, 49 Rutger
Mount, Joseph, shoemaker, 30 Cherry
Moulton, John, carver and gilder, 361 Pearl
Mowatt, John, merchant, 94 William
Mowatt, jun. John, merchant, 230 Pearl
Mower, James B. 10 Fair
Mozure, Caleb, 41 Barley
Muckle, Thomas, shipwright, Henry
Mugnie, Henry J. merchant-taylor, 85 Nassau
Muir, William, grocer, 90 Broad
Mulheran, Richard, merchant, 12 Peck-slip.
Mulheran, Elijah, 2 Birmingham-row.
Mullen, Ann, 191 William-street.
Mulligan, Hercules, 99 Liberty
Mulligan, John, attorney at law, office 21 Cedar
Mulner, James, mariner, 21 Batavia-lane.
Mumford, B. M. merchant, 28 Pine-street.
Mumford, David, merchant, 241 Pearl
Mumford, Gurdon, merchant, 37 William
Mumford, John P. merchant, 73 Stone
Mumford, W. C. merchant, 51 Pine
Munn, Stephen B. merchant, 103 Maiden-lane.
Munro, Joseph, oysterman, First-street.
Munro, Peter J. counsellor at law, 36 Broadway.
Munro and Ree, merchants, Jone's wharf.
Munro, John, merchant, 97 Greenwich-street.
Munson, Levy, marshal, 11 Green
Munson, Amos, shoemaker, 82 John
Munson, Silas, shoemaker, 99 Murray
Murdock, Samuel, labourer, 19 Warren
Murphey, Elizabeth, 7 Augustus
Murphey, Eleanor, boarding-house, 74 Maiden-lane.

Murphey, James, breeches-maker, Magazine-street.
Murphey, Isabella, mantuamaker, 7 Cedar
Murphey, widow Jemima, 91 Fair
Murphey, William, hairdresser, 299 Water
Murphey, John, cooper, 38 Barclay, & shop 21 Cooper.
Murphey, Mary, milliner, 411 Pearl
Murphey, Thomas, mariner, 30 Rutger
Murphey, widow, 24 Harman
Murphey, John, brewer, Magazine
Murney, Patrick, mariner, Magazine
Murray, John, broker, 64 Maiden-lane.
Murray, Peter, tobacconist, Pump-street.
Murray, Joseph, surgeon, 73 James
Murray, John B. merchant, 27 William
Murray and Mumford, merchant, 73 Stone
Murray, jun. John, merchant, 339 Pearl
Murray, Letty, 43 Cliff
Murray, Hugh R. grocer, 78 James
Murray, Jeremiah, mariner, 27 Cheapside.
Murray, Robert, merchant, 31 Warren-street.
Murray, John, merchant, 27 Beekman
Murray and Son, John, counting-house, 27 Beekman
Murray, William, shoemaker, 18 Cherry
Murray, John, grocer, 27 Harman
Murray, John, grocer, 245 Greenwich
Murray, Cæsar, whitewasher, 49 Cedar
Murray, John, grocer, 12 Chapel
Murrowny, Thomas, labourer, 98 Pearl
MUSEUM, (Baker's) in the Exchange.
Musgrove, Thomas, carpenter, 22 Robinson-street.
Mushroom, David, cartman, Henry
MUTUAL ASSURANCE COMPANY, office 140 Pearl
Myer, Mary, 64 Ann
Myers, Zebulon, smith, 6 E. George
Myers, Jacob, tea-waterman, Hester
Myers, Lydia, grocer, 43 Chamber
Myers, Henry, smith, 5 Murray
Myers, Jacob, baker, Eagle
Myers, James, 139 Chatham
Myers, John, tea-water man, Elizabeth
Myers, Christiana, 11 Murray
Myers, John R. 17 Dey

NEW-YORK DIRECTORY.

Myers, Jud. & S. coppersmiths, 71 John & 111 Pearl-l.
Myers, James, Little Catharine, corner Broadway.
Myers, William, milkman, 34 George-street.
Myers, Adolph, smith, 21 Catharine
Myers, Hazel, boot and shoemaker, Bowery-lane.
Myers, widow Rachel, 404 Pearl
Myers, Abraham and Mordecai, brokers, 404 Pearl
Myers, Charles, hairdresser, 82 Nassau
Myers, Lawrence, cartman, 52 Lombard
Myers, Manuel, spermaceti candle store, 62 Broad.
Myers, Cornelius, cartman, 41 Reed
Myers, Cornelius, smith, 43 Reed
Myers, Solomon, smith, 88 Harman
Myers, John, labourer, 67 Roosevelt
Myers, Frederick, tea-waterman, 63 Division
Myers, Rudolph, shoemaker, 11 Chapel
Myers, Daniel, sawyer, 138 Bowery-lane.
Myers, Garrit, labourer, 41 William-street.
Myers, Benjamin, bookbinder, 71 John
Mylander, Nicholas, tavern and clothier, 338 Water
Mylar, John, grocer and tavern, 57 George

N

Nabel, Barnet, baker, 20 Beaver-street.
Nack, Matthias, cartman, Barley
Nahs, Philip, 5 Chatham-row.
Nash, Bridget, Mulberry-street.
Nathan, Simon, merchant, 27 Water, & store 147 Pearl
Nathan, Joseph, 34 Whitehall.
Nations, John, sawyer, Lumber-street.
Navarro, Isaac, boatman, 60 Broad
Naw, R. 5 Frankfort
Naylon, Charles, shopkeeper, 186 William
Neafie, John, Jay
Neafie, Garrit, 90 Reed
Neal, Edward, labourer, Pope's-alley.
Neal, Joseph, shoemaker, 32 Rose-street.
Needham and Son, John, taylors, 10 Cherry
Needham, William, cartman, 8 Vesey
Needham, John, waterman, 67 George
Neal, Henry, carpenter, Cherry, Ship-yards.
Neilson, William, merchant, 80 Pearl-street.
Neilson, jun. William, 80 Pearl

Neilson, James H. 80 Pearl-street.
Neilson, William, mariner, Bayard
Neilson, James, labourer, Greenwich-road.
Neilson, William, labourer, Bedlow-street.
Neilson and Co. James, grocers, New Albany-bason.
Nesbit, sen. Samuel, physician, 62 Beekman-street.
Nesbit, jun. Samuel, physician, 62 Beekman
Nesbit, Archibald, grocer, 32 Warren
Nesbit, Hugh, shipwright, 8 Charlotte
Nestell, Michael, shopkeeper, 198 Broadway.
Nestell, Christian, baker, 29 Dey-street.
Nestler, Michael, butcher, Second
Nevil, John, grocer, 78 Wall
NEWARK stage-office, 5 Cortlandt
Newberry, John, cartman, 8 Augustus
Newby, Robert, malster, Greenwich-road.
NEW CITY TAVERN, 123 Broadway.
Newell, Andrew, cooper. 10 Crane-wharf.
Newell, John, mariner, Henry-street.
Newhouse, John, wheelwright, near Industry furnace.
Newkerk, John, baker, 49 Liberty-street.
Newkerk, Barnet, constable. 10 Liberty
Newport, James, distiller, 41 Partition, & 32 James
Newson, John, merchant, 176 Water
Newson, Robert, inspector of lumber, 141 Cherry
Newton, Joseph, carpenter, 109 Greenwich
Newton, William, merchant, 315 Pearl
Newton, Francis, labourer, 19 Fair
Newton, Richard, rigger and stivadore, 14 Harman
Newton, John, 64 Dey
Newton, H. dealer, 13 Oliver
NEW-YORK INSURANCE COMPANY office, 66 Wall
Nexsen and Son, Elias, merchants. 20 Burling-slip.
Nexsen, Catharine, 154 William-street.
Nexsen, Elias, merchant, 12 Liberty
Nexsen, William, accountant, 154 William
Nicholas, Henry, smith, 43 Chamber
Nichols, James, mariner, 52 Catharine
Nichols. William, smith, 89 Harman
Nichols and Son, Walter, grocers, 203 Water
Nichols, William, shipmaster, 43 Division
Nichols, John, rigger, 88 James

Nichols, Jacob, butcher, Third-street.
Nichols, Mary, teacheress, 267 Broadway.
Nichols, George, shipmaster, 18 Liberty-street.
Nichols, Elizabeth, mantuamaker, 22 Greenwich
Nichols, widow Margaret, boarding-house, 77 Cortlandt
Nichols, widow, 6 Chapel
Nichols, John, carver and gilder, Beekman
Nichols, Mary, 308 Broadway.
Nicholson, commodore James, 86 William-street.
Nickloie, Hester, 4 Garden
Nicoll, jun. Edward, merchant, 28 Greenwich
Nicoll, Augustus, china, glass, &c. store, 179 Water
Nicoll, William, grocer, Fisher
Nicoll, Alexander, smith, 24 Lombard
Nicoll, William, shipmaster, 24 Chapel
Nightingale, Joseph, mariner, 59 E. George
Nimmo, Alexander, shoemaker, 153 Greenwich
Nitchie, John, starch & hair powder maker, 38 Broad
Niven, Daniel, merchant-taylor, 5 Old-slip.
Niven, John, carpenter, 20 Lombard-street.
Nixon, Thomas, merchant, 161 Pearl
Nixon, John, 48 Cedar
Nixon, Richard, tavern, 37 Moore
Nixon, Richard, coppersmith, 92 Fair
Noah, E. broker, 40 Greenwich
Noble, George, cartman, 11 Moore
Noble, Robert, 44 Vesey
Nocus, Stephen, broker, 196 Broadway.
Noe, Mary, seamstress, 99 Harman-street.
Noe, John, shoemaker, 10 Catharine
Noe, Lemountis, 18 Broad
Noe, Samuel, shipwright, Charlotte
Noe, Elias, carpenter Henry
Nolden, Jacob, shoemaker, 34 Reed
Norman, William, Water

Norsworthy, Samuel, merchant, 418 Pearl-street.
North, Benjamin, carpenter, 39 Harman
North, Peggy, mantuamaker, 10 Cedar
North, widow, 10 Cedar
Northam, Abraham, Orange
Norton, Joseph, carpenter, 84 Murray
Norton and Brown, hardware store, 7 Burling-slip.
Norton, Henry, merchant, 7 Burling-slip.
Norwood, Andrew S. upholsterer, 127 William-street.
Norwood, Richard, custom-house measurer, 52 Gold
Norwood, Andrew, measurer of grain, 58 Beaver
Nostrandt, Peter, carpenter, 11 Rector
Nostrand, Daniel, cartman, First
Nostrand, Forster, tavern, 52 Bowery-lane.
Nostrand, George, smith, 6 Warren-street.
Nostrand, Garrit, cartman, Third
Nott, Nathaniel, carpenter and builder, 8 Hague
Nott, Sebastian, 241 Broadway.
Nott, Abraham, carpenter, 24 Harman-street.
Nourse, Thomas, labourer, 95 James
Nowlan, Thomas, shoemaker, 14 Chesnut
Nowlan, Thomas, labourer, 86 Fair
Nowland, Mathew, smith, 18 Rose
Nugent, Richard, grocer, 15 E. George
Nugent, Mitchel, carpenter, 63 E. George

O

Oakden, Joseph, pilot, 62 Gold-street.
Oake, widow, teacheress, 47 Chapel
Oakes, Thomas, potter, 90 Warren
Oakes, Henry, mason, 13 Reed
Oakley, George, grocer, 28 Division
Oakley, James, merchant-taylor, 165 Pearl
Oakley, John, shoemaker, Magazine
Oakley, Jesse, carpenter, Eagle
Oakley, Martin, labourer, Elizabeth
O'Brian, Jane, 63 E. George
O'Brian, Alexander, plaisterer, 5 Murray
O'Brian, Patrick, labourer, 41 Oliver
O'Brian, Rev. William, 18 Vesey
O'Brien, John, shipmaster, Skinner
O'Brien, Tanner, shopkeeper, 170 Broadway.
O'Conner, Hugh, merchant, 125 Front-street.

Odell, Reuben, windsor chairmaker, Barley-street.
Office Daily Advertiser, 71 Pine
Office Daily Gazette, 116 Pearl
Office Argus and Patriotic Register, 54 Wall
Office Diary and Register of the Times, 68 Pine
Office Minerva and Herald, 40 Pine
Office of the Time Piece, 26 Moore
Office of the Tablet, 358 Pearl
Office of the Museum, 3 Peck slip.
Office Gazette Français, 37 Barclay-street.
Office New-York Price-Current, 55 Liberty
Ogden, Joseph, taylor, 68 Cortlandt
Ogden, William, mason, 31 Barclay
Ogden, David A. counsellor at law, 68 Broadway.
Ogden, Benjamin, hairdresser, Chatham-street.
Ogden, Nathaniel N. 46 Cedar
Ogden, Charles L. merchant, 79 Broad
Ogden, Lewis, merchant, 73 Pearl
Ogden, William, merchant, 85 Greenwich
Ogden, David, merchant, 125 Pearl
Ogden, John, bricklayer, 54 Ann
Ogden, Thomas Ludlow, attorney at law, 77 Broad
Ogden, Jacob, physician, 43 Stone
Ogden, Andrew, merchant, 96 William
Ogden and Condit, merchants, 96 William
Ogilvie, William, clerk of court of probates, 69 Liberty
Ogilvie, Thomas, measurer of lumber, 33 Beekman
Ogilvie, Thomas, shipmaster, 125 Water
Ogilvie, Alexander, 2 Gold
Ogilvie, Peter, judge of probates, 69 Liberty
Ogilvie, Alexander, grocer, 118 Front
Ogilvie, Gabriel, silversmith, 35 Dey
Ogilvie, John, shipwright, First
Ogle, John, turner, 16 Harman
Ogsbury and Sons, Alexander, merchants, 77 William
Ogsbury, Alexander, merchant, 21 Murray
Ohle, William, at the City Tavern.
O'Jakey, Marian, tavern, 2 Crane-wharf.
Oliver, James, stonecutter, 59 Reed-street.
Oliver, Thomas, carpenter, 36 Harman
Oliver, William, mariner, First
Oliver, Alexander, labourer, Little Catharine

Oliver, Nicholas, carpenter, Barley-street.
Oliver, Isaac, ropemaker, Elizabeth
Oliver, Richard, cartman, 47 Barley
Oadiead, Lewis, merchant, 68 Water
Onderdonk, W. and B. merchants, 36 Fair
Onderdonk, John, physician, 57 John
O'Neal, Henry, weaver, Lumber
O'Nei, Thomas, grocer, 37 Roosevelt
Osborn, John, merchant, 25 Williams
Oram, James, printer, 33 Liberty
Oreet, widow, 56 Pearl
Ormond, John, carpenter, First
Ormond, William, mariner, 24 Bancker
Ormond, Thomas, machine-maker, 53 Barley
Orr, Robert, grocer, 17 James
Orr, Arthur, cartman, 16 Rector
Orr, Thomas, shoemaker, Winne
Orr, Thomas, mason, 3 Thomas
Orr, Thomas, mason, Barley
Orr, Henry, cartman, Broadway, near the furnace.
Orley, M. and H. tanners, 108 Gold-street.
Osborn, ——, shoemaker, 172 Division
Osborn, Lewis, cartman, Gibbs'-alley.
Osborn, John, shoemaker, Peil-street.
Osborn, Ichamer, shoe warehouse, 2 Beekman-flip.
Osborn, William, mariner, 22 Bancker-street.
Osborn, John, shoemaker, Little Ann
Osgood, Samuel, 9 Cherry
Oswald and Hertung, furriers, 83 Maiden-lane.
Oswald, Charles, furrier, 83 Maiden-lane.
Osrand, Charles, shipwright, 51 Cheapside.
Ostrander, Daniel, grocer, 377 Budlow-street.
Oswald, Philip, dry goods store, 113 Chatham
Ore for and Co. J. tallow-chandlers, 26 Ann
Overton, Andrew, china, glass, &c. store, 59 Water
Overing, Henry, 34 Chesnut
Overton, John, shoemaker, 86 Catharine
Overy, Joseph, cartman, 47 Barley
Owens, Humphrey, labourer, 109 Division

P

Paddil, George, cartman, 70 Murray-street.
Packer, John, shoemaker, Greenwich road.

Paddock, Peter, teacher, 150 Chatham-street.
Paff, Andrew, butcher, Bayard
Paff, John, musical store, 112 Broadway.
Page, Benjamin, 45 Partition-street.
Page, Samuel, inspector of provisions, 91 Broad
Page, jun. Samuel L. cooper, 22 Front
Page, Joseph, 70 Broadway.
Paget, Ann, skinner, corner of Hague-street.
Painter, Mary, huckster, 45 Chatham
Painter, George, labourer, Bedlow
Palmer, Thomas, Oliver
Palmer, Joseph, smith, 60 Harman
Palmer, Silas, shipwright, Charlotte
Palmer, Thomas, tavern, 44 Cortlandt
Palmer, Sarah, widow, 100 Liberty
Palmer, Edward, grocer, Pump
Palmer, William, carpenter, Bowery-lane.
Palmer, Lancaster, grocer, Bowery-lane.
Palmer, Timothy, hatter, 233 Water-street.
Palmer, Ashbel, cartman, Eagle
Palmer, William, painter and japanner, 106 Pearl
Palmes, Richard, shipmaster, 399 Pearl
Pancoast, Joseph, carpenter, Gibb's alley.
Pancoast, Solomon, carpenter, 14 Oliver
Pangburn, Isaac, cartman, Henry
Pangburn, Lewis, cartman, Henry
Panton, Francis, merchant, 59 Wall
Panton and Bradford's store, 42 Front
Panton, jun. Francis, merchant, 42 Front
Parage and Arjo, merchants, 57 Pearl
Paranque, Stephen, merchant, 44 William
Pardoe, William, 4 New
Paret, Stephen, fruiterer, 212 Greenwich
Parifh, ——, tinman, 249 Broadway.
Parifer, Philip, miniature painter, 252 William-street.
Parifer, Claude, painter, 37 Barclay
Park, John, baker, Cherry street, Ship-yards.
Park, Benjamin, mariner, 39 Harman-street.
Parker, Michael, carpenter, 28 Rutger
Parker, Isaac, shipwright, 30 Cheapside.
Parker, Joshua, taylor, 90 John-street.
Parker, William, grocer, 40 Augustus

NEW-YORK DIRECTORY.

Parker, John, sawyer, 15 Chapel-street.
Parker, Sarah, boarding-house, 12 Wall
Parker, Abigail, 5 Dey
Parker, Joseph, labourer, Henry
Parker, George, taylor, 316 Water
Parker, Adam, tavern, Bruce's-wharf.
Parker, James, dry goods store, 306 Water-street.
Parker, John, shoemaker, 83 Murray
Parker, Sidney, hatter, 207 Water
Parker, Peter, shipmaster, Division
Parker, George, carpenter, 119 Harman
Parker, John E. shoemaker, 10 Rose
Parker, James, labourer, 22 George
Parker, George, mason, 3 Chapel
Parker, Gabriel, shoemaker, 86 Fair
Parkinson, John, 5 Whitehall, & store 115 Greenwich
Parks, Peter, sexton Methodist church, Second
Parmerton, Rachel, 98 Pearl
Parsells, Thos. coach and chairmaker, 145 Broadway.
Parsells, Jacob, carpenter, 197 Broadway.
Parsells, Thomas, shoemaker, Mulberry-street.
Parsells, William, cartman, Winne
Parsells, widow, 12 Harman
Parsells, Thomas, boat-builder, 39 Bowery-lane.
Parsells, Richard, baker, Grand, corner First-street.
Parshall, James, accountant, 30 Vandewater
Parsons and Sons, James, merchants, 257 Pearl
Parsons, jun. James, merchant, 257 Pearl
Parsons, William, merchant, 235 Greenwich
Parsons, John, merchant, 257 Pearl
Parsons, ———, cartman, Henry
Pasone, Nathaniel, labourer, 53 Harman
Passman, Francis, grocer, 54 Frankfort
Partridge, John, boarding-house, 340 Water
Paterson, Robert, smith, 96 Liberty
Paterson, Jonathan, labourer, 12 Fair
Patrick, John, merchant, 36 William
Patrick and Todd's counting-house, 36 William
Patten, Johnstone, mason, 24 Beekman
Patten, James, smith, 30 Catharine
Patten, Edward, butcher, Rivers-lane
Patten, John, smith, 339 Water, & 36 Roosevelt-st.

Patterson, James B. harness maker, &c. 88 Water
Patterson, John, cooper, 10 Beaver
Patterson, Thomas, cartman, 30 Lombard
Patterson, John, grocer, 106 Chatham
Patterson, John, tinman, Hester
Paul, John, carpenter, 47 Barley
Paul, Thomas, taylor, 17 Cooper
Paul, Isaac, cartman, Greenwich-road
Paul, John, labourer, 8 Thomas-street.
Paul, Joseph, mariner, Birmingham-row.
Paul, John, labourer, 21 Barclay-street.
Paul, Bristow, sawyer, 49 Ann
Paulding, jun. William, attorney at law, 4 Cedar
Paulding, Eleanor, milliner, 112 Chatham
Paull, Joseph, cartman, 37 Chapel
Paxton, James, porter & punch house, 23 Cooper
Paxton, jun. John, auctioneer, &c. 142 Front
Paxton, Samuel, 44 Chapel
Payne, Thomas, cabinetmaker, 30 Beaver
Payne, James William, inspector of customs, 32 Fair
Payne, Joseph, boatman, Greenwich-road.
Peacock, William, shipwright, 50 Roosevelt
Peacock, Alexander, butcher, 42 Bowery-lane.
Peaceloek, David, sailmaker, 171 William-street.
Pearl, David, shipwright, 167 Division
Pearsall, Fell and Co. merchants, 237 Pearl
Pearsall, Son & Co. Thomas, merchants, 239 Pearl
Pearsall, Joseph, 254 Pearl
Pearsall, William, carpenter, 22 Oliver
Pearsall, Fell & Wittemore's card manuf. 131 Cherry
Pearsall, Robert, merchant, 268 Pearl
Pearsall, Nathaniel, ironmonger, 254 Pearl
Pearsall, Edmund & Robert W. merchants, 292 Pearl
Pearsee, Jonathan, 40 Nassau
Pearsee, jun. Jonathan, attorney at law, 40 Nassau
Pierce, Isaac, carpenter, Bowery-lane.
Pearseeman, Lucorn, labourer, Lumber-street.
Peaser, John, goldsmith and jeweller, 160 Pearl
Pearson, Francis, shipmaster, 62 Pine, and 131 Water
Pearse, John P. merchant, 4 Liberty
Pease, Kingsten, black ball maker, 8 Fayette

Peafell, Leonard, fruiterer, 243 Broadway.
Peafell, Frederick, carpenter, Greenwich-road.
Peck, Rebecca, wafher, Orange-ftreet.
Peck, William, merchant-taylor, 196 Water
Peck, Henry, grocer, 47 Fayette
Peck, Nathaniel, fhoemaker, faw-pits, Greenwich.
Peck, Hezekiah, cloathing ftore, 270 Water-ftreet.
Peckwell, widow, Charlotte
Pedley, Thomas, perfumer & hairdreffer, 219 Water
Peek, George, fhipwright, 416 Pearl
Peek and Dally, fhip chandlers, 227 Cherry
Peirfe, William, fhipwright, Henry
Peirfon, Mary, 46 Fair
Peirfon, Jofeph, meafurer of lumber, 93 Broad
Peirfon & Brothers, J. G. 17 Bridge, & ftore 23 Front
Peirfon and Houfeman, wire manufactory, 93 Broad
Peliffier, Victor, mufician 58 Ann
Pell, Mrs. 95 Pearl
Pell, Samuel, merchant, 95 Pearl
Pell, Gilbert, merchant, upper end of Lumber
Pell, Jonathan A. merchant, Lumber
Pell, Aaron, coach and chairmaker, 26 Broad
Pell & Co. Caleb, copperfmiths, 183 Water
Pell, widow, teacherefs 125 Divifion
Pell, Benjamin, merchant, 286 Pearl
Pell, Jabez, copperfmith, 9 Beekman-flip.
Pell, Jofhua, merchant, 181 Wafhington-ftreet.
Pell and Melick's ftore, 183 Wafhington,
Pell, Anthony, infurance broker, 95 Pearl
Pell, Gilbert, grocer, 50 Whitehall.
Pell, Caleb, foap & candle manufact. 41 Cheapfide.
Pelletreau, Ann, 56 John-ftreet.
Pelor, George, E. Rutger
Peltier, Francis, 33 Vefey
Peltue, Sarah, 21 Barclay
Pelton, William, fhoemaker, Third
Pember, Edward, picture frame maker, 215 William
Pender, Martin, fhoemaker, 27 Church
Pendleton, William, mariner, 47 Cliff
Pendleton, Nathaniel, attorney at law, 47 Naffau
Penfield, Daniel, merchant, 9 State
Penn, Lewis, grocer, 338 Broadway.

Pennell, Hay, wheelwright, 128 Bowery-lane.
Pennoyer, Lewis, carpenter, Harman-street.
Pennoyer, Wright, smith, Lumber
Pennoyer, Isaac, carpenter, Henry
Penny, Richard, hairdresser, 289 Water
Penny, Charles, pilot, Bedlow
Penny, Margaret, washer, Harman
Penny, Jonathan, washer, 114 Broad
Penny, Robert, mariner, Charlotte
Penny, James, cartman, Sixth
Penny, Sarah Ann, mantuamaker, 14 Thames
Pennycook, William, 8 Fair
Pennyhouse, John, 71 Chatham
Pentz, Adam, cooper, 95 Front, & house 8 Roosevelt
Pentz, Frederick, shoemaker, 24 Old-slip.
Pepper, John, tobacconist, Henry-street.
Pepper, Isaac, inspector of wood, 38 Harman
Peraut, A. P. 9 Upper Reed
Percy, Samuel, cartman, First
Perkins, William F. 94 Broad
Perkins, George, mariner, 229 William
Perriel, Christopher, labourer, Division
Perriere, Catharine, fruiterer, 71 Beekman
Perrin, John, butcher, 106 Bowery-lane.
Perrine, Benjamin, shoemaker, Birmingham-row.
Perrine, Robert, grocer, 3 Rector-street.
Perrine, widow, 224 William
Perrine, James, taylor, 111 Harman
Perrine, Abraham, shoemaker, Second
Perrot, John and James, grocers, 75 Fair
Perry, James, shipmaster, 35 Lumber
Perry, Nevers, cartman, saw-pits, Greenwich-road.
Perry, John, labourer, 65 Chatham-street.
Perr, William, mason and builder, 24 Gold
Pershine, John, shoewar house, 125 Water
Pessinger, John, butcher, Esther
Peters, Harry, china, glass, &c. store, 100 Maiden-lane.
Peters, John, merchant, 37 Greenwich-street.
Peters, John, taylor, 16 William
Peters, John C. hardware & jewellery store, 142 William
Peters, John, carpenter, 98 Harman
Peters, William, shipwright, 67 Harman.

Peters, Henry, taylor, 51 Partition-street.
Peterson, Peter, cartman, Norfolk
Peterson, Garrit, smith, Bayard
Peterson, Paul, tobacconist, 36 Vesey
Peterson, jun. Garrit, smith, 126 Chatham
Peterson, William, shoemaker, 5 Bowery-lane.
Peterson, John, cartman, 25 Chesnut-street.
Peterson, John, grocer, 24 Division
Peterson, Cornelius, smith, Division
Peterson, James, labourer, 18 Augustus
Petre, George, sugar-baker, Bayard
Pettinger, Andrew, labourer, 86 Bowery-lane.
Pettit, Thomas, silversmith, 6 Chapel-street.
Pettit, Abraham, mason, Pell
Pettit, William, tavern, 156 Fly-market.
Pettit, Joseph, tavern, 77 Vesey
Pettit, Robert, broker, 70 Cherry
Pfister and Macomb's counting-house, 81 Front
Phœbus, Rev. William, 3 Second
Phœbus and Valentine, merchants, 195 Broadway.
Phœnix, Daniel, mercht. & city treasurer, 138 Water-st.
Phœnix, Philip, taylor, 39 Augustus
PHILADELPHIA stage offices, Tontine and Old Coffee Houses; 118, 124, and 202 Broadway; 1, 3, 5, and 71 Cortlandt-street.
Philips, Henry, clothier, 54 Whitehall.
Philips, Frederick, 43 Pine-street.
Philips and Clark, druggists, 66 Maiden-lane.
Philips, Thomas, druggist, 66 Maiden-lane.
Philips, William, taylor, 55 Fair-street.
Philips, James, grocer, 358 Water
Philips, John C. labourer, Church
Philips, John, butcher, 25 Robinson
Philips and Baufher, hairdressers, 121 Cherry
Philips, Henry, hairdresser, 58 Roger
Philips, Jonathan, coachmaker, Cherry
Philips, Thomas, 29 Roosevelt
Philips, Jacob, shoemaker, Essex
Philips, George, mariner, 45 Cliff
Philips, John, carpenter, near Curtenius' furnace
Philips, Rev. J. academy, 117 Pearl street
Philips, Henry W. merchant, 40 Front

Philps, William, cabinetmaker, 31 Beekman-street.
Philps, Abraham, cartman, 12 Thomas
Phyfe, Duncan, cabinetmaker, 35 Partition
Pick, George, carpenter, 260 Pearl
Pickett, Libert, schoolmaster, 42 Warren
Pierce, Elizabeth, 179 Broadway.
Pierce, John, mariner, 57 Catharine-street.
Pierce, John, dry goods store, 383 Pearl
Pierce, Thomas, mariner, 83 Chatham
Pierpont, Hezekiah B. merchant, 63 Pine
Pierpont, widow, 69 Catharine
Pierfan, Phillip, jeweller, 252 William
Pierson, Thomas, shipwright, 121 Harman
Pierson, George, rigger, 25 Bancker
Pierson, David, carpenter, Thomas
Pierson, John, mariner, 35 Bancker,
Pierson, William, teacher, 24 Rutger
Pierson, Nicholas, umbrella-maker, Crofs
Pierson, Daniel, carpenter, 427 Pearl
Pierson, Caleb, printer, Henry
Pigget, Aaron, grocer, corner Second and Pump
Piggot, Robert, teacher, Eagle
Pike, W. H. dry goods store, 401 Pearl
Pilkenton, James, tanner, 45 George
Pilmore, Rev. Joseph, 47 Partition
Pine, Sylvanus, merchant, 263 William
Pine, Robert and Sylvanus, store Farmer's-wharf.
Pinkney, Elijah, grocer, Front-street, near Peck-slip.
Pinkney, Thomas, measurer, E. Rutger-street.
Pinkney, William, carpenter, Bowery-lane.
Pinks, widow, 13 E. George
Pinto, Abraham, 30 Mill-street.
Pinto, Rachel, 50 Stone
Pinto, Jesse, 30 Mill
Piper, Lovin, S. Murray
Piper, Frederick, labourer, Third
Piper, widow, First
Piquet, Peter, baker, 57 Bowery-lane.
Pitt, Nicholas, cartman, 41 Roosevelt
Pitt, John, Venetian blind manuf. &. 24 Maiden-lane.
Place, Joseph, boatman, 78 Murray
Place, Thomas, butcher, 130 Chatham

Place, Ephraim, shoemaker, Little Catharine-street.
Place, Jacob, shipwright, Bedlow
Place, Mary, teacheress, 40 James
Place, James, butcher, First
Plaine, James F. 222 Water
Plaintain, John, 303 Broadway.
Platt, William, painter, Pump-street.
Platt, William, lawyer, 49 Cedar
Platt, Stephen, cartman, Eagle
PLAYHOUSE, Chatham-row.
Plumb, David, cartman, 588 Pearl-street.
Plyrr, Peter, butcher, 34 Catharine
Poillon, John, grocer, 191 Washington
Poillon, Peter, grocer, Charlotte
Poillon, Peter P. merchant, 87 Maiden-lane.
Poineer, David, cartman, 50 Church-street.
Poineer, David, carpenter, 107 Gold
Poleg, Charles, cooper, 32 Bowery-lane.
Polhemus, Eldred, 13 Lumber-street.
Polhemus, Abraham, tanner and currier, 3 Jacob
Polhemus, Cornelius, cartman, Division
Polhemus, Jacob, shoemaker, 99 Warren
Polhemus, Francis, 7 Jacob
Polhemus, Jacob, Second
Pollard, William, accountant, 36 Beaver
Pollock, Carlile, merchant, 11 Whitehall.
Pollock, George, merchant, 91 Water-street.
Pollock, G. & H. counting-house, 3 Governeur's-alley,
Pollock, Hugh, merchant, 30 Greenwich-street.
Pollock, Ishacher, 62 Cherry
Pollom, Benedict, First
Pols, John B. grocer Division
Pool, John, sadler, 28 Church
Pool, Hannah, 40 Reed
Pool, Thomas, mariner, 27 Cheapside.
Pope, Henry, coach fringe manufact. 78 Maiden-lane
Pope, Thomas, builder, Greenwich-road.
Pordy, Thomas, grocer, 50 Reed-street.
Porter, Peter, labourer, 80 Reed
Porter, Jonathan, cartman, 28 Reed
Porter, Eldred, cartman, Henry
Porterfield, John, bellman, 4 Mulberry

NEW-YORK DIRECTORY.

Porterfield, Alexander, cartman, 13 Tryon-row.
Post & Sons, Wm. colour-shop, 160 Water-street.
Post, John I. upholsterer, 260 Water
Post, John, cooper and repacker, 262 Water
Post, Jotham, alderman, 23 Cherry
Post, William, butcher, Mulberry
Post, William, cartman, 76 Chamber
Post, Henry, 13 Fair
Post, Anthony, carpenter and builder, 96 Liberty
Post, Wright, surgeon, 40 John
Post, Richard, milkman, Eagle
Post, John, carpenter, 8 Thomas
Post, Thomas, cooper and repacker, 262 Water
Post, Henry, merchant 259 Pearl
Post, jun. Jotham, M. D. 28 Dey
Post, Joel, merchant, 23 Cherry
Post, John, cartman, 46 Chamber
Post, Marsells, hatter, 63 Dey
Post, Francis, cartman, 63 Dey
Post, William B. painter, 34 Vesey
Post, Peter, carpenter, 312 Broadway
POST-OFFICE, corner of Wall and William-street.
Potts, John, cartman, 59 Reed-street.
Pove, Nicholas, smith and farrier, 48 Robinson
Powell, Benjamin, boarding-house, 71 Cortlandt
Powell, Joseph, coachmaker, 73 Broad
Powell, James, sailmaker, 22 Stone
Powell, Henry, mariner, 69 E. George
Powell, Jacob and Thomas, grocers, Washington
Powers, widow, 4 Lombard
Powers, John, carpenter, 10 Harman
Powlis, Paules, cartman, 97 Reed
Powlis, Jacob, labourer, 56 Reed
Prall, Abraham, merchant, 167 Water
Prall, Ichabod, merchant, 165 Water
Prall, Isaac, plowwright, 10 E. George
Pratt, Isaac, cabinet-maker, 49 Harman
Pray, capt. John, Winne
Prentice, Thomas, carpenter, Greenwich-road.
Prentice, Jones, merchant, 184 Water-street.
Preston, Thomas, printer and glazier, 5 Catherine
Preten, John, mariner, Henry

Preten, John, mariner, E. Washington-street.
Pretlove, John, carpenter, Barley
Prey, widow, E. Washington
Preyer, Lewis, rigger, 16 Harman
Price, William, looking-glass manufactory, 85 Fair
Price, Simeon, nailmaker, Harman
Price, Reuben, labourer, 21 Bancker
Pride, Peter, carpenter, Little Ann
Pride, Robert, carpenter, 15 Beaver
Pride, John, carpenter, Little Ann
Prill, Christian, cartman, 60 Church
Prime, Nathaniel, merchant, 79 Greenwich
Primrose, John, leather-cutter, 231 William
Prince, Ruth, widow, 51 Fair
Prince, Benjamin, physician, 31 Chamber
Prince, Samuel, milliner, 125 William
Prince, Christopher, lumber merchant, 12 Barclay
Pringle, Thomas, taylor, 19 Division
Pringle, William, teacher, 19 Division
Prink, Peter, tea-waterman, Elex
Prior, Kirby and Co's. store, 259 Pearl
Prior, Thomas, sailmaker, 17 William
Prior, Edmund, merchant, 261 Pearl
Prior, James, mariner and tavern, 2 Dover
Prior, Phœbe, 36 Cliff
Pritchet, James, labourer, 40 Rose
Proudfit, Daniel, physician, 2 Pine
Proudfoot, Lawrence, accountant, 2 Liberty
Provoost, Right Rev. Samuel, D. D. 53 Nassau
Provoost, John, labourer, 31 Church
Provoost, Robert, painter, 11 Church
Provoost, John B. attorney at law, 32 William
PUBLIC STORE, 34 Front
Pudney, Sarah, huckster, 17 Dutch
Pugsly, Lucilla, tavern, 102 Fly-market
Puker, Ann, 10 Jacob-street.
Pullis, Abraham, cartman, First
Pullis, Henry, cartman, Division
Pullis, John, tavern, near the new jail, Greenwich-road.
Pullis, Cornelius, potter, Greenwich-road.
Pullis, George, shoemaker, Thomas, corner Chapel-E.
Pumphrey, Lloyd, shoemaker, First

Puntier, Samuel, grocer, 96 Gold-street.
Puntzius, John C. taylor, 27 George, and 24 Dey
Purdy, Samuel H. grocer, 62 Murray
Purdy, John, cartman, Little Catharine
Purdy, Benjamin, taylor and grocer, 30 Chamber
Purdy, Israel, grocer, corner of Barley and Chapel
Purdy, John, grocer, corner Hester-str. and Broadway.
Purdy, Monmouth, 395 Pearl-street.
Purdy, Mary, grocer, 81 Catharine
Purdy, Thomas, taylor, 275 Water
Purdy, William, cartman, 34 Barley
Purviss, William, plaisterer, 276 Greenwich
Purviss, Jane, mantuamaker, 276 Greenwich
Pye, Thomas, locksmith, Henry
Pyne, Joseph, shoemaker, 281 Water

Q

Quackenbos, John, cooper, 60 Broad-street.
Quackenbos, John, baker, 117 Chatham
Quackenbos, Isaac, shoemaker, 13 Nassau
Quackenbush, James, shopkeeper, 182 Greenwich
Querall, Joshua, baker, 20 Augustus
Quereau, Elias, baker, 11 Robinson
Quest, Thomas, taylor, 6 Cliff
Quick, Tunis, china, glass, &c. store, 1 Coenties-slip.
Quick, William, baker, 47 Broad-street.
Quick, James, baker, 57 Broad
Quick, widow, 29 Frankfort
Quick, widow, 7 Moore's-row.
Quick, jun. James, cloathing store, 88 Front
Quider, George, cabinetmaker, 46 Chapel
Quin, Robert, dry goods store, 14 Old-slip.
Quin, John, mariner, 46 E. George-street.
Quin, Tunis, labourer, 18 Barley
Quinion, Joseph, taylor, 15 Barclay
Quirk, Edward, hair and bread perfumer, 69 William

R

Ramage, Thomas, mariner, 23 Moore-street.
Ramsay, John, merchant, 133 Greenwich
Ramsay, jun. Charles, merchant, 20 William
Rand, Caleb, shipmaster, 323 Water
Randall, Jonah, shoemaker, Greenwich-road.
Randall, Levi, carpenter, E. Washington-street.
Randall, Thomas, labourer, 45 Robinson
Randall, widow of Capt. Thomas, 28 Whitehall
Randall, William, hairdresser, 118 Front
Randall, John, hairdresser, 193 Water, and 59 Ann
Randall, Thomas, mariner, Provost
Randeker, John, ropemaker, Petter
Randolph, Lewis, merchant-taylor, 92 Water
Randolph, Samuel, grocer, 9 George
Randolph, Samuel F. grocer, South
Rankin, John, grocer, 118 Chatham
Rankin, Robert, merchant, 83 Greenwich
Rankin, Edward, carpenter, 57 Reed
Ransier, Andrew, cedar cooper, Henry
Ransier, Frederick, cedar cooper, 218 Broadway.
Ransier, Jacob, cedar cooper, 7 Ann-street.
Ransley, John, shoemaker, 54 Partition
Ransom, Berzillai, cartman, 45 Bancker
Ransom, Joseph, mariner, 13 Oliver
Rapelye, Bernard, grocer, 70 Front
Rapley, Abraham, coachmaker, 185 Broadway.
Rathbridge, Thomas, tavern, 78 Pine-street.
Ratcliff, Samuel, taylor, Greenwich-road.
Ratcliff, John, labourer, 233 Greenwich street.
Rathbone, John, merchant, 35 Bowery-lane.
Ratlee, James, 20 Warren street.
Rattier, G. 43 Warren
Rausch, Frederick, musician, 260 Broadway.
Rauvou, Daniel, cartman, 75 Warman-street.
Raven, widow, 74 James
Raymer, Cornelius, administrator, 20 Beaver
Rawyer, Conrad, cartman, 52 Church
Ray, Mrs. 51 Vesey
Ray, Cornelius, state loan officer, 111 Broadway.
Ray, Andrew, cotton weaver, 30 Chamber-street.
Ray and Cozine, hairdressers, 127 Greenwich
Raymold, Mary, academy, Bowery-lane.

NEW-YORK DIRECTORY.

Raymond, Isaac, carpenter, 67 Henry-street.
Raymond, Henry, grocer, Lumber, corner Charlotte
Raymond, Andrew, 75 Harman
Raymond, Eliakim, 1 William
Rayner, David, bricklayer, 59 Lumber
Read, E. cartman, First
Read, Anthony, 10 Moore
Read, John, boot and shoemaker, 155 Water
Read, Samuel, 72 Vesey
Read, William, hairdresser, 131 Greenwich
Reading, James, butcher, Division
Reading, Ferdinand, boarding-house, 28 Front
Reauton, Cornelius, shoemaker, Mulberry
Reboul, John B. 141 Chatham
Rebuen, Emanuel, tobacconist, 13 Moore's-row.
Reden, Patrick, grocer, 222 William-street.
Reden, Henry, baker, 93 Gold
Redett, Mathew, boarding-house, 22 Warren
Reed, William, shipmaster, Charlotte
Reed, Samuel, brewer, 33 Lumber
Reed, Elizabeth, nurse, 15 Chesnut
Reed, Mathew, soap and candlemaker, 67 Cherry
Reed, William, grocer, 51 E. George
Reed, Henry, carpenter, 55 Cheapside.
Reed, Jane, 46 Fair-street.
Reelie, George, livery stabler, Beaver-lane.
Reedy, David, insurance-broker, 58 Wall-street.
Reeves, James, cooper, Cross
Reeves, William, grocer, 108 Broad
Reid, John, bookseller and stationer, 106 Water
Reid, William, boarding-house, Cherry-st. Ship-yards.
Reid, Samuel, sawyer, Henry-street.
Reid, William and Robert, hardware store, 442 Pearl
Reid, James, labourer, 60 Chatham
Reid, John, 75 Chatham
Reiley, Henry, bricklayer, 80 James
Reins, David, labourer, 56 Fair
Relas, John, constable, 5 Dey
Relbeck, Joanna, 19 James
Rulison, Jacob, labourer, 13 Rutger
Remington, William, merchant, 80 Fair
Remmery, William, boarding-house, Augustus

Remmey, John, stoneware manufacturer, Potter's-hill.
Remmey, Henry, stoneware manufacturer, 30 Reed-st.
Remmey, William, 198 Broadway.
Remsen, Peter, grocer, 31 Albany-pier.
Remsen, widow of Jacob, 61 Pearl-street.
Remsen, Henry, first teller in branch bank, 61 Pearl
Remsen, J. H. attorney at law & notary-public, 92 Pearl
Remsen, Cornelia, 61 Pearl
Remsen, George and Jeronimus, store 14 Front
Remsen, John, merchant, 18 Front, and house 29 Pearl
Remsen, Rem, merchant, 14 Front
Remsen, George, merchant, 32 Water
Remsen, Abraham, sawyer, 144 Chatham
Remsen, William, mason, 51 Whitehall.
Remsen, George H. merchant, 61 Pearl
Remsen, John, grocer, Bowery-lane.
Renault, Antoine, gilder, 27 Nassau-street.
Renney, David, taylor, 6 Cliff, and shop 102 John
Renvill, Joseph, milkman, 63 Harman
Renwick, William, merchant, 127 Pearl
Renwick and Gray's store, 127 Pearl
Repose, John, baker, 9 One street
Resler, David, soap and candlemaker, 212 Broadway.
Retler, Fred. soap and candlemaker, 347 Pearl-street.
Resley, John, shoemaker, 7 Harman
Retan, Harman, 36 Church
Revere, Jacob, labourer, 172 Division
Revere, John, lumber-yard, Lumber
Reynolds, Elnathan, tavern, 84 Catharine
Reynolds, Joseph, cartman, 153 Bowery-lane.
Reynolds, Samuel, flour-merchant, 45 Greenwich-st.
Reynolds, Jonah, taylor, 68 James
Reynolds, James, tavern, 232 Greenwich
Reynolds, Jonathan, shoemaker, Eagle
Reynolds, Rowland, shoemaker, 222 Water
Rhoam, Jacob, copper... ...
Rhinehart, Jacob, port... Jenny
Rhinelander, Fred. & Philip, merchts. 21 Greenwich
Rhinelander & Co. Bernard, brewers, G... ich
Rhinelander, William, sugar refiner, 230 Will street
Rhinelander, Philip, merchant, 22 George

Rhinelander and Brother, Ph. brewery, Barley-street.
Rhodes, William, merchant, 187 Pearl
Rhodes, Eleanor, 61 Reed
Rice, Elizabeth, 83 Roosevelt
Rice, Thomas, baker, 14 Frankfort
Rice, Thomas, carpenter, 180 Division
Rich, James, merchant-taylor, 166 Pearl
Rich, Henry, baker, 115 Greenwich
Rich, Stephen, grocer, 30 Barclay
Rich, Thomas, merchant, 65 Pine
Rich and Thomson's store, 121 Front
Rich, Ann, Barley
Rich, Thomas, mason, 79 Murray
Rich, Thomas L. taylor, 13 Lombard
Rich, Abraham, carpenter, 18 Thames
Richards, Samuel, joiner and carpenter, 6 Slote-lane
Richards, Smith, grocer, 62 Reed-street.
Richards, Jesse, cloathing store, 5 New-slip.
Richards & Co. George, merchants, 177 Water-strt.
Richards, Alex. lumber-merchant, Greenwich-road.
Richards, Benjamin, mariner, Jay street.
Richards, Stephen, enameller, 89 Greenwich
Richards, David, 155 Greenwich
Richards, Roger, hair-dresser, 4 New-slip.
Richardson, John, merchant, 163 Pearl-street.
Richardson, William, teller Bank N. Y. 25 Broadway.
Richardson, Thomas, teacher, 18 Nassau-street.
Richardson, Samuel, carpenter, Orange
Richardson, James, mariner, 4 Front
Richardson, John, dry goods store 143, William
Richardson, James, grocer, 110 Broad
Richardson, Charles I. attorney at law, 43 Chatham
Richardson, Robert, taylor, 41 Chatham
Richardson, Levi, carpenter, Charlotte
Richardson, Thomas, 16 Barclay
Richardson, John, Bayard's-lane.
Richardson, James, grocer, 80 Wall
Richardson, Gideon, 193 Pearl
Richey, Thomas, cartman, Sixth
Richey, John I. upholsterer, 93 John
Richey, ——, painter and glazier, 10 Brucker
Richeux, Lewis, 7 Frankfort

Ricker, John, shoemaker, 9 Augustus-street.
Ricker, George, grocer, 5 Chatham
Ricketts, Jacob, 142 Greenwich
Ricketts, Wm. & G. R. A. 142 Greenwich, & 51 Front
Ricketts' amphitheatre, 71 and 73 Greenwich
Ridabauck, Jacob, mason, 7 Chamber
Riddell, John, physician, 7 Chatham
Riddell, Robert, cooper, 88 Harman
Riddles, Mrs. boarding-house, 263 Pearl
Rider, Christian, cartman, 41 Robinson
Rider, Uriah, carpenter, Little Catharine
Rider, William, turner, 27 Partition
Rider, Valentine, boatman, 50 Barclay
Ridley, George, merchant-taylor, 130 Front
Ridley, John, accountant, 10 Ferry
Riffaud, Monsieur, boarding-house, 97 Broad
Rigby, William, feedsman, 21 Roosevelt
Riggs, Caleb S. counsellor at law, 18 Cedar
Riggs, Lydia, schoolmistress, 19 Pine
Riker and Sons, Henry, cabinetmakers, 378 Pearl
Riker, Gerardus, boatman, 79 Reed
Riker, Abraham, cabinetmaker, 378 Pearl
Riker, Mathew, cartman, 89 Reed
Riker, Tunis, Chapel
Riker, James, 148 Broadway.
Riker, James, smith, 63 Reed-street.
Riker, Martin, painter, 12 Rector
Riker, Richard, counsellor at law, 69 Pearl
Riker, John, 131 Chatham-street, corner James
Riker, Peter, 317 Pearl
Riker and Alexander, silversmiths, 350 Pearl
Riker, Sarah, mantuamaker, 10 Fair
Riker, Abraham, cartman, 0 Chapel
Riley, James, shipwright, Henry
Riley, James, cartman, Norfolk
Riley, Isaac, merchant, 49 Vesey
Riley, Edward, lawyer, 47 Pearl
Riley, Thomas, mason, Barley
Riley, John, tavern, 90 Front
Riley, Joseph, grocer, 63 Cherry
Riley, Terence, taylor, 51 Whitehall
Riley, Mathew, coppersmith, 39 Barclay-street.

Riley, widow, 191 Washington-street.
Riley, Deborah, 49 Whitehall
Riners, Peter, rigger, 64 Chatham-street.
Rinebecker, Henry, shopkeeper, 45 Pearl
Ring, Elias, dry goods store, 208 Greenwich
Ring, George, grocer, 34 Barley
Riordon, Mary, tavern, 4 Crane-wharf.
Ripton and Davis, shoemakers, Henry-street.
Ritter, Peter, hardware store, 1 Maiden-lane.
Ritter, Daniel, taylor, 248 Water-street.
Ritter, John P. dry goods store, 109 Chatham
Ritter, Michael, 84 Chatham
Ritter, Michael, 22 Pine, & store 140 Fly-market.
Ritter, John, taylor, 69 Nassau
Rivierre, Jane, 247 Broadway.
Rivington, James, Church, corner Warren
Roach, Charles, mariner, 25 Bancker
Roach, John, tavern, 17 E. George
Robart, Mary, 67 Beekman
Robb, John, carpenter, 26 Marketfield
Robeck, William, shipwright, 231 Greenwich
Robert, Daniel, physician, 45 Frankfort
Roberts, Nicholas, 435 Pearl
Roberts, Robert, 43 Rose
Roberts, William, hatter, 32 Bancker
Roberts, Daniel, baker, 33 Barclay
Roberts, Thomas, taylor, Orange
Roberts, Rev. George, 91 Broad
Roberts, Coonerhaut, grocery store, 1 Rector
Roberts, William, grocer, 2 Wall
Roberts, Robert, hatter, 131 Pearl
Roberts, Thomas, merchant, 134 Pearl
Roberts, John, engraver, 77 Pearl
Robertson, Alexander, merchant, 191 Pearl
Robertson, Thomas, brewer, 137 Chatham
Robertson, James, nail manufactory, 29 Catharine
Robertson, Joseph, cartman, Rex
Robertson, Archibald & Alex. limners, &c. 79 Liberty
Robertson, Richard, cartman, 15 Chapel
Robertson & Son, Robert, carpet store, 132 William
Robertson, Daniel, shoe seller, 210 Greenwich
Robertson, Maria, merchant taylores, 122 Water

Robertson, William, carpenter, 20 Bancker-street.
Robertson, widow, Charlotte
Robertson, Robert, merchant, 44 John
Robertson, Charles, merchant, 136 Pearl
Robertson, John Stark, 356 Broadway.
Robertson, Henry, mariner, 2 Ferry-street.
Robertson, John, shoemaker, 221 William
Robertson, James, merchant, 132 William
Robertson and Mackenzie, merchants, 188 Pearl
Robertson, Wm. grocer, near air-furnace, Greenwich.
Robertson, Eleanor, 1 Washington-street.
Robertson, Mrs. glover, 33 Augustus
Robins, Andrew, shipmaster, 80 Roosevelt
Robins, Enoch, mercht. 9 Rutger, & store 85 Front
Robins, Ezekiel, 174 Water
Robins, Elizabeth, 64 Fair
Robins, William, printer, 46 Lombard
Robinson & Hartshorne, commis. merchs. &c. 96 Wall
Robinson, Mary, tavern, 310 Water
Robinson, Wm. & S. 121 Water, & store 102 Wall
Robinson, John, livery-stable, 64 John
Robinson, James, builder, 52 Greenwich
Robinson, Thomas, shipmaster, 35 Liberty
Robinson, William T. merchant, 269 Pearl
Robinson, Joseph, grocer, 24 Front
Robinson, John, mariner, 3 Ferry
Robinson, John, shipmaster, 19 Fayette
Robinson, Wm. H. mercht. Avery's boarding-house.
Robinson, James, boatman, 91 Reed-street.
Robinson, John, bricklayer, 20 Thomas
Robinson, Henry, mariner, Reed
Robinson, Ann, 45 Roosevelt
Robinson, Calvin, cartman, Third
Robinson, Stephen, Cross
Robinson, James, shipwright, near Alms-house.
Roofor, George, tin-plate worker, 323 Water-street.
Robson, Mary, Bopshop, 302 Water
Robson, Michael, mason, 70 Chamber
Robson, John C. 31 Murray
Roches, Charles, Mulberry
Rockwell, Nathan H. 80 Chamber
Rosemont, John, labourer, 298 Broadway.

Rodgers, Robert, grocer, 4- Lombard-street.
Rodgers, Rev. J[ohn] D. D. 9 Pine
Rodgers, John R. B. M. D. 6 Nassau
Rodgers, Wiliam, boarding-house, 255 Pearl
Rodgers, Wm. grocer, 356 Water
Rodman, John, hoseer, 200 Pearl
Rodman, [...] 9 Cedar
Rodney, William [...]
Ro[...] Warren
Roderi[...]
Rodrig[...] 30 Maiden-lane.
Roe and Sinclair's store 248 Pearl-street.
Roe, John, merchant. 248 Pearl
Roe, Isaac F. merchant, 97 Greenwich
Roe, Benjamin, harness-maker, First
Roe, John, labourer, Third
Roe, Joseph, mariner, 61 Warren
Roe, Shoemaker, shoemaker, 71 Harman
Roebuck, Susannah, 6 Vesey
Rogers, Lewis, grocer, 28 Robinson
Rogers, Edward, tavern, Bruce's-wharf.
Rogers, Moses, merchant, 272 Pearl-street.
Rogers, John, merchant, 7 Beaver
Rogers and Co. Nehemiah. store 232 Pearl
Rogers, Henry, carpenter, 8 Banker
Rogers, Richard, naval officer, 21 Cortlandt
Rogers, Samuel, carpenter, 31 Barclay
Rogers, Nehemiah, merchant, 4 Dey
Rogers, Henry, merchant, 51 Dey
Rogers, Margaret, washer, 59 E. George
Rogers, John, shoemaker, 27 Lumber
Rogers, Henry, mariner, 27 Lumber
Rogers, Abigail, grocer, 6 Lumber
Rogers, L. glover and breeches-maker, 162 Broadway
Rogers, Aaron, merchant, 171 Water-street.
Rogers, [...] carpenter, 13 Thomas
Rogers, James, carpenter, 18 Chamber
Rogers, John, grocer, 74 James
Rogers, John, ship-wright, 5 Lumber
Rogers, John, patch[...]maker, 6 Lumber
Rogers, Hezekiah, [...]maker, 90 Harman
Rogers, Jedediah, boarding-house, 200 Pearl

Roget, Isaac, merchant, 111 Water-street.
Rollinson, William, engraver and seal-sinker, 17 New
Rolston, Mary, 47 Whiteha'l
Romaine, Jacob, cartman, 47 Division
Romaine, Jacob, teacher, 43 Murray
Romayne, Nicholas, M. D. 23 John
Romayne, Benjamin, store, 43 Partition
Romayne, Casparus, cartman, Elizabeth
Romayne, Simeon, wheelwright, Catharine
Romayne, Catharine, washer, Second
Romien, Andrew, 103 Beekman
Romine, Nicholas, smith, Bowery-lane.
Romine, jun. Nicholas, smith, Bowery-lane.
Romsey, Isaac, carpenter, Charlotte-street.
Ronalds, James, joiner, 36 Fair
Rooke, Christian, carpenter, 35 Chatham
Roome, John P. sailmaker, 76 Liberty
Roome, John I. porter-house, 58 Chatham
Roome, Jacob, merchant, 191 Broadway.
Roome, Rachel, 1 Temple-street.
Roome, Jacob, carpenter, Temple
Roome, William, painter, 78 Liberty
Roome, Nicholas, taylor, 14 Barclay
Roome, Catharine, 6 Lombard
Roorbach, John F. notary-public, &c. 87 Maiden-lane.
Roorbach, Frances, 4 Ferry-street.
Roorbach, Baron, boarding-house, 41 Dey
Roosevelt, Elbert, merchant, South
Roosevelt, James, merchant, 333 Pearl
Roosevelt, James I. merc. 99, & store 102 Maiden-lane.
Roosevelt, Cornelius, oil paints merchant, 87 Gold-st.
Roosevelt, James C. 34 Pine
Roosevelt, Margaret, 15 John
Roosevelt, John, 4 Roosevelt
Roosevelt, Oliver, painter, 95 Gold
Roosho, John, carpenter, 153 Chatham
Root, Reuben, carpenter, Fisher
Rosdale, widow, 255 Greenwich
Rose, John, marble polisher, 11 Barclay
Rose, Joseph, distiller, 273 Water
Rose, jun. Joseph, merchant, 24 Ferry
Rose, William L. attorney at law, 100 John

Rose, Talvendy Maria, 394 Pearl-street.
Rose, widow, 16 Jacob
Rose, John, carpenter, 27 George
Rose, Joel, cartman, Charlotte
Rose, Alexander, grocer and porter vaults, 15 Nassau
Rose, James, grocer, 377 Pearl
Roseaman, Richard, tinman, 55 Water
Rosenkrantz, Henry, baker, 11 Dutch
Rosett, David, taylor, 52 Roosevelt
Roshore, John, grocer, 41 Cedar
Ross, John, taylor, 8 Dutch
Ross, John R. marshal & turnkey new jail, 25 Reed
Ross, William, coachmaker, 208 Broadway.
Ross, Thos. tavern & boarding-house, 9 Crane-wharf.
Ross, Alexander, baker, 65 John-street, corner Gold
Ross, Hugh, grocer, Henry
Ross, John, hairdresser, 231 William
Ross, Jonathan, cartman, Division
Ross, John, stonecutter, 275 Greenwich
Ross, widow, 17 Skinner
Ross, David, labourer, 53 Barclay
Ross, David, accountant, Colden
Ross, William, cooper, Mulberry
Rosseli, Peter, shoemaker, 163 Division
Rossetter, Bryan, 217 Greenwich
Roulet & Brother, G. Rossier, merchs. 77 Greenwich
Rote, widow Martha, 38 Roosevelt
Roton, John, labourer, Broadway, near furnace.
Rourk, William, smith, 49 E. George-street.
Rous, Baptist, 116 Chatham
Rousseau, Charles, 37 Banker
Roux, Joseph N. Cross
Le Roux, Charles, 177 Broadway.
Rowe, widow, boarding-house, 13 E. George-street.
Rowland, Jonathan, shipmaster, Henry
Rowlandson, Wilson, shipwright, 67 E. George
Rowlandson & Whitaker, shipwrights, 67 E. George
Roy, Alexander, grocer, 33 Cliff, corner of Fair
Roy, John, carpenter, 43 Chamber
Rozier, J. A. B. French consul, 1 Water
Ruck, William, rigger, 27 Banker
Ruckell, John, baker, 10 Green

Ruckell, widow, Greenwich-road.
Ruckell, Philip, cartman, Chapel, corner Barley-strt.
Rudd, Samuel, teacher of languages, 91 Beekman
Ruff, Jennet, 2 Jacob
Rule, Elizabeth, 51 Reed
Rump, Jacob, carpenter, Barley
Rush, widow, First
Rushforth, William, shoemaker, 61 Cedar
Russell, Timothy, carpenter, 56 James
Russell, James, mason, 7 Rose
Russell, Samuel, tobacconist, 24 Catharine
Russell, Abraham, mason and builder, 153 Broadway.
Russell, James, mason, 48 Warren-street.
Russell, Joseph, tobacco manufactory, 112 Water
Russell, Richard, mason, Thomas
Russell, William, merchant, Cherry-strt. Ship-yards.
Russell, John H. gold and silversmith, 1 New-street.
Russell, Joseph, cartman, 104 Reed
Russell, Bartholomew, labourer, 54 Chapel
Russell, ———, shipmaster, 91 James
Russell, Robert, taylor, 18 Lombard
Russell, Richard, mason, Thomas
Russellier, Zacharias, branch pilot, 15 Ferry
Ruffin, John, cooper, First
Rustey, John, shoemaker, 10 Robinson
Rutgers, Col. Henry, E. Washington
Rutgers, Capt. Anthony, end of Chamber
Rutgers, Seaman & Ogden's counting-house, 79 Pearl
Rutgers, Nicholas G. merchant, 79 Pearl
Rutgers, Harman G. auctioneer, 128 Pearl
Rutherfurde, Walter, 219 Broadway.
Ruthven, John, ivory and hard wood turner, 30 John
Rutledge, William, builder and shipjoiner, 98 Front
Rutzer, John, shoemaker, 56 Whitehall
Rutzer, John, shoemaker, 62 Water-Street.
Ryan, Sarah, tavern, 108 Front
Ryan, Thomas, tobacconist, 210 Water
Ryan, Cornelius, cartman, Mulberry
Ryan, Philip, carpenter, 38 Augustus
Ryan, John, mariner, 54 Roosevelt
Ryan, William, mariner, 76 Gold
Ryan, Andrew, labourer, 33 Roosevelt

Ryar, Michael, cartman, 28 Reed-street.
Ryar, William, 17 Murray
Ryckman, Isaac, mariner, Henry
Ryckman, Albert, merchant, 26 George
Ryckman, Abraham, shoemaker, Broadway.
Ryckman, John, dry goods store, 424 Pearl-street.
Ryckman, Talbot, shoemaker, 41 Harman
Ryckman, James, cartman, Pump
Ryckman, Harman, shoemaker, Third
Ryckman, John, cabinetmaker, 208 Greenwich
Ryder, Mitchel, hatter, 205 Water
Ryers, Henry, painter, Winne
Ryers, Dennis, shoemaker, Bayard

S

Sackett, Richard, cabinetmaker, 233 Greenwich-street.
Sackett, Joseph, physician, 65 Partition
Sackett, Augustus, attorney at law, 110 Liberty
Sadler, Henry, merchant, 18 Cortlandt
Sadler and Co. Henry, counting-house, 74 Pine
Saffron, David, 22 Oliver
Sague, widow, 54 Rutger
Saidler and Waterbury, merchants, 131 Water
Saidler, James, merchant, 131 Water
St. John, Samuel, merchant-taylor, 126 Pearl
Salbardie, Francis, sugarmaker, 52 Barclay
Saliment, George F. professor of music, 39 Liberty
Salisbury, Elsy, boarding-house, 58 Water
Salmon, Helen, boarding-house, 153 Broadway.
Salmon, Sarah, 55 Ann-street.
Salter, Manasseh, merchant, 173 and 175 Broadway.
Salter, Thomas, merchant, 175 Broadway.
Salter, John, mariner, 58 Harman-street.
Salter, Thomas, mariner, Birmingham-row.
Saltonstall, Rich. R. merch. 94 Wall, & house 1 Gold-st.
Saltonstall, Harriot, 170 William
Saltus, Son and Co. ship-chandlers, 65 Front
Saltus, Solomon, merchant, 12 Stone
Sampson, Samuel, labourer, Bowery-lane.
Samuel, Augustus, baker, 7 E. George-street.
Sandford, Michael, cartman, 45 Chamber
Sandford, William, livery-stabler, 92 Chapel
Sandford, Peregrine, bootmaker, 46 William

Sandford, John, Greenwich-road.
Sandford, David, butcher, 194 Greenwich-street.
Sandford, Enoch, porter-house, 287 Water
Sandhaeven, Herman, 267 Broadway.
Sandilands, James, carpenter, Little Catharine
Sands, Stephen, cartman, 32 Barley
Sands, William, hairdresser, 112 Broad
Sands, Henry, attorney at law, 13 Cedar
Sands, Edward, grocer, 68 James
Sands, Joshua, collector of the port, 120 Pearl
Sands, Comfort, mercht. 13 Cedar, & house 26 Pine
Sands, Benjamin, hairdresser, 102 Liberty
Sands, Mary, 32 Beekman
Sanfay, Lewis, 3 Bowery-lane.
Santford, John, broker, 27 Cedar-street.
Sanxay, John, upholsterer, 59 Chamber
Sapineau, Mrs. dry goods store, 144 Front
Sarley, John, 36 Vesey
Sartre, ———, 11 Thames
Satterthwaite, Thomas W. merchant, 87 Water
Saunders, Margaret, Catharine, corner Henry
Saunders, Robert, printer, 58 Cedar
Saunders, Alexander, cabinetmaker, 13 William
Saunders, Mrs. milliner, 13 William
Saunders, Henry, tanner, 71 Warren
Saunders, widow of Thomas, 22 Gold
Saunders, Benjamin, merchant-taylor, 14 Cherry
Saunders, Christopher, cartman, 101 Reed
Saunders, Peter, cartman, Henry
Saunders, John, Cherry-str. & store Malcolm's wharf.
Saunders, John, labourer, Elizabeth-street.
Saunderson, James, mariner, 70 Ann
Sauntes, Ennis, tobacconist, 19 E. George
Savage, Richard, 75 John
Savage, James, grocer, 12 Beekman-slip.
Sawyer, Richard, mariner, Mulberry-street.
Sayre, John, silversmith, 273 Pearl
Sayre and Haggerty, merchants, 75 Maiden-lane.
Sayrles, Edward, mason, Henry-street.
Sayrs, Isaac, grocer, Charlotte
Saveand, John, 59 Catharine
Schenberry, John, sugar-baker, 3 E. George

Schenck, William P. boatman, Church-street.
Schenck, widow, sick nurse, 74 Liberty
Schenck, Peter A. merchant, 68 Front
Schenck, John, gold and silversmith, 133 Water
Schennet, Lewis, cartman, 347 Broadway.
Schermerhorn & Son, S. 31 Pearl, & store 62 Front-str.
Schermerhorn, Peter, ship-chandler, 220 & 224 Water
Schermerhorn, John P. ship-chandler, 187 Front
Schermerhorn, Cornelius, shipmaster, 39 Beekman
Schewsighauser, Nicholas, merchant, 15 Gold
Schieffelin, Jacob, 306 Pearl
Schlam, J. W. watchmaker, 25 George
Schmelzel, George, merchant, 181 Broadway.
Schoonmaker, John, cartman, Charlotte-street.
Schranton, Noah, blockmaker, E. Rutger
Schoft, John C. porter-house, 244 William
Schoots, Bernard, hair-dresser, 1 Bridge
Schroeppel, George C. merchant, Greenwich
Schrolder, Hendrick, colour maker, 64 Chatham
Schultz, Christian, Eagle
Schultz, jun. Christian, Eagle
Schultz and Nestell's brewery, Fourth
Schunkhu, John, grocer, 91 Nathu
Schurman, William, cartman, Third
Schuyler, Peter C. 23 William
Schuyler, Cornelius, butcher, Second
Schuyler and Hicks, merchants, 79 Malden-lane.
Schwertzholtz, I. C. piano-forte-maker, 25 Chatham
Scofield, Jesse, merchant taylor, 275 Water
Scofield, John, smith, Pump
Scofield, Hugh, labourer, 301 Broadway.
Scoles, John, engraver and bookseller, 6 Broad-street.
Scotland, John, cabinetmaker, 16 George
Scott and Seaman, merchants, 274 Pearl
Scott, James, merchant, 274 Pearl
Scott, Hector, merchant, 125 Pearl
Scott, Rachel, 24 George
Scott, James, carpenter, 34 Rose
Scott, Charles, labourer, Third
Scott, George, shopkeeper, 21 E. George
Scott, Mrs. 238 Broadway.
Scott, Mary, Little Clarence-street.

Scott, David, shoemaker, 10 Rose-street.
Scott, Charles, labourer, 66 Pearl
Scott, Wm. A. M. teacher of mathematics, 24 Cedar
Scott, Daniel, fringemaker, 251 William
Scott, Francis, labourer, 59 Catharine
Scott, widow, 45 E. George
Scott, Margaret, 9 Dey
Scott, James, calico-printer, 44 Barclay
Scott, Alexander, mason, Pump
Scott, George, labourer, Little Catharine
Scott, Mrs. seamstress, 29 Augustus
Scott, William, labourer, Little Catharine
Scott, Margaret, Magazine
Scriba, George, merchant, 23 Wall
Scudder, Samuel, revenue-officer, 73 Catharine
Scudder, Corbet, 58 Reed
Seabury, Edmund, 35 Vesey
Seacord, Jane, seamstress, 12 Cliff
Seal, George, cooper, 8 Depeyster
Sedleng, Andrew, taylor, 30 Nassau
Seaman, Henry, merchant, 164 Pearl
Seaman, Rich. mercht. 10 Cherry, & store Peck-slip.
Seaman, Valentine, M. D. 230 Water-street.
Seaman, Edmund, merchant, 24 Wall
Seaman and Co. Edmund, segar-house, 31 Pine
Seaman, Thomas, merchant-taylor, 252 Water
Seaman, Robert, grocer, 108 Bowery-lane.
Seaman, Jacob, grocer, corner New-slip & Water-st.
Seaman, John, 77 Beekman
Seaman and Sons, Willet, merchants, 296 Pearl
Seaman, James, accountant, 264 William
Seaman, Israel, merchant, 274 Pearl
Seaman, John, joiner, Division
Seaman and Van Keuren's store, 37 Front
Seaman, Henry, labourer, 37 Thomas
Seaman, Joseph, Greenwich-road.
Seaman, Ezekiel, mariner, Henry-street.
Seaman, widow, Henry
Seaman, Edmund, Engle
Seaman, Benjamin B. merchant, 73 Pearl
Seamle, Samuel, grocer, 72 James
Seamer, widow, 50 Augustus

Searing, Gilbert, cartman, Bowery-lane.
Sears, Moses, mason, 42 Augustus-street.
Sears, widow, 56 Maiden-lane.
Seaver, Luther, cooper, Fisher-street.
Seaward, Christopher, pilot, 89 Fair
Sebor, Jacob, merchant, 51 Beaver
Sebring, Isaac, merchant, 28 Wall
Sebring & Van Wyck, store, Coenties-sl. corner South-st.
Sebring, Cornelius B. smith, 31 Fair-street, & 16 John
Sebring, Peter, sailor, 16 John
Secor, David I. carpenter, 44 Barclay
Secor, Elijah, 148 Broadway.
Seelye, Jaben, grocer, Henry-street.
Segar, John, tavern, 6 Maiden-lane.
Seigone, John, tavern, 13 Moore-street.
Seifferth, George, labourer, 119 Chatham
Seiton, John, 31 Harman
Seixas, M. and T. merchants, 16 Marketfield
Seixas, Rev. Gershom, 20 Mill
Seixas, Benjamin, merchant, 76 Broad
Sell, Stephen, grocer, 43 James
Sergeant, James, cartman, 15 Rector
Sergeant, William, cartman, 47 Greenwich
Sergeant, widow, Beaver-lane.
Sergeant, Alling, shoe store, Front-st. near Crane-whf.
Serrur, Anthony, fruiterer, 123 Fly-market.
Service, Thomas, merchant, 183 Pearl-street.
Seton, Maitland and Co's. counting-house, 38 Mill
Seton, William M. merchant, 27 Wall
Seton, John Curson, merchant, 61 Stone
Seton, James, merchant, 67 Wall
Seymour, Isaac, musician, Barley
Seymour, ———, comedian, 26 Vesey
Shackerly and Co. Peter, carpenters, 103 Pearl
Shackerly, Mary, teach. ref., 103 Pearl
Shackerly, J. H. merc. 84 Maiden-lane, & 5 Liberty-st.
Shade, George, cartman, Pump-street.
Shaddock, Abraham, cartman, 18 Harman
Shaffer, Christian, taylor, First
Shampma, Andrew, cartman, 117 Division
Shanewolf, Frederick, hairdresser, 213 Broadway.

Shapter, Thomas, labourer, Bowery-lane.
Shareman, Henry, cartman, Harman-street.
Sharkey, John, tobacconist, Fisher
Sharp, widow, 89 Chamber
Sharp, Robert and John, merchants, 91 William
Sharples, James, portrait-painter, 272 Greenwich
Sharpless, Isaac, carpenter and builder, 443 Pearl
Sharpless, Aaron, grocer, 1 Cliff, corner of John
Sharrock, James, mason, E. George, corner Harman
Shatzel, sen. John M. boot & shoemaker, 96 Chatham
Shatzel, Michael, boot and shoemaker, 355 Water
Shatzel, William, shoemaker, 248 Water
Shatzel, Jacob, grocer, 35 Warren
Shaw, John C. merchant, 44 Beaver
Shaw, widow, Henry
Shaw, John, merchant, 9, and store 15 Pearl
Shaw, William, mariner, 84 James
Shaw, James, accountant, 15 Nassau
Shaw, James, merchant, 86 Maiden-lane.
Shay, Patrick, 4 Duane, and store 105 Front-street.
Shedden, William, merchant 99 Water
Shedden, Patrick and Co. counting-house, 99 Water
Sheerar, James, eating-house, 150 Fly-market.
Sheffield, Robert, shipmaster, E. Rutger-street.
Shelburne, Joseph, grocer, 309 Broadway.
Shelden, George, hairdresser, 81 Nassau-street.
Sheleigh, John, mariner, 74 Chamber
Shells, Jeremiah, labourer, 8 Moore's-row.
Shepherd, Thomas, hairdresser, 47 John-street.
Shepherd, John, shipwright, Lumber
Shepherd, John, taylor, 69 William
Shepherd, John, boatman, 12 Chapel
Shepherd, Stephen, breeches-maker, 96 Broadway.
Shepherd, Edward, teacher, 68 Broad-street.
Shepherd, Joseph, mariner, Mulberry
Shepherd, Eleanor, seamstress, 40 Beaver
Sherbrook, Miles, merchant, 25 Pearl
Sherer, Henry, gardener, First
Sherman, Nathan, carpenter, 80 Liberty
Sherman, Jacob, cartman, 5 Rose
Sherman, Joseph, carver and gilder, 12 James
Sherred, Jacob, painter, gilder, &c. 35 Broad

Sherwood, Joseph, carpenter, 69 Murray-street.
Sherwood, Seymour, rigger, 12 Chesnut
Sherwood, John, shipwright, Eagle
Sherwood, Mary, 12 Chesnut
Sherwood, Andrew, carpenter, 34 Thomas
Sherwood, Benjamin, grocer, 66 Vesey
Sherwood, Jehiel, cartman, 7 Bowery-lane.
Sherwood, Isaac, turner, 84 Chatham-street.
Sherwood, Benjamin, cooper, Magazine
Shields, James, labourer, 50 Church
Shields, Alexander, carpenter, Charlotte
Shields, Peter, mason, Charlotte
Shields, William, cartman, Lumber
Shields, William, tea-waterman, Bedlow
Shields, Edward, combmaker, 133 Chatham
Shields, Edward, cartman, Thomas
Shimmeal, Valentine, tanner & currier, 40 Frankfort
Ship, George, butcher, Bayard
Shipley, George, cabinetmaker, 195 Water
Shipman, William, 84 Partition
Shippey, Josiah, merchant, 25 Stone
Stites, Julius, cartman, 70 Warren
Shoe, Andrew, gardener, Orchard
Shoe, Andrew, cartman, Pump
Shoe, John, grocer, 9 Bowery lane.
Shoemaker, Abraham, dry goods store, 440 Pearl-str.
Shonburk, Henry, cartman, Second
Shonnard, George, silversmith, 414 Pearl
Shonnard, P. & A. plaister of Paris manuf. 98 James
Shonnard, Frederick, grocer, 80 Bowery-lane.
Shorton, Jane, 96 James-street.
Shotwell, Peter, oysterman, 79 Murray
Shotwell, widow, 102 Chamber
Shour, Oliver, carpenter, 448 Pearl
Shover, John, baker
Show, Madam, Pump
Showrt, William, cartman, 22 Chamber
Shrady, John, shoemaker, 86 Chatham
Shreve, Caleb, druggist, 155 Cherry
Shrigley, James, taylor, 25 Cliff
Shute, Richard, cartman, 37 Reed
Shute, widow, 10 Green

Shute, John, deputy-sheriff, 340 Broadway.
Shute, Henry, corner Magazine & Little Ann streets.
Shute, Jacob, cartman, Elizabeth
Shuter, James, merchant, 42 Dey, & store 82 Front-st.
Sibell, John, grocer, 33 Water
Sibley, Mary, schoolmistress, 12 Dutch
Sice, Michael, baker, 82 Fair
Sickeson, John, shoemaker, 34 Ann
Sickles, Garrit, shoemaker, 89 Division
Sickles, Henry, taylor, 57 Broad
Sickles, John H. merchant, 12 and 14 New
Sickles, widow, 7 New
Sickles, John, cooper, Bedlow
Sickles, Zachariah, cooper, Gibbs'-alley.
Sickles, widow, 70 Liberty-street.
Sickles, Henry, shoemaker, Mulberry
Sickles, John, clothier, 35 and 53 Maiden-lane.
Sickles, Daniel, cooper, Gibbs'-alley.
Sickles, Elias, smith, Bedlow
Sickles and M'Cloughan, cooperage, Stevens'-wharf.
Sidell, widow, shopkeeper, 56 Stone-street.
Sidell, John, merchant-taylor, 132 Pearl
Sidney, Joseph, cooper, 48 Cedar
Siebe, Henry, cabinetmaker, 11 Warren
Siemon, John, farrier, 103 William
Sigler, ———, taylor, 456 Pearl
Silkworth, Thomas, labourer, E. Washington
Silva, Ann, sezarmaker, near Cross
Silva, Joze Roiz, merch. 29 William, & store 79 Front
Silva, Joseph, mariner, 63 James
Sim, William, clerk in the loan-office, 23 New
Simlay, John, carpenter, 258 William
Simmemon, Godfrey, tobacconist, 51 Lumber
Simmon, David, mason, 39 Rose
Simmons, Robert, wheel-master, 83 John
Simmons, Walthon, sebrerer, 11 Chatham
Simmons, Wm. grocery & flour-store, 161 Fly-market.
Simmons, widow, Chapel-street.
Simmons, William, labourer, Greenwich-road.
Simmons, Jacob, 36 Rutger-street.
Simmons, Joshua, second
Simmons, Andrew, cartman, Little Catherine

NEW-YORK DIRECTORY.

Simond & Co. Lewis, 41 Beekman, & ſtore Stevens'-w f.
Simonſon, Simon, ſhoemaker, 49 Pearl-ſtreet.
Simonton, Henry and Jacob, grocers, 52 Front
Simonton, Jacob, carpenter, Eagle
Simonton, jacob, grocer, 26 Water
Simpſon, Solomon, merchant, 71 Broad
Simpſon, Dolly, waſher, 15 Ann
Simpſon, Jane, waſher, 94 Cherry
Simpſon, John, grocer, 344 Broadway.
Simpſon, Andrew, ſhipmaſter, 18 Fayette-ſtreet.
Simpſon, Lucretia, 19 Dutch
Simyton, widow, 5 Moore's-row.
Sinclair, John, merchant, Cherry-ſtreet, Shipyards.
Sinclair, James, ſhipmaſter, 5 Batavia-lane.
Sinclair, Hugh, grocer, 160 William-ſtreet.
Sinclair, Lawrence, teacher, Pump
Sinclair, Hector, carpenter, 11 Rector
Sinclair, John, labourer, 7 Hague
Sinclair, Mary, grocer, 325 Water
Sing, William, merchant, 4 Frankfort
Sipkins, Thomas, boatman, 14 Warren
Sipmar, Peter, labourer, 84 Fair
Sintus, Garrit, cooper, 10 Catharine
Sire, B. merchant, 45 Water
Siſe, Leonard, labourer, 27 Rooſevelt
Siſque, Daniel, labourer, 69 Diviſion
Siſſon, Preſerved, ſhipmaſter, 37 Cheapſide.
Sitcher, John, ſhoemaker, 19 Chapel-ſtreet.
Sitcher, Andrew, painter, 34 Lombard
Sitcher, William, 34 Lombard
Sitgreaves, George, teacher, 25 Markſtfield
Skaats, Rinier, chief marſhal, Federal-hall.
Skaats, Bartholomew, ſilverſmith, 40 Chapel-ſtreet.
Skaats, David, cartman, 69 Church
Skaats, Jacob, cooper, 6 Veſey
Skaats, widow, 75 Church
Skaats, Thomas, Chamber, near Alms-houſe.
Skelorn, W. G. chairmaker, 217 William-ſtreet.
Skelton, William, mariner, 24 Dancker
Skidmore, Paul, & G. merchts. 222 Pearl, & 121 Water
Skidmore, Lemier, grocer, 173 Greenwich.
Skillman, Joſeph, boatman, Pump

Skillin, Simeon, carver, 119 Cherry-street.
Skilman, Joseph, carpenter, 88 Chamber
Skinner, John, shoemaker, 52 Bancker
Skinner, Abraham, counsellor at law, 57 Pine
Skinner, Richard C. surgeon-dentist, 156 William
Skinner, Thomas, merchant, 109 Broad
Skinner, widow, 15 Lumber
Slack & Spencer's soap & candle manufactory, 8 Reed
Slade, Richard, shoemaker, Pump
Slater, William, labourer, 30 Rose
Sleep, John, mariner, 3 Bancker
Sleight & Bumstead, grocers, Cherry, corner George
Sleight and Co. John, merchants, 116 Liberty
Sleight, Mary, 43 Rose
Sleight, John, cartman, Henry
Sleight, Henry, carpenter, Henry
Slidell, jun. &Co. John, soap, &c. manuf. 50 Broadway.
Slidell, Michael, labourer, 56 Ann-street.
Slidell, Isaac, shoemaker, 56 Ann
Slidell, Joshua, measurer, 26 Warren
Slipper, Joseph, oil-case-maker, 10 Bayard
Sloan, Sarah, Little Catharine
Sloan, Richard, grocer, 282 Water
Slocum and Burling, merchants, 185 Water
Slocum, Christopher M. 185 Water
Sloman, Andrew, tanner, 100 Gold
Sloo, William, First
Slote, Isaac, sugar-refiner, 13 Thames
Slote, Peter, printer, 71 Chamber
Slover, Abraham, cabinetmaker, 94 Broad
Slover, Catharine, 94 Broad
Slowly, Mathew S. brewer, 46 Catharine
Smack, Christian, cartman, 18 Robinson
Small, Edward, slopshop, 202 Water
Small, William, grocer, Little Catharine
Smallen, Michael, tavern, 357 Pearl
Smart, John, sadler, 162 Water
Smith, Adam, labourer, Winne
Smith, Alexander, smith, 72 Murray
Smith, Arthur, mason, 204 Greenwich
Smith, Anna, 41 Rutger
Smith, Abraham, shoemaker, 290 Water

Smith, Alexander, merchant, 177 Pearl-street.
Smith, Anna, teacheress, 46 Warren
Smith, Albert, musical instrument maker, 86 John
Smith, Andrew, teacher, 5 and 9 Cedar
Smith, Alexander, smith, 58 Barclay
Smith, Benjamin, cartman, 50 Lombard
Smith, Benjamin, carpenter, 16 Reed
Smith, Benjamin, cooper, Charlotte
Smith, Benjamin, carpenter, 72 Chamber
Smith, Bethia, milliner, 16 Garden
Smith, Bernardus, taylor, 36 Gold
Smith, Caleb, merchant, 53 Beaver
Smith, Charles, 14 Dey
Smith, Charles, china and glass store, 272 Water
Smith, Christian, baker and tavern, 307 Broadway.
Smith, Charles, cabinetmaker, 239 Broadway.
Smith, Cornelius W. 83 Chamber-street.
Smith, Charles, bookseller, &c. 51 Maiden-lane.
Smith, Cornelius, Bull's ferry-house, 75 Vesey-street.
Smith, David, grocer, 194 Front
Smith, Daniel, merchant, 11 William
Smith, Esther, 52 Rose
Smith, Eliza, mantuamaker, 66 Vesey
Smith, Eben, carpenter, Little Catharine
Smith, Elihu H. physician, 45 Pine
Smith, E. taylor, Chatham
Smith, Edmund, merchant, 53 Gold
Smith, Fortune, labourer, Grand
Smith, George, rigger, 20 Ferry
Smith, Gilbert, cartman, 24 Thames
Smith, George, physician, 377 Bedlow
Smith, George, rigger, 21 Cliff
Smith, Gerardus, sailmaker, 15 Beaver, & loft 42 Front.
Smith, Grenville, merchant, 179 William
Smith, Gilbert H. physician, 31 Oliver
Smith, Henry, milkman, Pitt
Smith, Henry, painter, 325 Broadway.
Smith, Henry, labourer, 12 Roosevelt-street.
Smith, John, grocer, Mulberry
Smith, John, carpenter, 65 Harman
Smith, Jane, 53 Stone
Smith, John, cartman, 75 Harman

Smith, John, mariner, 3 Harman-street.
Smith, John, cartman, 23 Fayette
Smith, John Henry, merchant, 6 Bowery-lane.
Smith, John, mariner, 33 Rutger-street.
Smith, John, mariner, 15 E. George
Smith, John, merchant, 69 Barclay, & 183 Greenwich
Smith, John, butcher, Bowery-lane.
Smith, John, well-digger, 104 Bowery-lane.
Smith, John, pilot, 49 Cliff-street.
Smith, John, grocer, 67 Warren
Smith, John, coachmaker, Division
Smith, John, merchant, 140 William
Smith, John, butcher, 115 Bowery-lane.
Smith, John, cartman, 17 Rector street.
Smith, John, whitesmith, 17 Water
Smith, John, oval and round turner, 35 George
Smith, John, shipmaster, 24 Roosevelt
Smith, Joseph, corkcutter, 2 Crane-wharf.
Smith, Jacob, shoe store, 316 Pearl-street.
Smith, James, stonecutter, saw-pits, Greenwich-road.
Smith, James, attorney at law, 29 Cortlandt-street.
Smith, James A. tavern, 43 Vandewater
Smith, James, dry goods store, 442 Pearl
Smith, Jesse, mariner, 32 Bancker
Smith, Joseph, grocer, 78 Vesey
Smith, James R. merchant, 211 Pearl
Smith, Jacob, oval and round turner, 94 Beekman
Smith, Jacob, carpenter, 55 Ann
Smith, Joseph, shoemaker, 35 Partition
Smith, John, shipmaster, 67 Fair
Smith, James L. auctioneer, 81 Wall
Smith, Joseph, merchant-taylor, 42 Water
Smith, Lewis, constable, 3 Catharine
Smith, Luff, carpenter, Ly
Smith, Morris, physician, 33 Harman
Smith, Melancton, mer. 52 Greenwich, & office 43 Front
Smith, Moses, merchant, 21 Broad
Smith, Mary, teacheress, 8 Chapel
Smith, Maria, Cross
Smith, Morris, Little Catherine
Smith, Mary, boarding-house, 50 Broad
Smith, Mary, matron in the Hospital.

Smith, Nathaniel, carpenter, 72 Chamber-street.
Smith, Oliver W. merchant-taylor, 263 Water
Smith, Obadiah, mariner, 78 Catharine
Smith, Paschal N. mer. 30 Bowery, & office 36 Broad-
Smith, Philip, cartman, 18 Harman-street.
Smith, Patrick, mariner, 5 Moore's-row.
Smith, Platt, Greenwich-road.
Smith, Rich. tavern & boarding-house, 159 Fly-market.
Smith, Robert, cartman, 41 Oliver-street.
Smith, Richard, carpenter, 109 Division
Smith, Richard, labourer, Third
Smith, Ralph, carpenter, Pump
Smith, Richard, carpenter, 20 Vesey
Smith, Robert, mariner, E. Washington
Smith, Samuel, carpenter, Henry
Smith, Silas, cartman, Mulberry
Smith, Samuel, attorney at law, 53 Partition
Smith, Samuel, 61 Catharine
Smith, Stephen, hatter, 52 Water
Smith, Thomas, shipmaster, 19 Pearl
Smith, Thomas, blockmaker, &c. Front, Crane-wharf.
Smith, Thomas, taylor, 65 Barclay-street.
Smith, Thomas, blockmaker, Gibbs'-alley.
Smith, Thomas, dock-master, 144 Chatham-street.
Smith, Thomas, labourer, 80 Warren
Smith, Thomas, smith, 3 Dey
Smith, Thomas, attorney at law, 64 William
Smith, Timothy, chimney-office, 30 Ferry
Smith, Thomas, grocer, 152 Fly-market.
Smith, Thaddeus, boarding-house, 72 Vesey
Smith, Thomas Howell, grocer, 196 Front
Smith, T. R. ironmonger, 96 Beekman, & store 287 Pearl
Smith, William, cabinetmaker, Birmingham-row.
Smith, William, cartman, Mott-street.
Smith, William Henry, merchant, 52 Gold
Smith, William, silk dyer, 21 or 23 Chatham
Smith, Walter, merchant, 1 George
Smith, William, wool-comber, 18 Batavia-lane.
Smith, William, cartman, 27 Cliff-street.
Smith, William, blockmaker, Cherry, and 51 Oliver
Smith, William, rigger, 7 Harman
Smith, widow of Dr. William Pitt, 79 Beekman

NEW-YORK DIRECTORY.

Smith, widow, Essex-street.
Smith, widow, 84 Roosevelt
Smith and Co. David, merchants, 208 Water
Smith and Co. Charles, merchants, 130 Pearl
Smith and Co. Gamaliel, merchants, 36 Maiden-lane.
Smith and M'Kidop, dry goods store, 442 Pearl-street.
Smith and Demott, grocers, 58 E. George
Smith and Carll, merchants, 362 Front
Smith and Wyckoff's store, 211 Pearl
Smith and Creed, merchants, 97 Catharine
Smith, ——, mariner, Henry
Smithman, Catharine, fruiterer, 98 Harman
Smock, Cornelius, 16 Chapel
Smock, Cornelius, tavern, 12 Water
Smout, Geo. clothier, 151 Chatham, & 8 Bowery-lane.
Smuck, William, tea-waterman, Winne-street.
Smull, Ludovick, tea-waterman, Mulberry
Smyth, Andrew, merchant, 53 Beekman
Smyth and Moore, ironmongers, 3 Burling-slip.
Smyth, Mary, grocer, 16 Coenties-slip.
Snackenbergh, Chrisf. grocer, Bayard, corner Winne-st.
Sneden, Elijah, taylor, 87 Division
Sneden, Samuel, cartman and grocer, 9 Rector
Sneed, Ezekiel, butcher, Charlotte
Snegs, Mary, 11 Cliff
Snell, Thomas, shipmaster, 43 Frankfort
Snell, John, carpenter, 7 Cliff
Snodgrass, James, weaver, Lumber
Snow, Robert, accountant, 50 Pine
Snow, James, tavern, 253 Broadway.
Snow, Jane, 12 Batavia-lane.
Snow, Edmund, mariner, 6 E. George-street.
Snowdon, Charles, 130 Water.
Snowdon, widow, 25 Harman
Snowden, Geo. ship-chandler, 174 Front, & 56 Gold
Snyder, Jacob, carpenter, 7 Read
Snyder, Rebecca, Pope's-alley.
Snyder, widow, 39 Robinson-street.
Snyder, widow, near Cross
Solomon, Mark, butcher, 40 Greenwich
Solomon, Richard, cartman, near furnace, Broadway.
Sommerindyck, Mathew, grocer, 54 Broad-street.

NEW YORK DIRECTORY.

Somerindyck, Sarah, 20 George-street.
Somerville, Archibald, 88 Maiden-lane.
Somerville, Alexander, bookseller & stationer, 2 ...
Sommer, Mrs. corner of Wall and New-street.
Sommers, William, sailmaker, 39 Warren-street.
Sooy, Luke, dock-builder, Lumber
Souque, Michael, gold and silversmith, 177 Will.
Southworth, Elijah, watchmaker, 53 Water
Sovern, John, carpenter, 25 Barclay
Sowerby, James, grocer, Pump
Sparhawk, Susannah, milliner, 52 Cherry
Sparks, John, milkman, Little Ann
Sparkman, James, mariner, 27 Cheapside.
Sparling, George, gardener, Eagle-street.
Spatts, Richard, painter and glazier, 19 Rose
Spatts, ———, cabinetmaker, 1 Barley
Speed, Paul, livery-stabler, 60 New
Spence, James, 34 Whitehall
Spencer, Cornelius, rigger, 13 Cheapside.
Spencer, William, bricklayer, 28 Catharine-street
Spencer, William, nailor, 57 James
Sperry, John, merchant, 92 Maiden-lane.
Speyer, John, merchant, corner Stone & William st.
Spicer, Francis, butcher, 117 Bowery-lane.
Spicer, Peter, cartman, First-street.
Spier, John, cabinetmaker, 8 Cherry
Spier, Christopher, 24 Cedar
Spier, James, smith, 35 Day
Spier, Richard, brushmaker, 28 Vandewater
Spies, John, hatmaker, 76 Chatham
Spies, ———, tavern, Theatre-alley.
Spinley, Martin, 3 Rutger street.
Spragg, Samuel, cartman, 13 Cherry &c.
Spranger & Co. Peter R. sloe warehouse, 318 Pearl.
Spratt, John, labourer, ...
Sprent, William, grocer, Nicholas, corner ...
Springer, Joseph, carpenter, Barlow
Sprong, Jeremiah B. shoemaker, 21 Duneker
Sprofon and Martha, windsor chairmakers, 271 P...
Sprofon, John, chairmaker, Pump
Sprofon, John, grocer, Leonard
Sproat, John, shipmaster, 72 Roosevelt

Sproull, Thomas, labourer, 60 Chamber-street.
Sproull, Samuel, 63 Warren
Sprouls, Thomas, carpenter, 8 Cherry
Stackhouse, H. grocer, Catharine-slip, corner Water-st.
Stagg, John, store, 121 Greenwich-street.
Stagg, Thomas, merchant, 183 Greenwich
Stagg, Daniel, carpenter, 18 Roosevelt
Stagg, jun. Thomas, 271 Water, & store Rose's wharf.
Stagg, Abraham, cartman, 52 E. George-street.
Stagg, Thomas, cartman, Norfolk
Stagg, James, labourer, Warren
Stagg, John T. labourer, 43 Murray
Stagg, jun. John, grocer, 195 Greenwich
Stagg, Isaac, cartman, 46 Barclay
Stagg, Nicholas, labourer, Robinson
Stake, widow, corner of William and George
Stam, Peter, hatter, Little Catharine
Stamers, Thomas, mason, Charlotte
Stanbury, Charlotte, 73 Chatham
Stanbury, Isaac, grocer, Washington
Stanbury and Wood, ironmongers, 104 Water
Stanbury, Isaac, timber merchant, 68 Dey
Stanbury, Robert, tanner and currier, 107 Gold
Stanbury, Wood & Co. store, Front-str. Stevens'-whf.
Standerwick, Wm. grocer, Water-str. above New-slip.
Stanford, Rev. John, 81 Fair-street.
Stanley, Adam, wood-screw-maker, Henry
Stansbury, Jos. secretary, M. A. company, 140 Pearl
Stansbury and Haydock, merchants, 242 Pearl
Stansbury, Joseph M. merchant, 406 Pearl
Stansbury, Daniel, merchant, 406 Pearl
Stansbury, Jonas, 206 Greenwich
Stansbury, widow, 101 Gold
Stanton, jun. Robert, ship-chandler, corner Oliver-st.
Stanton, John, shipwright, 53 Cherry
Stanton, George, carpenter and builder, Brooklyn.
Stanton, Jasper, inspector of lime, 34 Partition-street.
Stanton, William, carpenter, 12 John
Stanton, Rebecca, 20 Warren
Stanton, Asa, cabinetmaker, 50 Oliver
Stanton, Robert, china and glass store, 96 Cherry
Stanwood, Lemuel, mariner, 4 Lumber

Staples, jun. John I. merchant, 169 Pearl-street.
Stark, widow, 11 Moore's-row.
Starling, James, cooper, 3 Bridge-street.
Starr, ——, shipmaster 67 James
Startin, Charles, merchant, 225 Broadway.
Stats, Elijah, cooper, Gibbs'-alley.
Stebbins, Simon, grocer, 4 Liberty-street.
Stebbs, John, waterman, Birmingham-row.
Steddiford, Hannah, 2 Chapel-street.
Steddiford, widow, 12 Vesey
Steddiford, G. auctioneer, 79 Wall, & house 65 Cedar
Steddiffne, John, shipmaster, Charlotte
Steel, Edward, shipmaster, 72 Greenwich
Steel, Caty, washer, 20 Murray
Steel, Benjamin, Bowery-lane.
Steel, Michael, milkman, Winne-street.
Steel, Stephen, 2 Pine
Steenbergh, Anthony, mason, 334 Broadway.
Steghefer, John, grocer, 48 Nassau-street.
Steinert, John, farrier, 46 Nassau
Stephens, David, trunkmaker, 72 Wall
Stephens, Benjamin, 185 Greenwich
Stephens, John, upholsterer, 90 Maiden-lane.
Stephens, George, stationer, 28 Cliff-street.
Stephens, Stephen, stationer, &c. 165 Pearl
Stephenson, James, nailor, 35 Barclay
Sterlitz, Joseph, merchant, 205 Pearl
Stevens, Joseph, 63 Liberty
Stevens, Ebenezer, 226 Water, & store Stevens'-wharf.
Stevens, John, 7 Broadway.
Stevens, Alexander, rigger, Magazine-street.
Stevens, John, carpenter, Colden, corner Augustus
Stevens, Lawrence, tea-waterman, Elizabeth
Stevens, Stephen, smith, saw-pits, Greenwich-road.
Stevens, ——, gardener, 1 Robe-street.
Stevens, James, sadler, and cap maker, 80 Broadway.
Stevenson, William, shipmaster, 61 Cliff
Stevenson, William, oysterman, 36 Vesey
Stevenson, John, shipmaster, 62 Roosevelt
Stevenson, Thomas, smith, 17 Gold
Stevenson, Benjamin, grocer, 200 William
Stevenson, Cornelius, 67 Broad.

Stevenson, widow, 45 Pearl-street.
Stevenson and Co. Hay, merchants, 167 Pearl
Stevenson, John, grocer, Greenwich, corner Duane
Stevenson and Saunderson's porter-vaults, 331 Pearl
Stevenson, Alexander, grocer, 279 Water
Stewart, Mrs. P. boarding-house, 55 Maiden-lane.
Stewart, John, shopkeeper, 58 Front
Stewart, Alex. mercht. 110 Front, & house 89 Water
Stewart and Co. Hugh, grocers, James
Stewart and Co. P. and C. merchants, 5 Burling-slip.
Stewart, Benj. caulker & shipwright, 172 Division-str.
Stewart, Robert & Hamilton, office, 55 Maiden-lane.
Stewart, Charles, merchant, 138 William-street.
Stewart, John, oysterman, Harman
Stewart, James A. merchant, 16 Broad
Stewart and Jones, ship-chandlers, 113 Front
Stewart, Charles, grocer, 29 Murray
Stewart, William, basketmaker, 44 Warren
Stewart, William, grocer, 60 L. George
Stewart, Alexander, baker, 8 Lombard
Stewart, Abraham, 29 Church
Stewart, Charles, 47 Augustus
Stewart, Thomas, Little Catharine
Stewart, Robert, carpenter, Cross
Stewart, James, merchant, 289 Broadway.
Stewart, James, pedlar, 276 Greenwich-street.
Stewart, Jennet, 51 Rutger
Stewart, John, carpenter, Charlotte
Stewart, James, grocer, Little Catharine
Steymets, Benjamin, 13 Thames
Steymets, William, taylor, 42 Cedar
Steymets, Isaac, embroiderer, saw-pits, Greenwich
Steymets, Ann, 24 Pine-street.
Stickler, Mary, First
Stiles, John, 17 Ann
Stiles, Mary, First
Stiles, William, carpenter, 61 Chapel
Stilwell, widow, of Elias, tavern, 155 Fly market.
Stilwell, John, carpenter, 45 Rutger-street.
Stilwell, Daniel, merchant-taylor, 221 Water
Stilwell & De Forest's hardware, &c. store, 169 Pearl
Stilwell and Powell, dry goods store, 393 Pearl

Stilwell, James, boarding-house, 31 Cooper-street.
Stine, Henry, cartman, 16 Warren
Stockbridge, Benjamin, schoolmaster, 25 Lumber
Stocker, Hugh, shipmaster, 15 Broadway.
Stocker, John, shipwright, E. Rutger-street.
Stockholm, Andrew, merchant, 34 Beaver
Stockwell, Elizabeth, boarding-house, 79 Fair
Stockwell, Samuel, constable, 2 Rider
Stockwell, Abraham, cooper, 27 Cliff
Stoddard, ——, shipmaster, 104 Cherry
Stokes & Lee, patent medicine store, 25 Maiden-lane.
Stone, Robert, ropemaker, Bayard-street.
Stonehouse, Catharine, 19 Cliff
Storey, William, shipmaster, 4 Rutger
Storey, James, tavern, 355 Pearl
Storm & Son, Thos. 1 Stone, & store 9 Coenties-slip.
Storm, Lewis, cabinetmaker, 432 Pearl-street.
Storm, widow, 62 Warren
Storms, Abraham, sugar-baker, Greenwich-road.
Storms, Garrit, dockbuilder, 32 Church-street.
Stoughton, Don Thos. Spanish Consul, 26 Greenwich
Stout, Seymour, shoemaker, 193 Water
Stout, Benjamin, 54 Maiden-lane.
Stout, widow, seamstress, 49 Partition-street.
Stout, John, shoemaker, 152 Water
Stout, Andrew, baker, 62 Partition
Stoutenburgh, Col. Isaac, 167 Greenwich
Stoutenburgh, John, merch 167 Greenwich, & 56 Dey
Stoutenburgh, Thomas, merchant, 118 William
Strachan, William, guager, 83 Pearl
Strader, widow, 1 James
Strang, Joseph, Mulberry
Srang, Joshua, E. Rutger
Strain, Daniel, cartman, Mulberry
Stratton, William, Bowery-lane.
Stratton, Latham, cooper, 5 Crane-wharf.
Stratton, Benjamin, cooper, 204 Front-street.
Stratton, Elizabeth, 42 Cedar
Stratton, jun. Benjamin, grocer and cooper, 204 Front
Strebeck, Rev. George, near the Alms-house.
Strickler, John, smith, New. corner Garden
Striker, John, milkman, 5 Augustus

Striker, John, labourer, Charlotte-street.
Striker, John, tallow-chandler, 55 Dey
Striker, Henry, taylor, 5 Augustus
Striker, Dennis, shoemaker, 70 Broad
Strinbeck, Lawrence, labourer, Charlotte
Stringham, Ann, 462 Pearl
Stringham, Daniel, labourer, Charlotte
Strong, Benjamin, merchant, 148 Water
Strong, Selah, merchant, 236 Water
Strong, Roger, attorney at law, 37 Nassau
Strong, Ambrose, labourer, Henry
Stroud, James, grocer, Charlotte
Struck, John, smith, 16 Murray
Struthers, William, smith, 240 Greenwich
Stuart, James, baker, corner of Rutger and Oliver
Stuart, James, grocer, 17 William
Stuart, jun. James, baker, 50 James
Stuart and Lay, watchmakers, 73 Wall
Stubbs, Charles, milkman, 83 Herman
Stumps, George, grocer, 143 Cherry
Sturges, jun. Jonathan, merch. 15 John, & 17 Front
Sturges, Strong, boarding-house, 5 Dover
Sturges, Nathaniel L. merchant-taylor, 186 Water
Sturman, Edward, shoemaker, First
Sturtevent, Eliphalet, moulder, Industry furnace.
Stutts, John, labourer, Orange-street.
Stuyvesant, jun. Peter, shoe-warehouse, 141 William
Suarth, James, mariner, 34 Vesey
Suffren, George, merchant, 4, and store 7, Depeyster
Sullivan, John, labourer, 45 Bancker
Sullivan, Edward, baker, 48 Frankfort
Sullivan, John, grocer, 83 Front
Sullivan, John, mariner, 57 Oliver
Summers, Patrick, tavern, 225 Water
SUPERVISOR'S OFFICE, 16 Nassau
SUPREME COURT CLERK'S OFFICE, Federal-hall
Surcia, John, labourer, First-street.
SURVEYOR OF THE CUSTOM'S OFFICE, 34 Front
Sutherland, Angus, cartman, 55 Augustus
Sutherland, William, carpenter, 97 Roosevelt
Sutherland, widow, tavern, 60 Broad
Sutherland, William, carpenter, First

Sutherland, James, mason, Little Catharine-street.
Sutton, James, cooper, 36 Gold
Sutton, George, carpenter, 17 Murray
Sutton, Joseph, cartman, Charlotte
Suydam, John, merchant, 35 Water
Suydam, Rinier, merchant, 4 Stone
Suydam and Wyckoff's store, 3 Coenties-slip.
Suydam and Heyer's store, 67 Front-street.
Suydam and Wells, merchants, 74 Water
Swain, Matt. grocer & shoemaker, 126 Bowery-Lane.
Swain, James, shoemaker, 31 Chapel-street.
Swain, widow, 49 Chapel
Swain, ——, mariner, 206 Greenwich
Swain, Christopher, shoemaker, Gibbs'-alley.
Swainell, Francis, silk stocking dresser, 30 Chapel-st.
Swan, James, shoemaker, 84 Harman
Swan, Charles, pilot, 16 Cliff
Swartwout, jun. Bernardus, merchant, 136 Greenwich
Swartwout, John, merchant, 43 Greenwich
Swartwout and Dumont's store, 66 Water
Swartwout, Elizabeth, 3 New Albany-bason.
Swartwout, John, labourer, 19 Thomas-street.
Swartwout, Abraham, grocer, 128 Broad
Swartz, Jacob, shoemaker, 199 William
Sween, Peter, labourer, Second
Sweeny, Thomas, shopkeeper, 113 Pearl
Sweeny, John, livery-stabler, 20 Lombard
Sweeny, Cornelius, carpenter, Mulberry
Sweet, Daniel, mariner, Barley
Swinbourn, widow, boarding-house, 15 Beekman
Swint, John, coppersmith, 30 Ann
Switzer, Peter, cutler, 10 Cliff
Swords, Thos. & Jas. printers & booksellers, 99 Pearl
Sykes, Philip, shoemaker, 46 Fair
Sykes, John, shoe warehouse, 115 William
Sylvester, Reuben, shoemaker, 340 Broadway.
Sypher, William, Catharine-lane.

T

Tabele, Jacob, joiner & cabinetmaker, 29 Fair-street.
Tabele, James, joiner and cabinetmaker, 7 Fair
Tabele, John, dry goods store, 132 Chatham
Tabele, William, 7 James-street.

Tait, William, smith, Greenwich-road.
Talbot, Col. 47 Vesey-street.
Talcott and Ellis, merchants, Stevens'-wharf.
Talman, Peter, merchant, 53 Cliff-street.
Talman, Samuel and Peter, merchants, 171 Front
Talman, Samuel, merchant, 41 Fair
Talman, Hermanus, hatter, 68 Vesey
Talman, John, shoemaker, 16 Chapel
Talmage, John, taylor, 130 Chatham
Tanner, Ann, 26 Nassau
Tanner, Benjamin, engraver, 26 Nassau
Tanner, John A. shipmaster, 8 Peck-slip.
Tanner, William, cooper, Essex-street.
Tanner, Thomas, mason, 19 Thomas
Tant, Thomas, mason, Third
Tap, Mrs. boarding-house, 89 Front
Tar, Henry, grocer, 21 Augustus
Tardie, Monsieur, 41 Beaver
Targay, James, cartman, 45 Barclay
Targay, John, carpenter, 45 Barclay
Targee, widow, 24 Gold
Targee, John, gold and silversmith, 24 Gold
Tarpin, George, mason, Orange
Tate, John, labourer, Sixth
Tate, Thomas, labourer, Sixth
Tate, John, taylor, Sixth
Tate, Patrick, labourer, 5 Moore's-row.
Tawzer, Esther, grocer, Winne-street.
Taylerson, Nicholas, agent, 450 Pearl
Taylor, Abner, labourer, 11 Reed
Taylor, Abraham, taylor, 55 John
Taylor, Allen, grocer, Barclay, corner Greenwich
Taylor, Archibald, taylor, 18 Augustus
Taylor, Benjamin, city-surveyor, 6 William
Taylor, David, cartman, 59 Chapel
Taylor, Edmund, 59 Robinson
Taylor, George, carpenter, Henry
Taylor, George, turner, Eagle
Taylor, Gilbert, grocer, Mott, corner of Pell
Taylor, Henry, cartman, 83 Murray
Taylor, James, smith, Mott
Taylor, Joseph, tavern, 158 Fly-market.

Taylor, Jeremiah B. carpenter, 25 Church-street.
Taylor, John, carpenter, 49 Church
Taylor, Justus, mariner, Bowery-lane.
Taylor, John, merchant, 185 Pearl-street.
Taylor, John, coppersmith, &c. 140 Maiden-lane.
Taylor, John, grocer, 103 Greenwich-street.
Taylor, John, tavern, 283 Water
Taylor, John, merchant, 44 Pine
Taylor, John, mariner, Catharine, corner Henry
Taylor, John, mariner, 11 Reed
Taylor, James, carpenter, 48 Barley
Taylor, John, grocer, 5 Harman
Taylor, James, shoemaker, Beaver-lane.
Taylor, John, near the Alms-house.
Taylor, Moses, grocer, 27 Broadway.
Taylor, Mrs. 40 William-street.
Taylor, Obadiah, 48 Barley
Taylor, Robert, shipwright, 1 Batavia-lane.
Taylor, Stephen, shoemaker, 53 Barclay-street.
Taylor, Solomon, boarding-house, 44 George
Taylor, Sarah, sick nurse, Beaver-lane.
Taylor, S. D. house & sign painter, 29 Roosevelt-st.
Taylor, Thomas, grocer, 85 Warren
Taylor, Violetta R. boarding-school, 34 Fair
Taylor, Willet, physician, 309 Pearl
Taylor, William, merchant, 44 Pine
Taylor, William, shoemaker, 104 Maiden-lane.
Tearly, Lawrence, mariner, 5 Tryon-row.
Teasman, John, teacher, Colden-street.
Teatreih, John, cabinetmaker, Eagle
Teer, Margaret, boarding-house, 281 Water
Teer, Mark, merchant-taylor, 110 Front
Telford, Francis, shipmaster, 23 Cliff
Teller, Tobias, smith, Henry
Teller, James, hatter, 1 Cherry, corner Pearl
Teller, jun. James, hatter, 19 Cheapside.
Temple, Sir John, British con. gen 156 Greenwich-st.
Templeton, Mrs. 3 Pine
Ten Brook, Henry, butcher, 50 Barclay
Ten Brook, John, merc. 101 Maiden-lane,& 18 Gold-st.
Ten Brook, Elizabeth, shopkeeper, 28 John-street.
Ten Brook, Henry, merch. 110 William, & 51 John

Ten Eyck, Richard A. printer, Garden-street.
Ten Eyck, Jane, schoolmistress, 63 Cedar
Ten Eyck, Andrew, block and pumpmaker, 71 Front
Ten Eyck, Daniel, 53 Broad
Ten Eyck, Philip, bookseller, 148 Pearl
Ten Eyck, John, merchant, store 32 Front
Ten Eyck, Richard, flour inspector, 37 Beaver
Ten Eyck, Sarah, boarding-house, 77 Pearl
Terme, Dennis, dry goods store, 49 Broad
Terrier, ———, 267 Greenwich
Terrill, William, merchant, 95 Broad
Terry, William, revenue measurer, 29 Water
Terry, John, mariner, 2 Roosevelt
Thacker, John, painter, William, corner Maiden-lane.
Thacker, John, painter, 26 Lombard-street.
Thall, Charles, cartman, Bedlow
Tharp, Cornelius, cartman, Winne
Tharp, Joseph, Leonard
Theall, Hezaiiah, porter-house, Cherry
Theall, Edward, cartman, Fisher
THEATRE, Chatham-row.
Thebaud, Joseph, merchant, 12 Beekman-street.
Thibou, Lewis, boot and shoemaker, 213 Water
Thomas, John, carpenter, 90 Warren
Thomas, Henry, oysterman, Washington
Thomas, Benjamin, shoemaker, 46 Cedar
Thomas, Evan, taylor, Orange
Thomas, John, brewer, Winne
Thomas, William, shipwright, 4 Bancker
Thomas, Sarah, washer, 247 William
Thomas, Abraham, sailmaker, 14 Rose
Thomas, Tom, oysterman, 82 James
Thomas, James, labourer, 87 Warren
Thomas, William, merchant, 159 Pearl
Thomas, Richard, mariner, 27 Rose
Thomas, E. teacher, 29 Gold
Thomas, William, mariner, 20 Division
Thomas, Griffith, mariner, 5 Cheapside.
Thompson, William, mariner, 20 Division-street.
Thompson, Ralph, carpenter, Bowery-lane.
Thompson, James, shipwright, Gibbs'-alley.
Thompson and Baptis, boat-builders, 321 Water street.

r

Thompson, John H. merchant, 35 Wall-street.
Thompson, James, coffee manufacturer, 23 Thames.
Thompson, William C. Tea-water-pump.
Thompson, James, city-marshall, 4 Ann-street.
Thompson, William, labourer, 22 Thames
Thompson, William, dock-master, 169 William
Thompson, John, hairdresser, 74 Liberty
Thompson, John, mariner, 8 Green
Thompson, Charles, marshall, 34 Church
Thompson, James, cartman, Bowery-lane.
Thompson, George, butcher, 448 Pearl-street.
Thompson, William, boat-builder, 90 James
Thompson, William, constable, 61 Division
Thompson, John, mason, Birmingham-row.
Thompson, Samuel, soap-boiler, 15 Barclay-street.
Thompson, Peter, grocer, 59 Barclay
Thompson, Samuel, mariner, 19 Fair
Thompson, Arthur, grocer, Upper Reed
Thompson, George, accountant, Little Catharine
Thompson, John, accountant, 310 Broadway.
Thompson, Philip, tavern, 388 Water-street.
Thompson, William A. counsellor at law, 188 Water
Thompson, James, carpenter, 5 Bancker
Thomson, James, merchant, 23 Fair
Thomson, Andrew, mason, 29 Roosevelt
Thomson, Robert, merchant, 45 Fair
Thomson, James, merchant, 197 Pearl
Thomson, John, merchant, 203 Pearl
Thomson, Alexander, carpenter, 85 Warren
Thomson, Alexander, merchant, 56 Wall
Thomson, Joseph, merchant, 65 Pine
Thorburn, Grant, hardware store, 22 Nassau
Thorley, William, grocer, 89 Warren
Thorn, widow, Second
Thorne, jun. Stephen, merchant, 22 Gold
Thorne, William, merchant, 33 Stone
Thorne, William, taylor, 17 Murray
Thorne, Robert, rigger, 15 Lumber
Thorne, William, merchant, 28 Peck-slip.
Thorne, Daniel, merchant, 33 Stone-street.
Thorne, Daniel and William, store, 25 Albany-pier
Thorne, Henry, boat-builder, 280 Water-street.

Thorne, Stephen, merchant, 19 Burling-slip.
Thorne, Samuel, shipwright, 88 Catharine-street.
Thorne, widow Elizabeth, 78 Catharine
Thorne, Isaac, shipwright, 19 Batavia-lane.
Thornton, John, grocer, 165 Fly-market.
Thornton, Allen, mariner, 7 Augustus-street.
Thornton, Gilbert, 106 Greenwich
Thorp, Joseph, cartman, 61 Chapel
Thorp, Daniel, cartman, 22 Rutger
Thorp, Daniel, boatman, 165 Washington
Thorp, Daniel, cartman, 27 Roosevelt
Throgmorton, John, mason, 7 Rose
Thurman, William M. silkdyer, 342 Pearl
Thurman, Ralph, accountant, 45 William
Thurman, John, merchant, 45 William
Thurston and King's store, 283 Pearl
Thurston, Jacob, mason, 102 Chamber
Thurston, William, smith, Pump
Thurston, Charles, carpenter, Pump
Thurston, William R. merchant, 27 Murray
Thurston and Bogert, ironmongers, 313 Pearl
Thurston, Woods, grocer, corner of Pump and Eng's
Thurston, John, merchant, 313 Pearl
Thurston, Benjamin, grocer, corner of First & Fisher
Thurston, John, mason, 102 Chamber
Thurston, Peter, carver and gilder, 41 Murray
Ties, John, ladies hairdresser, 63 Nassau
Tiebout, John, printer and bookseller, 358 Pearl
Tiebout, Cornelius, engraver, 273 Pearl
Tiebout, George, shipwright, 257 Greenwich
Tiebout, Albert, cartman, Catharine
Tiebout, Alexander, clock and watchmaker, 273 Pearl
Tiebout, widow, 40 Church
Tiernan, John, trusserer, 28 Beaver
Tier, Jacob,
Tier, John D.
Tiers, Valentine,
Tiers, Mathew,
Tiers, widow, 51 Bowery-lane.
Tier, Daniel, grocer, 55 Bowery-street.
Tier,
Tilling, George,

Tilford, Cornelius, mason, Elizabeth-street.
Tillary, James, physician, 86 Broadway.
Tilley, Jonah, grocer, 254 Water-street.
Tillinghast, Stephen, merchant, 48 Greenwich
Tillou, Francis, chamber chairmaker, 22 Stone
Tillou, Vincent, rush bottom chairmaker, 3 Broad
Tillou, Peter, rush bottom chairmaker, 40 Beaver
Tillou, Peter, grocer, 6 Ann
Tilton, Hutcheon, 14 E. George
Tilton, John, mariner, 12 Fair
Timons, James, calico-printer, 66 James
Timpson, Benjamin, gardener, 349 Broadway.
Timpson, ——, cabinetmaker, 247 Greenwich-street.
Timpson, Thomas, cabinetmaker, 70 John
Tinker, James, shipmaster, 37 George
Tinker, Joseph, shoemaker, 21 Fair
Tinney, William, accountant, 51 Stone
Tippet, George, cartman, Mulberry
Tisdale, Elkanah, miniature-painter, 8 John
Titford and Co. Isaac, druggists, 85 Maiden-lane.
Titur, George, grocer, First-street.
Titus and Ireland, grocers, 68 Partition
Titus, Charles, Broadway, near Union furnace.
Titus, Samuel, merchant, 32 William-street.
Titus, Henry, livery-stabler, 461 Pearl
Titus, John, merchant, 229 Pearl
Titus Joseph, carpenter, 16 Lumber
Titus, Gilbert, 15 Beekman-slip.
Tisyman, Abraham, taylor, Charlotte-street.
Tobin, Lawrence, labourer, Charlotte
Tobin, Francis, grocer, Orange
Tod and Seymour, merchants, 192 Water
Tod, David, merchant, 192 Water
Todd, sen. Adam, 362 Pearl
Todd, William B. merchant, 36 William
Todd, Coffin, Mulberry
Todd, William, 71 Liberty
Toletree, Robert, fidler, 322 Broadway.
Tom, Peter, cartman, 70 Murray-street.
Tom, Thomas, merchant, 17 Burling-slip.
Tom, John, 43 Beekman-street
Tombs, Andrew, shipmaster, New

Toadiny, Patrick, pedlar, 33 Warren-street.
Tomlinson, Bernard H. tavern, 25 Broad
Tomlinson, Christopher, tavern, at Rickett's circus.
Tomlinson and Co. Isaac, merchants, 8 Cooper-street.
Tomkins, William, whitesmith, 32 Ann
Tomkins, Enos, cartman, 115 Liberty
Tompkins, Daniel D. attorney at law, 1 Wall
Tonkin, Richard, mariner, 72 Murray
Tonnele, John, glover, 316 Water
TONTINE CITY TAVERN, 123 Broadway.
TONTINE COFFEE-HOUSE, corner Wall & Water sts.
Tooker, Daniel, tanner and currier, 7 Ferry-street.
Tooker, jun. Daniel, tanner, Skinner
Tooker, Elias, cartman, 53 Chamber
Tooker, Samuel, grocer, 13 Coenties-slip.
Torbart, Samuel, M. D. 1 Harman
Torbois, Isaac, painter, gilder, &c. 80 Liberty
Torrance, Hugh, grocer, 15 William
Torrey, John, carpenter, 74 Harman
Torrey, William, merchant, 515 Broadway.
Totten, William, grocer, 103 Division-street.
Totten, John, waterman, 27 Cheapside.
Totten, Silas, boarding-house, 115 William-street.
Totten, ——, cartman, 39 Chapel
Totten, Elizabeth, market-woman, 103 Division
Touce, Francis, smith, E. Rutger
Toulor, Moses, shipmaster, 19 Frankfort
Towers, widow, 27 Cherry
Towers, Roger, mariner, 84 Fair
Town, John, boarding-house, &c. at Hoboken.
TOWN CLERK'S OFFICE, Federal-hall.
Townley, John, grocer, 8 Lombard-street.
Townsend, Solomon, merchant, 225 Pearl
Townsend, Thomas S. 157 Fly-market.
Townsend, James, merchant, 282, & south 400 Pearl-st.
Townsend, George, merchant, 363 Pearl
Townsend & Franklin's flour store, Water, near Oliver
Townsend, George, merchant, 400 Pearl-street.
Townsend, William, carpenter, 28 Murray
Townsend, John, merchant, Cherry-street, Ship yards.
Townsend, Henry, grocer, Eagle-street.
Towe, Robert H. grocer, 70 N. st.

NEW-YORK DIRECTORY.

Tout, Robert, inspector of leather, 18 George-street.
Tozer, Daniel, pilot, 28 Stone.
Tracey, Thomas, grocer, Charlotte, corner Lumber
Trail, William, painter, 41 Barclay
Trappal, Michael, fleecy hosier, 45 Vandewater
Traver, widow, 28 Barclay
Travers, David, shipmaster, 65 Fair
Travers, Stephen, labourer, 12 Thomas
Tredwell, James, labourer, 29 Chamber
Tredwell, John, merchant, 218 Water
Tredwell, Wm. & J. physicians, 130 Fly-market.
Tredwell, Wm. A. livery-stabler, 5 & 47 Cortlandt-st.
Tredwell, William, boarding-house, 7 Cortlandt
Tredwell and Thorne, merchants, 176 Front
Tredwell & Co. John, china merchants, 22 Burling-slip.
Tredwell, A. merchant, 218 Water
Tree, Mary, hairdresser, 12 Old-slip.
Tremble, James, porter, Henry-street.
Tremble, Daniel, smith, 36 Pearl
Tremble, Moses, shipwright, 39 Cheapside
Tremble, ——, shipwright, Charlotte-street.
Trembly, Daniel, grocer, 68 Cortlandt
Trepan, Anthony, green grocer, 129 Fly-market.
Tribe, William, coppersmith, 14 Broad-street.
Trimbley, Alexander, cartman, 37 Barley
Trimper, Leticia, nurse, 52 E. George
Tripler, Christian, jeweller, 56 Beaver
Tripler, Thomas, accountant, 99 Cherry
Tripp, Lott, physician, 123 Fly-market.
Tripp, Lacey and Co. chandlers, 18 Ferry-street.
Trivett, James, shoemaker, 82 William
Trott, Benjamin, miniature-painter, 1 Wall
Troup, Robert, 44 Broadway.
Troup, John, shipmaster, 82 Roosevelt-street.
Troup, Henry, merchant, 26 George
Troup & Ryckman's china, glass, &c. store, 165 Front
Trowbridge, Isaac, bull's head tavern, 38 Bowery-lane.
Truelight, Frederick, cartman, 71 Chatham-street.
Tryon, Benjamin, mariner, 66 Harman
Tucker, Samuel, merchant, 219 William
Tucker, Abraham, victualler, 57 Whitehall
Tucker, Walter, carpenter, Little Ann

Tucker, Gideon, mason, 49 Reed-street.
Tucker, Richard J. merchant, 125 Front
Tuckerman, Isaac, labourer, 13 Oliver
Tuckness, John, baker, 60 Pearl
Tufts, Joshua B. grocer, 69 Partition
Turbit, Thomas, mason, 35 Chapel
Turcot, Peter, upholsterer, 311 Broadway.
Tureil, Ebenezer, 205 William-street.
Turk, Ahasuerus, turner, &c. 35 Nassau
Turlur, Daniel, labourer, E. Rutger
Turnbull, John & Richard, merchants, 90 William
Turnbull, Andrew, baker, 263 Broadway.
Turnbull, Col. George, 84 Broad-street.
Turnbull, John D. shipmaster, 1 Dover
Turner, John, cartman, 28 Vandewater
Turner, John, cartman, Lumber
Turner, John, merchant, 148 Broadway.
Torner, jun. John, merchant, 162 Pearl-street.
Turner, widow, 104 Reed
Turner, Mrs. milliner, 156 William
Turner, Alexander, cartman, Division
Turner, John, mason, 63 Chatham
Turner, Joseph, mariner, 68 James
Turner, Eleanor, 7 Moore's-row.
Turner, Robert, mariner, 114 Harman-street.
Turner, William, shoemaker, Barksy
Turney, Luke, smith, Chamber
Turss, John, cartman, 69 Reed
Turton, James, merchant, 6 Liberty
Tuthill, Daniel, carpenter, Orchard
Tuthill, Israel gardener, Mulberry
Tuthill, Daniel, teacher, 67 Roosevelt
Tuthill, Thomas, porter, 13 Reed
Tuttle, Daniel, cardmaker, 36 Division
Tuttle and Smith, taylors, 13 Catharine-slip.
Tuttle, Rebecca, boarding-house, 218 Water-street.
Tuttle, Uzal, carpenter, 88 Chamber
Tweedy, William, accountant 58 Front
Twitchings, Henry, grocer, 64 Front
Tylee, James, inspector of leather, 83 Chatham
Tylee, Nathaniel, mariner, 434 Pearl
Tyler, Jacob, teacher of navigation, 67 Cliff

Tyler, Joseph, comedian, Grey's gardens.
Tyler, Jacob, mariner, 12 Batavia-lane.
Tyson, John, shoemaker, Eagle-street.
Tyson, Cornelius, grocer, east side Catharine-slip.
Tyson, John, accountant, 3 Vandewater-street.

U

Ulshoeffer, George, musician and grocer, 3 John-str.
Underhill, Anthony L. 31 Dey
Underhill and son, David, merchants, 234 Water
Underhill, Samuel, merchant, 258 Pearl
Underhill, Joshua, merchant, 32 Vandewater
Underhill and Eustace, merchants, 167 Front
Underhill and Townsend, ironmongers, 231 Water
Underhill, Richardson, merchant, 51 Cliff
Underhill, Israel, grocer, Second
Underhill and Co. Richardson, 15 Crane-wharf.
Underhill, Townsend, merchant, 231 Water-street.
Underhill, Peter, taylor, 13 Oliver
Underwood, Phineas, milkman, Mott
UNION AIR FURNACE, 405 Broadway.
UNITED INSURANCE COMPANY OFFICE, 140 Pearl
Upton, Freeman, mariner, 30 Rose
Urch, widow, 73 Roosevelt
Ustick, Thomas, attorney at law, office, 56 John
Ustick, jun. William, merchant, 244 Pearl
Ustick, James, mariner, 53 Roosevelt
Utt, John, cooper, 30 Dey, & shop Hallett's-wharf.
Utt, Jonas, butcher, Greenwich-road, near air-furnace.
Utt, Peter, musical instrument maker, Chamber-str.

V

Vache, John, artificial florist, 28 Liberty-street.
Vail, Enos, grocer, Winne, corner Bayard
Vail, Joseph, chair maker, Grand
Valade, Lezand Pierre, Eagle
Vanden, Amar, 39 Warren
Vernon, Falconer, 34 Roosevelt
Valeau, Peter, shoemaker, Mulberry
Valeau, Samuel, cartman, 47 Augustus
Valeau, Isaiah, taylor, 55 Augustus
Valentine, John, cartman, Greenwich-road.
Valentine, Charles, grocer, 160 Greenwich-street.
Valentine, Abraham, grocer, 149 Fly-market.

Valentine, Jacob, flour merc. 199 Front, & 14 Peck-slip.
Valentine, Isaac, cartman, Cross-street.
Valentine, William, cooper, Fisher
Valentine, Caleb, grocer, 43 Dey
Valentine, Smith, 43 Dey
Valentine and Downing, grocers, &c. 63 Partition
Valentine, Henry, cartman, 9 Chapel
Valentine, John, cartman, Cross
Valentine, Robert, carpenter, 90 Chamber
Valet, Peter, gold-smith, 50 Fair
Valleau, William, shipbuilder, Corlaer's-hook.
Van Alen, Cornelius C. 8 Cortlandt-street.
Van Allen, Cornelius, coachmaker, 30 Barclay
Van Allen, Staats, carpenter, 60 Barclay
Van Allen, John, grocer, 6 Chatham-row.
Van Allen, Peter, shoemaker, Broadway.
Van Allen, Henry, tavern, Catharine-slip.
Van Allen, John, mariner, Catharine-slip.
Van Alst, George, cartman, 41 Rose-street.
Van Alst, John, block and pumpmaker, 175 William
Van Alst, Peter, grocer, 25 Peck-slip.
Van Alstyne, Thomas, painter, Magazine-street.
Van Alstyne, Abraham, grocer, 101 Washington
Van Antwerp, James, taylor, 48 Maiden-lane.
Van Antwerp, Daniel, measurer of grain, 33 Murray-st.
Van Antwerp, Nicholas, 59 Water, & store 41 Front
Van Buren, Mary, 65 Ann
Van Buren, Courtlandt, grocer, 139 Fly-market.
Van Buren, Beckman M. physician, Bowery-lane.
Van Buren, Michael, carpenter, 251 William
Van Buren, jun. Michael, carpenter, 251 William
Van Buren, Wm. china store, 72 New Albany bason.
Van Buren, Peter, gold & silversmith, 272 Pearl
Van Blarcom, Simeon, mason, 17 Chamber-street.
Van Blarcom, John, carpenter, 21 Partition
Van Buskirk, Lawrence, druggist, 16 Bowery-lane.
Van Dusel, Garret, Division
Van Brakle, James, shoemaker, 55 Division-street.
Van Bremer, Thomas, labourer, 6 Moore's-row.
Van Kirk, John, cartman, 4 Robinson-street.
Van Buskirk, Lucas, blkman, 35 Reed
Van Buskirk, jun. Abraham, merch. 177 Greenw.

Van Buskirk, Andrew, 4 Robinson-street.
Van Buskirk, Lawrence, cartman, 85 Reed
Van Cleek, Leonard, shipwright, Eagle
Van Cleek, Jeremiah, cartman, 135 Division
Van Cleek, Peter, labourer, 73 Harman
Van Clief, Benjamin, carpenter, 66 Harman
Van Cott, John, boatman, Essex
Van Cott, Cornelius, cartman, Eagle
Van Curah, Benjamin T. cartman, Harman
Van Curah, sen. Benjamin, cartman, Harman
Vandalfe, John, cartman, 38 Barley
Vandebarrick, Adam, butcher, Eagle
Vandenberg, John, cartman, 45 Barclay
Vandenburgh, Cornelius, butcher, Bowery-lane.
Vandenbroeck, R. J. 5 Wall-street.
Vandenhessel, I. C. 87 Liberty
Vanderbeck, Abraham, 17 Robinson
Vanderbeck, John, cartman, 87 Chamber
Vanderbeek, Conrad, cartman, 19 Barley
Vanderbilt, Oliver, boot & shoemaker, 124 Broadway.
Vanderbilt, jun. John, grocer, 153 Fly-market.
Vanderbilt, Jacob, shoemaker, Pump
Vanderbilt, Elizabeth, 26 Water
Vanderhoof, Henry, livery-stabler, 39 Vesey-street.
Vanderhoof, widow, 71 Warren
Vanderhoof, Peter, hatter, 49 Water
Vanderhoof, Miss, 14 James
Vanderhoof, John, cartman, 5 Rector
Vanderhoof, John, turner, Mulberry
Vanderhoof, John, butcher, Bayard
Vanderhoven, Cornelius, cartman, 59 Chapel
Vanderpool, John, sign-painter, gilder, &c. 75 Pearl
Vanderpool, William, mason, Winne
Vanderpool, Isaac, painter, 271 Greenwich
Vanderpool, Isaac, painter, 66 Dey
Vanderveer, William, ?, 3 Cortlandt
Vandervoort, Peter, accountant, 30 Fair
Vandervoort, Paul, mason, 28 Barclay
Vandervoort, Jacob, coachmaker, 39 Barclay
Vandervoort, William L. merchant, 12 No. ?
Van Deursen, widow, Margaret, 16 Cherry
Van Deursen, Catharine, boarding-house, 117 Water

Van Deursen, Andrew, butcher, Division-street.
Van Deursen, A. C. tallowchandler, 82 Broad
Van Deursen, Isaac, smith, 6 Chapel
Van Deursen, Isaac, smith, 61 Whitehall
Van Deursen, Jette, taylor, Cross
Vandewater, Henry, cabinetmaker, 24 Thames
Vandewater, Abraham, currier, 36 Ferry
Vandewater, William, 56 Chatham
Vandewater, Burger, 39 Bowery-lane.
Vandewater, Margaret, schoolmistress, 49 Broad-street.
Vandewater, William S. cooper, 51 Whitehall
Vandewater, Joseph, grocer, Pump
Vandewinter, John, coffee-man, 10 Cooper
Van Dine, Cornelius, boarding-house, 157 Front
Van Duel, Jacob, shipwright, 24 Fayette
Van Dyck, Isaac, cabinetmaker, 43 Maiden-lane.
Van Dyck, James, upholsterer, 58 Maiden-lane.
Van Dyk, Francis, chocolate-maker, 28 Beekman-strt.
Van Dyk and Shippey's counting-house, 50 Front
Van Dyk, John, chocolate & mustard manuf. 66 Broad
Van Dyk, James, merchant, 46 Broad
Van Dyne, James, hatter, 373 Pearl
Van Ever, widow, 51 Barley
Van Gelder, Abraham, grocer, 89 Bowery-lane.
Van Gelder, John, grocer, 83 Broadway.
Van Gelder, jun. Abraham, 63 Cortlandt-street.
Van Gelder, James, cartman, Winne
Van Gieson & Van Barcom, merchants, 98 William
Van Harlingen, Henry W. 25 William
Van Hook, Arondt, reading-room, 149 Water
Van Hook, Isaac, sexton Dutch-church, 55 Liberty
Van Holten, William, 193 Pearl
Van Horne, John, milkman, Chapel
Van Horne, Garrit, merchant, 129 Pearl
Van Horne and Clarkson, merchants, 129 Pearl
Van Horne, widow, 273 Pearl
Van Horne, Andrew, smith, Water, & house Fisher
Van Horne, David, Adjutant-General, 110 Liberty
Van Horne, David, mason, Winne
Van Horne, jun. Cornelius, cartman, Winne
Van Horne & Co. Augustus V. merchants, 81 Water
Van Horne, Magdalen, shopkeeper, 18 William

Van Horne, jun. Cornelius, cartman, Winne-street.
Van Houten, John, carpenter, 268 William
Van Houten, Peter, carpenter, Thomas
Van Houten, J. G. cartman, saw-pits, Greenwich-road.
Van Houten, Dennis, 38 Barley
Van Keuren, Benjamin B. grocer, 75 Reed
Van Keuren, Robert S. merchant, 37 Front
Van Keuren, Jacobus, cartman, Division
Van Kleeck, John L. grocer, 167 Washington
Van Lor, John, nail-maker, 84 Harman
Van Ness, widow, dry goods store, 386 Pearl
Van Nest, Abraham, sadler, &c. 111 Pearl
Van Nest, Deborah, 388 Pearl
Van Norden, Gabriel, grocer, 2 Maiden-lane.
Van Norden, D. smith, 1 Crane-whf. & 83 Roosevelt-st.
Van Norden, Luke, dry goods store, 11 Maiden-lane.
Van Norden, Theodorus W. grocer, 16 Maiden-lane.
Van Norden, John, cartman, Barley-street.
Van Norden, John, currier, 20 Vandewater
Van Nostrandt, Garrit, cartman, First
Van Nostrandt, Jacob, taylor, 112 Cherry
Van Orden, Charles, 47 Barley
Van Orden, John, tobacconist, 182 Greenwich
Van Pelt, Tunis, cooper, 58 Dey
Van Pelt, Jacob, carpenter, 55 Whitehall
Van Pelt, John, mason, 15 Frankfort
Van Pelt, jun. John, mason, 15 Frankfort
Van Pelt, Henry, mason, 27 Rutger
Van Pelt, Jacob, cartman, 62 Cedar
Van Ranst, John, paper-maker, 73 Bowery-lane.
Van Ranst, Abraham, 16 Roosevelt-street.
Van Rantz, Peter, sailmaker, 73 Bowery-lane.
Van Riper, John, grocer, 188 Greenwich-street.
Van Riper, Herman, carpenter, 12 Chamber
Van Shiver, Peter, carpenter, 104 Liberty
Van Sice, John, hairdresser, 44 Roosevelt
Van Solingen, Henry M. physician, 29 Maiden-lane.
Van Steenbergh, Samuel, teacher, 35 Cedar-street.
Van Steenbergh, John, shipwright, 27 Bancker
Van Sinderen, Adrian, merchant, 201 Pearl
Van Tassle, John, smith, Little Catharine
Van Tassle, Henry, cartman, Mulberry

Van Taftle, John, cartman, 46 Barley-ftreet.
Van Taftle, Peter, 82 Chamber
Van Tuyl and Son, And. merchants, 96 Maiden-lane.
Van Varick, John, baker, 53 Pearl-ftreet.
Van Varick, James, baker, 19 James
Van Veghter, John, boatman, Harman
Van Vleck, Ifaac, notary-public, Reed
Van Vleck, widow, 2 Chapel
Van Voorhis, Cornelius, infpector of wood, 78 Barclay
Van Voorhis, David, fhoemaker, 73 Warren
Van Voorhis & Son, Daniel, goldfmiths, 141 Broadway.
Van Vorft, Garrit, fhoemaker, 62 Reed-ftreet.
Van Wagganen, Garrit H. ironmonger, 5 Beekman-flip.
Van Wagganen, Jacob, 47 Liberty-ftreet.
Van Waggenen, jun. Jacob, failmaker, 2 Ferry
Van Wart, widow, 42 Liberty
Van Wart, William, cartman, 37 Robinfon
Van Wyck, Stephen, watchmaker, 275 Pearl
Van Wyck, Theodorus, merchant, 34 Greenwich
Van Wyck, Eldred, cartman, Eagle
Van Wyck, William, merchant, 16 Stone
Van Wyck and Phillips's ftore, 40 Front
Van Zandt, Jane, Elizabeth-ftreet, near Bunker-hill.
Van Zandt, Peter P. merchant, 180 Water-ftreet.
Van Zandt, Peter, merchant, 68 Chatham
Van Zandt, Mathew, merchant, 4 Burling-flip.
Van Zandt, Thomas, attorney at law, 59 John
Van Zandt, Mary, 37 William
Van Zandt and Co. Peter, merchants, 4 Burling-flip.
Van Zandt, James, 4 Burling-flip.
Van Zandt, Wynant, 35 William-ftreet.
Van Zandt, jun. Wynant, merchant, 177 Water
Van Zile, Peter, tanner, 37 Auguftus
Varet, Francis, 26 Reed
Varian, Michael, butcher, 6 Second
Varian, Jacob, butcher, 27 Divifion
Varian, Ifaac, butcher, 98 Bowery-lane.
Varian, Jacob, butcher, 113 Bowery-lane.
Varian, James, livery-ftabler, 39 Barclay
Varian, Wafhington, Elizabeth
Varick, widow, 5 New Albany bafon.
Varick, Eleanor, 1 Chapel-ftreet.

Varick, John, physician, 6 Cortlandt-street.
Varick, widow, milliner, 59 Dey
Varick, Abraham, merchant, 56 Water
Varick, Richard, mayor of the city, 108 Broadway.
Varnhagen, Godfrey, merchant, 213 William-street.
Vafs, William, cartman, 20 Batavia-lane.
Vaudes, ———, watchmaker, 89 Beekman-street.
Vaughan, Thomas, sawmaker, 75 Liberty
Vaughan, Valentine, cartman, 57 Murray
Veal, William, boat-builder, Bedlow
Veal, Thomas, ship-builder, Corlaer's hook.
Veitch, John, shipwright, 88 Harman-street.
Veitch, Walter, stonecutter, 24 Cedar
Veitch, James, spruce beer brewer, 28 Harman
VERMONT and ALBANY stage-office, 3 Cortlandt
Vergnes, Madam, 41 Cliff
Vermylia, John, merchant, 14 Vesey
Vermylia, Abraham, cartman, Division
Vermylia, William, carpenter, 44 Partition
Vermylia, Phoebe, boarding-house, 17 Fayette
Vermylia, John, cartman, Eagle
Vermylia, Sarah, 14 Vesey
Vermylia, Peter, cabinetmaker, Magazine
Vermylia, William, cartman, Crofs
Vermylia, John, cartman, Crofs
Vernon and Co. John, gold and silversmiths, 93 John
Verplanck, Gulian, merchant, 16 Wall
Verplanck, Mrs. 41 Wall
Verrett, John, cartman, 37 Lumber
Vervelan and Quick, coach painters, 5 Fair
Vetford, Joseph, carpenter, Henry
Viale, Augustin, 14 Cherry
Victor, ———, confectioner, 190 William
Vidal, Mrs. 56 Warren
Vidan, Mrs. 33 Vesey
Videll, Paul, merchant, 420 Pearl
Videto, John, carpenter, 220 Division
Vigham, James, labourer, Corlaer's hook.
Villee, Cornelius, infpec. of pot-ash, 23 Whitehall-str.
Villee, John, cartman, 59 Warren
Vinceador, Dutour, 345 Broadway.
Vincent, Carter, cartman, 22 Lombard-street.

Vincent, Wm. boarding-house, 101 Greenwich-strt.
Vinoles, Peter, confectioner, 58 Fair
Vitch, Anthony, 47 Barclay
Vogel, Mathew, butcher, 26 Division
Vork, Peter, Elizabeth-street, near Bunker-hill.
Voorhees, James, cartman, 77 Chamber-street.
Voorhis, Paul, carpenter, Hester
Voorhis, John, cartman, 50 Chapel
Voorhis, John, carpenter, 35 Lumber
Voorhis, Arnoldus, grocer, 42 Water
Voorhis, Elizabeth, 52 Stone
Voorhis, John, cartman, 66 Reed
Voorhis, Peter, grocer, 78 Vesey
Vos and Graves, merchants, 105 Water
Vosburgh, Harman, windsor chairmaker, 45 Chatham
Voshel, Daniel, shoemaker, 47 Chapel
Voss, John P. 60 Broadway.
Vory, James, coachmaker, 27 Reed-street.
Vory, John, 20 Reed
Vredenburgh, Jacob, 177 Washington
Vredenburgh, Cornelius, cartman, Cross
Vredenburgh, William I. 5 Stone
Vredenburgh, Margaret, 64 Gold
Vredenburgh, Isaac, shoemaker, 205 Broadway.
Vreeland, Jacob, cartman, Harman-street.
Vroom, George, cartman, Hester

W

Waddell, Robert R. merchant, 45 Pine-street.
Waddell, Isaac, taylor, Skinner
Waddington, Josh. merc. 172 Pearl, & store 134 Water
Wade, Robert, carpenter, Bowery-lane.
Wade and Co. William, merchants, 76 Water-street.
Wade, Edward, soap and candlemaker, 26 Catharine
Wade, jun. Edward, gilder, 61 Beekman
Wade, John, grocer,
Wade, Obadiah, cartman, Orange
Wade, Jonathan, cartman, Orange
Wagener, John, baker, 90 Beekman
Wagg, William, cooper, 424 Pearl
Wagenst, Michael, anchorsmith, 20 Ferry
Wagnett, David, grocer, 159 Pearl
Wainwood, Cato, sawyer, 57 Gold

NEW-YORK DIRECTORY.

Wainwright, Francis, druggist, 152 Pearl-street.
Wakeman, Jonathan S. smith, 39 Lumber
Wakeman, James, grocer, 30 Front
Walden, Jacob T. merchant, 305 Pearl
Walden, Thomas, 305 Pearl
Walden, Alexander P. 9 Dutch
Waldron, John, taylor, 3 Old-flip.
Waldron, David, livery-stabler, 20 Chamber-street.
Waldron, Oliver, carpenter, 61 James
Waldron, widow, Eagle
Waldron, William I. grocer, 61 Nassau
Waldron, Daniel, merchant, 207 Broadway.
Waldron, Alexander P. 30 Frankfort-street.
Waldron, Resolve, mariner, 1 Jacob
Waldron, Thomas J. grocer, 55 Bowery-lane.
Wale, Patrick, merchant, 53 Murray-street.
Walgrove, Garrit, cooper and cutler, 17 Pearl
Walgrove, Samuel, cisternmaker, 19 Dey
Walgrove, George, hay-weigher, Jay
Walker, David, 45 Whitehall
Walker, James, merchant, 68 Maiden-lane.
Walker, John, mason, Greenwich-road.
Walker, Abraham, taylor, Little Catharine-street.
Walker, Thomas, merchant, 276 Pearl
Walker, Peter, taylor, 25 Nassau
Walker, Sarah, washer, 298 Broadway.
Walker, John, brewer, 31 Lumber-street.
Walker, Samuel, 4 Caspel
Walker, Peter, taylor, 28 Cliff
Wall, Rev. George, 329 Broadway.
Wallace, William, mariner, 68 James-street.
Wallace, John, grocer, Washington
Wallace, Alexander, cartman, First
Wallace, John, mason, Orange
Walsdey, William, measurer of grain, 2 Old-flip.
Walsh, ———, mason, 20 George
Walsh, William, tallow-chandler, 95 Gold
Walsh, William, cartman, Bedlow
Walsh, James, painter, &c. Charlotte
Walsh, John, mariner, Pope's alley.
Walsh, Thomas, grocer, 74 Cedar
Walter, Andrew, carpenter, 10 Roosevelt

NEW-YORK DIRECTORY.

Walter, John, carpenter, Little Catharine-street.
Walton, William, 218 William
Walton, Abraham M. counsellor at law, 55 Wall
Walton, Robert, rigger, 137 Cherry
Walton, widow of Abraham, 269 Water
Walton, Gerard, 328 Pearl
Waltus, Daniel, physician, 44 Cherry
Wandell, William, grocer, 165 Washington
Wandell, Peter, boatman, 38 Harman
Wandell, James, measurer of grain, 80 Beckman
Wandell, Alexander, tavern, 35 Moore
Wandell, John, carpenter, 70 Harman
Wandell, William, cartman, 118 Harman
Ward, Thomas, shoemaker, Charlotte
Ward, Uzal, cartman, 91 Chamber
Ward, Mary, schoolmistress, 35 Rutger
Ward, Samuel, merchant, 320 Pearl
Ward, widow, 55 Church
Ward, Jasper, merchant, 29 Peck-slip.
Ward, Moses, merch. 135 Cherry, & store Pearl-strt.
Ward, Josiah, carpenter, Eagle
Ward, Jesse, cabinetmaker, 25 Frankfort
Ward, Thomas, shoe warehouse, 140 William
Ward, Alexander, oysterman, 85 Chamber
Ward, Abijah, carpenter, Division
Ward, George, 30 Church
Ward, Stephen, druggist, 310 Pearl
Ward, Francis, grocer, 249 Broadway.
Ward, Thomas, boarding-house, 3 Front-street.
Ward, Robert, cabinetmaker, Mott
Ward, John, cloathing store, 296 Water
Ward, Thomas, shoemaker, 55 Fair
Ward, Samuel C. merchant, 60 Maiden-lane.
Wardell, Robert, merchant, 169 Water-street.
Wardell, John, merchant, 169 Water
Wardell, Elizabeth, 63 Pearl
Wardell, Thomas, fisherman, 15 Fayette
Warcham, John, merchant, 355 Water
Waring, Thomas, hatter, 94 Broadway.
Waring and Eken's store, 17 Beekman-slip.
Waring, Sylvanus, smith, n. Rutger-street.
Waring, S. and E. hatters, 342 Pearl

NEW YORK DIRECTORY.

Warner, Geo. J. clock & watchmaker, 70 Maiden-lane.
Warner & Schuyler, watchmakers, &c. 70 Maiden-lane.
Warner, James, coach & harnefsmaker, 7 Barclay-str.
Warner & Co. G. failmakers, 14 Cedar, & loft 90 Water
Warner, Cornelius, carpenter, 31 Barclay
Warner, Charles, coach & harnefsmaker, 9 Barclay
Warner, William, 29 Barclay
Warner, Mofes, carpenter, 50 Chapel
Warner, William, fhipmafter, 66 Beekman
Warner, Michael, rigger, Mulberry
Warner, widow Jane, 66 Beekman
Warner, Matthias, grocer, 75 Divifion
Warner, Jofeph, mariner, Charlotte
Warner, Godfrey, cartman, Mulberry
Warner, Philip, carpenter, 27 Frankfort
Warner, widow, 67 Church
Warner, Jeremiah, grocer, 58 Frankfort
Warner, Jacob, harnefsmaker, 185 Broadway.
Warner, Leonard, carpenter, 14 Barclay ftreet.
Warner, Thomas, cabinetmaker, 3 Chapel
Warren, Thomas, merchant, 61 Maiden-lane.
Warren, John G. merchant, 28 Pearl, & ftore Old-Slip.
Warren, William, carpenter, 19 Barley-ftreet.
Warren, Mark, labourer, 80 Warren
Warren, Mary, perfumery, 146 William
Wafhburn, Edmund, Bedlow
Wafhburn, Jofeph, cartman, 67 Church
Warrington, William, fhipmafter, Gibbs'-alley.
WASHINGTON CHAPTER, Royal Arch Mafon's Lodge,
    66 Liberty-ftreet.
WATCH-HOUSES, 1 Broad, and 1 Divifion
Waterberry, Henry, fhoemaker, 9 Green
Waterberry, Gideon, fhoemaker, 86 James
Waterbury, Peter C. merchant, 62 Pine
Waterman, Jedediah, chocolate-maker, 322 Water
Waters, Thomas, oyfterman, 1 Rider
Waters, John, cartman, Effex
Waters, William, accountant, 56 Rutger
Waters, Garrit, fhipwright, 44 Auguftus
Waters, Smith, carpenter, 55 Murray
Waters, John, furveyor, Lumber
Waters, Cinfer, 48 Cedar

Waters, Andrew, brewer, Orange-street.
Waters, Daniel D. M.D. 49 Cherry
Waters, Jane, 46 Fair,
Watkeys, Edw. soap and candlemaker, 19 Nassau
Watkins, Charles, 26 Whitehall, & store 43 Front
Watkins, Joseph, ironmonger, Greenwich road.
Watkins, Samuel, physician & druggist, 314 Pearl-str.
Watkins, Mrs. 15 Church
Watson, jun. James, merchant, 44 Broad
Watson, William, 98 Beekman
Watson, James, merchant, 6 State
Watson, John, carpenter, 43 Rutger
Watson, Benjamin, shoemaker, 15 Oliver
Watson, Alexander, taylor & salesman, 204 Water
Watson, Abraham, physician, 50 Chamber
Watson, John, teacher, Mulberry
Watson, James & Samuel's store, 111 Front
Watson, widow, 38 Lombard
Watson, John, grocer, 11 Chapel
Watson, Elkanah, 214 Broadway.
Watson, James & Ebenezer, merchants, 36 Old-slip.
Watson and Leworthy, brush manufact. 319 Water-st.
Watson, Elizabeth, mantuamaker, 82 Fair
Wattles, George, merchant, 94 John
Watts, Robert, shipjoiner, 33 Bancker
Watts, John, 5 Broadway.
Watts, Charles, 116 Fly-market.
Watts, John, mariner, Bedlow-street.
Watts, James, carpenter, Henry
Watts, Alex. shoemaker, Greenwich, corner Cedar
Waud, Robert, cabinetmaker, Mott
Waugh, James, carpenter, Charlotte
Way, John, baker, 7 Harman
Way, James, paper-hanging manufactorer, 427 Pearl
Wayland, Seth, currier, 11 Rose
Wayland, Francis, currier, 50 Frankfort
Wayman, William, sadler, 4 Barley
Weatherhine, John N. cartman, 8 Augustus
Weatherspoon, Miss, tayloress, 3 Rector
Weaver, William, oysterman, 30 Lumber
Weaver, Jane, 17 Beekman
Weaver, Jacob, shipwright, 55 Rutger

Webb, John and Lewis, grocers, 221 Water-street.
Webb, Joseph, painter and glazier, 58 Warren.
Webb, Samuel, grocer, 57 Cherry
Webb, Orange, merchant, 81 Beekman
Webb, John, shipmaster, 78 Catharine
Webb, Pindar, shoemaker, 174 Division
Webb, Joseph D. 53 Vesey
Webbers, Woolverd, mason, 20 Rutger
Webster, George, marshal, 2 Rose
Webster, John, cartman, 25 Vandewater
Webster, jun. Noah, 40 Pine
Webster, Charlotte, teacheress, 38 Fair
Wedes, Michael, sawyer, Moore's-row.
Wedge, John, shoemaker, Little Ann-street.
Wedge, Elijah, bellman, 22 Mulberry
Wedman, Miss, milliner, 112 William
Weed, James, shipwright, Henry
Weed, Samuel, mason, Little Catharine
Weeden, Jonathan, Mulberry, & rope-walk, Orange
Weekman, Conrad, carpenter, 34 Augustus
Weeks, Stephen, grocer, Grand
Weeks, Catharine, 18 Liberty
Weeks, George, cartman, 54 Catharine
Weeks, Isaac, shoemaker, 6 Warren
Weeks, Benjamin, shipwright, upper end Lumber
Weeks, Robert, cartman, First
Weeks, James, merchant-taylor, 246 Water
Weeks, Ezra, carpenter and builder, 9 Frankfort
Weeks, John, shipwright, 70 E. George
Weeks, William, carpenter and joiner, 30 Cheapside.
Weeks, Stephen, cartman, Pump-street.
Weeks, John, labourer, Lumber
Weeks, Nathaniel, labourer, Little Catharine
Weeks, Jacob, cartman, Mulberry
Weeks, Gilbert, carpenter, Water
Weigh, ——, shipmaster, 8 Roosevelt
Weir, George, carpenter, 42 Partition
Weir and Co. Robert, merchants, 14 Gold
Weisenfels, Col. Frederick, 90 Warren
Weisenfels, George P. conveyancer, 63 Church
Weisenfels, Mrs. boarding-house, 73 Cortlandt
Welle, Robert, printer, 38 Harman

Welden, Jonathan, carpenter, 8 Roosevelt-street.
Weldon, William, 46 Chamber
Wellham, Robert, smith, 153 Greenwich
Wellham, Robert, grocer, 25 Vesey
Welling, William, wheelwright, Bowery-lane.
Wells, Abijah, cartman, 77 Reed-street.
Wells, John, attorney at law, 47 Pine
Wells, William, grocer, 33 Peck-slip.
Wells and Co. Lemuel, Jewellers, 158 Pearl-street.
Wells, Moses, shoemaker, 9 Vandewater
Wells, Hannah, 63 Pearl
Wells, Rev. Joshua, 10 E. George
Wells, John, mariner, 3 Lumber
Wells, Daniel and Nathaniel, grocers, South
Welsh, Thos. & Geo. painters & glaziers, 352 Water
Welsh, James, carpenter, 32 E. George
Welsh, Elizabeth, washer, 49 Lumber
Welsh, widow, seamstress, Moore's-row.
Welsh, William, cartman, Mott-street.
Welsh, Eleanor, washer, Mulberry
Welsh, Patrick, Mulberry
Welsh, Neil, Mulberry
Welsh, John G. shoemaker, 61 Ann
Welshman, Robert, mason, 94 Chamber
Welps, Peter, attorney at law, 74 Vesey
Welter, widow, Lumber
Wendover, Peter, sailmaker, 2 Lombard
Wendover, Stephen, merchant, 157 Pearl
Wendover, William, carpenter, 2 Lombard
Wenman, Bernard, silversmith, 52 Partition
Wenman, Daniel, carpenter, 18 Lombard
Wenman, Evert, taylor, 50 Partition
Went, Cort, grocer, 65 Chatham
Went, Christopher, torchmaker, &c. near the College.
Wentworth, Judah, boarding-house, 4 New-street.
Wentworth, William, attorney at law, 149 Water
Werth, John I. merchant, 22 Marketfield
Wessels and Woolsey, coopers, 3 Crane-wharf.
Wessels, Isaac, cabinetmaker, 61 Harman-street.
Wessels, Mathew, carpenter, 21 James
Wessels, Mary, washer, 3 Augustus
Wessels, James, measurer, Lumber

Wessels, Evert, 50 Lombard-street.
West, James, letter-carrier, 32 Broadway.
West, James, Pump-street.
West, Mrs. boarding-house, 208 Pearl
West, John, mason, 17 Chamber
West, John L. mariner, 13 Stone
West, Abner, combmaker, Division
West, Joseph, carpenter, 19 Chamber
West, John, carpenter, 155 Washington
West, John, carpenter, E. Washington
West, Edward, carpenter, 15 Fair
West, John, cartman, Winne
West, David, combmaker, Pell
Westerfield, Andrew, cooper, 29 Chapel
Western, Thos. piano-forte-maker, 64 Maiden-lane.
Westervelt, Benjamin, cartman, 17 Rector-street.
Westervelt, William, carpenter, 210 Greenwich
Westervelt, Peter, smith, 36 Thomas
Westervelt, Gardit, 37 Thomas
Westervelt, Benjamin, carpenter, First
Westervelt, Cornelius, cartman, 24 Thomas
Westervelt, John I. shopkeeper, 64 Vesey
Westervelt, widow, 73 Vesey
Westmire, Justice, shoemaker, Hester
Weston, Lemuel, mariner, 59 Cherry
Wetmore, Timothy F. M.D. 65 Cherry
Weyman and Son, Abner, clothiers, 30 Maiden-lane.
Whaites and Chartres, piano-forte makers, 19 Barclay
Whedon, Lovica, 42 Bancker
Wheeler, Solomon, grocer, Essex
Wheeler, John, cartman, 67 Reed
Wheeler, Mary, washer, 24 Augustus
Wheeler, Jonathan, cartman, 12 Fayette
Wheeler, Stephen, tavern, 52 Front
Wheeler, John, carter, 21 Catalip
Wheeler, John L. carpenter, 25 Thomas-street.
Wheeler, Richard, cartman, 11 Division
Wheeler, Ann, 29 Vesey
Wheeler, Eli, taylor, Vesie
Wheeler, Eliphalet, seaman, Second
Wheeler, Mathew, shoemaker, 30 Church
Whippo, John, grocer, 148 Bowery-lane.

Whippo, Miss Catharine, 356 Pearl-street.
Whitchurch, Thomas, 84 Chamber
Whitchurch, John, painter and glazier, 376 Pearl
White, Hartshorn, shoemaker, 24 Church
White, Brothers and Co. hat manufactory, 316 Pearl
White, Hezekiah, carpenter, 5 E. George
White, Joseph, 90 Chamber
White, Phœbe, mantuamaker, 13 Warren
White, John, shoemaker, 30 Warren
White, Thomas, taylor, 5 Moore
White, Ann, 33 Wall
White, Michael, shoemaker, 27 Vandewater
White, Thomas, merchant, 85 Water
White, Charles, retailer of mahogany, 80 Gold
White, Charles, shipmaster, 73 Roosevelt
White, Joseph, shipwright, 17 Lumber
White, Silas, inspector of lumber, 95 Catharine
White, jun. Silas, carpenter, Division
White, Peter, carpenter, Gibbs'-alley.
White, Henry, 21 Broadway.
White, sen. Thomas, 102 Bowery-lane.
White, jun. Thomas, baker, 100 Bowery-lane.
White, Francis, butcher, 100 Bowery-lane.
White, Eleanor, boarding-house, 124 Front-street.
White, Henry, accountant, 32 Whitehall
White, James, cartman, 24 E. George
White, George, conveyancer, 67 Chatham
White, Robert, mariner, 30 Rose
White, John, mariner, 81 Division
White, Cornelius, shipmaster, 14 Batavia-lane.
White, John, mariner, 69 Catharine-street.
White, William, mason, 26 Murray
White, widow, ironer, 50 Dey
White, John, butcher, 121 Bowery-lane.
White and Smith, hatters, Broad street.
White, John, merchant, 89 Water
White, John, clothing-store, 323 Water
White, ——, nurse, 5 Dutch
White, John, merchant, 93 Front
Whitecar, Rufus, shipwright, 65 E. George
Whiteland, John, butcher, First
Whitehead, William, cabinetmaker, 75 Pearl

Whitehead, Catharine, mantuamaker, 54 Chatham-st.
Whitehead, Elisha, merchant, 4 Vandewater
Whitelare, James, combmaker, 31 Augustus
Whitelaw, Thomas, mason, 86 Catharine
Whiteman, Henry, shopkeeper, 139 Broadway.
Whiteman, John, labourer, Bowery-lane.
Whiteman, Henry, shoemaker, 64 Cherry-street.
Whitfield, Hannah, 85 Roosevelt
Whitfield, Etty, 14 Beekman
Whitfield, Thomas, shipjoiner, 22 Rutger
Whitfield, George, boatbuilder, 85 Roosevelt
Whiting, Thomas, accountant, 171 William
Whitlock, James, carpenter, 265 William
Whitlock, Samuel L. shoemaker, 12 Chapel
Whitlock, William, shipmaster, 29 Frankfort
Whitlock, Joseph, 52 Vesey
Whitlock, James, taylor, 259 Greenwich
Whitlock, William, cardmaker, 51 Cheapside.
Whitlock, widow, Upper Reed-street.
Whitney, Asa, watchmaker, 104 Gold
Whitney, Isaac, baker, Gibbs'-alley.
Whitson, Richard, Eagle-street.
Whittemore, Thomas, merchant, 131 Cherry
Whittemore, Jacob, shipmaster, Third
Whittemore, Drake & Co. merchants, 129 Cherry
Whittemore, Robert, blockmaker, Jackson's wharf.
Whittingham, Richard, brass-founder, Henry
Whittle, Mary, milliner, 63 Gold-street.
Wicker, Philip, labourer, First
Wiggins, widow, grocer, 5 Ferry
Wiggins, Josiah, picture-frame-maker, 6 Hague
Wight, Archibald, carpenter, Little Catharine
Wilcox, Samuel, merchant, 7 Dey
Wiley, Alexander, taylor, 172 Greenwich
Wiley, Catharine, 16 William
Wiley, Alexander, marshal, 51 Augustus
Wiley, Robert, baker, 69 Catharine
Wiley, Ann, 44 Lombard
Wiley, Alexander, coachmaker, 203 Broadway.
Wiley, William, boatman, Sixth-street.
Wiley, Catharine, 53 Liberty
Wileyn, Samuel, rigger, 12 Harman.

Wilkes, George, taylor, 48 Reed-street.
Wilkes, Charles, cashier of the bank of N. Y. 32 Wall
Wikes, John, notary-public, 63 Stone
Wilkie, Edward, branch-pilot, 74 Wall
Wilkie, James, pilot, 60 Ann
Wilkie, Jeremiah, mason, Eagle
Wilkins, Jacob, 145 Washington
Wilkins, Martin S. counsellor at law, 3 Beaver
Wilkins, John, carpenter, Orange
Wilkinson, Catharine, 10 Dey
Wilkinson, Richard, mason, 259 Broadway.
Will, Henry, merchant, 125 Chatham-street.
Will, Rebecca, 67 Division
Will, Lawrence, well-digger, Mott
Willcocks, William, counsellor at law, 13 Broad
Willcocks, Ch. grocer, Bayard's-lane, cor. Elizabeth-st.
Willcocks, Peter, mason, 80 Lumber
Willess, William, hatter, 31 Maiden-lane.
Willet, Abraham, 55 John-street.
Willet, James, shoemaker, 14 Beckman
Willet, Marinus, 6 Barley
Willet, Taylor, smith, Henry
Willets & Co. Thomas, ironmongers, 136 Fly-market.
Willetts and Seaman, ironmongers, 142 Fly-market.
Willetts, Thomas, carpenter, 35 Bancker-street.
Willey, James, 35 Chapel
Williams, Thomas, shipwright, 337 Water
Williams, Joseph, shipmaster, 3 Hague
Williams, Cornelius, 40 Division
Williams, John, labourer, 10 James
Williams, Benjamin, smith, upper end of Broadway.
Williams, William, carpenter, 5 Hague-street.
Williams, Thomas, pilot, 58 Roosevelt
Williams, Cornelius, mason, Henry
Williams, Joseph, grocer, 125 Broad
Williams, Peter, tobacconist, 41 William
Williams, Christian, shoemaker, 216 William
Williams, Wm. china & glass store, 23 Maiden-lane.
Williams, John, porter-house, 6 John-street.
Williams, Andrew, carpenter, Winne
Williams, Nicholas, mariner, 90 Harman
Williams, Thomas, carpenter, 29 Thames

t

Williams, Belfast, 20 Batavia-lane.
Williams, Thomas, 61 Chatham-street.
Williams, Henry A. grocer, 102 Broad
Williams, Isaac, cartman, Second
Williams, David, ropemaker, Mulberry
Williams, Elam, cabinetmaker, 167 William
Williams, Mary, tayloress, 41 Ann
Williams, William, grocer, 171 Washington
Williams, Susan, Little Catharine
Williams, George, cartman, Winne
Williams, Samuel L. shoemaker, 209 Greenwich
Williams, Robert, potter, 54 Chatham
Williamson, David, nursery-man, Greenwich-road.
Williamson, Richard, grocer, 17 and 19 Old-slip.
Williamson, Tennis, mariner, Cherry-str. Ship-yards.
Williamson, Henry C. cabinetmaker, 7 Water-street.
Williamson, Thomas, comedian, 1 George
Williamson, John, mariner, 55 Roosevelt
Willis, William, soap and candlemaker, 25 Roosevelt
Willis, David, livery-stabler, 27 Whitehall
Willis, John, boarding-house, 71 Barclay
Willis, Henry, carpenter, 35 Bancker
Willis, William, bookbinder, 19 Cheapside.
Willson, Abraham, fur-merchant, 70 Water-street
Willson, John, labourer, 59 Reed
Willson, William, carpenter, Little Catharine
Willson, Hester, Elizabeth-street, near Bunker-hill.
Wilmerding, William, merchant, 88 Maiden-lane.
Wilmhurst, Richard, taylor, 54 Partition-street.
Wilmurt, John J. clock and watchmaker, 133 Water
Wilsey, widow and daughter, tayloresses, 69 Harman
Wilsey, Jacob, smith, 23 Barclay
Wilsey, Henry, mason, 65 Division
Wilson, John, Second
Wilson, T. tanner, 117 William
Wilson, Neven, flaxseed store 87, & cooperage 89 Front
Wilson, Thomas, sailmaker, 50 Roosevelt
Wilson, Wm, merchant, 217 Pearl, & house 16 Gold
Wilson, John, cartman, Mott
Wilson, Peter, butcher, Bowery-lane.
Wilson, Isaac, weaver, 41 Cherry-street
Wilson, John, cartman, Gibson-alley.

Wilson, Thomas, hairdresser, 46 Cherry-street.
Wilson, Harry, brewer, 85 Greenwich
Wilson, Sweeny, shipmaster, 14 Batavia-lane.
Wilson, Benjamin, tailor, 58 Rutger-street.
Wilson, John, shipmaster, 24 Oliver
Wilson, John, baker, 93 Fair
Wilson, Thomas, chairmaker, 43 Ann
Wilson, Joseph, mariner, 18 Baucker
Wilson, William, mariner, Charlotte
Wilson, Joseph, labourer, Eagle
Wilson, Mrs. 106 Greenwich
Wilson & Stephenson's millstone manuf. 40 Cortlandt
Wilson, William, stonecutter, 57 Dey
Wilson, Jacob, grocer, Catharine-slip.
Wilson, John, physician, 159 Front-street.
Wilson, Thomas, shoemaker, 26 Cliff
Wilson, Robert, printer, 102 Pearl
Wilt, Jacob A. cabinetmaker, 16 Frankfort
Wilt, George, butcher, 26 Frankfort
Wilt, Mrs. midwife, 26 Frankfort
Winans, Jemima, boarding-house, 4 Wall
Winans, Isaac R. sailmaker, 58 Wall
Winch and Co. grocers, 181 Washington
Winerell, James, grocer, 45 Roosevelt
Winchester, Morris, shipmaster, 32 Roosevelt
Winey, William, tea-waterman, 115 Division
Winnick, John, grocer, 93 Chamber
Winship, Samuel, tavern, 190 Greenwich
Winship, John, butcher, Bowery-lane.
Winslow, Thomas B. hatter, 71 Wall-street.
Winslow, Thomas, hairdresser, 70 Wall
Winstanly, William, portrait-painter, 9 Beekman
Winter & Co. Augusta, &c merchants, 120 William
Winter, Jacob, 23 Stone
Winter, Lawrence, 6 Batavia-lane.
Winter, ... New-street.
Winterup, ... merchant, 45 Wall
Winterly, Francis Bayard, 29 Wall
Winthrop, William, merchant, 52 Wall
Winthrop, John, northern, E. Washington
Winter, A. ....12 Ann
Wilby, ..., mason, Fayette

Wishart, Hugh, gold and silversmith, 319 Pearl-street.
Wisley, John, carpenter, Charlotte.
Witwill, Daniel, painter, 17 Bancker
Withington, Gothard and Shane, distillers, &c. Bedlow
Withington, John, china and glass store, 44 Cherry
Wittet, Thomas D. accountant, 66 Ann
Wolf, John A. 211 William
Wolf, David, merchant, 35 Fair
Wolhater, Anthony, gardener, Bowery-lane.
Wolhaupter, John, watchmaker, 41 Ann-street.
Wood, Isaac, butcher, Winne
Wood, Caleb, grocer, 9 Cooper
Wood and Dawson, grocers, 44 Front
Wood, Sarah, boarding-house, 13 Gold
Wood, Oliver, carpenter, 39 William
Wood, William, baker, 40 Beekman
Wood, John, grocer, 8 Robinson
Wood, Zophar, sievemaker, 322 Broadway.
Wood, Jeremiah, shoemaker, 15 Thomas-street.
Wood, Timothy, boot and shoe manufactory, 60 Wall
Wood, Dudley, Cross
Wood, Joseph, shoemaker, 1 Front
Wood, John, baker, 40 Beekman
Wood, Charles, grocer, 11 Chatham-row.
Wood, James, tin & hardware store, 175 Greenwich-st.
Wood, John, teacher, 44 Lombard
Wood, Stephen, cartman, Second
Wood, Israel, grocer, 187 Washington
Wood, William, 85 Reed
Wood, Robert and Daniel, grocers, 35 Herman
Wood, Andrew, shoemaker, 31 Cliff
Wood, James, shipwright, Mutual
Wood, Thurston, grocer, Pump
Wood, John, cartman, Third
Wood, A. grocer, 175 Washington
Wood, Ab. labourer, 47 Barley
Woodcock, John, whip-maker, 154 Chatham
Woodham, Capt. 32 Frankfort
Woodhull and Smith, merchants, 113 Maiden-lane.
Woodhull, Richard M. merchant, 55 Gold-street.
Woodhull and Rowe, grocers, New-slip.
Woodhull, William, carpenter, 14 Barger-street.

Woodhull, James and Gilbert, merchants, 61 John, and store 166 Front-street.
Woodruff, Samuel, housebuilder, 82 Chamber
Woodruff, James, hairdresser, 3 Liberty
Woods, John, merchant, 198 Water
Woods, James, attorney at law, 392 Pearl
Woods, R. & A. dry goods store, Pearl, corner Chatham
Woods, Thomas, labourer, 58 E. George
Woodward, Nathaniel, 37 Murray
Woodward, Peter, lumber-merchant, 30 Catharine
Woodward, John, coachmaker, 65 Nassau
Woodward, widow, 106 Division
Wooffendale, John, dentist, 154 Broadway.
Wool, Margaret, tayloress, 36 Lombard-street.
Wool, Jeremiah, 32 Broad
Wooley, Peter, shoemaker, 32 Church
Woolls, Stephen, comedian, 29 Dey
Woolsey, Andrew, taylor, 7 Chapel
Woolsey, Isaac, cartman, Eagle
Woolsey, Rev. Thomas, 70 Harman
Woolsey and Rogers, ironmongers, 235 Pearl
Woolsey, William W. merchant, 334 Pearl
Woolsey, George M. merchant, 52 Greenwich
Woolsey, Gerardus, cooper, 48 Augustus
Worckhert, George, baker, 19 James
Worden, Roger, shoemaker, 71 George
Worden, Samuel, labourer, 27 Bancker
Worker, Jacob, baker, 71 George
Worsley, Thomas, sailmaker, 52 Roosevelt
Wortindyke, Cornelius, 48 Chamber
Wortman, widow, 40 Barclay
Worts, Joshua, shipjoiner, Pell
Worts, William, carpenter, 13 Thomas
Wood, George, labourer, 28 Reed
Wood, Elizabeth, 35 Beaver
Wright, Augustus, tinmaker, 229 Water, & 105 Front
Wright, William, butcher, upper end of Mulberry
Wright, Samuel, carpenter, Crofs
Wright, Jordan, merchant, 298 Pearl
Wright, Stephen, carpenter, 201 Division
Wright, Gilbert and Gasey, bakers, Charlotte
Wright, Andrew, cabinetmaker, 5 Pine

Wright, Isaac, merchant, 300 Pearl-street.
Wright, Chs. merch. 298 Pearl, & store 3 Burling-slip.
Wright, William, cartman, Mulberry-street.
Wright, Rachael, 122 Bowery-lane.
Wright, Charles, merchant, 11 Cherry-street.
Wright, York, labourer, 18 Garden
Wunnenberg, Francis, furrier, 120 William
Wyatt, James, accountant, 30 George
Wycken, Cornelius, grocer, 143 Front
Wyckoff, Henry I. merchant, 10 Pearl
Wyckoff, John, mason, 71 Murray
Wyckoff, Albert, merchant, 36 Pine
Wylie, John, grocer, 51 Hartman
Wynkoop, Peter, tobacconist, 22 Roosevelt

Y

Yandall, Faithfull, tavern, Catharine-slip.
Yates, (R.) & G. Pollock's counting-house, 97 Front-st.
Yates, Adolphus, merchant, 5 Beaver
Yeamans, Ann. boarding-house, 120 Water
Yelverton, Andrew, shipwright, 49 Rutger
Yeoman, John, 5 Dutch
Yonge, John, shoemaker, 1 Frankfort
Yorkshire, Sarah, washer, 27 Vandewater
Youle, George, plumber and pewterer, 298 Water
Youle, John, ironfounder, air-furnace, Corlaer's hook.
Youle, Jane, 80 Beekman-street.
Youmen, Peter, carpenter, Fisher
Young, William, Barley
Young, James, cabinetmaker, 30 Augustus
Young, George, teacher of mathematics, 44 Stone
Young, Joseph, carpenter, 23 Ann
Young, John, baker, 30 Rose
Young, David, cartman, 10 Rose
Young, Abraham, porter, &c. 57 Chapel
Young, Nathaniel, lawyer, 5 Murray
Young, Thomas, cooper, 9 Rose
Young, widow, 20 Vandewater
Young, Jacob, cooper, 5 Rose
Young, Francis, shipmaster, 50 Roosevelt
Young, Thomas, shoemaker, 71 Dutch

NEW-YORK DIRECTORY.

Young, Robert, grocer, 27 Lumber-street.
Young, John, labourer, Elizabeth
Young, John, sadler, &c. 14 Gold
Youngs, James, teacher, 10 Gold

Z

Zeiss, John W. physician, 127 Chatham-street.
Zeller, Casper, gardener, Bowery-lane.
Zellers, Samuel, baker, 15 George-street.
Zuill, John, shipmaster, 22 Cherry
Zuntz, Alexander, auctioneer and broker, 62 Pearl

INDEX.

	Page.		Page.
TAMMANY society	2	Post-days at New-York	
Additional names	ibid	for the year 1798	35
Sick nurses	ibid	General Post-office	36
The Calender, calculated for the 23d year of American Independence	5	New-York fire engineers, wardens, firemen, &c.	37
		List of cartmen	43
Eclipses of the sun & moon	15	Errata to do.	86
French Calender	ibid	Record of inspectors of hay,	54
Table of high water	16	Record of porters and their respective stands in the city of New-York	ibid
Stamp duties	17		
Duties payable in the United States	20	Officers of the State of New-York	55
Bounties and tonnage	27		
Custom-house fees	28	Officers of the city and county of New-York	57
Surveyor's fees	ibid		
Vessels not belonging to the United States, where permitted to unload	29	Circuits and courts of Oyer and Terminer for 1798,	59
		Government of the United States	60
Mode of transacting business at the Custom-house, with sundry extracts from the revenue act.	ibid	Ministerial & consular appointments by the United States	61
		Ministerial & consular appointments to the United States	62
Duty of weighers	34		
Hours of doing business at the Custom-house	ibid	Officers of, and rules for doing business in the Bank of New-York, and the Branch Bank of the U. States in this city	63
Officers of the customs for the district of N. York	ibid		
Gaugers, weighers, measurers, &c.	ibid		

INDEX.

	Page.		Page.
Weight of Federal Coins	65	New-York coopers society	72
Officers of the Bank of the United States	ibid	N. York mariners friendly society	72
Do. of the Bank of Albany	ibid	Associated teachers	ibid
Mutual Assurance Company	ibid	Cincinnati	ibid
New-York Chamber of Commerce	ibid	St. George's society	ibid
N. Y. Insurance Company	66	St. Andrew's	73
United Insurance Company	ibid	St. Patrick's	ibid
N. York Western & Northern Canal Company	ibid	German	ibid
University of the State of New-York	ibid	Caledonian	74
Columbia College	67	Grand lodge of the State of New-York	ibid
Agricultural society	68	Different lodges	75—79
Society for the relief of distressed prisoners	ibid	Brigade of militia of the city and county of New-York	79—82
City dispensary	ibid	N. Y. regiment of artillery	82
New-York hospital	ibid	Brigade company of artillery	83
Manumission society	69	First & second troop of horse	ibid
Marine society	ibid	New-York rangers	ibid
Friary	70	Washington military society	ibid
St. Cecelia society	ibid	New-York society for promoting christian knowledge	ibid
Harmonical	ibid		
Columbian Anacreontic	71	N. York missionary society	84
Uranian musical	ibid	Rates of storage	ibid
General society of mechanics	ibid	Stages from New-York	85
		Hand in hand fire company	86

THE END.

THE publisher of the New-York Register and Directory thinks it necessary to make some apology for raising the price of it this year.—He last year reduced it lower than it had been sold at for some years previous—hoping that, by reducing the price, and increasing the quantity of information hitherto contained in it, to extend the sale—but finding it not to succeed, and that he was considerably a loser, he has this year been necessitated to come back his expences, and to make a small addition to the price—a desire of remuneration being his great moving principle.

$300 Dollars

May 25th 1798

www.ingramcontent.com/pod-product-compliance
Lightning Source LLC
Chambersburg PA
CBHW022043230426
43672CB00008B/1052